"DEFECTS"

Corporealities: Discourses of Disability

David T. Mitchell and Sharon L. Snyder, editors

"DEFECTS": Engendering the Modern Body

Helen Deutsch and Felicity Nussbaum, Editors

Ann Arbor

THE UNIVERSITY OF MICHIGAN PRESS

2002   2001   2000   2003   4   3   2   1

A CIP catalog record for this book is available from
the British Library.

Library of Congress Cataloging-in-Publication Data

Defects : engendering the modern body / Helen Deutsch and Felicity
    Nussbaum, editors.
      p.   cm. — (Corporealities)
    Includes bibliographical references and index.
    ISBN 0-472-09698-2 (cloth : acid-free paper)
    ISBN 0-472-06698-6 (pbk. : acid-free paper)
    1. Disability studies—Great Britain—History—17th century.   2.
Disability studies—Great Britain—History—18th century.   3.
Disability studies—France—History—17th century.   4. Disability
studies—France—History—18th century.   I. Deutsch, Helen, 1961–
II. Nussbaum, Felicity.   III. Series.
HV1568.25.G7D44   1999
363.4'0941—dc21   99-6767
                                                            CIP

For Michael Meranze, Marc Wilett,
and in memory of
Bean and Uncle Dave

Contents

Illustrations

Acknowledgments

This book began as a conversation between the two editors several years ago over dinner during a conference at the William Andrews Clark Memorial Library in Los Angeles. Both of us had professional and personal interests in disability, but it was the personal that served as the impetus for our impassioned conversation that evening. In the intervening years we have, fortuitously enough, become colleagues at the University of California, Los Angeles, and we jointly sponsored a conference at the Clark Library, "Deformity, Monstrosity, and Gender," in fall 1996. Several of the papers included in this volume were presented in another version at that conference while others were solicited specifically for this volume. We are grateful to the Clark Library and especially to Peter Reill for sponsoring the conference and for research support in bringing this collection to publication. The staff of the Center for Seventeenth and Eighteenth Century Studies, including Candis Snoddy, Nancy Connolly, and Marina Romani, has been unfailingly helpful. We have had expert assistance from Debra Bronstein, Norman Jones, and Anne Sheehan. The two editors each received fellowship support from the Henry E. Huntington Library and the National Endowment for the Humanities for related projects, and the time freed from teaching responsibilities helped bring this project to fruition more swiftly. The University of California Research Grant Council also supported our work.

Our intellectual and personal debts over the years are great, but we would particularly like to thank Carrie Bartkowiak, Joseph Bristow, Eva Cherniavsky, Lorna Clymer, Chris Contreras, Alexandria Currin, Diane Furtney, Lowell Gallagher, Jayne Lewis, Arthur Little, Laura Matsumoto, Anne Mellor, Jeredith Merrin, Tiffany Robbins, Judith Rosen, Valerie Smith, Janet Sorenson, Sheri Walker, and Alice Wexler.

Introduction

In the engraving from *Orthopaedia: or, the Art of Correcting and Preventing Deformities in Children* (1743) that graces the cover of this volume, a leafy curvaceous sapling, its shape imitated by a small promontory in the distance, seems to be locked together with a rigid measure in a gentle but firm embrace.[1] The fledgling tree thrives but requires training in order to fit itself to the standard by which it is judged. The pair exemplifies not only parent and child but also the marital couple, a doubling repeated visually in the two rocks rising on the bottom right. Though the straight stake seems to represent the masculine member and the crooked one the feminine, the viewer nevertheless awards aesthetic preference to the contorted trunk with its flourishing branches. Yoked together with the straight stick of wood to coax it into conformity, the healthy sapling's crooked nature will be rectified by the encircling rope. Though the engraving is intended to represent the art of correcting and preventing deformities in children and has come to represent the medical specialty of orthopedics, it also illustrates eighteenth-century attitudes toward another group of correctables, women, who charm because of their defects, while it depicts masculine science as offering moral and aesthetic criteria by which women and children are to be gauged. We take this engraving to be exemplary of the engendering of the modern body in its evocation of gender difference and in its encouraging of a universal standard of health and beauty.

This volume of essays is intended to define and contribute to an emerging area of disability studies in the early modern and Enlightenment periods, to trace its history, and to explore its interconnections with other imagined communities. We include here matters as diverse as femininity as monstrosity, ugliness as an aesthetic category, deafness and the theory of sign language, and the exotic deformed (eunuchs, mutes, and dwarfs). The essays focus on literary representations and other conceptual frameworks of culture in England and France over two centuries. As the essays demonstrate, in the seventeenth and eighteenth centuries a "defect" was both a cultural trope and a material condition that indelibly affected people's lives. "Defects" in-cluded having one of the senses impaired—blindness, deafness, or the in-ability to speak—as well as physical anomalies such as being lame or pos-sessing a humpback. By contrast, deformity's origins were more various—it could be man-made, accidental, or occur naturally—and a debate ensued concerning the amount of slippage possible between categories. Oliver Gold-smith, for example, testified to the belief that scars may be passed on through birth, as when a father's battle scar appears on his child so that "accidental deformities may become natural ones."[2] Most often, however, these cate-gories remained relatively distinct from each other.

Richard Steele's *Spectator* 17, from March 20, 1711, recommends that readers who are possessed of an uncomely face or body should form a self-mocking club that would help them adapt to their misfortune. Steele's essay includes a letter written by one "Alexander Carbuncle" that details the rules of the Ugly Club in the Act of Deformity. The requirement for admission, in addition to delivering a speech praising Aesop (an ancient known not only for his ability to allegorize the natural world but also for his physical defor-mity), is "a visible Quearity in [the potential member's] Aspect, or peculiar Cast of Countenance." *The Ugly Club: A Dramatic Caricature in One Act* (1798), a play based on the *Spectator* essay, perpetuates this level of hilarity concerning deformity. Peopled by such characters as Diaphanous, Tonnage, and Limp, the club gossips about the latest display of public ugliness, such as Ms. Touchwood's having lost two foreteeth, Mrs. Vizar's becoming disfigured with smallpox, and the recruitment of a new proselyte whose body resembles the letter *Z*. Deformity is the subject of comic camaraderie when the various club members celebrate their misshapen states in a lyric refrain:

> Come, Sons of Deformity, let's join hand in hand,
> Preserve unanimity, friendship, and love;
> 'Tis the sage who amends what so badly was plann'd,
> You've the sanction of Gods, and the fiat of Jove.
> > In our taste we agree,
> > Then our toast let it be—
> May our Club flourish ugly, united, and free!
> Repeated shouts of loud mirth the world shall apprize,
> That men may be happy without nose, feet, or eyes.[3]

This peculiar ironic refrain is of course a very unsatisfying expression of a collective identity for the disabled, at least those who are physically disfigured. Though in the mid-eighteenth century William Hay first concep-tualized and articulated an individual identity as a deformed man in his au-

tobiographical *Deformity: An Essay* (1754), shaping a unity among the physically disabled as a group and mustering its political force is largely a more
recent phenomenon. Connections among such groups in the early modern
period were most often drawn by the able-bodied, who made them into monsters, rather than being forged by the disabled themselves. James Paris Du
Plessis, for example, in *A Short History of Human Prodigies and Monstrous
Births*, presents atypical individuals without drawing any connections
among them. His vignettes of "freaks" in the London of 1731–33 include a
monstrous child with two heads, a man with a huge goiter, a hairy and moldy
woman, a child as large as an adult, a spotted Negro prince, a child shaped
like a lobster or a frog, dwarfs and giants, conjoined twins, and people with
appendages missing.[4] Freaks of nature as well as prodigies and monsters
were bonded together into an apparently coherent group, yet as Lorraine
Daston and Katharine Park have so aptly noted in regard to an earlier period, "The only thing they had in common was that each was anomalous."[5]
In the essays presented here, we are similarly linking together various persons in the eighteenth century who would have been considered to have possessed a defect. The connections are indeed arbitrary from the perspective of
the contemporary moment: pockmarked faces ravaged by smallpox, deafness, and giantism have little in common other than the fact that they were
perceived in the eighteenth century as marking the boundaries between the
increasingly significant categories of the typical and the atypical human being, the normal and the abnormal.

With increasing attention to the cultural construction of sex, gender, and
race, changes in the definitions of disability similarly reflect its implication
in societal expectations. Lennard J. Davis in this volume emphasizes disability's situatedness and its status as the object of perception, defining it as
a "disruption in the sensory field of the observer," and Kenny Fries also
stresses the spectacle of disability in his collection of writings by disabled
people entitled *Staring Back*.[6] Such articulations laudably move away from
definitions of disability that are limited to what an individual can or cannot
achieve, and move toward an investigation of cultural perceptions. We reject
definitions of disability as abnormality, lack, or absence that only contribute
to societal restrictions. If a disability pervades a large portion of a population, as in the case of the deaf community in Martha's Vineyard, does it cease
to be a disability because it is no longer perceived as unusual? In many instances disabilities both mental and physical (such as retardation, autism,
epilepsy, malformed or missing internal organs) are inconspicuous, and at-
tracting attention to them may paradoxically enhance opportunities for such
individuals. Part of our project in this volume is to question the reduction of

disability to the visible or sensory register, focusing instead upon the recip-
rocal relations within cultural contexts that render such definitions necessary
defenses, the groundwork for a situated identity from which to launch political action. The United Nations' definition of disability succinctly summarizes the way in which that interrelation shapes perceptions: "Handicap is
therefore a function of the relationship between disabled persons and their
environment. It occurs when they encounter cultural, physical, or social barriers which prevent their access to the various systems of society that are
available to other citizens. Thus, handicap is the loss or limitation of opportunities to take part in the life of the community on an equal level with
others."[7] What we wish to accentuate here is the material reality of disability, visible and invisible, even as it interacts with and is shaped in the nexus
of history, myth, and ideology.

Disability activists have recently contested the ways that the world's assumptions contract the range of responses to disability and instead have
sought to expand the horizon of expectations.[8] Civil rights legislation for the
disabled in the United States includes laws to mandate education in the least
restrictive environment in 1973 (Public Law 92-142) and to require archi-
tectural accessibility (Section 504, 1968), and these laws were important first
steps toward the Americans with Disabilities Act (1990). An aging population is becoming grudgingly if increasingly aware that one in five "normates"
(a term that Rosemarie Garland Thomson coins to distinguish those who
think of themselves as definitive human beings)[9] has a disability, will develop
a disability, or will have a child affected by disability in their lifetimes. Yet
on a global scale even most disabled Americans are enormously privileged,
and attention to worldwide barriers to education, healthcare, and employment is just emerging.

The physically or mentally "defective" have largely been ignored in early
modern and Enlightenment studies, in spite of numerous prominent examples in literature, and disability studies is just beginning to extend its interests to genealogies of the earlier periods.[10] Swift's Lemuel Gulliver in his giant incarnation and as a pigmy exhibited for money is among the most
obvious examples from literature. The lesser-known *Memoirs of Martin
Scriblerus* includes discussions of conjoined, or "Siamese," twins joined at
the back, the little Black Prince, and the "Man-mimicking Manteger."
Alexander Pope's own diminished height, humpback, and general frailty
made him a curiosity, and his *Dunciad* (1728) teems with monstrosities.
Mary Toft's birthing rabbits was a hoax that appealed to the popular imagination in the first half of the eighteenth century. In addition, the deaf-mute
Duncan Campbell attracted Eliza Haywood's attention and that of several

other commentators during the early decades of the eighteenth century because of his second sight and his ability to use sign language. Sarah Scott's colony of the maimed served the women of *Millenium Hall* (1762), and she linked ugliness to virtue in her midcentury translation of a French novel, *Agreeable Ugliness: Or, the Triumph of the Graces* (1754). Scott in particular displayed heightened awareness of the occurrence of physical deformities. The philanthropic Lady Ellison in *The History of Sir George Ellison* (1766), also written by Scott, manages to decrease the incidence of disability by her attention to infant care: "This may seem a trifling circumstance, but was much otherwise in effect, as it proved of great service to their health, and rendered them strong and well-shaped; . . . for in fifteen years after she began this practice, there was scarcely a crooked young person to be seen within ten miles of her house."[11] Damaged literary heroines include Henry Fielding's *Amelia* (1751), who met with an accident that injured her nose, and the learned but lame and pockmarked Eugenia in Frances Burney's *Camilla* (1796). Samuel Johnson famously commented upon the similarity between students at Braidwood's school for the deaf and the Highlanders at the conclusion to his *Journey to the Western Islands of Scotland* (1775). And Jane Austen's *Persuasion* (1818) turns the humble Mrs. Smith, confined and a "cripple," into a perceptive witness who recognizes what no other character understands: that Mr. Elliot is really a treacherous man whom the heroine should avoid. Once she accepts Captain Wentworth as her true love, Anne joins the tradition of fictional heroines who become beautiful in order to merit marriage, and her father's fear that a freckled complexion will be a detriment to a woman's future prospects is appeased.

Perhaps no defect was more feared or more common for eighteenth-century women than smallpox. *Inoculation; or Beauty's Triumph: A Poem, in Two Cantos* by Henry Jones (176), is an ode to beauty and a poem of praise for Daniel Sutton's inoculation against smallpox. According to the poem, Sutton's "nobler and unmatch'd Discovery" is superior to Columbus's discovery of America because saving a human life bears more value than diamond quarries or gold mines. Yet the poem also inauspiciously reveals that the remedy has economic significance. Canto 2 reduces the global issues to the romantic involvement of a youth and a virgin. Sent to the Indies in pursuit of wealth, Strephon returns home to seek his beloved Flavia. Eager to behold her beautiful face, he is instead struck dumb at "the Tomb of her departed Beauty" after her bout with smallpox. She shouts, "And was it then my Face alone you lov'd!" (18). Thunderstruck and paralyzed by her scarred face, Strephon shuns Flavia, only to have her later reappear with her dazzling beauty miraculously restored: "When Phoenix-like her new

Complexion rose, / With tenfold Splendor, and amaz'd the World" (23). The explicit moral of the poem is that this tragic tale would have been averted if Flavia had been inoculated. But the poem is also instructive about the powerful social effects this defect wrought in the eighteenth century, especially upon gendered relationships. It repeats a common theme, that defect or ugliness is fascinatingly close to beauty in that it rivets the spectator who views it.

In the real rather than the imagined early modern world, the exact number of persons who would have been counted among the defective or the deformed is difficult to determine since definitions shifted significantly through history. Certainly there are frequent mentions in literary history of impaired senses—of blindness, deafness, the inability to speak, or mental retardation. In addition, men permanently injured from the British and French wars and in labor-related accidents were numerous even during the preindustrial period. Smallpox scars marred women's beauty, but syphilis, rickets, and other disabling illnesses had equally visible effects. Prenatal care was woefully inadequate, and early modern childbirth practices also resulted in many infants being diseased or injured at birth. On the other hand, babies now resuscitated or kept alive with high-level technology would have died shortly after birth in the eighteenth century. Just what portion of the population would be labeled mentally ill or deficient vacillated, though not consistently, with the growth of greater social sympathy and benevolence in the later eighteenth century, a period during which, nevertheless, the absence or presence of physical or mental defect helped to define the very nature of the human species. In fact, the history of disability is intricately bound up with the formation of other aspects of European modernity including the development of class, race, gender, and sexual norms both at home and in the emergent empire.

In the medieval period, miracles and prodigies were imagined to be at once part of the natural order and divine signs from God, but in the early modern period this preternatural realm of strange events and unusual beings began to provoke multiple interpretations. As the miraculous event was redefined as a natural fact, cultural meaning was constructed and contested upon evidence. When the authority of the witness to such an event was scrutinized, that authority in large part determined the validity of the claim as to whether a miracle was a natural wonder or something deserving of careful investigation. Since scientific explanation and correspondence to natural law for marvels and prodigies increasingly were demanded, "preternatural phenomena los[t] their religious meaning as signs."[12] But sometimes both explanations were entertained: "The cause of a monstrous birth might be both the bestiality of the parents *and* divine displeasure at such sinful acts."[13] "Miracles" then became subject to public debate and controversy over their origin and meaning. In the later sixteenth and seventeenth centuries books of secrets and natural wonders proliferated, resulting in Francis Bacon's attempt to distinguish carefully between natural marvels and those of supernatural origin, though the divisions often proved to be tenuous and unreliable. As Rosemarie Garland Thomson argues, "a narrative of the marvelous" thus evolved into "a narrative of the deviant" so that "wonder becomes error" and a prodigy becomes "nature's sport or the freak of nature."[14] Conflating superstition with science, books of prodigies and monsters were enormously popular in the Renaissance, and by the turn of the eighteenth century, such beings and occurrences were increasingly the subject of strictly scientific examination and investigation. These books raised troubling questions about what actually constituted valid evidence, and how it would be evaluated and classified. By the mid-eighteenth century, wonders, increasingly believed to be the province of enthusiastic and superstitious vulgar folk, diverged from a more enlightened curiosity that spurred "serious" philosophic and scientific inquiry.[15]

Midcentury also witnessed the secularization of monsters through the scientific categorization of the human and the systematizing of natural history. As trading and colonial efforts extended beyond the Americas to Africa, Asia, and the South Pacific, the scientific classification of living creatures began to take its modern shape. The travel writing that resulted from exploration conjured up marvels and wonders, but it also increasingly attempted "objective" descriptions of curiosities and rarities as well as of "Other" populations. Linnaeus's *Systema Naturae,* first published in 1735, reached multiple editions during the century. In the tenth edition of 1758, *homo sapiens* was divided into the wild man, American, European, Asiatic, and African. Another species, *homo monstrosus,* included both natural and man-made monsters,[16] classified by climate or manner:

Small, active, timid	*Mountaineer.*
Large, indolent	*Patagonian* [South American Indians].
Less fertile	*Hottentot.*
Beardless	*American.*
Head conic [macrocephalic]	*Chinese.*
Head flattened [plagiocephalic]	*Canadian.*[17]

In Linnaeus's formulation the huge, dwarfed, misshapen, or eunuchlike beings all dwell outside of Europe, in the New World, Africa, and Asia—with the important exception of the excessively thin European maiden, omitted from the preceding list, which was presented in the first English translation of the treatise in 1802. This aberrant European—and female—form included

Junceae puellae abdomine attenuato: Europae, "rush-like girls with narrowed stomach: in Europe."[18] Although European persons with various physical anomalies, conjoined twins, midgets, and giants were regularly exhibited at fairs and marketplaces during the early modern period, in this geography of defect, the European character seems to exclude bodily irregularities, and other geographical regions give rise to anomalies peculiar to a particular "race."

The history of monstrosity and human defects must be complicated, then, we argue, with the emergence of racial and gender difference. Mixing distinct species together is at the crux of understandings of monstrosity when, for example, women are believed to mate with "drills" or cats with rats: "the monstrous Productions, that are so frequently to be met with in Nature, will find it hard, even in the race of Animals to determine by the Pedigrees of what *Species* every Animal's Issue is; and be at a loss about the real Essence, which he thinks certainly conveyed by Generation, and has alone a right to the specifick name."[19] In the mid-eighteenth century Henry Baker, a fellow of the Royal Society, and Pierre Louis Moreau de Maupertuis argued that an accidental variation or defect in one person might infect a whole race of men with abnormality. Both men reached this finding after investigating cases of "startling human deformities, polydactylism for Maupertuis and a peculiar prickly skin for Baker."[20] Baker reported the case of the Porcupine-man, Edward Lambert, whose warty brown barklike skin turned white and smooth after having contracted smallpox and after having been salivated.[21] Lambert's six children, all of whom were possessed of the same skin, witnessed to the way that an entirely new race could be propagated by a single aberrant being. In short, even monstrous complexion, or so eighteenth-century men of science believed, could be inherited. According to Baker, if "the accidental original be forgotten, 'tis not improbable they might be deemed a different species of mankind: a consideration, which would almost lead one to imagine, that if mankind were all produced from one and the same stock, the black skins of the negroes, and many of their differences of the like kind, might possibly have been originally owing to some such accidental cause."[22] In addition, as Nicholas Mirzoeff points out in this volume, emancipatory discourse surrounding deaf education was contemporaneous with the emergent abolitionist movement. These and other examples indicate the ways in which formulations of monstrosity connected with the racialization of the European character and were harnessed in the service of polygenetic theories.

Maupertuis argues that in addition to creating differences of complexion, mutation and migration brought about entire races of giants and dwarfs:

"Men of excessive stature, and others of excessive littleness, are species of monsters; but monsters which can become peoples, were one to apply himself to multiplying them." He continues: "However many giants, however many dwarfs, however many blacks, may have been born among other men; pride or fear would have armed against them the greater part of mankind; and the more numerous species would have relegated these deformed races to the least habitable climates of the Earth. The Dwarfs will have retired toward the arctic pole: the Giants will have inhabited the Magellanic lands: the Blacks will have peopled the torrid zone."[23] Abnormality is thus indicative of a species apart, and it is punished by being relegated to hot climates; mutant forms are in Linnaeus's categories, like race, given geographic specificity. The deformed, then, are easily intermingled and made synonymous with the racialized since dwarfs, giants, and blacks together compose "deformed races." Pollution or degeneration of the "race" also created social disorder and contamination of the social body. For Oliver Goldsmith in *An History of the Earth,* extreme climate contributes toward degeneration of an entire population, "as their persons are thus naturally deformed, at least to our imaginations, their minds are equally incapable of strong exertions. The climate seems to relax their mental powers still more than those of the body; they are, therefore, in general, found to be stupid, indolent, and mischievous."[24] Accident, mutation, and climate all breed potential deformity.

Theories of degeneracy also figure in the shift from emphasis on inherited rank or status to the formation of a self-conscious middling class. Ann Russell Stoler raises the important question of whether the discourse of degeneracy—of the belief in the increasingly defective nature of an entire population—serves as a "vehicle of bourgeois empowerment" (32) or is more likely a middle-class "representation of 'powerlessness' within a 'seemingly self-possessed imperious discourse'" (32). "This [bourgeois] class must be seen . . . as being occupied, from the mid-eighteenth century on, with creating its own sexuality and forming a specific body based on it, a 'class' body with its health, hygiene, descent, and race."[25] The history of disability, while of little interest to Foucault, is nevertheless implicated in his *History of Sexuality,* for the regulation of children extends to the publication of popular medical directives that address correcting physical impairments in children. According to Stoler's analysis of Foucault's work, issues of race are "embedded in early discourses on sexuality, but not yet in explicit form. In the making of a bourgeois 'class' body in the eighteenth century, a new field of discourse emerged concerned with 'body hygiene, the art of longevity, ways of having healthy children and of keeping them alive as long as possible' that 'attest to the correlation of this concern with the body and sex to a type of "racism"' from which modern racism derives.[26] Stoler productively aligns theories of degeneracy with racism and sexuality in the late eighteenth century. There are also, we argue, manifestations of deviation and degeneracy that emerge in the early modern period in conjunction with the body politic.

The struggles over the representation of deformity and normalcy are contests over ways of making meaning that have real effects on people's lives in the past and will continue to do so in the future. In this way ideology, rather than being simply a mystifying force that belies the truth, is itself both constitutive of and reflective of the material reality that is disability. We welcome the critical exchange that results from debates within and without the disabled community as a means of strengthening theoretical understandings and encouraging the analysis necessary for social change. Beyond Foucault's formulations of power and knowledge we wish to draw attention to the systemic aspects of disability under varied historical conditions as they connect with issues of social class, global economic disparities, and patriarchy.

Our aim is especially to ally deformity, disability, and gender studies during this period. Thomas Laqueur's reversal of Freud's claim that "anatomy is destiny," and his narrative of the eighteenth-century replacement of a single-sex "metaphysics of hierarchy" with a two-sex "physiology of incommensurability," in which the nature of woman (defined by Aristotle as monstrous) shifts from that of a lesser, colder man to another sex and flesh, provides part of the basis for the undoing of such totalities, though we find references to woman as fair defect well beyond the early modern period.[27] Londa Schiebinger's work on debates within the medical community on the nature of femininity, and her tracing of the sexualization of the entire human body in eighteenth-century science, culminating in the emergence of a distinctly female skeleton, demonstrates powerfully how much was at stake politically in the constitution of a newly naturalized femininity. Schiebinger argues convincingly for the imbrication of sexual and racial difference in a culture of emerging empire.[28]

In keeping with this model of sexual incommensurability, women and men figure differently in cultural equations concerning the reproduction of defects. For example, while monstrosity may be associated with the male imagination's extraordinary creativity, women are accused of imagining themselves into bearing monstrous children. Women who conceived during menses, who gaze on strawberries or beasts or terrifying sights, were believed to be liable to give birth to malformed or spotted children. Alternatively, the kinds of corporeal contributions from each parent determine the perfection or imperfection of the child: "If some particles are too distant, of a form too little suitable, or too weak in affinity to unite with those with which they should be united, there is born a monster with deficiency *(monstre par dé-faut)*. But if it happens that superfluous particles nevertheless find their place, and unite with the particles whose union was already sufficient, there is a monster with extra parts *(monstre par exces)*."[29] The origins of defect were the focal point of eighteenth-century controversies about the role of each parent in creating life, and battles over the hierarchy of the sexes were waged between preformationists—who believed that the homunculus existed in miniature in the sperm or egg, and epigenicists, who believed that both sexes contributed genetic material to the embryo.[30] Especially pertinent to our period is the construction of the relationship between sexual difference and anomalous bodies by scientific and social institutions at their inception.

A number of the essays included here explore the disquieting connections between indeterminate sexual categories and deformity from the most obvious examples of hermaphrodites and eunuchs to the questions about cross-gendering posed by Amazons and fops. Sexual difference is sometimes simply made equivalent to deformity or monstrosity so that women are, by their very nature, deemed to be defective. Women's monstrosity figures centrally in, for example, a misogynist satire such as *The Female Monster:*

> This Venom spreads thro' all the Female-kind;
> Shew me a Woman, I'll a Monster find.
> They're false by Nature, and by Nature taught,
> The Treachery that *Eve* so dearly bought.[31]

Women's deformity or perfection may be interpreted as an index to their virtue—the more ugly or contorted they are, the more virtuous they are inclined to be. Virtue transforms aesthetic sensibility and redefines beauty's tyranny of the visual, so that "the Law of Virtue is the Law of true Taste, and of the Beautiful."[32] Most blemishes nevertheless caused women's value to decline on the marriage market or to make them altogether unmarriageable. Sometimes defined as an imperfection that interferes with the perception of beauty, deformity can be disguised with cosmetics, and various eighteenth-century texts impart such advice: "Upon this principle we now proceed to the means of acquiring and preserving beauty by *natural* means: for hitherto we have only endeavoured to teach the method of disguising deformity, or palliating defects by the assistance of art." Women seek by such artifice to encourage civility and sociability, "as when united with virtue it [beauty] constitutes the happiness of polished society."[33]

The author of *Hebe; or, the Art of Preserving Beauty, and Correcting Deformity* also strikingly recognizes that deformity and beauty reflect their cultural context. Deformity is influenced by taste, varying within different regions of the world where what is judged as a defect may in fact be a sign of beauty: "Hence we may learn, not to regard many things as deformities, because differing from our taste and habit, when they may, in reality, be perfections, though in an order, or a class of beauty, we are not sufficiently acquainted with."[34] According to this treatise, the most beautiful women are believed to be Grecian, Turkish, and Circassian rather than English, but the eyes characteristic of a Chinese woman, for example, imagined on an Englishwoman would make her appear deformed.[35] Here the encompassing vision of empire takes the place of an omniscient and divine providence that would assign deformity a seemingly natural place within an emerging worldwide aesthetic order.[36] Though cultural relativism is recognized, this imperial vision affords privilege to symmetry and whiteness as visible signs of beauty.

There is also a *shared* monstrosity between women and the deformed of both sexes that is not simply or easily adjudicated and that often signals gender fluidity. "Defects of nature" are frequently feminized or imagined as something categorically distinct from manliness and masculinity. For men, on the other hand, deformity is often associated with oversexed effeminacy or impotence. Since the female condition would seem to be aligned with natural defect, men fear that "defect" is an emasculating contradiction to the empowering and mutually constitutive character traits of aesthetic taste and of civic humanism. In David Hume's essay "Of the Delicacy of Taste and Passion," the ability to discern deformity reveals the capacity for aesthetic discrimination in a language that is itself curiously feminine: "There is a *delicacy* of *taste* observable in some men, which very much resembles this *delicacy* of *passion,* and produces the same sensibility to beauty and deformity of every kind, as that does to prosperity and adversity, obligations and injuries."[37] Beauty and normalcy derive from symmetry and regularity; and their characteristics vary depending upon gendered expectations: "Is it not full as unseemly a sight, to behold a *Woman* giving the word of command to her troops, leading them up to combat in battle array, and giving them the signal of onset, as to see a *Man* knotting, knitting, handling a distaff, or embroidering his wife's petticoat? The reason is, that every thing unnatural and out of character is offensive. . . . [W]hat makes a *Woman* elegant, makes a *Man* deformed."[38] Female deformity is distinct from male defects, but both conform to a bourgeois aesthetic of gender difference. The regulation of the normative class body in the early modern period extended even beneath the skin and beyond, for in encompassing the heart and sensibility, moral philosophers, along with medical and penal reformers, sought to define a "moral monstrosity" that would locate inhumane examples of the upper and lower classes beyond the limits of the human.[39] In short, the regulation of the body of which the definition of disability is a part may compose a cluster of conceptual structures that the emergent middle class worriedly adopted in order to consolidate, promote, and represent its power.

We might further characterize the period of our inquiry, with the help of a variety of scholars, as a transitional era of "new science" that attempts, beginning with Francis Bacon's imperative to natural philosophers to assemble "a compilation, or particular natural history, . . . of all monsters and prodigious births of nature; of every thing, in short which is new, rare, and unusual in nature[,]" to envision difference in order to normalize it.[40] For Bacon, the monster is no longer a portent of divine intention but rather "a point of reference that allows the naturalist to identify the overreaching regularity of the rest of organic life," "a benchmark for the rational study and understanding of the universe."[41] Georges Canguilhem has described this transformation as encapsulated in the etymological shift of *anomaly*, from a descriptive term meaning "uneven, rough, irregular," to the proscriptive "outside the law,"[42] in which "the irregular submits to the rule, the prodigy to the predictable."[43] Lorraine Daston and Katherine Park outline a history of monstrosity that begins with "divine prodigies," shifts to "natural wonders," and ends with the moment when "by the end of the seventeenth century, monsters had lost their autonomy as a subject of scientific study . . . and had been integrated into the medical discipline of comparative anatomy and embryology," becoming a form of pathology.[44] Marie-Hélène Huet concentrates on the Enlightenment replacement of the maternal imagination's unnatural and licentious mimicking of art that results in monstrous birth with the scientist's paternal and natural law that ordains the study of teratology.[45] However we describe it, at the moment when attempts are made to define difference as natural fact—no longer as a sign for divine or preternatural agency—it is revealed as the norm's inverse reflection. The same paradox applies, as we will see, to eighteenth-century notions of femininity, in which the characters of women can only be considered, as Alexander Pope declares in his *Moral Essays*, "as contradistinguished from the other Sex," at worst monstrously devoid of form, at best lesser men.[46] The essays in this volume, on topics as diverse as female old age, ugliness and female virtue, and the cultural affinity between women, monsters, and eunuchs, interrogate the double bind of a femininity that, like monstrosity, is situated both within and without emerging orders of cultural self-definition. As Andrew Curran and Patrick Graille have argued, "Since the monstrous birth was no longer classified as being against or outside of nature, its very corporeality impinged on present reality." To write about monsters in the eighteenth century, a transitional era preceding teratology's complete scientific regulation of the monster, was to lose empirical certainty.[47] It would seem that a kind of knowledge emerged in the Enlightenment that exposed the unknown only to recognize itself in that which it most despised and feared.

To naturalize the monster, in short, was to threaten the coherent legibility of corporeality itself: "the monster was, in many ways, the anatomical corroboration of the breakdown of objective truth."[48] To penetrate the monster's mystery through dissection, as John Hunter's pursuit of Charles Byrne, the Irish Giant (1761–83), reminds us, was an attempt to reestablish that objectivity. Hunter, an eighteenth-century British surgeon, man-midwife, physician, professor of anatomy, naturalist, and avid collector, was particularly in need of monstrous corpses to dissect and display as specimens in his museum. The following narrative from an early-nineteenth-century biography illustrates his insatiability for novelty, which "often led him to pay more than its worth for an object he desired to make his own":

> Byrne, or O'Brien, the famous Irish giant, died in 1783. He had been in a declining state of health for some time previously, and Hunter, anxious to procure his skeleton, set his man Howison to keep watch on his movements, that he might be sure of securing his body at his death. Byrne learned this, and as he had a horror of being dissected, determined to take such precautions as should ensure his not falling into the hands of the doctors: he accordingly left strict orders that his body should be watched day and night, until a leaden coffin could be made, in which it was to be inclosed, and carried out to sea and sunk. Byrne died soon after, and, in compliance with his directions, the undertaker engaged some men to watch the body alternately. Howison soon learned this, found out the house where these men went to drink off duty, and gave information to Hunter, who forthwith proceeded thither with the view of bribing them, to allow the body to be carried off. He had an interview with one of the party at the ale-house, and began by offering him fifty pounds if he would allow the body to be kidnapped: the man agreed, provided his companions would consent, and went out to consult them. He returned shortly, saying that they must have a hundred pounds. Hunter consented to this, and thought the affair settled; but the men finding him so eager, soon came back with an increased demand, which was also agreed to; when further difficulties were found, and larger and larger demands made, until, it is said, they raised the price to five hundred pounds! The money was borrowed from Pidcock to pay them; and in the dead of night the body was removed in a hackney coach, and after having been carried through several streets, was transferred to Hunter's own carriage, and conveyed immediately to Earl's Court. Fearing lest a discovery should take place, Hunter did not choose to risk the delay which the ordinary mode of preparing a skeleton would require; accordingly, the body was cut to pieces, and the flesh separated by boiling; hence

has arisen the brown colour of the bones, which in all other respects form a magnificent skeleton.[49]

The doctor's excessive desire for a magnificent display piece, and the giant's terrified need to keep his body intact, are curiously reminiscent of a different genre of narrative. In Samuel Richardson's sentimental opus *Clarissa* (1747–48), the libertine Lovelace's need to know, to possess the body of the virtuous heroine, thereby—or so he erroneously surmises—exposing the mortal woman hiding beneath the paragon of femininity, exceeds her confinement and her rape: he plots after her death to embalm her heart and keep it in a jar before his eyes. Clarissa, whose will is honored only in death, triumphs, her coffin borne by maidens only, her flesh seemingly immune to decay. Byrne's defeat is immortalized in Hunter's museum, the center of the osteological collection of the Royal College of Surgeons in London, his bones stained by the surgeon's guilty haste.[50]

Yet these twin narratives of illicit desire, abduction, and bodily possession reveal an uncanny alliance between monstrosity and femininity, between scientific truth and sentimental fiction, an alliance based on a common fascination with the anomalous. Richardson's novelistic battle of the sexes serves as a kind of terrifying subtext for our initial story of a struggle between the scientific subject's rage for classification and his object's longing for self-possession. Each desire is the other's double, and whether the document that results is scientific treatise or literary narrative, each supplements and mirrors the other. Whether the anomaly be the exceptionally virtuous heroine or the exceptionally tall man, both the libertine and the surgeon unite in a common curiosity—a scientific mission tinged with supernatural wonder and sexual importunity—to see beneath the surface of apparent mystery. For both, the desire to know is eternally drawn to and thwarted by the corporeal and the visual.[51] Each exemplifies the drive for knowledge as a desire to *see* "parts of nature previously deemed private, thereby forging additional links with sexual-cum-intellectual penetration and with the violence of the dissecting room."[52] In both cases curiosity aims to destroy what it seeks by reducing anomaly—through dissection's revelations—to the norm. In our period, in further development of the complexities of corporeal vision, we can also consider John Bender's work on the late-eighteenth-century culture of sensibility's merging of the medical-anatomical and novelistic-aesthetic gazes in the construction of the realistic novel and third-person indirect discourse's sophisticated simulation of interiority,[53] or Barbara Maria Stafford's analysis of anatomy as constitutive of the eighteenth-century worldview.[54] When science turns its anatomical gaze toward the exceptional body and toward the woman, such covert identification, such corporeal sympathy, is all the more threatening. And look science must, for, as Marie Hélène Huet puts it, "monstrosity always reveals a truth," a compromising truth often linked to bodies marked by class, race, or gender.[55]

The body, in other words, makes potential monsters of us all. In a period that puzzled over the bodily location of the soul and the number of souls present in conjoined twins,[56] and that articulated a powerfully political metaphor of nervous organization in order to retain man's place on the great chain of being,[57] women's less-valued nervous systems subjected them to the constant threat of excess and incoherence, exhibiting the "*psychological effect of a moral fault*" as old as Aristotle.[58] But as both Dennis Todd and Huet have shown, anxieties about monstrosity, while frequently projected upon the bodies of women—in Todd's detailed study of the farm woman Mary Toft, who held the eighteenth-century scientific community spellbound by claiming to have given birth to a litter of rabbits, and in Huet's tracing of the monster-creating maternal imagination to the birth of teratology and the myth of the self-creating Romantic male author—reveal masculine anxieties about the irresistible dominion of the body over the mind and the instability of claims of identity, integrity, and reason.

In Huet's account, monstrosity, like femininity, and like the imagination, is contagious and uncontainable; the truth it reveals at the book's close is the monstrous father's self-reflection in a maternal mirror, his abject affinity with the mother that lies behind the unnatural desire to replace her and to reproduce alone. Huet's book can be said to be a history of the varying and enduring incarnations of "the belief that progeny was art and art a monstrous progeny."[59] Whether the monstrous work of art be an infant that deviates from the laws of paternal resemblance, or a female likeness so perfect that it eludes the father and the certification of his signature, for the artist of monstrosity, there is no escaping the awareness of being authored by another, by the enveloping body of the mother. For Dennis Todd's early-eighteenth-century men of letters (including Swift, Pope, and a host of doctors and courtiers), the impressionable female imagination not only gives birth to the defective but is also a vehicle of enthusiasm in any body, reducing abstract ideas to seductive corporeal forms, and rendering into airy fantasy real objects. Creating delusion and incoherence, the body becomes a dehumanizing vehicle of social isolation. For these gentlemen of letters, the very ambition to signify oneself, to cut a figure in the world, becomes potentially feminizing and inherently monstrous. The horrific double of Mary Toft's unnatural breeding is masculine ambition, the grotesque human hybrid of reason possessed by the imagination's appetites.[60] We might also link Todd's reading of the fear of the corporeal imagination with Lennard J. Davis's description in *Enforcing Normalcy* of the Enlightenment decorporealization of language that resulted in the marginalization of the deaf. Defect in these accounts at once threatens individuality with its difference, and more powerfully, threatens by its lack of difference. It is itself the verification of one's humanity and the sign of individuality, the desire to signify oneself gone beyond natural bounds.[61]

The origins of monstrosity in the history of science similarly link anatomy's revelations to the secrets of embryology and the womb. For John Hunter's elder brother and pathbreaking anatomy professor William Hunter, also the most important man-midwife of his day, renowned for his strikingly realistic anatomical engravings of the pregnant uterus, anatomy "is to the physician and surgeon what geometry is to the astronomer. It discovers and ascertains truth; overturns superstition and vulgar error; and checks the enthusiasm of theorists and sects in medicine, to whom perhaps more of the human species have fallen a sacrifice, than to the sword itself, or pestilence."[62] In an age devoid of sophisticated techniques of imaging the body's interior, medical museums abounding with verisimilar "preparations" of human interiors such as the Hunters' provided an opportunity to learn the norm from witnessing as many deviant examples as possible. Anatomy was at the heart of empiricism, of the belief that to see with one's own eyes was to be free of the superstition, error, and enthusiasm that characterized the vulgar crowd who gawked at freak shows, and the unenlightened past that read monsters as divine warnings. Hunter's language haunts science with fears of religious and political disorder that threaten as much as physical plagues, hinting that the prodigy beyond science's universals shadows the unique particular that is science's very essence.[63] As Stephen Pender describes seventeenth-century scientific views of monstrosity, "monstrous human bodies may be thought of as the sites across which singularity was, by an almost alchemical process, made to signify the normative rather than the deviant."[64]

The Enlightenment, a period obsessed with synchronic display of the unusual in the *wunderkammer,* or curiosity cabinet, saw natural history not as a process but rather as a universal collection of the fittest. According to Foucault, from this perspective monsters "form . . . the background noise, as it were, the endless murmur of nature[,]" static and fixed in their display. While Foucault ignores Enlightenment identifications of the monstrous with the savage and primitive, and thus monstrosity's temporal location in the prehistorical, his account of the necessary fixity of exceptional beings in the Enlightenment gaze is a powerful one: "It is so impossible for *natural history* to conceive of the *history of nature,* the epistemological arrangement delineated by the table and the continuum is so fundamental, that becoming can occupy nothing but an intermediary place measured out for it solely by the requirements of the whole. . . . Thus, against the background of the continuum, the monster provides an account, as though in caricature, of the genesis of differences."[65] Such a collection, like Hunter's museum, itself a display of scientific authority and national identity, affects to transcend time and contingency, even mortality, in the service of a self-enclosed spectacle of mastery, a totality perilously based on unique specimens.[66]

However much the drive to secularization and scientific classification might have prevailed in learned circles during the early modern period, its consciousness was haunted by wonder and irreducible mystery. The discourse of defect during the early modern period is one important means with which to verify Terry Castle's claim that the eighteenth century invented the uncanny.[67] Stephen Pender and others have argued that Park and Daston's narrative of the transformation from prodigy to pathology was never completed, that scientific curiosity and awestruck wonder coexisted in the learned community.[68] In the centuries-old tradition of Bartholemew Fair and other popular marketplaces that Paul Semonin describes, "the monsters were normal and their extraordinary form became part of a spectacle of the unnatural, the grotesque, and the lewd," a comic spectacle that can be linked to the "antick" caricatural mode of Breughel and Hogarth revised by British caricaturists of the end of the century.[69] Such grotesque visions, as Barbara Stafford has shown in her analysis of late-eighteenth-century caricature of bodies distorted by pain, resurrect the "ancient" in "antick" modes of representation and with their "comic horror" confront the self in the monstrous other with laughter rather than shame.[70] While the urge to read deformity as either divine warning or scientific pathology can be seen as a fear-driven denial of such affinities, this comic laughter at the monstrous other, an acceptance that lowers all humanity to the level of the animal, curiously quells that fear.

One of the major themes of the essays assembled here is the questioning of the visually objectified nature of defect. Many of the authors challenge the early modern period's fetishization of difference, its need to know difference through envisioning it. Yet such curiosity, as our essays show, paradoxically affords the opportunity for new forms of potentially subversive subjectivities and interiorities. The anecdote of Hunter serves both as historical tableau and monitory parable for our contribution to the contemporary criticism of defect, deformity, and monstrosity. The strange resemblances it uncovers illustrate the method of the essays in this volume: all employ a mode of historical inquiry that undoes past definitions in order to open present questions. We hope by such inquiry to distinguish ourselves from the scientific founders of medical museums, themselves so intent on separating themselves from the masses who flocked to see marvels at Bartholemew Fair.[71] And we also distinguish ourselves from the recent important volume *Monster Theory,* whose editor reads monstrosity from Beowulf through Jurassic Park as the return of history's repressed, foregrounding the monster's uncanny ahistoricity and questioning history's truth.[72] Our volume insists upon the early modern period's importance for the study of disability and defect because this was an era that legislated differences of sex, race, and able-bodiedness under the aegis of the "natural." It also attempts to elicit careful connections and distinctions among the various emergent modern definitions of defect, disability, deformity, and monstrosity. These newly instituted differences provided a one-way mirror, even a key, to an emergent norm, a norm we hope to restore to its troubled historical particularity. For many Enlightenment thinkers, science's thwarted drive to define monstrosity left literature as the proper venue for the display of monsters in all their ambiguity.[73] Our brand of literary and cultural criticism hopes to worry the tenuous link between literature and science, between "subjective" and "objective" forms of knowledge, so crucial to Enlightenment modes of vision. In the process we hope to begin to restore to "natural history" what it would not write, the beginnings of a genealogy of human nature.

Concluding the introduction to *Making Sex,* Thomas Laqueur confesses to a "most obvious and persistent omission in this book: a sustained account of experience in the body," a claim that Stephen Pender echoes when he observes that "there is little direct evidence detailing the ways in which *monsters themselves* felt about their deformity."[74] We hope that the essays in this volume will continue the effort toward such a subjectification of the objectified body, begun in part by our own earlier work—Helen Deutsch's study of Alexander Pope's ambiguously gendered manipulation of a couplet of deformity and form in *Resemblance and Disgrace,* and Felicity Nussbaum's exploration of the potentially revolutionary alliance of deformity and femininity in exotic and English feminotopias in *Torrid Zones.*[75] The writers in this volume read dialectics of difference in order to let monsters interrogate their makers and the "defective" query the margins that define them. When William Hay declares with pride that his curved back conforms to the shape of Hogarth's line of feminine beauty, he begins such an interrogation in terms that we pursue. We have chosen to organize our essays under three recurrent and often overlapping rubrics of "defect": disability, monstrosity, and imperfection. We close this introduction by tracing our authors' engagement with a related set of intersecting and evolving categories in the eighteenth century: namely, the various differences, including especially gender, race, and nation, that cross and unite these classifications of physical difference.

The cultural construction of femininity as natural monstrosity is examined in detail by Elizabeth Heckendorn Cook, Felicity Nussbaum, Robert W. Jones, and Jill Campbell; to varying degrees, these authors examine from within the experience of possessing a female body in eighteenth-century culture. For the virtuous young woman of Cook's essay, to be singular, to express a desire of her own, is to be a monster. Cook investigates the ideological contradictions inherent in the science of eighteenth-century botany (a pursuit often recommended for women), whose practitioners' investigations into the often scandalous sexual behavior of plants forced them to read a divide between sex and gender, a divide that her examination of the works of Erasmus Darwin deconstructs in detail. Cook analyzes the paradoxes of disparate genres in Darwin: his conduct book for girls designed to instruct them in virtuous "involuntary motions," and the generic monstrosity of his epic poem cum scientific treatise, *The Loves of the Plants,* in which different parts of the text battle for control over interpretation of natural—and monstrous—plant sexuality. Nussbaum's essay examines the various plots of female deformity, desire, and racial difference in play in early eighteenth-century British culture at large and in prose works by Aphra Behn and Eliza Haywood in particular. In her account, the ideological association of women with the disabled and the exotic deformed is at once forged and undone by the writings of a particularly monstrous form of woman, the female author. Robert Jones's insightful reading of Sarah Scott's novel *Agreeable Ugliness* similarly considers the contradictory relationship of female identity to beauty in Scott's work. If in Cook's account, female singularity is construed as freakish, in Jones's analysis, singularity, here called "ugliness," is the mark of middle-class female virtue, as long as, paradoxically, it remains indistinguishable from the father's image as "a nonidentity, a near resemblance." For women to be monstrous in Scott they must provoke desire in the eyes of men; the question of female desire remains, in Scott's work, largely unanswered, but for the feminotopia of *Millenium Hall.* Jones's essay shows us Scott's attempt to negotiate with propriety and dignity a woman's adult and adulterating leap into public life, a leap that, as Harriet Guest's work on the female middle-class appropriation of the aristocratic ethic of retirement has demonstrated, risks putting virtuous interiority on display.[76] Jill Campbell's meditation on the "acquired deformity" of old age collapses nature and culture, first exploring how cultural anxieties about aging were projected onto the bodies of older women depicted as monstrously grotesque, noting how the temporal process of mortality common to all human beings is fetishized as a woman's loss of visual beauty. A transmogrification that takes a lifetime is imagined in such projections as an instant, as the complexities of temporal experience disappear into the simultaneity of the visual. Campbell goes on to consider the lived experience of Lady Mary Wortley Montagu, who contemplates her beauty lost to smallpox in poems written early and late in her career. Here the social invisibility of female old age allows for the articulation of that which society finds too monstrous even to define, female desire.

Barbara M. Benedict, Lennard J. Davis, Helen Deutsch, Nicholas Mirzoeff, and Stephen Pender question the politics of visibility governing definitions of defect in related ways, all tending toward an examination of norms of masculinity, subjectivity, and cultural authority. For Stephen Pender this questioning begins by historicizing a concept of monstrosity that recent scholarship has too often fixed and universalized as its own mirror of alterity. Outlining a history of human exhibition in England in the "age of curiosity," the seventeenth and eighteenth centuries, Pender also tells a story of rising anxiety over fraud, imposture, and excessive credulity. Pender demonstrates the class dynamics involved in the emergence of the new science and its reform of curiosity, arguing that science incorporated the threat of wonder while pretending to reject it in the form of popular gullibility: thus "science," even Bacon himself admitted, "is a monster." Asserting that "there was more continuity than change in the history of human exhibition in England," Pender concludes with a discussion of William Hay's mid-eighteenth-century autobiographical *Deformity: An Essay,* considering Hay's attempt to revise what has endured as a "residual faith in the somatic exterior as a reliable index to the soul," and to transform the visible deformity that Bacon had argued was an inevitable cause of human evil into a sign that demands interpretation. From this perspective deformity is the sign of human individuality itself, and its meanings are the stuff of history.

Lennard J. Davis and Helen Deutsch both examine the figure of the powerful and charismatic man of letters Samuel Johnson, a monumental cultural authority who was also physically disabled, in order to illuminate early modern definitions of disability. For Davis, the contemporary fascination with Johnson occurs at a transitional moment in Britain, when earlier definitions of monstrosity as spectacle cede in the nineteenth century to a version of disability as a character-defining moral virtue or shortcoming to be heroically overcome. Johnson and Amelia, Henry Fielding's famously noseless mid-century novel heroine, are marked by their defects yet cannot fully possess them: "Their bodies bear the mark but not the sign." Davis analyzes a period in which disability as a "disruption in the sensory field" had not yet become the stuff of interiority. Deutsch turns to Johnson as an exemplary case of the eighteenth-century association of masculine disability with cultural authority. In her argument, the spectacle of Johnson's nervous tics performs and thus masters anxieties about authorship and agency shared by Johnson and his viewers. By attempting to restore to view the spectacle of Johnson's body that so fascinated his contemporaries, Deutsch also situates that disabled body at the formative center of Johnson's formidable literary achievement, asking in the process what has been at stake for later generations of Johnsonians in making that body disappear. In an enthralling case study of Renwick Williams, branded "The Monster" of 1790 and arrested and imprisoned for public and verbal assaults on women (particularly on their clothes), Barbara Benedict examines a figure who, at a moment of great social anxiety in England, is made to embody monstrosity conceived as masculinity itself. At this moment, Benedict argues, the traditional trope of monstrosity as wonder, "challenging science in explaining deviation . . . was deployed to define the unregulated part of humanity itself." Provoking "the first instance of a trial prosecuting a hate crime against women," depicted as a predatory yet effete aristocrat, while feared as a bestial working-class incendiary, the figure of Renwick Williams also exemplifed the terrifying nature of modern monstrosity, which conflated older definitions of the natural and legible evil of the bodily deformed with an aberrancy that wore the guise of a gentleman. Benedict demonstrates the haunted nature of a particular historical moment desperately in need of exceptional beings in order to regulate potential social disorder through the promulgation and control of gendered norms. Examining a parallel crisis of vision, Nicholas Mirzoeff focuses on the tableau of the discovery of deaf sign language in eighteenth-century France in order to restore an alternate deaf subjectivity beyond the subsequent definitions of deafness as monstrosity, a subjectivity inherent in "the silences . . . of the historical record in pursuit of the history of the other," and in "the face-to-face ethical encounter . . . that the discourse of monstrosity seeks to prevent." Juxtaposing his historical account with the work of a contemporary deaf artist Joseph Grigely, Mirzoeff's subject matter and method characterize a form of inquiry that is profoundly dialogic in its recognition of alterity and inspiring in its call for the individual reader's own perceptual transformation.

Though a number of the essays consider the relationship of the boundaries of the human to the formation of national pride, Joel Reed examines these ideas most explicitly. Reed's consideration of Anglo-Irish antiquarianism, on the borders of science, aesthetics, wonder, and religious martyrology, understands nationality itself as a kind of macabre perversion when articulated by the colonized for an English audience that has set the limits of scientific comprehension and of British citizenship. The anonymity and interchangeability of individual citizens that characterizes modern nationalism is belied here by the monstrosity of a liminal Anglo-Irish identity that must insist on both individual particularity and scientific universality, both national pride and admission into an international (and significantly English) scholarly community. Combining a "pantheon of admirable men" with a "gallery of freaks," these writers confuse the boundaries of individuality, thereby exposing the monstrosity inherent in subsequent constructions of uniform nationhood. Finally, Cora Kaplan's afterword considers women writers such as Wollstonecraft, Brontë, Craik, and Woolf who twist the conjunctions of monstrosity, race, and gender to wrest bourgeois feminist agency and autonomy from them. Such women both advance their progressive agenda and distinguish themselves from a repulsive femininity, even, in the case of Woolf, apparently advocating the destruction of mentally impaired people. Thus a certain strain of feminism, a liberal feminism that this volume wishes to contest and transform, competes with disability rather than aligns itself with its interests.

In short, the essays gathered together in this volume show that the functions that the defective and the monstrous served in culture in the past and in the present are multiple and contradictory, though they threaten to solidify into cultural norms that demarcate the limits of the human. Norbert Elias has described how, as a category of the normal evolves, the socially aberrant are pushed increasingly to the margins in order to "civilize" the social body.[77] The aberrant are akin to all those who inhabit the margins—"races" other than European, women, those of uncertain gender, the laboring classes—as the nation and the modern body associated with it begin to cohere. Our goal is to heighten the visibility of the "defective" even as we seek to shift the terms by which we acknowledge that we are they.

NOTES

1. *Orthopaedia: or, the Art of Correcting and Preventing Deformities in Children: By Such Means as may easily be put in Practice by* PARENTS *themselves, and all such as are employed in Educating* CHILDREN. *To which is added A* DEFENCE *of the* ORTHOPAEDIA, *by way of* SUPPLEMENT, *by the* AUTHOR, translated from the French of M. Andry, professor of Medicine in the Royal College and Senior Dean of the Faculty of Physick at Paris, 2 vols. (London, 1743), 2:211.

2. Oliver Goldsmith, *An History of the Earth* (London, 1774), 2:239.

3. *The Ugly Club: A Dramatic Caricature in One Act performed on the 6th of June, 1798, at The Theatre-Royal, Drury Lane,* founded on the Seventeenth Number of the Spectator by Edmund Spenser the Younger (London, 1798), 40.

4. *A Short History of Human Prodigies and Monstrous Births, or Dwarfs, Sleepers, Giants, Strong Men, Hermaphrodites, Numerous Births, and Extream Old Age &c*, compiled by James Paris Du Plessis, BL Sloane MS. 5246.

5. Katharine Park and Lorraine Daston, "Unnatural Conceptions: The Study of Monsters in Sixteenth- and Seventeenth-Century France and England," *Past and Present* 92 (August 1981): 51.

6. Kenny Fries, ed., *Staring Back: The Disability Experience from the Inside Out* (New York: Penguin, 1997).

7. Susan Wendell, *The Rejected Body: Feminist Philosophical Reflections on Disability* (New York: Routledge, 1996), 13ff., cites the UN definition and offers a helpful critique of its premises.

8. We are grateful to Alexandria Currin, a teacher at Jowonio, an inclusive preschool in Syracuse, New York, for her help in formulating this point.

9. Rosemarie Garland Thomson, *Extraordinary Bodies: Figuring Physical Disability in American Culture and Literature* (New York: Columbia University Press, 1997), 8.

10. In a related development in twentieth-century autobiography studies, G. Thomas Couser foregrounds "the relation of illness narratives to other forms of life writing and to the discourses of illness and disability," in *Recovering Bodies: Illness, Disability, and Life Writing* (Madison: University of Wisconsin Press, 1997), 13.

11. Sarah Scott, *Sir George Ellison*, ed. Betty Rizzo (Lexington: University Press of Kentucky, 1996), 197.

12. Lorraine Daston, "Marvelous Facts and Miraculous Evidence in Early Modern Europe," *Critical Inquiry* 18, no. 1 (1991): 108. Similarly, Nicolas Vlahogiannis discusses the use of disability as sign of divine punishment in the classical world, a definition that placed the disabled, at once heroic and abject, on the margins of humanity. "Disabling Bodies," in *Changing Bodies, Changing Meanings*, ed. Dominic Montserrat (London: Routledge, 1998), 13–36.

13. Daston, "Marvelous Facts," 112–13.

14. Rosemarie Garland Thomson, ed., *Freakery: Cultural Spectacles of the Extraordinary Body* (New York and London: New York University Press, 1996), 3, 4.

15. Lorraine Daston and Katharine Park, *Wonders and the Order of Nature, 1150–1750* (New York: Zone, 1998), 305 and chap. 9.

16. Mary Louise Pratt, *Imperial Eyes: Travel Writing and Transculturation* (London: Routledge, 1992), mentions the category of monsters but does not discuss its significance. See also George Louis Leclerc Buffon, *Natural History, General and Particular* (London, 1780).

17. Charles Linné [Linnaeus], *A General System of Nature, through the Three Grand Kingdoms of Animals, Vegetables, and Minerals, Systematically Divided*, trans. William Turton, M.D., 7 vols. (London: Lackington, Allen, and Company, 1802), 1:9. See also Pratt, *Imperial Eyes*, 32.

18. Translated in Thomas Bendyshe, "The History of Anthropology," in *Memoirs* (Anthropological Society of London, 1863–64), 1:426.

19. John Locke, *Essay concerning Human Understanding*, bk. 3, chap. 6, sec. 23. For a history of monstrosity that begins with the biblical prohibitions against bes-

tiality, see Arnold I. Davidson, "The Horror of Monsters," in *The Boundaries of Humanity: Humans, Animals, Machines*, ed. James J. Sheehan and Morton Sosna (Berkeley and Los Angeles: University of California Press, 1991), 36–67.

20. Winthrop Jordan, *White over Black: American Attitudes toward the Negro, 1550–1812* (Chapel Hill: University of North Carolina Press, 1968), 244.

21. Henry Baker, "A Supplement to the Account of a distempered Skin," *Philosophical Transactions* 19, no. 424, pt. 1 (1755): 21–24. Salivation entailed producing excess excretions by administering mercury.

22. Baker, "Supplement," 23.

23. [Pierre Louis Moreau de] Maupertuis, *Vénus Physique, contenant deux dissertations, l'une sur l'origine des hommes et des animaux; et l'autre sur l'origine des noirs* (La Haye, 1745), pt. 2, chap. 7, in *Forerunners of Darwin: 1745–1859*, ed. Bentley Glass, Owsei Temkin, and William Straus Jr. (Baltimore: Johns Hopkins Press, 1959), 77.

24. Goldsmith, *History of the Earth*, 2:228.

25. Ann Laura Stoler, *Race and the Education of Desire: Foucault's* History of Sexuality *and the Colonial Order of Things* (Durham: Duke University Press, 1995), 29. Stoler is citing Michel Foucault, *The History of Sexuality*, vol. 1, trans. Robert Hurley (1978; rpt., New York: Random House, 1990), 125.

26. Stoler, *Race and the Education*, 29.

27. Thomas Laqueur, *Making Sex: Body and Gender from the Greeks to Freud* (Cambridge: Harvard University Press, 1990), 6.

28. Londa Schiebinger, "The Anatomy of Difference: Race and Sex in Eighteenth-Century Science," *Eighteenth-Century Studies* 23 (1990): 387–406, and *The Mind Has No Sex? Women in the Origins of Modern Science* (Cambridge: Harvard University Press, 1989), 189–213. For Schiebinger's expansion of Laqueur, see *Mind Has No Sex?* 190–91.

29. Maupertuis, *Vénus Physique*, pt. 1, chap. 17.

30. For the political and social ramifications of these debates, see Marie-Hélène Huet, *Monstrous Imagination* (Cambridge: Harvard University Press, 1993), chaps. 1 and 2; and Ludmilla Jordanova, "Gender, Generation, and Science: William Hunter's Obstetrical Atlas," in *William Hunter and the Eighteenth-Century Medical World*, ed. W. F. Bynum and Roy Porter (Cambridge: Cambridge University Press, 1985), 402–12.

31. *The Female Monster or, The Second Part of the World turn'd Topsy Turvey. A Satyr* (London, 1705).

32. *A Discourse Concerning Propriety of Manners, Taste and Beauty. Being an Introduction to a Work Hereafter to be published intituled* [sic] *Moral Beauty and Deformity, exemplified and contrasted in two Living Characters* (London, 1751).

33. *Hebe; or, the Art of Preserving Beauty, and Correcting Deformity; Being a Complete Treatise on the Various Defects of the Human Body, with the most approved Methods of Prevention and Cure; and the Preservation of Health and Beauty in General* (London, 1786), 165.

34. *Hebe*, 15.

35. *Hebe*, 11.

36. See, for an example of a divine order which encompasses and sees beyond

monsters, Michel de Montaigne, *The Complete Essays of Montaigne*, trans. Donald M. Frame (1958; rpt., Stanford: Stanford University Press, 1981), 539. For the eighteenth-century deist version of such providence, see Andrew Curran and Patrick Graille, "The Faces of Eighteenth-Century Monstrosity," *Eighteenth-Century Life* 21 (May 1997): 1–15.

37. David Hume, *Essays Moral, Political, and Literary*, ed. Eugene F. Miller, rev. ed. (Indianapolis: Liberty Fund, 1987), 4.

38. *Beauty's Triumph, or, the Superiority of the Fair Sex Invariably Proved*, 3 parts (London, 1751), 151.

39. James A. Steintrager, "Perfectly Inhuman: Moral Monstrosity in Eighteenth-Century Discourse," *Eighteenth-Century Life* 21 (May 1997): 114–32. See also Michel Foucault, *Discipline and Punish*, trans. Alan Sheridan (1977; rpt., New York: Vintage, 1979).

40. Francis Bacon, *Novum Organum*, quoted in Park and Daston, "Unnatural Conceptions," 1.

41. Curran and Graille, "Faces of Monstrosity," 1.

42. Georges Canguilhem, *On the Normal and the Pathological*, trans. Carolyn Fawcett in collaboration with Robert S. Cohen (1978; rpt., New York: Zone, 1991), 31–32.

43. Georges Canguilhem, *La connaisance de la vie* (Paris: Vrin, 1965), 177, quoted in Huet, *Monstrous Imagination*, 102.

44. Park and Daston, "Unnatural Conceptions," 23.

45. Huet, *Monstrous Imagination*, esp. 103–28.

46. Alexander Pope, "Argument" of *To a Lady, Of the Characters of Women* (1735), *The Poems of Alexander Pope*, ed. John Butt (New Haven: Yale University Press, 1963), 559. This poem accompanies three epistles devoted to the different characters of men.

47. Curran and Graille, "Faces of Monstrosity," 7.

48. Curran and Graille, "Faces of Monstrosity," 3.

49. Drewrey Ottley, *The Life of John Hunter, F.R.S.*, in *The Works of John Hunter, F.R.S.*, ed. James F. Palmer, 4 vols. (London, 1835), 1:106–7.

50. Byrne had been exhibited in his native Ireland before coming to London. A boot, shoe, stocking, and a glove once in his possession are also on display at the Royal College of Surgeons. In his portrait of John Hunter, Sir Joshua Reynolds depicts the giant's lower limbs in the background. See Fiona Haslam, *From Hogarth to Rowlandson: Medicine in Art in Eighteenth-Century Britain* (Liverpool: Liverpool University Press, 1996), 285–86. When Byrne's skull was opened in 1911, his pituitary gland was found to be greatly enlarged. He thus takes his place in medical history as instrumental in revealing the cause of giantism. J. Dobson, "Charles Byrne: The Irish Giant," *Annals of Surgery* 13 (1953): 63–65, cited in Haslam, 315.

51. On the experimental impulse at the heart of sensibility that links libertines with scientists, see Ann Jessie Van Sant, *Eighteenth-Century Sensibility and the Novel: The Senses in Social Context* (Cambridge: Cambridge University Press, 1993). For a recent fictional rewriting of this curious desire and its victim, see Elizabeth McCracken's recent novel *The Giant's House* (New York: Avon Books, 1996), in which

a librarian meets and falls in love with a young man who is a giant. She gives him books about his condition—realizing reluctantly that the category of her research must be "freaks"—and the story of Hunter and Byrne fuels his nightmares.

52. Jordanova, "Gender, Generation, and Science" 401. Jordanova's discussion of William Hunter's visual epistemology, in which "all was known by means of sight," and all of nature was a self-evident surface to be revealed through violence, is equally applicable to John Hunter, who was William's most famous student, successor, and rival as anatomist.

53. John Bender, "Impersonal Violence: The Penetrating Gaze and the Field of Narration in *Caleb Williams*," in *Vision and Textuality*, ed. Stephen Melville and Bill Readings (Durham: Duke University Press, 1995), 256–81.

54. Barbara Maria Stafford, *Body Criticism: Imaging the Unseen in Enlightenment Art and Medicine* (Cambridge: MIT Press, 1991).

55. Huet, *Monstrous Imagination*, 128.

56. See Stephen Pender, "'No Monsters at the Resurrection': Inside Some Conjoined Twins," in *Monster Theory: Reading Culture*, ed. Jeffrey Jerome Cohen (Minneapolis: University of Minnesota, 1996), 143–67, for an analysis of seventeenth-century views of conjoined twins; and Dennis Todd, *Imagining Monsters: Miscreations of the Self in Eighteenth-Century England* (Chicago: University of Chicago Press, 1995), 126–39, for eighteenth-century perspectives.

57. On the political ideology of the nervous system, see Karl Figlio, "The Metaphor of Organization," *History of Science* 14 (March 1976): 17–53. For its gendered politics, see Van Sant, *Eighteenth-Century Sensibility;* Barbara Duden, *The Woman beneath the Skin: A Doctor's Patients in Eighteenth-Century Germany*, trans. Thomas Dunlap (Cambridge: Harvard University Press, 1991); John Mullan, *Sentiment and Sociability* (Oxford: Clarendon Press, 1988); and Claudia L. Johnson, *Equivocal Beings: Politics, Gender, and Sentimentality in the 1790s* (Chicago: University of Chicago Press, 1995).

58. Michel Foucault, *Madness and Civilization*, trans. Richard Howard (1965; reprint, New York: Vintage, 1988), 158.

59. Huet, *Monstrous Imagination*, 10.

60. Todd, *Imagining Monsters*, esp. 64–139. It is important to note that Todd curiously ignores the gendering of the mind-body problem posed by monstrosity, a problem that he nevertheless so carefully analyzes.

61. Lennard J. Davis, *Enforcing Normalcy: Disability, Deafness, and the Body* (London: Verso, 1995).

62. *Two Introductory Lectures: Delivered by Dr. William Hunter to his Last Course of Anatomical Lectures at his Theatre in Windmill-Street: As they were left corrected for the Press by himself. To which are added, some papers relating to Dr. Hunter's Intended Plan, for establishing a Museum in London, for the Improvement of Anatomy, Surgery, and Physic* (London, 1784), 117. For an analysis of Hunter's obstetrical atlas in the context of contemporary medical, social, aesthetic, and political thought, see Jordanova, "Gender, Generation, and Science."

63. Daston, "Marvelous Facts," 94–95.

64. Pender, "No Monsters at the Resurrection," 150.

65. Michel Foucault, *The Order of Things: An Archaeology of the Human Sciences* (1970; rpt., New York: Vintage, 1994), 155, 157.

66. On Charles Wilson Peale's museum as an American totality designed to defeat mortality, see Edward L. Schwarzschild, "Death-Defying/Defining Spectacles: Charles Wilson Peale as Early American Freak Showman," in Thomson, *Freakery*, 82–96.

67. Terry Castle, *The Female Thermometer: Eighteenth-Century Culture and the Invention of the Uncanny* (New York: Oxford University Press, 1995), 8–9.

68. See Pender, "No Monsters at the Resurrection"; and Paul Semonin, "Monsters in the Marketplace: The Exhibition of Human Oddities in Early Modern England," in Thomson, *Freakery*, 72.

69. Semonin, "Monsters in the Marketplace," 77.

70. Semonin, "Monsters in the Marketplace," 80. On caricature, see Stafford, *Body Criticism*, 178–99.

71. For the beginnings of an analysis of the British culture of curiosity, see Barbara M. Benedict, "The 'Curious Attitude' in Eighteenth-Century Britain: Observing and Owning," *Eighteenth-Century Life* 14 (November 1990): 59–98; Richard D. Altick, *The Shows of London* (Cambridge, MA: Belknap Press, 1978).

72. Cohen, *Monster Theory*, 1–25.

73. Curran and Graille, "Faces of Monstrosity," 8–11.

74. Laqueur, *Making Sex*, 23; Pender, "No Monsters at the Resurrection," 163.

75. Helen Deutsch, *Resemblance and Disgrace: Alexander Pope and the Deformation of Culture* (Cambridge: Harvard University Press, 1996); and Felicity A. Nussbaum, *Torrid Zones: Maternity, Sexuality, and Empire in Eighteenth-Century English Narratives* (Baltimore: Johns Hopkins University Press, 1995).

76. See Harriet Guest, "A Double Lustre: Femininity and Sociable Commerce, 1730–1760," *Eighteenth-Century Studies* 23 (1990): 479–501.

77. Norbert Elias, *The Civilizing Process*, trans. Edmund Jephcott, 2 vols. (New York: Pantheon, 1978).

PART 1 Disability

Dumb Virgins, Blind Ladies, and Eunuchs: Fictions of Defect

Felicity Nussbaum

> Not every Man or Woman was design'd
> To propagate and multiply their Kind;
> Forbid we rightly the Deform'd and Foul,
> To clothe with ill-shaped Limbs the heav'nly Soul.
> —Claudius Quillet, *Callipaedia: or,*
> *the Art of Getting Beautiful Children*

According to a feminist vindication popular throughout the eighteenth century, Aristotle, who "pretends that *women* are neither more or less than *Monsters*," regards the sex as deformed amphibious things.[1] The author of the defence of women's rights counters the assumption that sexual difference should be construed as defect: "Each [sex] was perfect in its Way; and it was necessary they should be disposed as we see them, and every Thing that depends upon their respective constitutions, is to be consider'd as Part of their Perfection. It is therefore, without Foundation, that some imagine the Women are not so perfect as the Men, and represent that as a Defect, which is an essential Appendage to their Sex, without which they could not answer the Intent of their Creation."[2] The "Appendage to their sex" (called an "Essential Portion of their Sex" in an earlier version) refers to women's reproductive organs, and in particular the womb, construed in the earlier Aristotelian and Galenic models to be an interior penis that constitutes the salient biological difference.[3] Echoing Alexander Pope's sentiment in *Epistle to a Lady,* "Fine by defect, and delicately weak" (line 44), the tract suggests that the culture defines woman as a defective man, less than a man and lacking perfection, because she is less vigorous and strong. Unlike men's appendage, hers is not palpable or easily observable. The essence of womanhood is her womb, hidden and interior, rather than the more visible female organs. This mysterious female difference is misconstrued, the tract suggests, as deformity. But, *Female Rights Vindicated* asserts, men habitually and misogynistically deem women's flaws to be natural and intrinsic to their sexual difference. Defect is not only the lack of a penis but the presence of the wrong thing.

Woman's excess or appendage—the reproductive womb—embodies failed femininity within a striking dynamic of similarity and difference. Further complicating femininity's definition is the concept that a woman's value within the sexual economy arises from another sign of biological difference, her external beauty. Speaking of female attractiveness in *Female Rights Vindicated,* the author notes, "If one would judge of its Worth by the Sentiments and Passions it excites, which is the common Method of estimating every Thing, it would be found to be surpass'd by nought, either in Praise or Effect; so greatly are the Passions agitated, fortified, mixed, and diversified by the Impressions of Beauty" (94). Thus woman's difference is both "Merchantable" and the object of contempt, both precious and demeaned, both visible and invisible, her "defect" valued as the object of envy, yet the site of monstrous excess.

Here I want to consider the alignment between gender and defect in several eighteenth-century fictions written by women in the context of these vindications to assess the ways that deformity and disfigurement helped both to articulate sexual difference and to muddy its binaries. Female subjectivity and women writers in particular are the source of increased cultural anxieties about "natural" boundaries between the sexes and thus help constitute the problem they describe and attack. In particular I will be discussing fictions that resist these conceptual frameworks of femininity as defect. The early women writers Aphra Behn and Eliza Haywood, I suggest, offer particularly vexed fictive examples of femininity as monstrosity. In the context of misogynist tracts and the responses to them, these fictions refine and counter the prevailing constructions of femininity as aberration. Their arguments also extend to the much desired but mutilated man, the eunuch, who veers away so radically from the conquering economic hero crucial to the formation of a British identity. A defective man is often taken to be a mere imitation of femininity since defect bears a linguistic and cultural equivalency to womanhood. In this construction, lack signifies femaleness, while substance signals masculinity. As *Female Rights Vindicated* puts it, "When a Man is to be ridiculed for Pusillanimity, he is called effeminate, meaning he is as cowardly and weak as a Woman. When on the other Hand, a Woman is to be praised for her uncommon Courage, for her Strength, or even intellectual Capacity, she is compared to a Man. These Expressions, so favourable to the Men, fail not to contribute, in a great Measure, to the high Opinion that is entertained of them" (92). Natural anomalies, man-made monsters, and imaginary beings test the limits of gender and of the human as definitions of the modern body emerge. These gradations of categories set in play fascinating oppositions that help to shape normalcy, including those between reproductive and nonreproductive beings, and between those deformities for which sufferers are held morally responsible and those deformities suffered by the innocent.

Another set of oppositions arises between internal and external defect. *Beauty's Triumph* (1751) claims that even women's elaborate artifices cannot adequately disguise their blemishes. In the refutation of Sophia's arguments for women's superiority, part 2 asserts men's natural moral superiority by handing the woman in question a pocket mirror. Here the cultural meaning of "blemishes" slips between the metaphorical and the material, between that of character and of a more literal physical disfigurement: "By shewing you to yourselves in a true light, [the reflection] will, I hope, enable you to improve the real excellencies, and to remove out of sight all the blemishes you may discover in yourselves. And as patches and paint will be useless to hide the defects . . . it may possibly set you on finding out better expedients to prevent the ill effects of them, than the daubing disguise of affectation."[4] Anatomists of the later eighteenth and early nineteenth centuries often literally erased blemishes in the interests of molding representations of the body into idealized versions. Anatomist Bernard Albinus urged his peers to "draw a handsome face, and if there happens to be any blemish in it, they [would] mend it in the picture," and Samuel Thomas von Soemmerring preferred to select the most perfect anatomical models for representation.[5] Depicting blemishes interfered with the idealized depiction of womanhood, but cosmetics were only a temporary and unsatisfactory solution to helping women escape their inherently flawed state. In short, defects for both sexes were deemed substantive as well as superficial, but women's blemishes in particular were frequently believed to reveal the outward manifestation of internal deficiency.

The misogynist male narrator in *Beauty's Triumph*, part 2, ironically links "blemish" both to women's beauty and to anatomical essentialism. Recalling the assignment of defect to the womb, Salacia is exemplary of a mother whose blemishes result in the creation of deformed and monstrous children: "she possesses all the blemishes which compose the perfections of her sex, in so high a degree, that we could not but acknowledge her worthy of something very like our esteem, if all these feminine accomplishments were not eclipsed by one more, which absorbs all the rest: she is sensible that the chief

end she was made for is to breed" (95–96). In this passage, blemishes paradoxically constitute the perfection of womanhood, but the ability to give
birth, the most potent marker of sexual difference, here corresponds with
monstrosity and moral perversion. Though women are responsible for re-
producing the species, their principal deformity rests in their incapacity to
bear healthy "normal" babies: "That WOMEN *are no more to be trusted
than their WOMBS:* these being not more liable to miscarry of their fruits,
than they of the trust we deposit in them" (124). A particularly defective nature suffuses a mother's deformity into her progeny or, alternatively, threatens to makes her barren, though even apparently "normal" mothers may
give birth to defective children. Yet another logical possibility is that deformity makes a prostitute of women such as the hideous Calvia, "too old and
batter'd to produce even a monster" (98), whose home became known as a
public stew.[6] As a prostitute, she is aligned with women's disfiguring sexuality. The womb—in misogynist tracts, the sign of woman's ineradicable defect and the sign of her difference—either replicates its monstrosity in the
children it spews forth or is condemned to forfeit its reproductive function.
Woman's monstrous inadequacy, her freakishness, results from being a
woman, from having a womb, whether she bears children or she is unable
to bear them.

The eighteenth-century controversies surrounding the question of the potency of the maternal imagination also raised the specter of extraordinary
female power over producing "normal" offspring.[7] *Orthopaedia: or, the Art
of Correcting and Preventing Deformities in Children* extended the commonplace warning that men should not have intercourse with their wives
during menstruation to connect such activity with birthing deformed children.[8] Even Mary Wollstonecraft couples what she believes to be a cultural
tendency toward effeminacy with a high incidence of mental retardation
among the privileged classes, and she asserts that championing women's
virtue produces healthy "normal" babies of the middling class. While bearing healthy children may excuse and justify woman's "defect," her intrinsic
femaleness also aligns itself with disfigurement. The defect of womanhood that is concentrated within the womb has the potential to migrate or
to overflow to other parts of the body and even to other bodies. Inherently
and essentially defective because women possess wombs, their reproductive
power embodies the extraordinary potential to deform the human race by
breeding monsters, and the entire category of the female embodies the difference that deforms. Beyond the inherent defect of the sex, *particular*
women bear a double defect in also being blind, lame, deaf, ugly, or scarred.
Women of both sorts—the general run of femininity and the particular case

of anomalous beings—throughout the century focus cultural anxieties about links between normalcy and gender in fictions of defect as diverse as Henry Fielding's noseless *Amelia*, Sarah Scott's ladies permanently blemished from smallpox, and Frances Burney's lame, pockmarked, and humpbacked Eugenia.

Deformity, like *defect*, is a word with eighteenth-century currency. William Hay, a humpbacked member of the House of Commons, first articulated an identity as a disabled person in *Deformity: An Essay* (1754), in which he refers at length to Hogarth's discourse, *Analysis of Beauty*. Hay employs Hogarth's admiration of the curved line to redefine as aesthetically pleasing the curvature of his spine. *Deformity* frequently serves as the opposite of beauty in, for example, the title of the treatise *Hebe; or, the Art of Preserving Beauty, and Correcting Deformity* (1786). A missing eyebrow, large nose, wandering eye, hare lip, wide mouth, chin hair, freckles, and birthmarks signify deformities. Characterized by asymmetrical or misshapen bodies, the author defines deformity as an unnatural and correctable condition, "not as a total privation of beauty, but as a want of congruity in the parts, or rather an inability in them to answer their natural design; as when one arm or leg is longer than the other; when the back is hunched, when the eyes squint, and such similar defects: which, however, are not to be opposed as a contrast to beauty; for the unfortunate object may, in every other part of his body, be exactly well-made, and perfectly agreeable."[9] This problem of anatomical malformation, especially characteristic of women's bodies, may be deemed to be either accidental, man-made, or attributable to inadequate child care and poor health habits. Deformity may disguise or soften itself with artistry or cosmetics, but its permanency and intractability evoke pity, while ugliness inspires moral questioning. Beauty would seem to be within reach of the deformed, while ugliness is endemic and obdurate. A misshapen woman who strives toward virtue may transform herself into a less malformed figure. Whether the outer shell reflects the inner character, or whether disfigurement is judged biological in origin and thus unchangeable, determines whether our response is to be compassionate or condemnatory: "In a Word, if these Defects are trifling, or only the Appearances of such, it is imprudent or malicious to take Notice of them; nevertheless this is the general Practice of the Men with respect to the Women."[10] Deformity is akin to ugliness but not necessarily the opposite of beauty, though ugliness encodes evil and malevolence: "Whereas *ugliness*, which I look upon to be . . . the proper contrast to beauty, may exist in the human form without deformity; nor can I think the ideas necessarily connected. Ugliness always excites our aversion to the object in which it resides; deformity as generally calls up our commiseration."[11] In short, ugliness often corresponds to an inscrutable inner evil, while deformity—"an inability to answer nature's design"—excites compassion rather than contempt, since the defects of character are often perceived to be remediable.

Two tales of defect by Aphra Behn published in 1700, *The Dumb Virgin: or, The Force of Imagination* and *The Unfortunate Bride: Or, The Blind Lady a Beauty*, demonstrate both that all femininity is deformed or monstrous by definition and that a particular subclass of defective women who populate these fictions is especially disquieting.[12] At one level these doubly defective women stand in for all femininity; at another level they represent women who defy femininity, women writers. In these novellas the unstable relationship of beauty to virtue, of defect to lust, displays the linkages between gender and defect. In *The Dumb Virgin*, a wealthy Venetian senator's wife expresses unbridled desire for a paradisal island in the Adriatic Sea, an idyllic seat of pleasure and a market for beauty and gallantry. In this tale of woe, the cause of defective children is Renaldo's yielding to his wife's excessive desires rather than taking command. An attack by Turkish pirates brings the apparent drowning of her infant son and results eventually in her bearing defective daughters. The eldest, Belvideera, a physically deformed daughter "addicted to study" (344), is addressed as a neutered child without an identifiable gender: "its limbs were distorted, its back bent, and tho the face was the freest from deformity, yet had it no beauty to recompence the dissymetry of the other parts" (344). Her femininity is curiously lost because of the unmistakable crippling of her body. The mother's imagination, especially the erotic desire for something exotic and unfamiliar, and her unrealized fears of being taken captive and enslaved, produces defect; but defect also interrupts or complicates desire.

Saddened and uncommunicative because of her grief, Belvideera's mother dies in giving birth to a second daughter, Maria, who is beautiful but unable to speak, "which defect the learn'd attributed to the silence and melancholy of the Mother, as the deformity of the other was to the extravagance of her frights" (344). In both cases her reproductive power is compromised by immoderate desire, and her womb, the defective appendage, makes manifest the mother's hidden faults and produces a more definitive secondary category of flawed femininity in the second generation. In Maria's case the defect of speechlessness, as in the generality of womanhood, is made invisible by her natural disguise of female beauty; in Belvideera's case, as in the group constituted by defect, her facility with words distracts auditors from the painfully obvious flaw. The loving father diligently tends to the daughters' education so that Belvideera, a wit, compensates for her natural impediments by becoming a linguistic prodigy. Maria's defect results from the mother's timidity, while the eldest daughter's deformity arises from bold desire, thus setting forth a distinction between the cause of defect and deformity, though such distinctions are not consistently maintained in these two novellas. The beautiful but nonverbal Maria, skilled at sign language, rewards her father's devoted attentions by exhibiting charm and grace. Paradoxically, others find themselves struck dumb by her beauty or blinded by her piercing gaze. She possesses such a commanding presence that when a painter finds himself incapacitated by her beauty and powerful gaze, Maria resorts to completing the portrait herself. Maria embodies the creative woman who, silenced in traditional ways and excluded from conventional femininity, finds the means to express herself through art. Strong suggestions of narcissism emanate around Maria from the self-portrait she paints to the extraordinary description of her hair as "linkt in amorous twinings" (351). Her dazzling radiance is so extreme that it can only be viewed in the shade. Belvideera's tongue, in spite of her physical deformity, carries a force as compelling as Maria's eyes. As such she typifies the learned Amazonian whose femininity throughout the eighteenth century is questioned and who is often placed outside the usual sexual traffic or represented as a freakish man-woman.

In *The Dumb Virgin's* subplot, a suitor named Dangerfield "with no disguise but a *Turkish* Turbant on" (346) courts Maria, though both sisters, one beautiful but silent and the other ugly but brilliant, become competitors for him.[13] The uncomely Belvideera at first jealously prevents Dangerfield from learning about her sister's muteness. Though Maria pulses with sensual heat, "her breasts with an easy heaving show'd the smoothness of her Soul and of her Skin" (351); her searing beauty inflicts metaphoric wounds on her lover, for her love cannot be expressed verbally. The mute Maria curses the handicap, explained at the masquerade as a penance for unnamed sins, that prevents her from voicing her passion. One sister's contorted limbs are weighed against the other sister's being "dumb" as the women debate whether disfigurement or muteness is the greater public shame, yet both seem united in their sexual desire for Dangerfield and in their fear that their aberrant femininity excludes them from successfully circulating within the sexual economy.

When various sword fights ensue, Dangerfield, hoist on his own petard, is caught between his love for Maria's beauty and Belvideera's wit. Overwhelmed by her beauty, he declares his surfeit of passion for Maria. Swooning into his arms, she scribbles a message revealing her mute state to which he responds, *"Dumb,* (he cryed out) *naturally Dumb? O ye niggard powers, why was such a wondrous piece of Art left imperfect?"* (353–54). Maria figures the very state of being woman in the disturbing contrast between her remarkable external beauty and her silent interior flaw. This romantic tragedy inspires women to believe that handicaps, handicaps that exceed the defect of being a woman, need not be an impediment to love but may preclude marriage. Maria's inability to resist Dangerfield's malevolent charm leads her finally to succumb to his sexual assault. In Dangerfield's dying moments, a dagger birthmark he bears reveals that he is actually the son who supposedly had drowned in the Adriatic Sea. This bodily defect signifies the deeply tainted nature of love, the mother's legacy to her son, and Maria's figurative blindness leads to a greater monstrosity—incest. The recognition dawns that Maria had slept with her brother as "a violent impulse broke the ligament that doubled in her Tongue." She cries out, "Oh! Incest, Incest" (359), kills herself on her brother's sword, and the narrator, herself a playwright, is struck dumb, made speechless, when the heroine's tongue is loosened.

Ros Ballaster has argued of *The Dumb Virgin* that "Maria's entry to subjectivity/speech is then coterminous with her death and with her recognition of her desire as incestuous,"[14] but Maria's subjectivity is not confined to speech. To suggest that Behn constructs Maria without a subjectivity unwittingly replicates the idea of woman as a defect of nature. In Behn's tale the disability that defines woman as woman does not completely disempower her, and though Maria struggles to make her wishes known, she is not without will. Maria successfully employs sign language ("her silent conversation," 345) and communicates intimately with her sister. In fact, the narrator suggests that their elegant use of the form was original. The silent Maria conveys a wide range of human emotions including desire, envy, and surprise through painting, writing, body movements, clothing, and manners. Though her tongue is incapable of revealing her feelings in spoken words, she is able to communicate a fully developed subjectivity: "The language of her Eyes sufficiently paid the loss of her Tongue, and there was something so commanding in her look, that it struck every beholder as dumb as herself" (345). Both subject and object, she in fact turns the tables to disable spectators with her stunning looks. Similarly, the leveling effect of a masquerade that they all attend allows Maria to compete for men without having to talk, and it is also the turning point in creating jealous envy between the sisters: "Poor *Maria* never before envied her Sister the advantage of speech, or never deplor'd the loss of her own with more regret" (348). Though Maria flirtatiously affects an inability to communicate her love, Dangerfield has no doubt of his conquest over her heart.

Maria's recognition of her incestuous desire for her brother prevents marriage; and the unattractive Belvideera, assigning her fortune to an uncle, re-signs herself to a reclusive virginity typical of a learned lady. In *The Dumb Virgin,* then, physical deformity, ugliness, and verbal impairment seem to forestall marriage, marriage that could reproduce only monstrosity, but these characteristics do not preclude illicit desire or unorthodox subjectivity. Orig-inally muted and silenced, Maria's release into speech coincides with her recognition of another kind of monstrosity. She is only freed to speak her subjectivity through incest that would, if fully realized, thwart the traditional patriarchal transfer of property. In short, in the novella the more encom-passing category of women reproduces defect through sexual desire, while defective overreaching ladies, a subclass, defy their defect but die calling the very name of monstrosity ("Incest!").

Beyond the persistent strand of misogynist satire against learned ladies in the eighteenth century, the language of deformity and female subjectivity ex-tends easily to characterize eighteenth-century women writers and their lit-erary productions as monstrous, mutilated, and compromised. Sometimes the connection is literal, as in the example of the deformed poet Mary Chan-dler (1687–1745), who established a milliner's shop to support herself; or the blind poet Priscilla Pointon Pickering (ca. 1740–1801), who celebrated her marriage to a saddler in "Letter to Sister, Giving an Account of the Au-thor's Wedding-Day."[15] But more often, able-bodied women acting on the Restoration stage or publishing in the literary marketplace are simply as-sumed to be defects of nature by definition. Mutilation and deformity are implicated in their perverse desires. We think, for example, of the grotesque image of Eliza Haywood "with cow-like udders, and with ox-like eyes," her works compared to "two babes of love close clinging to her waste" in Pope's *Dunciad* (2.149–58).[16] This enduring image of the woman writer as the monstrous and repulsive prize bestowed on the winner of a pissing contest should be given equal weight, I think, with the more familiar epithets such as *whore, heteroclite,* and *bluestocking* applied to eighteenth-century women novelists. Women's empowerment in this period, whether it derives from beauty's empire, linguistic skill, or political and military victory, is deeply bonded to defect and deformity. In the second tale of defect, *The Unfortu-nate Bride; or, the Blind Lady A Beauty,* again Behn pairs beauty with dis-ability, and two lovely cousins, Celesia and Belvira, desire the same man. The language of love in this tale of blindness is ironically visual, and Frankwit was "so amiable . . . that every Virgin that had Eyes, knew too she had a Heart, and knew as surely she should lose it. His *Cupid* could not be reputed blind" (325). The visual metaphors are ridiculous in the extreme: "her beau-teous image danced before him," "he saw his Deity in every Bush," "there were pulses beating in their Eyes" (326), and "he only valued the smiling Babies in *Belvira's* Eyes" (327). After these constant references to the eyes, the female voice of the narrator coyly inserts that she had forgotten to mention that Celesia was visually impaired: "*Celesia* was an heiress, the only Child of a rich *Turkey* Merchant, who when he dyed left her fifty thousand pound in Money, and some Estate in land; but, poor creature, she was blind to all these riches, having been born without the use of sight, though in all other respects charming to a wonder" (327). Being blind is not equated with sexual virtue, but it does make Celesia oblivious to earthly wealth. Celesia, according to Frankwit, possesses a *"charming Blindness"* (328), and, like Maria in *The Dumb Virgin,* she is able to conquer lovers even with a significant handicap: *"You, fair Maid, require no Eyes to conquer"* (328).

When childhood sweethearts Frankwit and Belvira seek Celesia's advice as to whether they should marry, Celesia confesses her own attraction to Frankwit. Reminding us of the incestuous love in *The Dumb Virgin,* sexual expectation is likened to "A Monster which enjoyment could not satisfy" (329). Celesia's blindness, unlike ugliness or physical deformity, does not detract from her charms, and her powers of understanding, in the tradition of the blind prophet, are quite formidable: "Sight is fancy," according to Celesia. When Frankwit determines to marry Belvira, Celesia "thought herself most unhappy that she had not eyes to weep with too; but if she had, such was the greatness of her grief, that sure she would have soon grown blind with weeping" (329). Though Frankwit protests his undying devotion to Belvira in an epistolary poem, the narrator treats the lover's remonstrations of fidelity with skepticism. Frankwit makes a brief trip to Cambridge, and Celesia miraculously recovers her sight in his absence through the ministrations of an aged matron: "her eyes flow'd more bright with the lustrous beams, as if they were to shine out; now all that glancing, radiancy which had been so long kept secret, and as if, as soon as the cloud of blindness once was broke, nothing but lightnings were to flash for ever after" (331).

The plot thickens as Frankwit lodges in Cambridge with a wealthy blackamoor, Moorea, who intercepts the lovers' letters. Moorea is racialized as a she-devil whose name also implies a religious other: "the Black *Moorea,* black in her mind, and dark, as well as in her body" (332). A widow who had been left six thousands pounds per annum by her knighted husband, her jealous treachery eventually allows the blind, beautiful Celesia and the man who is "a much softer beauty" to be united in marriage, and it leads to the death of Belvira. Moorea, complicit in the evil that befalls the other characters, sends false news of Frankwit's death. When the bewitched Frankwit fails to return, his friend, the rich and manly Wildvil, marries Belvira. The narrator, a mutual acquaintance of Moorea and Belvira, discovers the foul play wrought by the blackamoor widow and triumphs over the racial other's schemes by sending the offending letters to the newly married Belvira. In a predicament reminiscent of the staggering effects of incest in *The Dumb Virgin,* her writing powers fail her. Frankwit is struck speechless by the events that transpired, kills Wildvil in a fit of jealousy, and accidentally inflicts a mortal wound on his beloved Belvira. The paralyzing effects extend to the narrator, who professes to be stymied by the pathetic scene. Celesia, too, longs to be struck blind again so that she will not have to witness the brutality. Yet Moorea may also be interpreted as releasing the blind woman into the sexual economy, and the narrator understood as disingenuously wishing to have Celesia's blindness restored in order to resume the narrative. Must women be defective in order to possess and narrate a story?

Regaining her sight allows Celesia to become a legitimate competitor for Frankwit, whom she marries after Belvira's death, an option apparently unavailable to a sightless woman. Celesia cannot become the object of love until its rightful recipient (Belvira) is murdered, and the black Moorea intervenes in her behalf, an evil woman who nevertheless expedites the marriage of the formerly blind virgin, since Belvira in her dying moments enjoins Celesia and Frankwit to wed. But the restitution of Celesia's sight, losing her defect, also wreaks havoc, since her marriage is predicated on jealousy, deceit, and murder. Behn's doleful tale suggests that it is best for a rich and beautiful woman to remain disabled, without vision, teeming with erotic desire, even though the consequence is that she will be unable to marry. In each of these novels, the release from the defect of nature (muteness or blindness) brings misery and chaos. Defects need not render desire untenable; in fact, they may fan women's passions. Desiring women are themselves figured as defective and monstrous, and they are punished by bearing deformed children and breeding incest. In these two tales, neither the able-bodied category of "women" or more literally deformed women can be released from the defective essence of femininity.

Samuel Johnson asserts in *The Adventurer* 115 (11 December 1753) that "The revolution of years has now produced a generation of Amazons of the pen, who with the spirit of their predecessors have set masculine tyranny at defiance . . . and seem resolved to contest the usurpations of virility."[17] Though in *Idler* 87 Johnson ironically protests, "There is, I think, no class of English women from whom we are in any danger of Amazonian usurpation," and, "To dye with husbands or to live without them are the two extremes which (the prudence and moderation) of European ladies have, in all ages, equally declined," he protests too much:

> I do not mean to censure the ladies of England as defective in knowledge or in spirit, when I suppose them unlikely to revive the military honours of their sex. The character of the ancient Amazons was rather terrible than lovely; the hand could not be very delicate that was only employed in drawing the bow and brandishing the battle-axe; their power was maintained by cruelty, their courage was deformed by ferocity, and their example only shews that men and women live best together.[18]

Combining the female other and the native other, these Amazonian rulers' mutilated bodies personify monstrous femininity, perverse sexuality, aberrant maternity, and the opposite of the proper lady, yet a generation of Amazons seems to prevail. Johnson's Amazons are learned ladies, women of science, in an increasingly familiar conjunction of deformity and women's writing. Johnson had, of course, earlier translated Abbé de Guyon's *Dissertation on the Amazons* (1740); other midcentury texts that focus on the Amazon include Anna Meades's *The History of Cleanthes, an Englishman, and Celemene, the Illustrious Amazonian Princess* (1757); Hannah Snell's *The Female Soldier* (1750); and the anonymous *The British Amazon* (1753). Most famously in Charlotte Lennox's *The Female Quixote* (1752), the very title of which exemplifies "man-woman," Thalestris, queen of the Amazons, figures prominently as a satiric model for the romantic heroine.

Amazons are, of course, widowed warrior women who colonized Asia and built the city of Ephesus. Temporarily defeated by Hercules and Theseus, they murdered their guards and escaped. These barbarous and nomadic natives of Scythia (ancient European and Asiatic Russia) are governing women who amputate or cauterize their left breasts in order to become better marksmen. Actual ruling women in the contemporary moment of the eighteenth century are imagined to wage war in the Caucasus or to live primarily in Africa, where they "kill all the Boys they bring forth, and train up their Girls to military Exploits."[19] Amazons represent an entire "race" of exotic women who are deformed in several senses—sexually perverse, physically mutilated, and possessing a womb, but disinclined to marry and reproduce in the conventional manner. They engage in reproduction but inappropriately and brazenly so. As we have seen, woman's essentially defective nature arises by definition and also when she gives evidence of being insufficiently feminine, and the Amazon personifies this doubly impossible position.

The Amazon, a powerful yet mutilated warrior woman, is a specifically monstrous emblem of women's entry into the public sphere; her defective male counterpart, the eunuch, figures as man's fear of what may result from exercising that power. Defective women are so closely aligned in the cultural imagination with eunuchs, those "ecchoes of virility," according to the mythology, that it is they who allegedly introduce the practice of castration. In fact, the atrophy of male organs and the loss of masculine attributes characterized a disease that came to be known as "Scythian," named for the Amazon's legendary home, and "Scythian insanity" showed itself in a man's acting and dressing like woman. Linking Amazons to eunuchs as exotic and sometimes racialized deformed beings, *Eunuchism Display'd* (1718) recounts the commonplace legend that Semiramis, queen of the Assyrians, having dressed as a man and having led her troops to victory, introduced the practice of castration in order to demonstrate her political power over her lovers, and other legendary manly queens mutilate and maim young boys: "Perhaps this Dress gave Birth to those Reports, that *Semiramis* had made imperfect Men, half-Men, and so on, till at last it was conjectured, that she effectually made People undergo the cruel Ceremony of Castration" (4).[20] Semiramis brought up her son as a girl, took men to her bed, and then executed them.[21] In this cultural parable, male deformity misogynistically results from female authority. David Hume, for example, recounts the legend of Scythian Amazons conspiring against sleeping men to make them defective in another way, to blind them, and to free the women from pleasing men through fashion and display: "It was, therefore, agreed to put out the eyes of the whole male sex, and thereby resign in all future time the vanity which they could draw from their beauty, in order to secure their authority."[22] Merely being associated with powerful women transforms men into metaphoric eunuchs, weak and listless men, if not literally castrated beings. The misogynist gentleman who declares men's superiority in *Beauty's Triumph* indicts those fellow males who act effeminate or simply speak with women: "If there are a few degenerate creatures, who . . . by conversing with *Womankind,* putting on their foibles, and affecting to be like them, degrade themselves of manhood, commence intellectual eunuchs, and deserve no more to be reputed of the same sex with us" (159). As in the instances cited earlier, reproductive capacity or its failure seems critical to definitions of defect. Enfeebled masculinity—enervated, luxurious, and sodomite, and a particular threat to an English nation poised for military victory and continued imperial expansion—finds its most monstrous manifestation in the eunuch. Women seem doomed to being construed as defective and troubling beings whether or not they possess this reproductive ability, since giving birth may simply confirm their monstrosity, while men's ability to penetrate and spend their seed protects them from charges of feminine defect.

The vindications asserting women's equality throughout the eighteenth century also raise the specter of hermaphroditism and sexual ambiguity because women's sovereignty in both feminist and misogynist texts rests uneasily upon unmanning men. The author of *Beauty's Triumph* likens women to impersonations of "that copy of themselves," Sporus, an effeminate being who is famously "between *that* and *this*" (107). Sporus, the neutered male wife, parallels the female husband:

> All the World knows the History of *Sporus*, whom *Nero* caused to be gelt, and whose Folly was so extravagant, that he endeavoured to change his Sex; he made him wear Woman's Cloaths, and afterward married him with the usual Formalities, settled a Dowry upon him, gave him the nuptial Veil, and kept him in his Palace in quality of a Woman, which gave birth to this pleasant Saying, *That the World would have been happy had his Father* Domitian *had such a Wife.* In short, he caused this *Sporus* to be drest like an Empress, had him carried in a Litter, and attended him to all the Assemblies and publick Fairs of *Greece*, and at *Rome* to the *Sigillaria*, and Squares of the City, where he kissed him every Moment.[23]

In verses adapted from Pope's portrayal of Lord Hervey as Sporus in *Beauty's Triumph*, even a man-made eunuch or a natural hermaphrodite is better than a woman: "How well the masterly limner knew them [women], who snatch'd from them the graces he so skilfully bestowed on *Sporus*, that copy of themselves, inspired too by them, as they by *Satan!*" (107):

> *Whether in florid impotence they speak,*
> *And, as the prompter breathes, the puppets squeak;*
> *Or,* Eve's *true spawn, and tools of th'ancient toad,*
> *In puns, or politics, or tales, or lyes,*
> *Or spite, or smut, or rhymes, or blasphemies:*
> *Their wit all see-saw, between* that *and* this;
> *Now high, now low,* now forward, now remiss;
> *And* each herself *one* dull *antithesis.*
> *Amphibious things! That, acting either part,*
> *The trifling head, or the corrupted heart,*
> Bullies at cards, and flirts when *at the board,*
> *Now* jilt *like dames, now* swear *like any lord.*
> (107–8)

His gender status seriously at issue, Sporus is a profoundly inadequate copy of women. Resembling the general class of women in possessing an intrinsic defect, the eunuch is also a third sex, "neither Male nor Female, but a Prodigy in Nature" (7) whose wit, like his sexuality, is impossibly compromised. Eunuchs may be born eunuchs, their testicles "lank and flabby," or they may, like Sporus, have their testicles removed either before or after puberty, making them man-made or artificial monsters.[24] Just as the extent to which women are responsible for their defects affects the extent of our compassion, *Beauty's Triumph* argues that whether a eunuch is voluntarily or involuntarily castrated determines the nature of our moral response:

> These are imperfect Creatures, in a Word, Monsters, to whom Nature indeed has been sparing of nothing, but the Avarice, Luxury, or Malice of Men, have disfigured and deformed. If they have sometimes been raised to the highest Pinnacles of human Glory, and bask'd in the Sunshine of this World; the People look'd upon them as so many Erroneous Productions of the depraved and corrupted Minds of Princes, who elevated them to those High States of Honour, and when they appeared in Publick, they only encreased and augmented the Hatred and Aversion the People had for them, who laughed at them amongst themselves, calling them old Women, &c. (95–96)

As we have seen, all women are intrinsically defective, yet some carry the supplementary burden of ugliness, malformation, or disability. Their innocence of creating these additional flaws, and their attentiveness to overcoming them through virtuous behavior, associates them with eunuchs who may have voluntarily accepted castration; and at the same time because their defect is "natural," it disassociates them from the eunuchs whose bodies may be marked by a vicious act intentionally perpetrated upon them. Natural defect and man-made defect do not run strictly parallel. A man in a woman's clothing, Sporus costumed as Nero's wife is a precious yet inferior object, a substitute for a woman and preferable to her. A diminished man masquerading as an imitation of a woman—inherently defective—ranks more highly than she, and the man-made eunuch whom Nero had gelded rises to a place superior to women who retain their natural reproductive capability. In spite of his impotence, his inability to reproduce, he possesses a cultural value that exceeds that of a natural woman. A eunuch could be categorized as a natural or man-made deformity, both the object of derision and a prized rarity because of his castrato voice. The affectation of femininity perverts manliness, though the exchange value of both women and eunuchs is high. Women are also judged defective because of their capacity to reproduce, while eunuchs are judged defective because of their inability to reproduce; both in a sense possess deformed reproductive organs for which they are paradoxically in demand.

Often the object of sexual derision in Restoration comedy, eunuchs were frequently treated with more dignity in Restoration tragedy as agents of considerable political power. The author of *Eunuchism Display'd* wonders about this paradox: "I cannot well comprehend how any one who is mutilated, and degraded (if I may so say) from the quality of a Man, should on that Account be *more precious than he was before.*"[25] This double attitude of adulation and contempt, of awe and disdain, toward the eunuch replicates the combination of idealization and misogyny for eighteenth-century women and brings to the foreground the artificial social nature of such a defect. These contradictions escape resolution, for to reconcile them would be to recognize the artificial and contingent status of these categories. It is precisely that constructedness which Amazons, eunuchs, ugly women, or deformed persons of any sort make visible. Yet because femininity as well as deformity is also gaining its own substantial subjectivity in the eighteenth century through women writers, the pressure to define womanhood as either deformity or its absence increases while exposing such a resolution as inadequate since defect signifies both difference and its attraction.

Unlike Aphra Behn's narratives of female defect, *The Dumb Virgin* and *The Blind Lady a Beauty*, Eliza Haywood's *Philidore and Placentia, or L'Amour trop Delicat* (London 1727) is a romance that incorporates the deformity of a Christian eunuch. A fantasy of female power, the first section of the novel set in England mirrors the second section placed in a seraglio. In the novella (as Michael McKeon has pointed out), personal merit rests on one's financial fortune, on movable property rather than landed wealth. Without mentioning the eunuch, McKeon recognizes that commodity exchange in the novel is an endless circuit in which the movement toward completion and consumption, a perpetual imagining of an end that must never come, becomes an end in itself.[26] The eunuch, I suggest, is both a conduit toward the completion of traditional male-female desire and the emblem of the inability to achieve its fullest resolution. The eunuch is *himself* a commodity as well as the nonreproductive circuit through which women are exchanged.

No eunuch appears in the first section of *Philidore and Placentia*, which focuses on an aggressively sensual Haywood heroine who is in love with Philidore, of noble family but poor. Philidore burns with a violent suppressed desire that cannot be realized because of the disparity in their two fortunes. As in the Behn novellas, the defective is from the beginning intertwined with Eastern exoticism. Philidore darkens himself to what is termed an Egyptian color and transforms himself into a humble and groveling servant who silently worships his adored object of affection. But his "native whiteness" soon begins to show through his disguise, and the impassioned Placentia is charmed "insensible of the danger."[27] Placentia rewards him for rescuing her from ravaging ruffians by making him groom of her chambers, for she sees "the gentleman through the disguise of rusticity" (172). An erotic exchange between them arouses desire but cannot satisfy it.

Bemoaning the fact that she is rejected by her slave, Placentia desperately attempts to seduce him. At first adopting a manly threat of force, she later shifts tactics and faints while in dishabille. Revived, she proposes marriage in spite of his birth, his identity remaining a mystery, but he steadfastly refuses and flees to Turkey to bury his broken heart. In these scenes of seduction, the woman is the sexual aggressor who openly declares her passion and makes a proposal of marriage regardless of the lover's lack of fortune.

In the story that constitutes the second part of the novel, Philidore during his adventures in Turkey encounters a beautiful mysterious man, disguised in blood and dust, who reveals himself to be a Christian eunuch, thus distinguishing himself from the Turkish eunuchs of the seraglio. Their apparent kinship is both nationalist and religious: in spite of the eunuch's turban, Philidore rightly believes him to be English and Christian. The eunuch pleads, "If you are a man of honor and a European, as your habit makes me hope you are, assist an unfortunate Christian oppressed by these barbarians" (187). The magnetic attraction between Philidore and the eunuch is palpable: "Yet was he attached to him by an impulse which he could not at that time account for. Though this was the first moment of their meeting, already did he love him with a brother's tenderness" (188), a feeling that rivals only Philidore's feelings for Placentia. The homoerotic undertones remain subdued, but the affection and passion Philidore expresses for the "lovely stranger" resemble those of a lover. The homoerotic potential is displaced and overcome by stronger heterosexual desire: "And though he had the extremest tenderness for this Christian eunuch that one man can possibly have for another, yet he found no difficulty to part with him, in all probability, forever, when the interest of Placentia was in dispute" (209). To clarify the eunuch's sexual orientation, and to erase these implications of homoerotic desire between the two men, Philidore recovers a picture of a beautiful woman from the effects of the stranger, and only then, by witnessing a medical examination, discovers that "this beautiful person had been deprived of his manhood" (192), not in order to obtain a position in the seraglio, but as a punishment. Since the eunuch was involuntarily castrated, relegated to the nonreproductive economy, our sympathies are appropriately engaged in his behalf. The beautiful exotic stranger embodies both an idealized man and a monstrous eunuch who finally spills out the history of his emasculation. The eunuch's narrative reminds us of a similar juxtaposition between beauty and defect in Behn's lovely mute heroine Maria, whose loosened tongue allowed her to speak of monstrosity. The occasion of being made defective or recognizing its monstrosity releases narrative. Women writers in articulating their deformity are released into an exposition of its history. Woman's "deformed" subjectivity, like the subjectivity of the Christian eunuch as Haywood narrates it, is recounted, resisted, and redefined even as it is constituted by defect.

In Haywood's *Philidore and Placentia* the Christian eunuch, like the female sex he is alleged to personify and parody, is both beautiful and deformed. Of ancient and honorable family, the eunuch, the last surviving male heir and himself an exotic, collects rarities and, as one would expect from an effeminate, attends to fashion. Shipwrecked and captured by Persian pirates, purchased as a favorite by the Bashaw of Lipera, he soon recognized that even before he became a eunuch, he was a feminized commodity at the Bashaw's disposal who possessed use-value like "a fine garden, a palace, a rich jewel, or any other thing which affords him delight. He [the bashaw] thinks of those whom ill fortune has reduced to be his slaves but as part of the furniture of his house, something he has bought for his use." To his peril he falls in love with the loose and sensual beauty of Arithea, one of the Bashaw's wives, in the seraglio.[28] When the Bashaw considers freeing him, he is so disordered by infatuation that he refuses to leave. Both the seraglio and his enslavement are metaphors for the power that love wields in making him forget national loyalties. He enters the forbidden walls of the seraglio disguised as a mute, already taking on the mark of the defective, and he risks slavery and exile at his peril. Unsatisfied, Arithea relentlessly upbraids him for his cold European nature and his failure to confront the Bashaw, just as Philidore had failed to be sufficiently aggressive with Placentia in part 1.

The European, then, besotted with love, is the failed agent of Arithea's release from confinement and polygamy. The luxurious and indolent seraglio, charged with Eastern sensuality and wildness, inspires mad passion. At the very moment of potential climax between the illicit lovers, slaves capture the European and make him a eunuch, leaving him "nothing but the name of man." The reader imagines lack and mutilation. All this demonstrates the alleged barbarity of the Bashaw and the East, but it also suggests the terrible consequences of a desire misplaced onto the elusive Eastern woman: "Thus wretched, thus become the scorn of both sexes and incapable of being owned by either" (206).

In the conclusion Philidore, still in Turkey, suddenly becomes heir to a great fortune, and the economic impediment to his marriage with Placentia is at last removed. In a plot that parallels the eunuch's story, Placentia, having followed Philidore to Turkey, resurfaces as having been enslaved by a Persian merchant. Now dispossessed of her fortune, she turns the tables on Phili-dore and refuses to marry him, but the Christian eunuch is revealed to be the barren Baron Bellamont, her brother who is returning home to claim his in-heritance. The Christian eunuch offers Placentia a third of his newly acquired estate, though his being a eunuch and unable to produce children to com-pete for the fortune as heirs is kept secret in order to ensure her accepting the fortune. Placentia is firmly resituated within the marriage economy, and her capacity to bear heirs is reinstated. Men who are outside the heterosex-ual economy, aligned with women in their defective nature, are different from them in that masculinity is deformed by virtue of an inability to re-produce, while woman's status is ambivalent and inclusive of both since her reproductive organ is the very site of her defect. In a very substantial way, "woman" is a eunuch.[29]

Ultimately, however, deformity or defect are firmly attributed to a male body rather than a female one in Haywood's tale, and the eunuch's defect is the cruel consequence of desiring a woman of the seraglio, a religious and national other, and for which the eunuch is condemned to a life outside the reproductive economy. Marriage between two passionate European lovers, alternately without fortune, takes place on the back of the eunuch, a defec-tive imitation of a man, so that money and value are partially transferred to the hands of a woman instead. The Christian eunuch's misplaced desire for an Eastern woman, a woman of the seraglio, emasculates him, enriches the European woman, and enables her marriage that had previously been con-strained by economic factors. There is not a hint in Haywood's novella of *women*'s being genuinely defective; rather her heroines are sexually aggres-sive, berate men for their cowardice, and are rewarded with sufficient for-tune because a subclass of men is rendered impotent and relegated outside the reproductive economy. In Behn's tales, *women* both intrinsically and ex-ternally defective are depicted as outside of such circulation. Haywood's tale seems to argue that women's empowerment may not be synonymous with their sexual, physical, or moral deformity and that femininity need not be tantamount to monstrosity, though women's economic empowerment de-pends on man's castration in the cause of love, just as Semiramis's political authority required the emasculation of her suitors.

During the eighteenth century, I suggest, femininity as perfect differ-ence, an inferior perfection, competes with femininity as defect. Amazon-ian women and eunuchs are the flawed beings who become the collectibles of empire along with giants, pygmies, mermaids, hermaphrodites, and mutes. Yet they are also the terrifying emblems of duplicity and gendered uncertainty reflecting England's anxieties about its national manliness and its capacity to engage in the necessary rapacity for empire building. They, like the eunuch, represent the perpetuation and frustration of desire, and the displacement of its imperial designs. The interrelations among these mutant categories are metaphors for cultural and historical change that are indicative of women's increasingly possessing what men wished to delimit—their formidable entrance into the publishing marketplace, economic viability, and the recognition that their defect, reproductive power, could be manipulated for the transfer of wealth, social status, and political power. In the eighteenth century, women are inscribing a subjectivity that contests a model of femininity that is produced only in relation to conventional forms of masculinity and also queries the concept of a double defect; it contests in myriad ways the concept of the feminine, of the female, and of the exceptional woman as defective, deformed, and monstrous, even among the earliest practitioners of women's writing.

Femininity, then, both circulates inside the reproductive economy and is excluded from it. The shared monstrosity between women and the "defective" of both sexes is not easily undone, now or in the eighteenth century, though Donna Haraway has argued that the discourses of dismemberment and suffering open up the possibility of a nongeneric, feminist, cyborgian humanity. In Haraway's mythology, that "brokenness" may even signify hope since she calls for a language of connection outside Enlightenment thought (and its humanism) that would create bonds between inappropriate/d others. Haraway takes Sojourner Truth's heretical declaration, "Ain't I a Woman?" as a prime example because it turns her exclusion and difference from the universal human "into an organon for placing the painful realities and practices of de-construction, dis-identification, and dis-memberment in the service of a newly articulated humanity."[30] But, I suggest, beyond the vexed problem of identifying dismemberment with suffering, and making Truth into the Other, Haraway's utopian vision that would turn suffering to hope, individual dismemberment to collective wholeness, is constrained by its simple reversal of terms. To avoid this reversal means that we will have to produce, steadily and carefully, the history and genealogy of disability, defect, and deformity in their multiplicity in order to avoid replicating the seductive but finally pernicious view that the handicapped bear a special mystical responsibility to bring more ordinary folk closer to Truth or the equally problematic view that those who exceed the social construction of gender—as in the case of Sojourner Truth or of early modern women writers such as Aphra Behn and Eliza Haywood—exemplify defect and deformity.

NOTES

1. *Female Rights Vindicated; or the Equality of the Sexes Morally and Physically proved*, By a Lady (London, 1758), 115. This is a later version of *Beauty's Triumph, Or, the Superiority of the Fair Sex invincibly proved*, 3 parts (London, 1751). Also known as the "Sophia pamphlets" (1739), these and other translations of Poullain de la Barre's *De l'égalité des deux sexes* (1673), widely disseminated and regularly revised throughout the eighteenth century, typically included rhetorical contests between a misogynist and a feminist.

2. *Female Rights Vindicated*, 89.

3. The earlier version is François Poullain de La Barre, *The Woman as Good as the Man; or, The Equality of Both Sexes*, trans. A. L., ed. Gerald M. MacLean (Detroit: Wayne State University Press, 1988), 131. Thomas Laqueur, *Making Sex: Body and Gender from the Greeks to Freud* (Cambridge: Harvard University Press, 1990), explains that women's internal organs were imagined to be defective male appendages because they failed to descend.

4. *Beauty's Triumph*, 71. Part 2 by a Gentleman is entitled "Being an ATTEMPT to refute SOPHIA's Arguments; And to probe the Natural Right of the Men to Sovereign Authority over the Other Sex," 65. Subsequent references to *Beauty's Triumph* are given in the text.

5. Bernard Albinus, *Table of the Skeleton and Muscles of the Human Body* (London, 1749). See Londa Schiebinger, *The Mind Has No Sex? Women in the Origins of Modern Science* (Cambridge: Harvard University Press, 1989), 203.

6. For the concept of the prostitute as man-woman, see Felicity A. Nussbaum, *Torrid Zones: Maternity, Sexuality, and Empire in Eighteenth-Century English Narratives* (Baltimore: Johns Hopkins University Press, 1995).

7. On maternal power to deform fetuses, see Julia Epstein, "Dangerous Wombs," in *Altered Conditions: Disease, Medicine, and Storytelling* (Routledge: New York, 1995), 123–56: "Assigning responsibility for the horror of defective or malformed births affected inheritance, social organization, and political power. In a social system dependent on male lineage, it was more than just ideologically convenient to displace this responsibility onto the bodies and minds of women" (151).

8. *Orthopaedia: or, the Art of Correcting and Preventing Deformities in Children*, trans. from the French of M. Andry (London, 1743), 29.

9. *Hebe; or, the Art of Preserving Beauty, and Correcting Deformity* (London, 1786), 13–14.

10. *Female Rights Vindicated*, 102.

11. *Hebe*, 13–14.

12. Aphra Behn, *The Works of Aphra Behn*, ed. Janet Todd (Columbus: Ohio State University Press, 1995), 3:321–60. All subsequent references are to this text. Jacqueline Pearson, "Slave Princes and Lady Monsters: Gender and Ethnic Difference in the Work of Aphra Behn," in *Aphra Behn Studies*, ed. Janet Todd (Cambridge: Cambridge University Press, 1996), 219–34, considers two Mexican Jewish heiress monsters, a giant and a little one, in *The Rover*, part II (1681). Pearson suggests that

one category of oppression is often simply substituted for another, an assertion that the essays in this volume question.

13. Janet Todd in her edition suggests that the fictional suitor calls to mind Thomas Dangerfield, who participated in the Meal-Tub Plot, a Protestant attempt to counter the Popish Plot. Both the real and the fictional Dangerfield disguised themselves in Turkish costume (*Works of Aphra Behn*, 3:336).

14. Ros Ballaster, *Seductive Forms: Women's Amatory Fiction from 1684 to 1740* (Oxford: Clarendon Press, 1992).

15. See Roger Lonsdale, ed., *Eighteenth-Century Women Poets: An Oxford Anthology* (Oxford: Oxford University Press, 1989), 275–76.

16. Catherine Ingrassia, "Women Writing/Writing Women: Pope, Dulness, and 'Feminization' in the *Dunciad*," *Eighteenth-Century Life* 14 (November 1990): 40–58, extends Pope's fears to men and interprets the *Dunciad* as "a symbolically emasculated man's personal and professional anxiety about the increasing power of creative and mercenary male and female writers."

17. Samuel Johnson, *The Idler and the Adventurer,* in *The Yale Edition of the Works of Samuel Johnson,* ed. W. J. Bate, John M. Bullitt, and L. F. Powell (New Haven: Yale University Press, 1963), no. 115, December 11, 1753, 2:457–58.

18. Samuel Johnson, *Idler* 87, 2:272. As Addison writes in *Spectator* 434 (July 18, 1712), "No Woman was to be married till she had killed her Man," in Joseph Addison and Richard Steele, *The Spectator,* ed. Donald F. Bond, 5 vols (Oxford: Oxford University Press, 1965), 4:24.

19. *Female Rights Vindicated,* 20. The Amazon's military heroics serve as a displacement of the cultural terror surrounding effeminacy and luxury, and as Laura Brown has argued in *The Ends of Empire: Women and Ideology in Early Eighteenth-Century English Literature* (Ithaca: Cornell University Press, 1993), attributing violence to women helps men avoid acknowledging the violence of empire. The Amazon comes to represent both the native and the "alter ego of the male imperialist" at once (131).

20. The reference to Semiramis also appears in John Bulwer, *Anthropometamorphosis: Man Transformed* (1650; London, 1653), 353. On the connections between ruling women and eunuchs, see especially Dympna Callaghan, "The Castrator's Song: Female Impersonation on the Early Modern Stage," *Journal of Medieval and Early Modern Studies* 26, no. 2 (spring 1996): 321–53.

21. Callaghan, noting a similar myth in John Bulwer's *Anthropometamorphosis,* writes that the passage reveals, however, that in phallic logic, there always lurks the possibility that women, precisely because they do not have a penis and testicles, could castrate men without expecting retaliation. "In desiring men who are like herself, Semiramis implicitly presents . . . also the possibility of an erotic preference for a man devoid of the sexual use of his penis, a choice which threatens to make virility redundant" ("The Castrator's Song," 326).

22. David Hume, "Of Love and Marriage," in *Essays Moral, Political, and Literary,* ed. Eugene F. Miller, rev. ed. (Indianapolis: Liberty Fund, 1987), 559. Hume's essay is a plea for sexual equality and equanimity since sexual division derives from Jupiter's punishing the rebellion of the prosperous Androgynes by creating two kinds of imperfect beings.

23. *Eunuchism Display'd, Describing all the different Sorts of Eunuchs; the Esteem they have met with in the World, and how they came to be made so. Wherein principally is examin'd whether they are capable of Marriage, and if they ought to be suffer'd to enter into that State* (London, 1718), 75.

24. According to Enid and Richard Peschel, "The Castrati in Opera," *Opera Quarterly* 4 (1986), eunuchs' physical anomalies extended beyond the genitals. They "had subcutaneous fat localized to the hips, buttocks, and breasts, sometimes had fatty deposits on the lateral portions of the eyelids, had pale and oftentimes swollen and wrinkled skin, and possessed abnormally long arms and legs, resulting in what is technically called a 'eunuchoid appearance'" (27), cited in Beth Kowaleski-Wallace, "Shunning the Bearded Kiss: Castrati and the Definition of Female Sexuality," *Prose Studies* 15, no. 2 (1992): 153–70, who importantly emphasizes the nonphallic sexual threat that eunuchs represent. See also Jill Campbell, "'When Men Women Turn:' Gender Reversals in Fielding's Plays," in *The New Eighteenth Century: Theory/Politics/English Literature*, ed. Felicity Nussbaum and Laura Brown (New York: Methuen, 1987): 62–83; and Yvonne Noble, "Castrati, Balzac, and Barthes' *S/Z*," *Comparative Drama* 31, no. 1 (1997–98): 28–41.

25. *Eunuchism Display'd*, 106.

26. Michael McKeon, *The Origins of the English Novel, 1600–1740* (Baltimore: Johns Hopkins University Press, 1987), 260–61.

27. Eliza Haywood, *Philidore and Placentia; or, L'Amour trop Delicat*, in *Four before Richardson: Selected English Novels, 1720–1727*, ed. W. H. McBurney (Lincoln: University of Nebraska Press, 1963), 162. All subsequent references in the text are to this edition.

28. Arithea's beauty is white and rosy, not at all like the darkness of the Orient. For discussion of notions of skin color, see Felicity Nussbaum, "Women and Race: 'A Difference of Complexion,'" in *Women and Literature in Britain, 1700–1800*, ed. Vivien Jones (Cambridge: Cambridge University Press, forthcoming 1999).

29. Kowaleski-Wallace, "Shunning the Bearded Kiss," 163–67, discusses the close identification between Frances Burney as a woman writer and the castrato Pacchierotti, though she focuses on the social perceptions of mutilation rather than the analogies that defective organs in the two sexes inspire.

30. Donna Haraway, "Ecco Homo, Ain't (Ar'n't) I a Woman, and Inappropriate/d Others: The Human in a Post-Humanist Landscape," in *Feminists Theorize the Political*, ed. Judith Butler and Joan W. Scott (New York: Routledge, 1992), 86–100.

Dr. Johnson, Amelia, and the Discourse of Disability in the Eighteenth Century

Lennard J. Davis

> [I]t was requisite to a Whore to be Handsome, well shap'd,
> have a good Mien, and a graceful Behaviour; but that for a
>   Wife,
> no Deformity would shock the Fancy.
> —Daniel Defoe, *Moll Flanders*

Samuel Johnson was a person with multiple disabilities. He was blind in one eye and had poor vision in the other. He was also deaf in one ear. These disabilities were the result of childhood tuberculosis of the lymphatic system, known then as "scrofula." In addition, he had prominent scars on the neck from incisions of his lymph nodes in treatment of this tubercular attack.[1] His face was further ravaged extensively by smallpox.

Johnson was also intermittently mentally ill, suffering from profound, often debilitating depression with suicidal impulses. In addition he evidenced what might be diagnosed as an obsessive-compulsive disorder that manifested itself in hypochondria, phobic and ritualistic behaviors,[2] compulsive picking of the skin on his hands, crushing anxiety attacks, and so on. Perhaps related were the physical tics and convulsive actions he manifested. As described by Boswell,

> he commonly held his hand to one side towards his right shoulder, and shook it in a tremulous manner, moving his body backwards and forwards, and rubbing his left knee in the same direction, with the palm of his hand. In the intervals of articulating he made various sounds with his mouth, sometimes as if ruminating, or what is called chewing the cud, sometimes giving a half whistle, sometimes making his tongue play backwards from the roof of his mouth, as if clucking like a hen, and sometimes protruding it against his upper gums in front, as if pronouncing quickly under his breath, *too, too, too*.[3]

When Hogarth first met Johnson, he remarked that he saw a man "shaking his head and rolling himself about in a strange, ridiculous manner" and concluded that Johnson "was an ideot, whom his relations had put under the care of Mr. [Samuel] Richardson" (1:147). Alexander Pope wrote that his attempts to get Johnson a job as tutor failed because Johnson had "an infirmity of the convulsive kind, that attacks him sometimes, so as to make him a sad Spectacle" (1:143). Johnson's tics and throat cluckings, as well as other behaviors, were almost certainly symptoms of what is now called Tourette's syndrome.[4]

In his early twenties as well as his fifties, Johnson suffered severe mental breakdowns and depressions so total that often he could not get out of bed. He became paranoid during these times, refusing to see people he did not trust. A contemporary described him during one of his breakdowns sitting in silence: "[He] looked miserable; his lips moved, tho he was not speaking; he could not sit long at a time. . . . [He] walked up and down the room, sometimes into the next room, and returned immediately . . . dreadful to see.[5] In later life, he suffered a stroke that caused aphasia and agraphia, congestive heart failure, kidney disease, severe arthritis that made it difficult to walk, emphysema, and increasing deafness, as well as a hydrocele of the testes.

If Johnson had lived during the twentieth century, he most probably would have been institutionalized, given shock therapy, or more recently put on a regimen of antidepressants. Without treatment, he might well have ended up on the streets. More tellingly for our purposes, his biography would have focused on these ailments, disfigurements, and so on. He would have become his illnesses and deformities. While his contemporaries clearly note his eccentricities, Johnson is not pathologized.

The question I wish to explore is why his contemporaries refer to his disabilities only in a casual and literary manner[6]—tending to see him as a brilliant man who had some oddities rather than as a seriously disabled person. Why, as Julia Epstein asks, did Johnson never write about his own mannerisms when he did write about other aspects of his illness?[7] On the other hand, why do we know about these disabilities at all? Shakespeare, for example, lived fewer than two hundred years earlier, yet one has almost no knowledge of his appearance, let alone whether he had disabilities. His body is not a factor in our thinking about his subjectivity, and standards of normality do not apply to our judgment. John Milton wrote about his blindness in his poetry, but our detailed knowledge of the medical issues is limited. Clearly, standards of biography change, and one can point to an increasing interest in the individual and the author, but I think there are more factors at work than simply the growth of individualism.

I would argue that this evolving interest in disability, and the paradoxical aestheticizing of it in Johnson's life, is actually part of a historical and cultural transition in which the modern discourse of disability became consolidated. In this liminal period, we can see traces of both earlier and later formulations of disability. In other words, we can see the contradiction of an earlier sense in which disability per se did not exist and of a later one in which disability is a modality used to explain a great deal.

In order to understand this phenomenon better, let us look at the reception of disability in this period and earlier. To do this I need to qualify what I mean by disability. Disability is not so much the lack of a sense or the presence of a physical or mental impairment as it is the reception and construction of that difference. Contemporary theoreticians of disability distinguish between an impairment and a disability. An impairment is a physical fact, but a disability is a social construction. For example, lack of mobility is an impairment, but an environment without ramps turns that impairment into a disability. In other words, a disability must be socially constructed; there must be an analysis of what it means to have or lack certain functions, appearance, and so on. For the sake of this argument, I define physical disability as a disruption in the sensory field of the observer.[8] Disability, in this sense, is located in the observer, not the observed, and is therefore more about the viewer than about the person using a cane or a wheelchair. The term *disability* is a categorization tied to the development of discourses that aim to cure, remediate, or catalog variations in bodies. Thus, disability is part of a continuum that includes differences in gender, as well as bodily features indicative of race, sexual preference, and even of class.[9]

Notably, researchers in disability have a difficult time documenting disability before the mid-eighteenth century. Obviously this is not because persons with disabilities were lacking. Indeed, it is probable that the figure of 15 percent, now generally accepted as the percentage of people with disabilities in the United States and throughout the world, would have held in the past.[10] In fact we might estimate upward of 25 percent of the population was disabled, given the lack of modern medicine and so on. It is estimated now that in some third-world countries upward of 50 percent of the population is either disabled or cares for people with disabilities, and this figure would have held true as well for countries like England before the advent of modern medicine. In short, disability affects a very large number of people now and in the past.

Although there may have been a great number of people with disabilities, one must, however, assume that disability was not an operative category before the eighteenth century. Some researchers have made the point that in preindustrial countries disability is not as relevant a category as it is under factory conditions where the interchangeability of standardized workers is paramount. People with visual, auditory, or mobility differences can be incorporated into a preindustrial society. Thus, in some sense, their disabilities are not remarkable. One only has to think of Nora Groce's account of deafness on Martha's Vineyard, *Everyone Here Spoke Sign Language,* in which few contemporary informants could recall which citizens of the island in the past had been deaf since the entire community had learned sign language to accommodate extensive hereditary deafness.[11]

To make the historical point, let us consider King James I. Almost no one knows or mentions, even in his lifetime, that he was a person with disabilities. His public representations and other documents almost never cite or represent what apparently only two contemporaries noted. Anthony Weldon, a contemporary Englishman and critic of James writes that

> his tongue [was] too large for his mouth, which ever made him speak full in the mouth, and made his drink very uncomely, as if eating his drink, which came out into the cup of each side of his mouth. . . . his legs were very weake, having had as was thought some foul play in his youth, or rather before he was born,[12] that he was not able to stand at seven years of age, that weaknesse made him ever leaning on other mens shoulders; his walke was ever circular, his fingers ever in that walke fidling about his cod-piece.[13]

M. de Fontenay, a French ambassador and one of the few writers to confirm this observation, wrote that "his carriage is ungainly, his steps erratic and vagabond, even in his own chamber. . . . he is feeble in frame, and . . . he cannot work for a long time at business."[14]

One would assume that such debilities would have been noted by other writers, but in most descriptions of James I, no mention is made of such, and the rest of the contemporary accounts read like that of the ambassador from Venice: "He is sufficiently tall, of noble presence, his physical constitution robust, and he is at pains to preserve it by taking much exercise at the chase."[15] This lack of attention to James's ambulatory difficulties and to his somewhat convulsive behavior gives us some indication that this type of disability is not seen as remarkable, mentioned by only two of scores of commentators and contemporary historians.

Rather than disability, what is called to readers' attention before the eighteenth century is *deformity.* The word seems to have been in use since the beginning of print, according to the *Oxford English Dictionary,* and is the operative word in defining some aspects of physical disability. Disability as the observation of the absence of a sense, a limb, or an ability is much less remarked on than deformity as a major category, a dramatic physical event or bodily configuration like giantism, dwarfism, or hunchback formations. Even so, only a few writers comment on the subject at all—notably Castiglione, Montaigne, and Bacon, writing briefly on "deformity" and "monsters." And of course we have Shakespeare's *Richard III.* Castiglione, in *The Courtier,* stresses that physical ugliness or deformity, while not necessarily a punishment from Nature, is often seen as such.

> Thus everyone tries hard to conceal his natural defects of mind or body, as we see in the case of the blind, the lame, the crippled and all those who are maimed or ugly. For although these defects can be imputed to Nature, yet no one likes to think he has them, since then it seems that Nature herself has caused them deliberately as a seal and token of wickedness.[16]

Thus Castiglione ends up ratifying the notion that deformity is a sign of evil. Montaigne in his essays seems mainly interested in the idea that deformed people, particularly women with crooked spines or lame men like Hephaestus, are hypersexual, and that deformity often occurs because the pregnant mother's imagination is shocked by some event into producing a marked or deformed child. Montaigne also sees monstrous births as signs of divine intention,[17] as Castiglione sees physical defects as punishments by Nature. Meanwhile, Bacon, as a rationalist, sees deformity "not as a sign" of divine intervention or marking of the body, but as a "cause" of personality and behavior. For Bacon, deformed people are ambitious, "void of natural affection," good spies, and advantaged in "rising" in court.[18] Shakespeare, clearly holding to all these opinions, depicts Richard III as a crooked-backed, limping sexual villain, a spying, usurping plotter. His behavior is a result of his appearance, as he says, "since I cannot prove a lover, . . . I am determined to prove a villain."[19]

While mentions of deformity are sporadic, they tend to uphold certain time-honored beliefs, such as the notion that deformity can be traced to a moment in utero. Without a genetic explanation for births of people with disabilities, the Empedoclean paradigm, which attributed birth defects to the mother's imagination, held sway, as Marie-Hélène Huet has painstakingly documented.[20] Thus deformity is caused by a moment, an instance, as when Richard describes himself as "deformed, unfinish'd, sent before my time / Into the breathing world, scarce half made up."[21] His self-image is of a loaf half-baked, deformed by not enough time in the womb.[22]

While not much attention was paid to people with disabilities, there was during the late seventeenth and early eighteenth centuries an inordinate attention paid to natural "wonders," that is to dramatic instances of deformity. These wonders tended to fall into the category of *lusus naturae,* including giants, dwarfs, hermaphrodites, Siamese twins, hirsute women, and other kinds of anomalous births. While we now tend to consider any anomalous birth as part of the category of disability, this grouping together of birth anomalies and disability did not exist much before the nineteenth century. Our modern concept of normality requires that all deviations from the norm be treated equally, but under the previous discursive grid, anomalous, strange births were distinguished from disabilities that were acquired, particularly through disease.

But even dramatic deformities, such as those exhibited for money at Bartholomew Fair and other locations, which tended to capture the attention of writers, were met with a strangely calm affect. Montaigne's accounts of monsters in his essay on the subject are written laconically.[23] Those who saw monsters in the seventeenth and eighteenth centuries did not spell out their reactions in any great emotional detail. A Mr. Hooke seeing a giantess wrote, "saw the Dutch woman in Bartholomew fair, very strange"; a Mr. Thoresby writes, "After dinner with Mr. Gale, walked into Southwark to see the Italian gentleman with two heads; that growing out of his side has long black hair."[24] Dennis Todd attributes this blasé tone to the fact that these "are records of men imbued with the spirit of Baconian science." But, given that these reactions are the rule over time rather than the exception, I think a better explanation is required. We want to recall, for example, that Jonathan Swift, upon hearing of Mary Toft's giving birth to rabbits, sent a letter to Mrs. Howard:

> I have been five days turning over old Books to discover the meaning of those monstrous Births you mention. That of the four black Rabbits seems to threaten some dark Court Intrigue, and perhaps some change in the Administration [,] for the Rabbit is an undermining animal that loves to work in the dark. The Blackness denotes the Bishops, whereof some of the last you have made, are persons of such dangerous Parts and profound Abilityes. But Rabbits being cloathed in Furs may perhaps glance at the Judges.[25]

While Swift, that man of reason, may be mocking an irrational tradition here, he signals its continuing strength by referring to the notion of monstrous births as signs from heaven, as did Montaigne, two hundred years earlier, who comments on seeing a monstrous child with a headless conjoined twin that this occurrence "might well furnish a favorable prognostic to the king that he will maintain under the union of his laws these various parts and factions of our state."[26] These two approaches—the deformed as creatures of their mother's imagination or as signs of divine intention—were the regnant paradigms for the category of the births of people with disabilities. These ways of thinking about people born with disabilities seem to be the operative explanatory devices though the middle of the eighteenth century. Thus the blandness we pick up is a function of the unremarkable common quality of most physical differences.

What we do see in the second half of the eighteenth century is a remarkable appearance of the disabled person in print as author and character. Deafness, particularly, seems to be discovered as a discrete category of disability. We can track this interest by noting that the number of schools for the deaf increases from zero at the beginning of the century to a dozen in 1789 to sixty in 1822.[27] Deafness and blindness become the subject of study by philosophers, linguists, and educators. Even the category of "monster" becomes refined and delineated into a discourse, finally arriving at Saint-Hilaire's founding of the science of teratology and the attempt to produce monsters through teratogeny in the nineteenth century. These events are tied up with the development of the concepts of the normal, the abnormal, the anomalous, and so on.

William Hay's publication of *Deformity: An Essay* may be used to mark this watershed. Hay, a member of Parliament, had spinal deformities and described himself as "scarce five Feet high," with a "Back [that] was bent in my Mother's Womb."[28] Hay's work, although influential, does not do much to reform the concepts of deformity that preceded his work. Rather, Hay ends up reiterating (although humanizing and questioning to a degree) stereotypes about people with disabilities, including the notion that the disability results from an extraordinary shock or event during gestation. He also maintains the distinction between deformity and disability, seeing spinal deformity and the accompanying dwarfism as fitting into the remarkable or even wondrous category more than blindness, deafness, or lameness. As he writes, "it is not easy to say why one Species of Deformity should be more ridiculous than another, or why the Mob should be more merry with a crooked Man, than one that is deaf, lame, squinting, or purblind."[29] Here Hay makes distinctions between types of deformity, rather than seeing blindness, for example, as linked to spinal deformity. He also notes that the mob will mock a birth deformity like his more than degenerative disabilities that might, for example, accompany old age. Hay appears to occupy a liminal position in his analysis between discourses of wonder and deformity and a discourse of disability.[30]

In regard to Dr. Johnson we can see better how this tension between older systems of classification and newer ones plays out. In the *Life of Johnson* Boswell simultaneously mentions and then downplays Johnson's disabilities.[31] For example, while Boswell does note Johnson's scrofulous childhood, he takes great pains to point out that Johnson could see very well and that though he was blind in one eye "its appearance was little different from that of the other" (1:41). Hester Thrale echoes this point, saying of his blind eye that "this defect however was never visible, both Eyes look exactly alike."[32]

Given the extent of Johnson's multiple disabilities, rather little mention is made of them even by Boswell and his contemporaries. For example, portraits of Johnson edit out his disabilities; only his death mask shows the rather dramatic scars on his neck. In the *Life of Johnson,* at Boswell's first meeting with Johnson, the biographer mentions his "slovenly" dress and "uncouth" surroundings, but nothing else. Tellingly, however, the first discussion between the two of them is about madness and Christopher Smart, the poet who had been confined to a madhouse. Of Johnson's eyesight, Boswell writes, "How false and contemptible then are all the remarks which have been made to the prejudice either of his candour or of his philosophy, founded upon a supposition that he was almost blind" (*Life,* 1:42).[33] Of Johnson's depression, hypochondria, and paranoia, Boswell says that "there is surely a clear distinction between a disorder which affects only the imagination and spirits, while the judgement is sound, and a disorder by which the judgement itself is impaired." Boswell is in part defending Johnson against "those who wish to depreciate him . . . since his death" by laying hold of "this circumstance" (1:66). Johnson himself seemed to be of the opposite opinion, often fearing himself mad.[34] This fear is perhaps closer to the truth than Boswell's protective defense. Although Boswell wants to make a distinction between impairment of "imagination and spirit" and impairment of "judgement," traditional categorizations of the mentally ill were not so nice in their discerning. As Jonathan Andrews notes, "Early modern writers made little distinction between idiocy and chronically progressed conditions of mental enfeeblement."[35] Andrews points out that while the term "idiot" and "fool" were used in the country parishes, the same terms in metropolitan parishes were equivalent to "distracted" and "lunatic."[36] Johnson himself must have been aware of the slippage possible between his condition of profound bouts of distracted depression and the degenerative possibilities inherent in that condition.

What we may be observing here are the effects of the formation of a new discursive category of disability. With it goes several contradictions. This new category is seen as continuous, running the gamut from physical impairments to deformity to monstrosity to madness. Linked to this development is an institutional, medicalized apparatus to house, segregate, isolate, or fix people with disabilities. Part of this fixing involves the clinical gaze that replaces the stare of wonder. The disabled person now is seen, drawn, illustrated, dissected, legally placed, morally and ethically determined. Mental illness is categorized into types and subtypes. The concept of normality is invented along with the bell curve and statistics.[37] As Huet points out, once disability is linked to genetics, we see a shift in the way people with disabilities are categorized. No longer is disability something tied to an individual event, like the mother's witnessing a violent crime, but to a genetic entity or a group defect—ethnic, racial, national, or class-related. Women continued to be blamed for birth defects, particularly those from undesirable socioeconomic groups. Further, in terms of cultural symbolic production, images of the disabled person are linked to specific kinds of moralized narrative. People with impairments now are seen as deserving or nondeserving. The undeserving disabled are the villains, the poor who develop disabilities through their laziness or lack of care, fakes, and the like. Among these are the literary villains, limping, one-eyed, one-armed evil men. The deserving literary disabled are often women, children, or older people, sickly and struggling to triumph over their disability. Built into the literary discourse of disability is this contradiction. Disability implies weakness or evil as well as personal culpability and the effect of divine justice, but at the same time disability is random, impersonal, and something over which the individual sufferer triumphs. In some sense this contradiction is a pentimento of the two opposing, historically divergent readings of disability—deformity as sign or punishment versus disability as impersonal affliction randomly assigned throughout the population. In the earlier version, unless the deformity is wondrous, it is ignored or erased. In the latter, it must be commented on, noted, treated, and inscribed into an economy of bodily traits.

In the case of Dr. Johnson, we can see both systems in action. On the one side Boswell and Thrale note his disabilities, but on the other they forget them, as do Sir Joshua Reynolds and other portrait painters. For example, Thrale talks of Johnson's mentioning "the Evil which greatly afflicted him in his Childhood, & left such Marks as even now greatly disfigure his Countenance."[38] But in another place writes of "his appearance":

> His Stature was remarkably high, and Limbs exceedingly large; his Strength was more than common I believe & his Activity was greater than his Size gave one Cause to expect, his Features were strongly marked, though his Complexion was fair, a Circumstance somewhat unusual.[39]

And in another:

> Mr. Johnson's bodily Strength & Figure has not yet been mentioned; His Height was five Foot eleven without Shoes, his Neck short, his Bones large &

Fig. 1. *Samuel Johnson.* Mezzotint engraved by James Watson in 1770, after the portrait from the life by Sir Joshua Reynolds in 1769. In this most notable attempt to represent what is now considered Johnson's disability, Reynolds has chosen to portray Johnson's squint and attempts to transform his subject's hand gesticulations into a sort of Ciceronian rhetorical emphasis or gesture of spiritual interiority. Interpretations of the image have varied dramatically over the past two hundred years. (Reproduced by permission of the Huntington Library, San Marino, California.)

His Shoulders broad; his Leg and Foot eminently handsome, his hand handsome too, in spite of Dirt, & of such Deformity as perpetual picking his Fingers necessarily produced: his Countenance was rugged.[40]

Remarkably, the description of his person never mentions his facial disfigurements detailed earlier. This description and erasure is done under the pressure of the new injunction, as it were, to include disability or normality as a functional category in the formation of the subject. Indeed, we know more about Dr. Johnson's health than almost anyone before him, according to one physician-scholar who states that "we can follow his case history from before birth through his autopsy two days after death."[41] We even know about the abscess Dr. Johnson had on his buttock three weeks after he was born, as well as the swollen testicle he had to have drained in his last month. This incredible level of intimacy with his body, demanded by a new standard of biography and a new attitude toward disability, must also be disavowed or resisted. Hence the erasure and the contradictions by Boswell of the symbolic significance of blindness or insanity. In other words, given the ideology of normality and the hypersignification of images of disability, Johnson must not and cannot be allowed to signify as would a character in a novel if he or she were blind, deaf, or physically impaired in some way. Narrative must not be allowed to transubstantiate the physical into the moral both because of Boswell's respect for Johnson and because the discourse of disability is not fully in place to transmute the physical into the medical.

But by the nineteenth century, when Macaulay writes of Johnson, he can permit this narrative transformation. He writes clinically of Johnson as a child:

> The boy's features which were originally noble and not irregular, were distorted by his malady. His cheeks were deeply scarred. He lost for some time the sight of one eye; and he saw but very imperfectly with the other. But the force of his mind overcame every impediment. Indolent as he was, he acquired knowledge with such ease and rapidity that at every school to which he was sent he was soon the best scholar.[42]

Here we see the appearance of the familiar narrative trope of disability—the triumph over adversity. Macaulay develops this trope further, detailing Johnson's mental illness, now seen as genetic, hereditary. I will quote at length to show the extent of the commentary on disability. Macaulay describes "the sufferings of an unsound body and an unsound mind":

> Before the young man left the university, his hereditary malady had broken forth in a singularly cruel form. He had become an incurable hypochondriac. He said long after that he had been mad all his life, or at least not perfectly sane; and, in truth, eccentricities less strange than his have often been thought grounds sufficient for absolving felons, and for setting aside wills. His grimaces, his gestures, his mutterings, sometimes diverted and sometimes terrified people who did not know him. At a dinner table he would, in a fit of absence, stoop down and twitch off a lady's shoe. He would amaze a drawing-room by suddenly ejaculating a clause of the Lord's Prayer. He would conceive an unintelligible aversion to a particular alley, and perform a great circuit rather than see the hateful place. He would set his heart on touching every post in the streets through which he walked. If by any chance he missed a post, he would go back a hundred yards and repair the omission. Under the influence of his disease, his senses became morbidly torpid, and his imagination morbidly active. At one time he would stand poring on the town clock without being able to tell the hour. At another, he would distinctly hear his mother, who was many miles off, calling him by his name. But this was not the worst. A deep melancholy took possession of him, and gave a dark tinge to all his views of human nature and of human destiny.[43]

Macaulay goes on to describe Johnson's depression. What should impress us about his account is the extensive detail of the consideration. Johnson is narrativized into his disability.[44] Yet the operative trope remains his triumph over disability: "With such infirmities of body and mind, this celebrated man was left, at two-and-twenty, to fight his way through the world."[45] Fight he does, as do all deserving people with disabilities, and the fight becomes emblematic for all of us, just as the league of dying or disabled characters from Tiny Tim of "A Christmas Carol" to Philip Carey in *Of Human Bondage* to Christy Brown of *My Left Foot* serve the cause of ableist society, in this way.[46]

I want to turn now from Dr. Johnson to a literary character with a disfigurement—Fielding's Amelia. In so doing, I am retreating to midcentury in order to provide an example that represents both a literary disability as well as a physical one. When Henry Fielding published *Amelia* in 1751, he expected a huge success. So did many others who bought the book on the basis of having read *Joseph Andrews* and *Tom Jones*. But the bawdiness, humor, and satire were missing. In fact, the novel became the laughingstock of the general public. But the greatest ridicule sprung from one minor point. The eponymous heroine of the book was introduced as having little or no nose. Mr. Booth, her husband, says of her:

> However it was, I assure you, the accident which deprived her of the admiration of others, made the first great impression on my heart in her favour. The injury done to her beauty by the overturning of a chaise, by which, as you may well remember, her lovely nose was beat all to pieces, gave me an Assurance that the Woman who had been so much adored for the Charms of her Person, deserved a much higher Adoration to be paid to her mind.[47]

Amelia's noselessness is brought to the attention of the reader as well as of other characters in the beginning of the novel. Particularly, Amelia is ridiculed by other young ladies who "have turned their heads aside, unable to support their secret triumph, and burst into a loud laugh in her hearing." Jokes are made at her expense: "she will never more turn up her nose at her betters." Her loss of nose is also seen as a "loss of exquisite beauty," which is the same as "the loss of fortune, power, glory" (67). Yet Mr. Booth, her husband-to-be, is taken with her, although—or because—she wears a mask. He begs her to show him her face, and when she does he says "Upon my Soul, Madam you never appeared to me so lovely as at this Instant" (68).

Amelia is a long-suffering wife to an errant and problematic husband. Her facial mutilation is in keeping with a moral trope of Griselda-like affliction. The problem with her lack of a nose, however, arose specifically because, as is well known, in the first edition Fielding does not mention Amelia's nose being repaired, yet Amelia is treated as if she were beautiful throughout the rest of the novel. The reviewer for *London Magazine* pointed out that an "imperfection" of the novel "in our opinion, is, that the author should have taken care to have had Amelia's nose so compleatly cured, and set to rights,

Fig. 2. Samuel Johnson in his seventies, by John Opie. In keeping with the nineteenth-century narrativizing of disability as heroic triumph, this engraver has chosen to place Opie's realistic portrait of the aging Johnson upon a pedestal that portrays Hercules slaying the monstrous Hydra. (Reproduced by permission of the Huntington Library, San Marino, California.)

after its being *beat all to pieces,* by the help of some eminent surgeon, that not so much as a scar remained, and that she shone forth in all her beauty as much after that accident as before."[48] Many reviewers attacked Fielding for this point alone. In France the following year, Matthew Maty's review in *Journal Britannique* noted, "It is not made clear how she recovered a member so essential to a beautiful face; but apparently a clever surgeon fixed it because after her marriage there is hardly a man who does not become amorous with her or a woman who does not envy her."[49] Bonnel Thornton wrote a parody of the novel in his *Drury-Lane Journal.* In it Booth comes home to his Amelia, but this time with his nose flattened as well:

> She then clap'd him down upon a chair, and was going to wipe his mouth with her muckender: but what was her consternation, when she found his high-arch'd Roman Nose, that heretofore resembled the bridge of a fiddle, had been beat all to pieces! As herself had before lost the handle of her face, she now truly sympathis'd with him in their mutual want of snout.[50]

In William Kenrick's parody of *Macbeth,* the three Weird Sisters throw various texts into the pot, including *Amelia,* saying, "To add to these and make a pois'nous Stench, Here take 4 Ounces of a *noseless wench.*"[51] Samuel Foote, an old adversary of Fielding, inserted a frontispiece to the published version of his play *Taste,* which ridiculed Fielding at several points, portraying the bust of Praxiteles' Venus of Paphos, a statue whose nose has been destroyed. Fielding, in defense of his novel, staged a mock-trial in the *Covent-Garden Journal* in which he has a prosecutor address an imaginary court with a list of accusations that ends with "Lastly, That she is a Beauty WITHOUT A NOSE, I say again, WITHOUT A NOSE. This we shall prove by many Witnesses."[52]

I have taken much time to review what many already know—that this little detail was not a flash in the pan but a sustained issue. Contemporaries were aware that "his fair heroine's nose has, in my opinion, been too severely handled by some modern critics,"[53] or that "Amelia's Nose, was an Omission of the Author's which has occasioned a vast deal of *low wit* and has been a standing Joke here."[54] Why should Fielding's career have tottered on the bridge of Amelia's nose?

Perhaps the issue was intensified by people's knowledge of Fielding's personal life. Fielding's heroine is based on his first wife, Charlotte Craddock. He took the name Amelia from his deceased daughter. This much Samuel Richardson recognized in a letter in which he deprecated Fielding for lack of invention: "Amelia, even to her noselessness, is again his first wife."[55] Charlotte had suffered the same accident in a chaise and had her nose fixed by a surgeon. As Johnson commented, when

> the Town had found out that Amelia had performed all her Wonders with a broken Nose, which Fielding had forgotten to cure, & had broken indeed for no other Reason than to impress himself with an Idea of his favourite Wife, who had once met with a similar Accident, & whose Character he had meant to exhibit under the Name of Amelia; thus did this oddity spoyl the Sale of one of the first Performances in the World of its Kind.[56]

So what was the joke all about? There was evident glee that Fielding had in-advertently forgot to fix his fictional character's nose. The contrast between a woman who deserved praise, especially for beauty, and the fact of nose-lessness was clearly too much of a contradiction, too risible. Fielding changed his text in the second edition, clearly smarting under the critique, by adding a physician who repairs Amelia's nose.

But the issue, as with the case of Johnson, involves a complex clashing of paradigms. If noselessness, or disability, represents or signifies a failing or a lack, then Amelia becomes, through this signification, an example of defor-mity—a deformed character. Indeed, perhaps not so strangely, Fielding be-gins his novel with the appearance of a noseless woman who encounters Booth when he arrives in prison:

> The first Person who accosted him was called *Blear-Eyed Moll;* a Woman of no very comely Appearance. Her Eye (for she had but one) when she derived her Nick-name was such, as that Nick-name bespoke. . . . Nose she had none, for *Venus,* envious perhaps of her former Charms, had carried off the gristly Part and some earthy Damsel, perhaps from the same Envy, had levelled the Bone with the rest of her Face: Indeed it was far beneath the Bones of Cheeks, which rose proportionally higher than is usual. (28)

Blear-Eyed Moll is punished by both goddess and mortal with disfigure-ment—punished because of her sexual charms, and in reality punished by the retributive force of syphilis. Noselessness is a common image for the ef-fects of venereal disease, as Ned Ward indicates when he points out "the abundance of both Sexes had sacrificed to the God *Priapus,* & had unluck-ily fallen into Aethiopian Fashion of Flat Faces." He lists in this "Noseless Society" many "poor scarify'd Bawds."[57] Not only is Moll noseless, but she is distorted as well. Her remaining eye is crossed and yellowed, and "About half a dozen ebony Teeth fortified that large and long Canal, which Nature has cut from Ear to Ear, at the Bottom of which was a Chin, preposterously short, Nature having turned up the bottom, instead of suffering it to grow to its due Length." Her corpulence is mentioned along with the fact that "her vast Breasts had long since forsaken their native Home, and had settled them-selves a little below the Girdle" (28).

How odd that this novel should have two noseless women, when most novels do not have even one. Moll seems in some sense the necessary re-pressed Other of Amelia. She too is noseless, but her noselessness is made to signify in a narrative sense, in the sense in which such details in a novel should. And, as with Amelia, Moll's noselessness is tied up with the issue of feminine envy. For Fielding, the iconography of the deformed, grotesque, morally and physically corrupt female is perfect. Yet, though he tried to isolate this negative picture from the idealized Amelia, his textual parapraxis opened the floodgates of ridicule, revealing the necessity of the imposed binary of good/bad, beautiful/deformed, in the regulation of female bodies. The danger of the uncontrolled female body, expressed in the uncontrollable nature of deformity, is the punishment meted out to Moll in the projection of female envy. Hence, Moll exists as the grotesque, deformed female, so that Amelia can remain pure. The problem was that Fielding violated the mutually exclusive categories by "forgetting" to fix Amelia's nose.

But how accidental is this forgetting? All critics have seen Fielding's parapraxis as an unmotivated event; something that simply slipped his mind. But would it not be much more canny to see Fielding's slip as revealing a repressed fact about femininity under patriarchy and disability under ableism?

In the latter case, what we see is the slippage from the earlier, still persisting, model in which deformity reflects inner vice or divine judgment, to the latter one in which disability is seen as moral virtue, especially in its overcoming. Novels of the second half of the eighteenth century begin to take up the role of enforcing normalcy by producing images of the perfect and disabled body.[58] Here in the world of fiction, or cultural symbolic production, the disability signifies.

Amelia was not the only novel in which female characters were depicted as becoming facially disfigured. Sarah Scott, who herself had smallpox, features two major heroines—Harriot Trentham in *Millenium Hall* and Louisa Tunstall in *The History of Sir George Ellison*—who lose their beauty to facial scarring. Frances Burney presents Eugenia in *Camilla* who also is disfigured in childhood by smallpox and a fall. However, these women, in the new pattern, may find the disfigurement a blessing rather than a curse. For example, Harriot Trentham "became perfectly contented with the alteration this cruel distemper had made in her. . . . She has often said she looks on this accident as a reward for the good she had done."[59] In effect, disfigurement and disability become a positive virtue, particularly in women, children, and the elderly, that signals spiritual and moral dignity achieved through suffering. This trope continues through the nineteenth century, for example, with Esther Summerson in *Bleak House*, disfigured by smallpox, not as punishment for her sins, but as a mark of female suffering and spiritual transcendence over the body.[60]

So Amelia and Dr. Johnson, caught between these two paradigms, are described with their disabilities, but not really allowed to have them. Their bodies bear the mark but not the sign. They are neither normal nor abnormal.

They signify, and yet they do not. Their message is written on the flesh and yet, in some sense, more aptly written on the page. Looking backward from the eighteenth century, we see an absence of a discourse of disability—a world of variously marked unexceptional bodies and a Bartholomew Fair of signs and wonders. Looking ahead, we see the systematized, divided structure of normal and abnormal bodies whose various disabilities are to be institutionalized, treated, and made into a semiology of metonymic meanings. Dr. Johnson, Amelia, and many others suffer that moment where paradigms clash at night.

NOTES

1. Mrs. Thrale writes that the childhood tuberculosis, known as scrofula or "The King's Evil," "left such Marks as even now greatly disfigure his Countenance, besides the irreparable damage it has done to the Auricular Organs; & I suppose 'tis owing to that horrible disorder too that he never could make use but of one Eye, this defect however was never visible, both Eyes look exactly alike." Hester Thrale, *Dr. Johnson by Mrs. Thrale: The "Anecdotes" of Mrs. Piozzi in Their Original Form*, ed. Richard Ingrams (London: Chatto and Windus, 1984), 5.

2. His compulsive behavior included activities such as "touching the posts as he passed, and going back if he missed one; adjusting his steps so that his foot would touch a threshold at a particular moment; blowing out his breath loudly like a whale when he finished a lengthy remark or a dispute, as if to punctuate it and give it finality; treading the floor as if measuring it and also testing its firmness or stability; or making patterns with his heels and toes, as Miss Reynolds said, 'as if endeavouring to form a triangle or some geometrical figure.'" W. Jackson Bate, *Samuel Johnson* (New York: Harcourt Brace Jovanovich, 1978), 382.

3. James Boswell, *Life of Samuel Johnson*, ed. George Birkbeck Hill, rev. by L. F. Powell (Oxford, 1934–50), 1:485. All subsequent references are to this edition and are given in the text.

4. This thesis is discussed by Julia Epstein in *Altered Conditions: Disease, Medicine, and Storytelling* (New York: Routledge, 1995), 65–66. The syndrome was first reported in 1885 by Dr. Georges Gilles de la Tourette, a French physician interested in neurology. It is characterized by uncontrollable facial and bodily tics, compulsive grunting vocalizations, in some cases profane verbalizations, and incessant, obsessive exploration of the environment.

5. James Boswell, *Correspondence and Other Papers of James Boswell Related to the Making of the Life of Johnson*, ed. Marshall Waingrow (New York: McGraw-Hill, 1951), 24.

6. Julia Epstein in *Altered Conditions* makes this point, stressing that Johnson's literary fame is linked to the aestheticization of Johnson's maladies (67). She comments on and notes the difference between this kind of writing which serves to monumentalize Johnson's body and mental prowess and later clinical writings (or

pathographies) which treat the physical difference as symptoms. While I agree with Epstein's notion of a split between an earlier nonmedicalized way of seeing the body and the later discourse which medicalizes disability, I want to point out that the aesthetic impulse Epstein describes is not simply a writerly tendency but part of larger cultural way of regarding disability.

7. Epstein, *Altered Conditions*, 67.

8. William Hay defines disability in a similar way: "Bodily Deformity is visible to every Eye." *Deformity: An Essay* (London, 1754), 2.

9. It is important that we not cut off disability from these other manifestations. The connections are not obvious initially, but consider Aristotle's dictum that women are deformed males (*Generation of Animals,* trans. A. L. Peck [Cambridge: Harvard University Press, 1944], 4:104). Later versions have it that women are disabled men. Or add to this the idea that non-Europeans were "monsters" that could be exhibited in fairs along with dwarfs and giants, that homosexuality could be regarded as a medical disability, and that lower-class workers could be seen as physically imperfect, deformed by work, or working at such jobs because they were deformed.

10. Adrienne Asch and Michelle Fine, "Disability beyond Stigma: Social Interaction, Discrimination, and Activism," *Journal of Social Issues* 44, no. 1 (1988): 5.

11. Nora Ellen Groce, *Everyone Here Spoke Sign Language: Hereditary Deafness on Martha's Vineyard* (Cambridge: Harvard University Press, 1985).

12. This alludes to the murder of David Rizzio in the presence of a pregnant Mary Stuart. Here upheld is the classical belief that deformities were caused by the mother's looking on something disturbing or impressive during her pregnancy, as has been noted by Marie-Hélène Huet, *Monstrous Imagination* (Cambridge: Harvard University Press, 1993), and Julia Epstein in *Altered Conditions.*

13. Robert Ashton, ed., *James I by His Contemporaries* (London: Hutchinson and Co., 1969), 12.

14. Ashton, *James I,* 2–3.

15. Ashton, *James I,* 8.

16. Baldesar Castiglione, *The Book of the Courtier,* trans. George Bull (London: Penguin, 1967), 289.

17. Michel de Montaigne, *The Complete Essays of Montaigne,* trans. Donald M. Frame (1958; rpt., Stanford, Calif.: Stanford University Press, 1965), 791, 539.

18. Francis Bacon, *A Selection of His Works* (New York: Odyssey, 1965), 158–59.

19. William Shakespeare, *The Complete Works,* ed. Alfred Harbage (London: Penguin, 1969), 1.1.28–30.

20. Huet, *Monstrous Imagination.*

21. Shakespeare, *Richard III,* 1.120–21.

22. The baking analogy appears with a somewhat different spin in an eighteenth-century work:

As when the Wheaten Mass is work'd to Dough,
Or swells with Leaven in the Kneading-Trough,
It takes whatever Marks the Maker gives,
And from the Baker's hand its Form receives.

So works the Fancy on the Female Mold,
And Women shou'd beware what they behold.

Claude Quillet, *Callipaedia; or, The Art of Getting Beautiful Children: Written in Latin by the Abbott Claude Quillet. Done into English Verse by Several Hands* (1708–10; rpt., Philadelphia: American Antiquarian Publishing Company, 1872), 53–54. More recently, scientists have lent some credence to the notion of the mother's diet or cravings having an effect on the adult child's health or physical well-being. The *New York Times* reported that adults with heart disease may have developed the disease not because of hereditary influences but rather as a result of their mother's diet during pregnancy (October 10, 1996, C1).

23. Montaigne, *Complete Essays,* 538–39.

24. Dennis Todd, *Imagining Monsters: Miscreations of the Self in Eighteenth-Century England* (Chicago: University of Chicago Press, 1995), 154.

25. Todd, *Imagining Monsters,* viii.

26. Montaigne, *Complete Essays,* 539.

27. Lennard J. Davis, *Enforcing Normalcy: Disability, Deafness, and the Body* (London: Verso, 1995), 52.

28. Hay, *Deformity,* 4.

29. Hay, *Deformity,* 34.

30. The remarkable aspect of his work is that it is one of the first works written by a person with disabilities about disabilities. Pierre Desloges, a deaf person, some fifteen years later writes a book about his deafness. In other words, although persons with disabilities may still uphold stereotypes about disability, they nevertheless are speaking themselves.

31. Boswell's motivation in countering other critical versions of Johnson's life is clearly operative here. Unfortunately, I cannot here deal with Boswell's motivation in detail; neither do I include research concerning the telling revisions that Boswell made in his manuscript or varying accounts of Johnson given in Boswell's journal versus his public accounts.

32. Thrale, *Dr. Johnson,* 5.

33. He might be referring to a book interestingly titled *Deformities of Dr. Samuel Johnson.* The author, James Thomson Callender, attacks not the physical deformities of Johnson but his literary ones. The book includes eighty-nine pages of line-by-line corrections of Johnson's putative errors. Callender refers to Johnson's physical condition only twice, quite indirectly. Callender states that "his personal appearance cannot much recommend him" and refers to "the weakness of his vision." *Deformities of Dr. Samuel Johnson* (1782; rpt., Los Angeles: William Andrews Clark Memorial Library, 1971), iv.

34. I am operating under the assumption that madness is a disability. It is so defined, for example, in the Americans with Disabilities Act of 1990. However, it is entirely possible that in the eighteenth century madness was considered completely differently from disability. If Foucault is correct in *Madness and Civilization: A History of Insanity in the Age of Reason,* trans. Richard Howard (New York: Random House, 1973), madness was considered a defect in reasoning power or rationality.

This defect might be ascribed an epistemological rather than a physical basis—and so might not be considered a "defect" or "disability." For more recent work on this subject, see David Wright and Anne Digby, *From Idiocy to Mental Deficiency: Historical Perspectives on People with Learning Disabilities* (London: Routledge, 1996).

35. Jonathan Andrews, "Identifying and Providing for the Mentally Disabled in Early Modern London" in Wright and Digby, *From Idiocy to Mental Deficiency*, 70.

36. Andrews, "Identifying and Providing," 71.

37. For more on this see my *Enforcing Normalcy*, 23–49; Rosemarie Thomson's *Extraordinary Bodies: Figuring Physical Disability in American Culture and Literature* (New York: Columbia University Press, 1997); James W. Trent Jr., *Inventing the Feeble Mind: A History of Mental Retardation in the United States* (Berkeley and Los Angeles: University of California Press, 1994); Harlan Lane, *When the Mind Hears* (New York: Random House, 1984); Douglas C. Baynton, *Forbidden Signs: American Culture and the Campaign against Sign Language* (Chicago: University of Chicago Press, 1996); Michel Foucault, *The Birth of the Clinic: An Archeology of Medical Perception*, trans. A. M. Sheridan (New York: Pantheon, 1973).

38. Thrale, *Dr. Johnson*, 5.

39. Thrale, *Dr. Johnson*, 68.

40. Thrale, *Dr. Johnson*, 47.

41. Peter Pinco Chase, "The Ailments and Physicians of Dr. Johnson," *Yale Journal of Biology and Medicine* 23, no. 5 (April 1951): 370.

42. Thomas Babington Macaulay, *Life of Samuel Johnson* (Boston: Ginn and Company, Atheneum Press, 1904), 2.

43. Macaulay, *Life of Samuel Johnson*, 4–5.

44. Rather than dismissing or apologizing for Johnson's Tourette's syndrome, a disability studies approach might show how the syndrome enabled Johnson to compile his dictionary. The obsessive-compulsive behavior would aid him in the repetitive activities required.

45. Macaulay, *Life of Samuel Johnson*, 5.

46. Alternatives to the "triumph over disability" scenario are ones in which the morality and uplift is not built in a mandatory way into the story. Contemporary memoirs and fiction by authors like Nancy Mairs, *Remembering the Bone House* (New York: Harper and Row, 1989); Kenny Fries, *Body Remember* (New York: Dutton, 1997); Anne Finger, *Basic Skills* (Columbia: University of Missouri Press, 1986); Michael Bérubé, *Life as We Know It* (New York: Random House, 1996) and others provide us good examples.

47. Henry Fielding, *Amelia* (Oxford: Oxford University Press, 1983), 66. Subsequent references are given in the text.

48. Ronald Paulson and Thomas Lockwood, eds., *Henry Fielding: The Critical Heritage* (London: Routledge and Kegan Paul, 1969), 303.

49. Paulson and Lockwood, *Henry Fielding*, 327.

50. Paulson and Lockwood, *Henry Fielding*, 323.

51. Paulson and Lockwood, *Henry Fielding*, 333.

52. Paulson and Lockwood, *Henry Fielding*, 315.

53. Paulson and Lockwood, *Henry Fielding*, 349.

54. Paulson and Lockwood, *Henry Fielding*, 348.

55. Paulson and Lockwood, *Henry Fielding*, 335.

56. Thrale, *Dr. Johnson*, 102–3.

57. Cited in Philip Stevick, "The Augustan Nose," *University of Toronto Quarterly* 34, no. 2 (1965): 111.

58. See my *Enforcing Normalcy* for a fuller development of these ideas, as well as my "Who Put the *The* in the Novel?: Identity Politics and Disability in Novel Studies," *Novel* 31, no. 3 (summer 1998): 317–34.

59. Sarah Scott, *Millenium Hall* (Harmondsworth, England: Penguin, 1986), 199.

60. It is possible that disability served some positive, adaptive function for eighteenth- and nineteenth-century women. As invalids or "sick" women, females could avoid undesirable aspects of caregiving and attain greater privacy, perhaps even a sickroom of one's own, which would permit concentrated uninterrupted intellectual and creative work.

Paper, Picture, Sign: Conversations between the Deaf, the Hard of Hearing, and Others

Nicholas Mirzoeff

In late modern culture, it ought to be possible for the deaf, the hearing, and the hard-of-hearing to get along. Despite the panoply of communications devices now available, the spoken and heard voice remains the dominant metaphor for intelligence. Hearing remains so normalized as a standard component of humanity that no other means of communication is considered authentic. When Jacques Derrida writes of the phonocentrism of Western culture, he means that stalemated negotiations are described as a dialogue of the deaf, that being hard-of-hearing is seen as equivalent to senility and that deafness is a kind of monstrosity.[1] Yet for all the absolutism implied in such characterizations, there is no hard line between the deaf and the hearing but rather an intermediary zone of the hard-of-hearing, not belonging to the sign language culture of the profoundly deaf and yet not quite at home in the hearing majority, in which different people use many different means of communication and expression. Further, the profoundly deaf and the hearing have always conversed with each other. Before the discovery of antibiotics, deafness in its various degrees was far more common than it is today, as it was a side effect of such diseases as scarlet fever, mumps, smallpox, and even the common cold. It is still the case that most people are at one or two degrees of separation (to borrow a phrase from John Guare) from a deaf or hard-of-hearing person.[2] The deaf, sign language, and the hard-of-hearing exist in a border zone between visibility and invisibility that brings into relief the continued tensions generated by the coexistence of postmodern visual culture with Enlightenment rationality. It has been the hope of much work in Deaf studies, including my own, that these borders could be breached by making Deaf history "visible," that is to say, by detailing the various crimes and misdemeanors of the hearing toward the Deaf. In a different register, this was also the belief of the Deaf artists, critics, and writers of the late eighteenth and nineteenth centuries.

However, despite national media attention for Deaf issues in the past decade, Deaf and disability issues have continued to be marginalized in sharp distinction to those of concern to African Americans and other minority groups. In part this is, as it has always been, a question of numbers. Yet in an academy that rightly devotes considerable attention to transsexual people, there ought to be room for the significant issues raised by sign language and Deaf culture and history. I begin to suspect that it is in part the very way that this history has been written that accounts for its inability to resonate on the wider academic stage. In this essay, I have sought to write less from the perspective of revealing past wrongs than in the fashion Michel Foucault described as genealogy. Thus, the past failure to deal with what are again contemporary issues reveals the poverty of the discursive structures that both cause the "problem" and offer "solutions." For Foucault, the classic example of this process was the persistence of the disciplinary penal system even though the belief in rehabilitation that inspired it had evaporated. For liberal penal reform to insist on a greater emphasis on rehabilitation was, then, simply to reiterate the logic of the penal system itself. By the same token, to insist on the equality or superiority of sign language as a system of communication is to engage with the debate on the terms created by phonocentrism. Instead, we need to seek ways to sustain difference *as* difference, that which Derrida has called *différance*. In this endeavor, more history is not the solution. Rather, we need to reopen the question of what it might mean to hold conversations between the Deaf, the hard-of hearing, and others.

The deaf have always conversed with each other using signed languages, which were first noted by Plato. The early modern period saw dramatic changes both in hearing attitudes to the deaf and within deaf culture and language. The result was the first state-sponsored education for the deaf in France (1791) and the United States (1814) using signed languages to teach national languages. This transformation has been widely recounted in deaf history,[3] but certain fundamental questions remain open: how was this encounter possible? Who really educated the deaf in the eighteenth century before sign languages were properly understood by the hearing? How can we retrieve the traces of their signed language to each other? And how did the hearing begin their conversations with the deaf? I will explore these questions in dialogue with the work of the contemporary deaf artist Joseph Grigely, whose extended series *Conversations with the Hearing* is the inspiration for this piece. In the *Conversations*, Grigely turns the written scraps of conversation that arise when the hearing people he is interacting with

Fig. 3. Anon., *International Congress of the Deaf* (Paris, 1889). The deaf organized extensively to resist the anti–sign language position of hearing educators of the deaf in the late nineteenth century, as this group photograph of an international congress of the deaf in 1889 shows. (Courtesy of Institut National des Jeunes Sourds, Paris.)

speak in ways that he cannot lip-read into conceptual art. Here I place the early modern picturing of deafness and the late modern revival of interest in sign language and deaf culture in conversation with Grigely's work, discussed and quoted in the italicized sections. The Enlightenment pictured deafness as a new form of difference. Grigely pictures communication between the deaf and the hearing. The resistance to picturing the deaf as different was and is to picture them as monsters. For sign pictures language, which modern culture has tried to present as the pure presence of thought, as ineffable and unknowable.

As modernism tries to work out its crisis that we call postmodernism, the hearing have once again begun to "see" sign language after an interval of over a century since the Milan Congress of 1880 outlawed the use of sign in deaf education. While this renewed openness is to be welcomed, there is nonetheless a danger that the linguistic purpose of sign language has become lost as it becomes a "warm fuzzy," suitable for all kinds of advertising. This strategy reached its nadir with a Dr. Scholl advertisement for wart remover, endorsed by a signing woman who could not "afford" to have her hands blemished by warts. Here the pathology that hearing culture attributes to deafness has been displaced and condensed into a wart, of all things. In common with other activists and scholars,[4] I have been concerned to try to write deaf history, as a case study not of pathology but of the cultural construction of "centers" and "margins" and of how certain groups came to be excluded from the ranks of the civilized. I do not want to frame the deaf as monstrous or even as disabled but as a culture whose existence poses significant questions for the majority, phonocentric culture. Many Enlightenment thinkers regarded the deaf as machines, incapable of independent thought. One of Kant's less celebrated universals was the necessity of speech to reason. Thus he argued that a deaf person "can never achieve more than an analogue of reason."[5]

There was another side to the Enlightenment. In a working-class district of Paris in the early 1770s, a Jansenist priest named Charles-Michel de l'Epée observed two deaf women signing to each other. For Epée the deaf suddenly became visible: "Men similar to us but reduced in some ways to the condition of beasts, as long as no-one worked to free them from the gloomy shadows in which they were enslaved." Epée was inspired by this encounter to establish a school for the deaf, as many had done before him. He organized "displays" of sign language that made both himself and the deaf celebrated as Enlightenment heroes. His originality lay in the fact that he was the first hearing person to educate the deaf using a signed language derived from deaf sign language. Furthermore, he sought to educate the deaf poor, whereas most previous efforts at deaf education had aimed at the deaf children of the nobility. As his analogy indicates, this moment of clarity was enabled by the emancipatory discourse created around the Atlantic slave trade, most famously by the abbé Raynal. So while Epée has long been praised for being the "father" of the deaf, he could only "see" them through an abolitionist lens, initiating the curious mix of race and gender with which hearing people have often viewed the deaf. I have always suspected, with no hard evidence to support it, that Epée was also hard-of-hearing, if only because so many other individuals who have been associated with deaf and disability issues are at this one degree of separation.

It is still difficult for hearing people to see the deaf. The Americans with Disabilities Act of 1990 included deafness as a category of disability, much to the surprise of many deaf people who see themselves as a distinct lan-

Fig. 4. Marlet, *Les Sourds Muets* (1805). One of many popular prints showing the displays of sign language by the pupils of the abbés Epée and Sicard. (Courtesy of Institut National des Jeunes Sourds, Paris.)

guage-based culture rather than as "hearing-impaired." For that reason many deaf prefer to write of themselves as Deaf, indicating the cultural claim that is being made. This Deaf culture was to a significant degree the creation of institutes for the deaf that arose all over Europe and the United States in the early nineteenth century, inspired by Epée's example. During the French Revolution, the radical Prieur de la Marne successfully proposed the establishment of a meritocratic Institute for the Deaf in Paris using the sign language method: "The deaf have a language of signs which can be considered one of the most fortunate discoveries of the human spirit. It perfectly replaces, and with the greatest rapidity, the organ of speech. . . . If one were ever to realize the much desired project of a universal language, this would perhaps be that which would merit preference" (47). Prieur's language was so exactly that which was to become central to the deaf culture that grew up around the new Institute that one is tempted to suggest he may have been coached by a deaf person. One of the most successful pupils of the new Institute was Laurent Clerc, who was brought to the United States by Thomas

Gallaudet to assist in the creation of a college for the deaf that has become Gallaudet University. There is a sense, then, in which the very existence of national sign languages is the direct result of Epée's moment of recognition.

Although Epée himself was never fully conversant in sign language, after his death he became an embodied sign for sign language. That is to say, the deaf would commemorate Epée, for all his faults, as a way of celebrating the possibilities of sign language itself. The Central Society for the Deaf, an important Parisian deaf pressure-group set up in the 1830s, centered its activities around an annual banquet on Epée's birthday, attended by such disparate hearing figures as the radical Ledru-Rollin and the photographer Louis Daguerre. The deaf painter Frédéric Peyson was a leading member of the Society, and it was no coincidence that his first salon painting was entitled *Last Moments of the abbé de l'Epée* (1839). Critics immediately appreciated that his work was a tribute not just to Epée but to sign language itself. Indeed, during the nineteenth century over one hundred deaf people became professional artists in France, coached in the studios of the Institute, and they all followed Peyson's example. By the time a museum was opened at the Institute in 1890, over 180 portraits of Epée were available for display.

Of all these works, the most celebrated was Felix Martin's sculpture of Epée, first exhibited at the Salon of 1876 and installed at the Institute for the Deaf in 1879. Martin retained Epée's own emancipatory discourse by depicting the priest initiating a deaf boy into finger spelling. Although the child was represented as half Epée's size according to the conventions of such liberation iconography, he was not marked with any visible "racial" signs of inferiority, as nineteenth-century anthropology would have liked. For this work, Martin was awarded France's highest civilian honor, the Légion d'Honeur, by the interior minister at a special ceremony at the Institute. The statue remained a venue for deaf celebrations and meetings, especially on the key day of Epée's birthday. What they were celebrating was Epée as the "inventor" of sign language, a politically acceptable way to defend deaf culture against the increasing hostility of the oralists, those who would teach the deaf to speak and outlaw sign language. Indeed, even the installation of Martin's statue was taken as an opportunity to call for the relegation of the outdated sign language method to the past, and inaugurate the modern era of oralism. The deaf continued to assert the modernity of sign language, enshrined as a Republican activity by the creation of the Institute during the Revolution. Martin used the plinth panels of his statue to remind his audience of this argument by representing the key scene of Epée's encounter with the deaf women.

He is approached one night in New York City by a man who makes a circular gesture around his stomach. Rather than assume he knew what was meant, Grigely asks him to write it down: "The man seemed a little surprised by my request but he took it seriously and started to write. The letters came slowly: M-O-N and then he stopped. He seemed confused as if he wasn't sure what came next. There was a long pause and then he crossed out the unfinished word and tried to start again. He wrote an M but stopped and didn't continue. He paused again. And then he crossed out the M." Grigely asks: "What was his life like? Metonymized by effort and erasure, by inscription and cancellation, one can begin to imagine what was otherwise unimaginable. Hope, jobs, things like that. The letters crossed out. The immense space between speech and writing. The gesture that began it all, the gesture to which we return."

Grigely reencounters the Other, just as Epée did, but from the perspective of the literate, signing deaf person. Grigely seems to echo the nineteenth-century deaf critic Ferdinand Bérthier on mimicry, a theory of sign language and gesture: "thought is reflected whole as if in a mirror, complete with its most delicate contours. It materializes there, so to speak."

In their different ways, Grigely and Epée recognized that they did *not* understand what was being signed. As Geoff Bennington has argued: "The only communication worth the name takes place . . . when I do not have immediately available to me the means to decode a transparent message."[6] Epée's moment was what philosopher Emmanuel Levinas has called the moment of ethics, or alterity. That is to say, he did not try and reduce the Other to being the Same but recognized the presence of difference. In Levinas's view, ethics occur by "the putting into question of my spontaneity by the presence of the Other."[7] In this instance, the casual assumption of the hearing that the deaf can have no language was put into question by the visible presence of the signs made by the deaf women. Elizabeth Grosz reminds us that alterity "always asserts itself outside of and unforeseen by the subject. (It is what surprises and astonishes.) Second, alterity is always an *excess*, an unabsorbable remainder or residue, a 'force' that exposes the subject's limits." In both cases, the encounter with alterity is marked by the excess of signed language, the supplement to speech that exposes the insufficiency of oral language. Levinas emphasizes that Western epistemology has sought to negate alterity by reducing otherness to the Same—by making the deaf speak, for example.

This transmutation of alterity into sameness had frequently occurred in the by then traditional assumption of explorers and philosophers that "primitive" languages like sign language were immediately intelligible. When Columbus arrived at Cuba he thought he had reached Japan: "And I believe that it is so according to the signs that all the Indians of these islands and those that I have with me make (because I do not understand them through speech, [and] that it is the island of Cipango of which marvelous things are told." As Stephen Greenblatt remarks, "the sightings are important only in relation to what Columbus already knows and what he can write about them on the basis of that knowledge."[8] During the French Revolution, Epée's successor at the Institute for the Deaf, the abbé Sicard, trained anthropologists heading to Australia in sign language in the belief that the indigenous people would undoubtedly understand it. In the age of high Victorian imperialism all manner of real and improvised sign languages were used to help the Europeans communicate with their new subject peoples. Today scientists earnestly teach sign language to gorillas, acting on the unspoken belief that sign is a primitive and simple language system. Gorillas are thus the "same" as humans in some sense because they can make use of American Sign Language handshapes. In this sense, sign language becomes the unstable mark of simian similarity and difference with the hearing/human. Indeed, insofar as Western humanism presupposes that the human condition is defined by spoken language, it is sign language that attests to the tangential relation of both the deaf and gorillas to humanity. For oralists like the Italian Giulio Ferri in the early twentieth century, "the violent and spasmodic mimicry [of the deaf] . . . can at least serve as an argument to establish their consanguinuity with the famous Primates."

The other operation that may be performed is to transform the Other into a monster, the abject, not the Other to the ego but something that simply is not. Monstrosity is, as Dennis Todd has pointed out, a discourse of self-identity, not alterity.[9] As soon as periodicals and newspapers were established in early modern Europe, they featured reports of monstrous births and other mythical events. Every edition of the learned seventeenth-century *Journal des Savants,* in which the philosophy of René Descartes was disseminated, would contain such reports. As popular newspapers developed in France, they borrowed this feature from the learned press. On February 27, 1777, Parisians could read,

> A natural phenomenon has been reported which is most extraordinary. It would seem that the wife of Sieur de Barentin, the first President of the Cour des Aides, has recently given birth to a bush which has been identified as a currant bush, although it was not bearing currants at the time—only cherries—so it is said. This monstrous new species bore absolutely no resemblance to anything human and was quite inanimate. This strange birth has obviously been the cause of great sorrow to all the family.[10]

What did the Barentin family actually see when they reported this mulberry bush? Like Columbus, they saw what they wanted to see and reduced the

Other to the Same, a mass of the abject. Despite this long history, contemporary self-appointed prophets of cultural apocalypse point to tabloids such as the *Weekly World News* as incontrovertible evidence of the cultural decline of the West.

> *Grigely uses silk-screened pages from the* Weekly World News *to indicate the survival of early modern scientific discourses of monstrosity in popular culture. Like Warhol's use of commercial imagery, his replication of this seemingly most disposable of media transforms it into a matter for reflection. Why have we come to expect all newborns to conform to a grid of normality in terms of physical appearance? Why are we surprised when teenagers later go to all manner of extremes from anorexia to body piercing and tattooing to affirm or deny that idealized body image?*

The Barentin family's experience took place a few years after Epée had "seen" sign language's alterity. Why was one form of seeing so different to the other? It was necessary for something to cross the gap between the viewer (with hearing) and the viewed (without) in order that the third thing, sign language, could be seen. Epée's encounter was modern, in a way that Columbus's and the Barentins' were not. It was above all urban; taking place as a part of those wanderings that a parish priest might make across a city like the *flâneur* or the Situationists after him. It was modern because as Heidegger argued, the definitive episode of the modern is its ability to picture the

Fig. 5. Joseph Grigely, *Colt Born with Human Face*, silk-screened from the tabloid *Weekly World News.* (Courtesy of the artist.)

world: "the fact that the world becomes picture at all is what distinguishes the essence of the modern age."[11] Until the visual was understood as being as complex a system as print, sign could not be seen by the hearing as a complex system for sending messages, only as a simple pantomime. Epée's challenge, as the deaf recognized, was to acknowledge his failure to understand.

Who taught the deaf? It was not the hearing instructors, who, in Bérthier's phrase "took the deaf from their villages and taught them Latin to prepare to speak French." Indeed Sicard admitted as much: "It is important to say that it was neither myself nor my illustrious master [Epée] who invented the language of the deaf. . . . [A] speaking man should not involve himself in inventing signs or in giving them abstract values" (58). The Institute for the Deaf gained its prestige from two prodigies, Jean Massieu and Laurent Clerc. Clerc learned from Massieu, who taught him directly from 1797 to 1802. Who taught Massieu? Sicard claimed that it was he who did so. In fact, a local priest named Saint-Sernin led the class in Bordeaux where Massieu learned French. There were sixteen deaf students, including three women, two of whom were Jean's sisters Jeanne and Blanche. The deaf taught themselves, taking the opportunity presented by the schools to create standardized sign language from disparate sources and then learn the French equivalents. Clerc later described how this process functioned in the New York asylum: "The signs which they employed were a combination of those used by the Indians, of those they had learnt from some of our own [French] pupils, together with what they had gathered from the works of the Abbé de l'Epée, and Sicard, and those of the English instructors." By the 1830s, these hybrid languages had evolved in the Institutes for the Deaf into standardized, complex languages. The hearing instructors in the Institute for the Deaf recognized that: "In our Institute, they converse in signs without their teachers being able to penetrate the subject of their discussion. . . . It is certain that there exists in our building a tradition of signs, which is the invention of the deaf" (109). In the manner of the classic disciplinary institution chronicled by Foucault, power created resistance.[12] The French Revolution sought to number and order the deaf in order to render them assimilable to the mainstream. Ironically, their impulse created a standard French sign language that in turn enabled American sign language to develop and become national.

Joseph Grigely, *The History of Deaf People*

> *"When you look through piles of photographs of 19th and 20th century deaf institutes, you can find a lot of images of children being taught to speak. But*

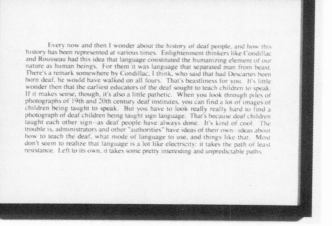

Every now and then I wonder about the history of deaf people, and how this history has been represented at various times. Enlightenment thinkers like Condillac and Rousseau had this idea that language constituted the humanizing element of our nature as human beings. For them it was language that separated man from beast. There's a remark somewhere by Condillac, I think, who said that had Descartes been born deaf, he would have walked on all fours. That's beastliness for you. It's little wonder then that the earliest educators of the deaf sought to teach children to speak. If it makes sense, though, it's also a little pathetic. When you look through piles of photographs of 19th and 20th century deaf institutes, you can find a lot of images of children being taught to speak. But you have to look really really hard to find a photograph of deaf children being taught sign language. That's because deaf children taught each other sign--as deaf people have always done. It's kind of cool. The trouble is, administrators and other "authorities" have ideas of their own--ideas about how to teach the deaf, what mode of language to use, and things like that. Most don't seem to realize that language is a lot like electricity: it takes the path of least resistance. Left to its own, it takes some pretty interesting and unpredictable paths.

Fig. 6. Joseph Grigely, *The History of Deaf People.* Here Grigely appropriates a nineteenth-century depiction of deaf education. (Courtesy of the artist.)

you have to look really hard to find a photograph of deaf children being
taught sign language. That's because deaf children taught each other sign—as
deaf people always have done. . . . Language is a lot like electricity: it takes
the path of least resistance." Photography and film could have been used from
the 1830s onward to educate children in sign language. But because these me-
dia claimed the "natural" transparency of speech, they were in fact used for
oral instruction, showing lip movements. By contrast, the evidently artificial
medium of video has become the means of record for sign, especially the sign
language poetry movement.

During the French Revolution, some radical sections of the Jacobin group
came to understand that the deaf were their own educators. During a debate
in the Convention on the future of the institute, Nicolas Raffron, a radical
Jacobin, questioned the need for hearing instructors. "They [the deaf] have a
language of their own," he argued. "Those whom I knew already understood
their language of signs very well, even though the abbé de l'Epée had not yet
opened his school" (62). Perier, a deputy of the abbé Sicard, and a teacher at
the institute, defended the school against this attack: "The Deaf-Mute is always a savage, always close to ferocity, and always on the point of becoming
a monster" (62). Even after birth, the "savage" deaf could mutate into monstrous forms without the restraining hand of the disciplinary Institute. Perier
compared the deaf to those he called "savages" in Africa, arguing that just as
slavery had recently been abolished, "the deaf will be restored to civilization,
just as the men of color are about to be restored to their rights" (62). Here is
the dialectic of the Enlightenment. On the one hand, the Institute would permit the deaf to develop their sign language culture, create a vibrant deaf intellectual elite in the nineteenth century and provide training for deaf writers
and artists who flourished from 1830 to 1900. On the other hand, by including the deaf in the discourse of monstrosity, primitivism, and savagery,
the way was opened for future eugenicists like Alexander Graham Bell to
warn of the creation of a "deaf variety of the human race" (225).

The same impulse that led to the establishment of sign language education in 1795 would bring about its abolition at the Milan Congress of 1880.
Whereas the French Revolution had believed that institutions would restrain
the growth of monsters, Bell now argued that the deaf schools were a literal
breeding-ground for deviancy. Bell further raised the specter that a signing,
deaf nation might be established in the West of America, noting ominously
that "24 deaf mutes, with their families, have already arrived [in Manitoba]
and have settled upon the land. More are expected next year." The use of
sign language would lead to more marriages, more deaf people, and eventually a "deaf variety of the human race" might be established in the American West. A conversation with the Deaf might mean very different things to

different spectators. Its current fashionable status with advertisers—especially, in a moment of intense irony, AT&T, founded by the arch oralist Alexander Graham Bell—should not be taken as the end of this argument but a swing in this cycle of modernity. Although sign language has again achieved a degree of legitimacy with hearing professionals and as a legitimate language in academic institutions, medical doctors are energetically advocating the use of cochlear implants as a "cure" for deafness. At the same time, the future of the residential school for the Deaf is again open to question, for they run against the grain of liberal and conservative beliefs alike, whether expressed in terms of "integration," "mainstreaming," or "welfare-dependency." Registrations at Gallaudet University, the federally funded university for the deaf where all instruction is provided in sign language, have fallen considerably as other universities have improved their provision for deaf students. Should one lament the decline of Gallaudet or celebrate the seeming success of deaf/hearing integration?

Let us return to the beginning, the attempted conversation between the deaf and the hearing. The difference between the deaf and hearing sides of this exchange of looks is crossed by desire, that polymorphous and perverse disrupter of neat divides. Here I want to draw a distinction between the desire that constitutes individuals as subjects and the desire actually experienced by individuals. Jacques Lacan's model of the subject's being constituted by lack or insufficiency has become widely accepted among visual theorists. In trying to explain Lacan's notion of desire, Michel de Certeau wrote: "A Midrash once said, 'Praying is speaking to the wall.' Lacan turns speech into a conception close to this rabbinical austerity. The Other is there, but we can expect nothing from it except the desire which is produced by being deprived of it."[13] Or one might say, speaking to the deaf. For as Judith Mayne has emphasized, there is a difference between the theoretical subject and the actual viewer.[14] In other words, while the ego may be formed in a process of splitting that creates an awareness of lack, what I want can be *creative.* Desire is central to language. It is above all central to the acquisition of language, as psychoanalysts have documented in their differing ways. It is equally important in the acquisition of second languages, as Alice Kaplan has emphasized: "Whatever the method, only desire can make a student learn a language, desire and necessity."[15] However, the cumbersome nature of so much signed education in the nineteenth century and oral education for the deaf today might almost be designed to extinguish this desire to learn.

To turn these aphorisms into more concrete form, I want to look at two moments involving the deaf intellectual Laurent Clerc. One of the manuscripts in the Laurent Clerc Archives, which have now found their way into

Fig. 7. Jérôme-Martin Langlois, *The Abbé Sicard Instructing his Deaf Pupils* (1814). Langlois was a student of the leading neoclassical painter Jacques-Louis David, who found the "heroism of modern life" (Baudelaire) at the Institute for the Deaf. (Courtesy of the Institut National des Jeunes Sourds, Paris.)

Sterling Memorial Library at Yale, is a note by the neoclassical artist Jérôme-Martin Langlois, a student of David. He undertook two paintings in the Institute, in direct adherence to Leonardo da Vinci's advice to artists that they should learn to imitate the sign language of the deaf. In the note, Langlois signals his intention to paint the sleeping Clerc, an image he compared to Joseph-Marie Vien's picture of a Capucin nun. Before he could complete the sketch, Clerc woke up. It is intriguing that Langlois's seemingly private thought has fetched up in Clerc's archive. Was it in fact a curious note from the artist to his subject? Langlois's reference to Vien's painting is odd: why did the sleeping boy suggest a virginal woman? Was it a displacement of a more obvious artistic reference from the period, Girodet's *Endymion*, which showed an overtly sexualized young man asleep? The myth tells that Selene, goddess of the moon, kept Endymion eternally asleep in order that she could enjoy his beauty. In the same way, Langlois had wanted to keep Clerc asleep so that he could capture his image. By rationalizing it as the image of a nun, he tried to void his desire of sexual content but perhaps stands convicted of overcompensation. What he wanted to do was picture the Other motivated by his sudden flash of desire for that Other.

> *I found out about the Clerc Archives at Yale in Harlan Lane's wonderful footnotes. In the depressing fashion of contemporary archives, you can only read them on microfilm. Clerc visited England with Sicard during the Peace of Amiens in 1814. His passport is preserved in the archive. It is covered with a conversation with a hearing woman. I sent a photocopy to Joseph Grigely in 1993, knowing that he would be interested. I didn't know he had made it into one of his "Conversations," until he sent me a slide of the piece in 1997 (fig. 3).*
>
> *In the text I am quoted as calling this "the earliest encounter between a Deaf person and An Other," implying both that it was recorded and that it marks a two-way exchange. Clerc flirts with an Englishwoman. Their conversation proceeds by some mime, some lip-reading, and these surviving written traces. He begins by asking, "What hotel do you lodge in Dieppe?" and she replies, "Loire." He then hints at something he wishes to say: "If I did know English better, I could say to you but I don't know anything en français." Some time later, the conversation takes a distinctly romantic turn. Clerc admits: "Yes I have wept much for her." She asks, "Would you have married her," and he replies, "That is impossible because she is noble." On the edge, in the margins of deaf/hearing conversations, he notes, "She has not said it to me."*

What was it that Clerc wanted to read? In the margins of this passport, a dance of desire and inscription was played out, similar to that implied in Langlois's note. The deaf and the hearing desired each other in ways that could not be said but could be painted or written. As historians we have the traces of this event but must accept that it cannot be fully reconstituted. I am not saying that writing such histories is impossible but rather that we have to gaze respectfully into the gaps, the silences, and the walls in the historical record in pursuit of the history of the Other. For nineteenth-century modernists, this gap of intelligibility was unacceptable and was closed by force. Do we postmodernists have sufficient restraint to allow the Other to be the Other, or are we compulsively bound to reenact the failures of modernity? As Lacan says in his seminar on ethics, "reality is precarious."[16] It is known

Fig. 8. Joseph Grigely, *Conversations with the Hearing.* A photocopy of a "conversation" between Laurent Clerc and an unknown English woman, found by the author in the Laurent Clerc Archives, Yale University, and adapted by Joseph Grigely. (Courtesy of the artist.)

not as the product of self-analysis but in the face-to-face ethical encounter between the reality principle and the pleasure principle, between self and other, that the discourse of monstrosity seeks to prevent.

Envoi

As a child, I spent many dreary hours being tested. Seated in a soundproof booth, I wore headphones that filled my right hearing ear with white noise, while ever louder noises were pumped into my deaf left ear in a futile attempt to force it to register sound. What was always overlooked was the child in between the deaf/pathological ear and the hearing/normal ear. Hearing and deafness are for the most part in-between conditions. While the profoundly deaf in the United States number in the tens of thousands, there are 21 million people who are hard of hearing, including President Clinton, who came out as hard-of-hearing in October 1997. Yet this 10 percent of the population is not seen as a constituency by anyone except the manufacturers of hearing aids. For deafness is constituted by the hearing as a shame culture. I have lost count of the times people have said to me things like "you can hear if you want to," or "I'm bored of repeating myself to you." On the other hand, when a distinguished visiting speaker spoke so quietly at a New York university that he could not be heard in a small room, no one had the courage to ask him to speak up because, in my opinion, they were embarrassed to admit they could not hear. But the ASL sign "hard-of-hearing" can also be used to refer to "someone who deviates" from the Deaf cultural world.[17] While the profoundly Deaf have had Deaf Pride for a generation, it is time for those of us who are hard-of-hearing to stop being ashamed. After so many demolitions of the binary opposition, it is time to stop simply opposing deaf to hearing and to look at the points in between where so many people are. There should be good amplification at all classes, lectures, and public events, as well as ASL interpretation as a right, not a privilege. Let us talk loudly, turn the TV up, ask people to repeat themselves and be damned.

NOTES

1. Jacques Derrida, *Of Grammatology*, trans. Gayatri Chakravorty Spivak (Baltimore: Johns Hopkins University Press, 1976).

2. John Guare, *Six Degrees of Separation* (New York: Vintage Books, 1990).

3. The classic history of the deaf is Harlan Lane, *When the Mind Hears: A History of the Deaf* (New York: Random House, 1984). All references to early modern deaf history in this essay are taken from my book, *Silent Poetry: Deafness, Sign and Visual Culture in Modern France* (Princeton: Princeton University Press, 1995), unless otherwise attributed. All further references to this book will be cited parenthetically.

4. See *The Disability Studies Reader*, ed. Lennard J. Davis (New York: Routledge, 1997) for a representative sample.

5. Immanuel Kant, *Anthropology from a Pragmatic Point of View*, trans. Mary J. Gregor (The Hague: Nijhoff, 1974).

6. Geoff Bennington, *Legislations* (London: Verso, 1994).

7. Emmanuel Levinas, *Difficult Freedom: Essays on Judaism*, trans. Seán Hand (Baltimore: Johns Hopkins University Press, 1990), 8.

8. Stephen Greenblatt, *Marvelous Possessions: The Wonder of the New World* (Chicago: University of Chicago Press, 1991), quoted from *The 'Diario' of Christopher Columbus's First Voyage to America, 1492–1493*, trans. by Oliver Dunn and James E. Kelley Jr. (Norman: University of Oklahoma Press, 1989), 75, from Greenblatt, 88. See similar observations by Basil Davidson on the case of Africa in "Africa

and the Invention of Racism," in *The Search for Africa: History, Culture, Politics* (New York: Times Books, 1994), 42–64.

9. Dennis Todd, *Imagining Monsters: Miscreations of the Self in Eighteenth-Century England* (Chicago: University of Chicago Press, 1995), 136.

10. Quoted by Arlette Farge, *Fragile Lives: Violence, Power, and Solidarity in Eighteenth-Century Paris* (Cambridge: Harvard University Press, 1993), 233.

11. Martin Heidegger, "The Age of the World Picture," in *The Question concerning Technology*, trans. William Lovitt (New York: Garland, 1977).

12. Michel Foucault, *Discipline and Punish: The Birth of the Prison*, trans. Alan Sheridan (New York: Pantheon Books, 1977).

13. Michel de Certeau, *Heterologies: Discourse on the Other*, trans. Brian Massumi (Minneapolis: University of Minnesota Press, 1986), 50.

14. Judith Mayne, *Cinema and Spectatorship* (New York: Routledge, 1993), 36.

15. Alice Kaplan, *French Lessons* (Chicago: University of Chicago Press, 1993), 131.

16. Jacques Lacan, *Seminar 1: The Ethics of Psychoanalysis*, trans. Jacques-Alain Miller (New York: W. W. Norton, 1988).

17. Carol Padden and Tom Humphries, *Deaf in America: Voices from a Culture* (Cambridge: Harvard University Press, 1988), 41.

PART 2 Monstrosity

In the Bodyshop: Human Exhibition in Early Modern England

Stephen Pender

"Let that man consider the discomfort of Deformitie," Thomas Bedford wrote in October 1635, "How lyable it is daily to exprobration through the evill custome of wicked men, more ready to cast it in the teeth, than condole or commiserate" with those whom God has touched with "the black-finger of Deformity." The occasion for these reflections was the birth of "strange and wonderfull" conjoined twins to John Persons and his wife in the village of Stonehouse, Plymouth, England. News of these "two bodies joyned together in one common skin" spread quickly; "Towne and Countrey" gathered to gawk at the stillborn twins. Bedford was indignant. In his funeral oration, appended to a thorough physical description of the twins in *A True and Certaine Relation of a Strange-Birth*, Bedford censured his audience for spiritual lassitude and idle curiosity. To Bedford, the birth, as the "speciall handy-worke of God," was clearly a "Lesson": in "altering or hindering the course of Nature," God calls man to "an observation of his Providence." Yet "Nature is deafe, and Reason dull in these occasions," Bedford insisted; while astrologers, philosophers, and physicians might offer "reasons for the coalition of these two twinnes into one," faith alone was susceptible to the monster's pedagogy. Bedford's paean to faith registered his anxiety about the perverse speculation inspired by monstrous births; since our delight is measured by our desires, and none would desire a "mishapen Birth," it was precisely the "pleasure" taken in gazing at monsters that irked him. "Defect or excesse" in the body, Bedford wrote, "must needs breed griefe, because it createth trouble." Yet the "common sort," to Bedford, "make no further use of these Prodigies and Strange-births, than as a matter of wonder and table-talk: . . . It was not thus in the better Ages of the world." Most vexing to Bedford in his own "irreligious" age was the lucrative trade and exhibition of monsters. He questioned whether "Monsters and mishapen births may lawfully be carried up and downe the country for sights to make a gaine by? Whether the Birth being once dead, may be kept from the grave for the former ends? Whether the parents of such births may sel them to another[?]" Living monsters, "fit for none imployment," were put on display; dead monsters, Bedford lamented, were "prostituted to the covetousnesse of any." Since few greeted human anomaly "with sorrow of Heart, and Humiliation," and many would rather "make a benefit of such births," public exhibition was one of the genuine "discomforts of deformity."[1]

A True and Certaine Relation of a Strange-Birth exemplifies many of the concerns and apprehensions about prodigies and monsters in early modern England. Bringing a "provincial" event to the attention of literate Londoners, Bedford's discussion of the relation between the soul and the body, first and second causes, providence and sin, curiosity and the problems of public display is typical. Although he was wrong about the past, for it seems monsters and prodigies were a continual source of fascination from antiquity to the Renaissance,[2] the deformed bodies of the twins provided Bedford with potent vehicles for his own spiritual pedagogy. In particular, in his concern about the contemporary "wonder and table-talk" of the common sort he was not alone. Anxiety about the popularity and effects of human exhibition in the early modern period was common. However, recent scholarship on monsters and the monstrous in early modern England has, for the most part, ignored Bedford's bête noire.[3] Rather, scholars have focused on deformity as a mobile, ahistorical concept that embodies our prurience or disrupts our perceptions of "the human"; monsters are conceived as mirrors in which we see our boundaries, our narcissism, or our questions about received images of self. As an evolving cluster of metaphors and distinctions, the monstrous has been seen as a trope of aspersion, an ever-present threat used to disarm political or religious opponents. Whether so-called monsters or freaks are enlisted for their capacity to "throw doubt on life's ability to teach us order," to formalize and embody the "unthought," or, rather more grandly, to chart the contours of change in Western culture, human deformity, figured as a kind of return of the repressed, now has its own minor culture industry.[4] From early enquiries that sought to shed light on unexplored recesses of modern culture, to an enterprise that sees in a symptom the totalizing narrative of modernity, monsters have been used and abused to satisfy the interests of contemporary critics. Indeed, somatic difference has been used to call into crisis almost the totality of our epistemological and ontological insights into the past.[5] Collections and symposia attest to this accelerated investment, as does the recent production of a Broadway musical, Side Show, based on the lives of conjoined twins Daisy and Violet Hilton.[6]

Scholarship concerned specifically with human exhibition has been on the whole more historical in nature, and here I offer a contribution to this body of work by mapping out the local history of human exhibition in early modern England. My enquiry is divided into two parts. The first sketches a history of human exhibition in England in the "age of curiosity." In the second, I study manifestations of the anxiety that developed in the seventeenth century related to imposture, fraudulent exhibition, and false monsters. Throughout, my concern is to suggest that attitudes toward human exhibition reflect several emergent practices: English natural philosophy, the reform of curiosity, and a renewed anthropological attention to the human body. I conclude by arguing that there was more continuity than change in the history of human exhibition in England. Bedford's derisive remarks about the "wonder" of the "common sort" are echoed over one hundred years later by William Hay in his autobiography, *Deformity: An Essay* (1754); attention to the human body as a mark of difference, and a residual faith in the somatic exterior as a reliable index to the soul, remained more or less constant throughout the early modern period. Human exhibition, I argue, was a vehicle for this continuity.

"Bartholomew-Babyes"

In the early seventeenth century, England seemed a fecund matrix of monsters.[7] Proto-Catholic and future bishop Geoffrey Goodman, intervening in the vigorous debate about the senescence of the world, declared in 1616, "Monsters are rare and seldom appear to us . . . [although] Affrica be a fruitfull mother of monsters." But others disagreed.[8] Sir Thomas Browne wrote, "There is all *Africa,* and her prodigies in us."[9] By midcentury, some believed that "England [had] *grown* Affrica" due to the frequent appearance of prodigies and the attention they received, though scanty records and the political texture of the debate about "monsterous England" in the sixteenth and seventeenth centuries obscure our inquiries.[10] Clearly, the expansion of printing brought prodigies to the attention of a wide audience; chroniclers and pamphleteers, in particular, had vested interests in perpetuating the view that England was overrun with monsters.[11] In 1633, Henry Reynolds held that popular poets, ignorant about the "mysteries and hidden properties of Nature," were no better than "illiterate Empyricks": they trafficked in "whissles, painted rattles and such like Bartholomew-babyes." The "mont'ibanke Rimers of the time," he implied, wrote about nothing but curiosities and monsters.[12] Reynolds's rancor was occasioned perhaps by the popularity of ballads and broadsides advertising the latest prodigy; he was not alone in his disgust.

By 1667, Thomas Sprat lamented that the "wild amuzing [of] mens minds, with *Prodigies*, and conceits of *Providence*, has been one of the most considerable causes of those spiritual distractions, of which our Country has long bin the *Theater*." To Sprat, the amusement with prodigies was "a vanity, to which the English seem to have bin subject above all others."[13] Despite Sprat's hyperbole, symptomatic of recent social upheaval as well as the future bishop's reaction to religious "enthusiasm," England's situation was not unique: sports of nature *(lusus naturae, jeux de nature)* were popular both as curiosities and subjects of "scientific" investigation in most western European cultures. Neither was England alone in its attention to human deformity and human exhibition.[14] Scholars have demonstrated the popularity of human exhibition in this period, suggesting that by 1600 monsters were popular attractions at fairs, public houses, and coffeehouses. Yet, with the possible exception of Richard Altick, whose important study is concerned with London over three centuries, no scholar has yet offered a comprehensive history of human exhibition. Although a cursory glance at the evidence here confirms English participation in a European phenomenon, a comparative study is not my purpose; rather, I offer an outline of the history of human exhibition in England between about 1560 and 1740.[15]

In 1552 in Middleton Stony, Kent, conjoined twins were born to John Kenner and his wife. The birth was sensational; a ballad was published immediately, and the birth was mentioned in contemporary chronicles and diaries.[16] Engaged in correspondence about another set of conjoined twins, a secretary of the Royal Society cited the birth as late as 1664.[17] The attention paid to this monstrous birth was extraordinary; it marks perhaps the beginning of a popular "amuzement" with prodigies. Indeed, various later writers looked to the mid–sixteenth century as an impressively prodigious period. Mentioning unusual births of both humans and animals, Holinshed noted for 1562 that in "no age at anye time hath ther be sene so many and so great and straunge wonderous sygnes everye wher aborad as within these few years."[18] Although the interpretations of these events differed, reformers and papists, learned and lewd, believed recent events—the birth of monstrous humans and animals, the appearance of comets and meteors—signs of divine indignation or imminent apocalypse. The world itself had grown progressively monstrous; prodigies, contemporaries assumed, embodied God's displeasure with England's profligacy. In such a conflicted period, the local potency of the monstrous—expressed either in the "rhetoric of monstrosity" or in the use of prodigies as political tools—was not lost on the English.[19]

In recent work on monsters in the early modern period, there has been little effort to see in the publications of the "pot-poets" who retailed their wares on the streets of London—"stories of some men of Tyburn, or a strange monster out of Germany," according to John Earle—evidence of human exhibition. While the English became more aware of the resonance of monstrous metaphors, to describe, say, moral turpitude or the evils of Roman Catholicism, the real bodies of so-called freaks were put on display in parlors, taverns, churches, and cabinets. In *The True Fourme and Shape of a Monsterous Chyld* (1565), William Elderton advised his readers that "this Childe was brought up to London, wheare it was seene of dyvers worshipfull man and women of the Cytie. And also of the Countrey." In the following year, a ballad entitled *The True Discription of a Childe with Ruffes* (1566) functioned as an advertisement for the exhibition: "This Childe beforesaid (the day of the date underwritten) was to be seene in Glene Alley in Sothwark beeing alive and x weeks olde and iiii. dayes not unlikely to live long." In 1609, a pamphlet mentioned "a huge deformed fish, that would groan and roar contrary to his kind, which by many people was seene at the Swanne within Newgate." The same text noted the situation at the birth of a deformed human baby (not dissimilar, we might assume, to the Persons example): "Not many hours passed, before the reports of this strange byrth was bruited abroad and the eares of the inhabitants there-about dwelling, so filled with the newes thereof, that they came in multitudes to behold it, in such aboundance that it was wonderfull."[20] By 1617, in an anonymous pamphlet on a seemingly "unpossible" monstrous birth, the author spent several paragraphs castigating the public for their lack of piety. Londoners, "siting idly at their doores, gaping and gazing," the author insisted satirically, were less prone to hear a sermon than they were a "winters tale" or see a monster.[21] There is clear evidence that by the early seventeenth century the birth of a monstrous child was an important public event; many had been "eye witnesses" to "abortive and prodigious births."[22]

Although the records are sparse for the sixteenth century, by comparison, the amount of evidence for the lucrative trade and display of monsters is plentiful in the seventeenth century. Perhaps most famously in this period, Johannes Baptista Lazarus Colloredo, a Genoan *thoracopagus parasiticus*, was exhibited in most of the courts of Europe. Lazarus, whose autositic brother Johannes emerged from his thorax, had exhibited himself in Germany, Spain and France, as one English ballad put it, and was on display in England and Scotland from 1637 until 1642; he was also mentioned in medical dissertations.[23] In 1664, an ostler, John Waterman, displayed his conjoined daughters quite profitably. The twins were dissected, embalmed, and brought to London for exhibition. Waterman "(being a poore man) had twenty pounds given him the first day [of exhibition], by persons of quality."[24] The Waterman twins may have died, Pepys suggests, by "being showed too much to people." By 1670, as one correspondent to the *Philosophical Transactions of the Royal Society* avers, the parents of prodigies demanded great sums of money for the privilege of permitting the dissection and display of their dead children.[25] A merchant who documented the birth of conjoined twins in Ostend in 1682 claimed, "Their Parents are offered a great Sum of Money for them to be carried about: They told us, they did intend (after the Holy Days, so called) to carry their Children to *Bridges* [Bruges?], and it may from thence to the Cities of Holland." "Many people came to see them and gave 3 *Stivers* apeice."[26] In the case of a two-headed monster born in Exeter, October 5, 1682, the child was buried, then disinterred for public display (see fig. 9). The monster "lived not long, but was buried and taken up again on the 10th Instant [that is, of October], and many hundreds now resort to see it." Another account suggests that after its birth, the child "was soon buried, but after taken up again, and exposed to the view of numerous Spectators, to the great advantage of the Parents."[27] In the transactions of the Royal Society, the efforts of correspondents desirous of an accurate description (or indeed the purchase) of anomalous births were repeatedly frustrated by the crowds of onlookers curious to see these "unusual accidents."[28] In 1680, a monster born near Taunton was seen by five hundred people a day.[29] The trade in dead monstrosities was wide indeed, encompassing both the public exhibition of human bodies to the multitude who flocked to see curiosities and the natural philosophers who collected bodies or fragments of bodies thought rare or curious.

By mid-seventeenth century, the exhibition of rarities was extremely popular both at fairs (Sturbridge and Bartholomew, for example) and in the streets and taverns of London. Robert Boyle noted that "the Multitude flocks to see" those "vast exotic Animals" that "Men give money to be allow'd to gaze on." Boyle himself had been to see elephants.[30] Ned Ward thought the various shapes in which human nature throws itself were plentiful indeed, including the impossible shapes of the posture-masters. Anthony Wood complained that the "folly" of laughing at worthwhile things and gazing at curiosities characterized "an age given to brutish pleasure and atheisme," and Boyle insisted that there was "nothing so sacred or so true that impudent and facetious men do not make a shift to break a jest upon."[31] Even legitimately interesting rarities, Wood implied, were subject to common derision. By midcentury, John Spencer believed the frequent exhibition of monsters

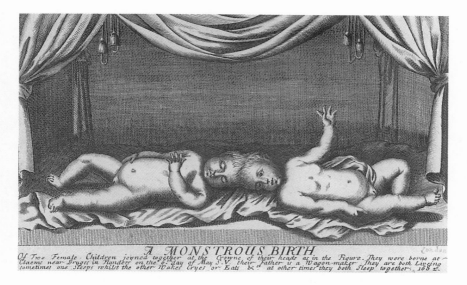

Fig. 9. From *A True Relation of the Birth of a Monster Born at Exeter, Having Two Perfect Heads* (London, 1682). A two-headed monster born in Exeter, October 5, 1682, "lived not long, but was buried and taken up again . . . and many hundreds now resort to see it." (Reproduced by permission of the British Library.)

and other anomalies undermined the state by giving "every pitiful Prodigy-monger . . . credit enough with the People."[32]

Yet it was not just "the People" who interested themselves in prodigies, rarities, and monsters. The virtuosi, gentlemen-amateur practitioners of natural philosophy in seventeenth-century England, were deeply invested in curiosities, as William Eamon has shown. Their attention to natural and artificial "trifles" and "conceits," he argues, was an endorsement of curiosity, for the very same reasons that Augustine had included it among his catalog of sins.[33] Following Bacon, the virtuosi pried into nature's secrets, into nature distressed and altered, in order to uncover its underlying forms; for them, admiration and wonder were the very parents of philosophy. The human body was a significant part of the virtuoso inquiry into the secrets of nature. As Sprat insisted in the *History of the Royal Society,* the "long studying of the *Spirits,* of the *Bloud,* of the *Nourishment,* of the parts, or the *Diseases,* of the *Advantages,* of the accidents which belong to *humane bodies*" were all "within their Province."[34] The body—deformed, dissected, or pathologized—figured largely in the investigations of the physicians and natural philosophers who formed the Society. Pepys's and Evelyn's penchants for popular entertainments, human exhibition, and dissections are well known; Pepys saw dissections, and Evelyn, who suggested a medal be made of *thoracopagus* Johannes Lazarus Baptista Colloredo, donated "the Principal veins, arteries, and Nerves, both of the *Limbs* and *Viscera*" to the Royal Society; other natural philosophers and physicians, including the famous Dr. Swammerdam, donated skeletons, preserved fetuses, and organs.[35] Less well known are the frequent visits to popular entertainments and museums of another member of the Royal Society, Ralph Thoresby, who also had a significant cabinet of his own.

Thoresby's penchant for curiosities was intense. In 1683, Thoresby went "to see a most wonderful woman, but about two feet long, though twenty-one years old . . . [who is] said to have no bone in her but the head, though I suppose a mistake. This seems to me as prodigious as the monstrously great man" (a giant whose height he was to measure). Though Thoresby registers skepticism about the claims of the monster-monger who had brought this sight to London, his incredulity does not blunt the thrill of seeing the dwarf. Throughout his life, he visited cabinets and other collections of curiosities and, with a group of justices from the north of England, saw an astonishing posture-master who threw his body into strange shapes. Thoresby was especially fascinated with John Valerius, a man born without hands who could perform several quotidian acts that appeared outside his range of dexterity.[36] Thoresby visited Valerius and collected several specimens of his writing in 1709; in March 1710 Thoresby "carried [his] children to see Hans Valery, (aged 40,) the German, who, though born without hands or arms, writes different hands and languages with his feet and mouth."[37] Thoresby's return to see Valerius with his children gives us some access into the audience for monsters: his children would have seen Valerius with their father, and Thoresby himself had souvenirs—pictures of Valerius with his writing on verso—to take away with him.[38] Thoresby's concern with curiosities and human exhibition typifies the practices of the virtuosi.

As well as a form of "esoteric consumerism,"[39] Thoresby's collection of Valerius's artifacts points to the traffic between public exhibition and the considerably more private spaces of museums and collections. Thoresby was a frequent visitor to anatomical and private collections. In the 1680s he managed to see "a skull of the most prodigious thickness, and a horn out of a woman's forehead" and many "skeletons and stuffed skins."[40] From a tradition that reaches back to reliquary collections at churches like Canterbury,

the body parts of exceptional human beings were prized as the numinous remains of those who were either indisputably holy or who stretched the limits of the human.[41] Monsters figured prominently in cabinets; dwarfs were
sometimes docents. Famous collections, like the Leiden anatomical theater,
displayed the skin, bones and organs of notorious criminals or anomalous
medical cases, tinged with the colors of memento mori. In the anatomical
theater at Delft, for example, there were two examples of conjoined twins,
"strange aberrations and accidents," and several premature births set up in
a glass container.[42] Ned Ward was indignant about the state of Royal Society's repository, which contained, among other "musty relics and philosophical toys," "abortives put up in pickle."[43] Both European and English
cabinets contained monstrous human and animal remains. Dr. Colepresse of
Devonshire, a correspondent of the Royal Society, dissected a two-headed
lamb. "The Monster dyed, and is now in my Custody, after it hath been dried
in an Oven and by the Sun."[44] After a woman gave birth to two eggs in 1639
in Norway, for example, one egg was given to the famous Olaus Worm, "in
whose Study it is reserved to be seen of as many as please." In fact, the presence of human remains in collections, exhibitions, and museums dramatically increased during the seventeenth and early eighteenth centuries.[45]
While Zacharias Conrad von Uffenbach could privately view Claudius du
Puy's curiosities, both alive and dead, during his visit to London in 1710 (and
remark that they were "strewn about in great disorder"), the less auspicious
James Paris Du Plessis, Pepys's servant at York, had to be content to see a
pictorial representation of du Puy's embalmed twins, presumably in a tavern
or coffeehouse.[46]

As we saw with Thoresby's visit to Valerius, artifacts associated with human anomaly were also prized. William Hay, a member of Parliament who
was dwarfish and hunchback, wrote in 1754 that since his "Flesh will afford
but little Manure," upon death his body was to be opened, and "if a Stone
should be found in my Bladder (as I imagine it will) I desire it may be preserved among Sir *Hans Sloane*'s Collection."[47] When the famous dwarf
Joseph Boruwlaski performed in London in 1786, the duke of Marlborough
requested one of his shoes in order to "place it in his cabinet among other
rarities."[48] Fragments, bodies, and artifacts were traded back and forth between spaces of collection and exhibition. Richard Bradley gave readers of
his natural history the opportunity to survey "the several Curiosities I have
mentioned" by directing them "to those Cabinets where each respective Subject is lodg'd."[49]

From the 1560s until the eighteenth century, with some regularity, the
English were exposed to rarities, curiosities, and human and animal defor-

mity. Living and dead monsters were sold, traded, and displayed; embalmed, they were conspicuous in early collections, including the Royal Society's repository.[50] Sprat's claim that the English were "amuzed" with prodigies seems only a slight exaggeration. As we have seen, human deformity engrossed both the learned and the vulgar; the English amusement with monsters took several forms. The early exhibition of human and animal deformity intensified anxiety about moral turpitude and imminent apocalypse, symptoms perhaps of the protracted English negotiation with the Reformation. Gradually, writing concerning human exhibition began to manifest fears about the nature and constituents of popular culture, as well as religious trepidation; perceived credulity was balanced with calls to reform, fervent skepticism, and ribald satire. Even the virtuosi, who were careful to present their monster-gazing as legitimate scientific inquiry, did not escape censure. In 1708, for example, the famous Hungarian twins, Helen and Judith, joined at the buttocks, were on display in London. Seeing the children at Charing Cross, Jonathan Swift, perhaps parodying the handbills printed to advertise the show, wrote that they were bound to "cause many speculations" and raise an "abundance of questions in divinity, law and physic."[51] The virtuoso reaction to the twins, and to "*Monster-mongers*," became the object of Swift's acerbic wit, as we shall see. The rather more fantastic case of Mary Toft inspired a similar range of reaction.[52] Now that I have outlined some of the aspects of human exhibition in early modern England, it remains to trace some of the educated reactions to these "Strange-Births" and "abortives put up in pickle."

"Fabulous Experiments, Idle Secrets, and Frivolous Impostures"

In 1611, Henry Peacham, schoolmaster and grammarian, posed a rather disconcerting question. "Why," he asked, "doe the rude vulgar so hastily post in madnesse / To gaze at trifles, and toyes not worthy the viewing?"[53] Peacham's comments register both the perceived capriciousness and credulity of vulgar curiosity—the "wonder and table-talk" of the common sort—and the confusion among the learned about the utility of the study of preternatural phenomena. If it is madness to gaze at trifles and toys, why study monsters? If some of the central subjects of natural philosophy and history were treated in early newspapers, ballads, and broadsides, how was it possible to distance the careful, natural philosophical study of human anomaly from the table talk of the people? Indeed, as some scholars have argued, both wonder books and the writings of natural philosophers "clearly share a taste for the rare and singular for its own sake."[54] Works directed toward the "curious" treated the same subjects, including monsters, from the perspectives of "the new science." However, contemporary natural philosophers did attempt to differentiate their inquiries from the "rude vulgar." If natural philosophers shared a taste for the rare with the "middling sort," they also worried about imposture, fraud, and the religious and political valences of human exhibition. In this section of the paper, I trace the scrutiny of human exhibition by those who saw it as a symptom of spiritual languor, a political threat, trifling scientific inquiry, or popular credulity. I consider the attitudes of the educated toward imposture and fraud, as well as some of the ways in which the virtuoso preoccupation with monsters was satirized. It seems the birth and subsequent display of deformed human beings, as Bedford implied, bred less grief than trouble.

In January 1600, a monster was born to a yeoman's daughter after an incestuous relation. Writing against "the sinnes of Incest, Onanisme, Whoredome, Adulterie & Fornication," the author of *A Most Straunge and True Discourse* argued that the monster was the result of "the grosse iniquitie of the people."[55] The people are "naturally enclined and desirous of the means that may further the sinne that we are most enclined unto: as close companying together, dalyance, sight, touching, talking lewdly of the actions of generation, writing of letters, making and reading of lewde and wanton bookes, ballads of love and pamphlets that tend that way" (sigs. B3v–B4r). Noting that there had been a bifurcation of teratological material—popular accounts became, to this author, less concerned with sin—the author claimed that the people had neglected "wise & grave histories . . . & of reading what monstrous births God hath sent unto many both in this Realm, & in other places: which might make us to tremble and quake, when wee shall but reade and heare of them." The author suggested a corrective course of reading to stem the tide of "lewde and wanton bookes"; his syllabus is telling.[56]

This pamphlet is symptomatic of a number of concerns embodied in seventeenth-century teratological ephemera. Often the authors of pamphlets and broadsides were concerned at once to advertise their prodigies *and* correct the wayward curiosity of the vulgar. Like Bedford, the author of *A Most Straunge and True Discourse* was careful to establish the truth of the birth; he included a detailed description of the body of the infant and the circumstances of the sexual relationship that resulted in the monster.[57] His main point, however, was, like Bedford's, to chastise the "people" for their sinfulness. The early anti–Roman Catholic sentiments embodied in monster pamphlets and broadsides were still present in the seventeenth century; yet with the author of *Most Straunge and True Discourse,* Bedford, and others, a new concern with "policing" popular culture emerged. Human exhibition, as the pamphlet suggested, was part of a nexus of cultural practices—gambling, game playing, and theatergoing—that were attacked in the early part of the century. Francis Bacon was perhaps the most well known advocate of such a position.

Although Bacon called for a "collection or particular natural history of all prodigies and monstrous births of nature," from the outset he was cautious to excise from such a history incredible, untrustworthy reports—he did not want a "book . . . filled with fabulous experiments, idle secrets, and frivolous impostures, for pleasure and novelty"—since once "an untruth" is "made common . . . it is never overthrown or retracted." Other declared Baconians followed suit. Naturalists may "much advantage men, by exciting and assisting their *curiosity* to *discover,*" wrote Joseph Glanvill, but such excitation must be strictly limited to the credible.[58] Once an untruth was made "common," that is, the property of the people, it was intractable. And the people, as Bacon suggested in his *Essays,* were poor judges of the truth.[59] By 1650, the author of another teratological pamphlet, setting down his "discourse . . . to draw out instructions for learning, and information [for] the unlearned, and simpler sort," claimed that most "misconstrue" the meaning of prodigies; thirty years later, Christopher Nesse concurred.[60] As natural philosophers learned more about generation and began to disavow the devil's (but not God's) hand in the production of preternatural phenomena, there was a general perception that the "lower orders" were becoming unrepentantly credulous. Bacon's suspicion of popular opinion was echoed in sentiments commonplace in the seventeenth century.

Apparently the common sort were dangerously gullible. Viewing or reading the records of authentic monstrous births was problematic enough; believing in potential frauds and imposters, the people diminished the luster of utility and knowledge natural philosophers sought to establish and sustain. "Bartholomew faire babies," often wildly exaggerated displays of monsters or outright frauds, had the potential to alter the reception of *real* anomalous births, undermining their possible value as "lessons." Wresting monster-gazing and curiosity from the lower orders meant revitalizing individual inquiry and testimony against the delusions of the crowd.[61] The "solid reason of one man, is as sufficient as the clamor of a whole Nation," but men and women in aggregate are "errour it selfe." The mob is a "confusion of knaves and fooles, and a farraginous concurrence of all conditions, tempers, sex, and ages"; thus "it is but naturall if their determinations be monstrous, and many wayes inconsistent with truth." The first human beings fell, according to Sir Thomas Browne, due to Eve's lack of "suspition of imposture."[62]

Set apart from common gaping, then, was the practice of the diligent natural philosopher, whom Robert Boyle exemplified. "[W]eak Intellectuals," according to Boyle, were satisfied with "Babies and Whistles," just as poets unacquainted with natural history contented themselves to write about "Bartholomew-babyes." The "contemplation of Nature," however, "is an Imployment, which both the Possessors of the sublimest Reason, and those of the severest Virtue, have not onely allowed, but cultivated."[63] For Boyle and the other advocates of natural philosophy, an extremely important component of the virtuoso's vision was the ability to "discover the subtil cheats and collusions of imposters," since, in the words of one pamphlet, "Too many have been deceived and cheated of their Money."[64] Monsters "carried up and downe the country for sights to make a gaine by," as Bedford put it, became more problematic in this antagonistic context. Indeed, as Simon Schaffer has argued, the profitability of wonder itself was severely limited by the end of the eighteenth century; eventually, wonder, and its close cousin, curiosity, were seen as threats.[65] Fraudulent human exhibition contributed to this reassessment.

Boyle's apprehension has a history. In perhaps the most popular medical text in both England and France in the late sixteenth and early seventeenth centuries, Ambroise Paré warned against indigents who dissembled deformity in order to bolster alms giving. The "subtle devices of begging companions" and the craft of the devil are somewhat alike, he wrote in 1573, citing a number of cases in which beggars had altered their bodies in order to solicit the charity of the parish or passers-by. Using bovine or porcine bladders or stomachs, or, in one case, the limb of a recently deceased pauper, various "crafty beggars" feigned illness or monstrosity. Rather gruesomely, some were not content with crippling themselves, but "have stolen children, have broken or dislocated their armes and legges, have cut out their tongues, have depressed their chest, or whole breast, that with these, as their owne children, begging up and downe the country, they may get the more reliefe." Similarly, in 1634 Fortunio Liceti excoriated those "Bohémiens," by which he probably meant Gypsies, who raided the charnel house for body parts or amputated parts of themselves to give the impression of frightening monstrosity ("pour donner un aspect monstrueux horrible").[66] Most maddening to Paré, however, was the popular network that had developed for the exchange of chicanery. These beggars "part the kingdome amongst themselves as into Provinces" and "communicate by letters one to another, what newes or new quaint devises there are to conceale of advance their roguery."

In order to accomplish their ends, Paré claimed, "they have invented a new language onely knowne to themselves, so to discourse together and not bee understood by others." To the last statement, Paré's English translator added, "We here vulgarly terme it [the new language] *Canting.*"[67] Though this practice was not "of late invention," to Paré and his contemporaries, it was evidently an acute problem in the late sixteenth and early seventeenth centuries.[68]

The practice was not confined to beggars. On October 10, 1627, Sir Henry Herbert, master of revels, friend of John Evelyn, and brother to the poet George Herbert, licensed the unfortunate showman Humfrey Bromley "& 3 assistants to show a childe with 3 heads for a yr."[69] Two weeks later, under pressure from the mayor of London, Hugh Hamersly, Bromley presented the following letter to the Company of Barber-Surgeons of London:

> Whereas Sr Henry Herbert Knight Mr of the Revells hath authorized the bearer hereof Humfrey Bromley to shew a Child presented to be naturallie borne haveing Twoe heades ffower Armes and three legg[es] wch I suppose not to be borne of any woeman or to be the perfect substance of a child in respect whereof I forbeare to p[er]mit the said Humfrey Bromley to make show thereof within the lib[er]ties of this Cittye untill such tyme as I maye be truely satisfied from you whether the same child be of the substance is pretended Therefore I desire you that upon advised view of the said Child you truly certifie mee in writing under yor hand[s] whether the same be really a child as is presented. . . . I maye not unadvisedly suffer his Ma[jes]t[y's] subject[s] to be deceyved thereby.[70]

Deception it certainly was, nor was it Bromley's first. In June 1616, Bromley and his wife were instructed to leave Norwich for the exhibition of a deformed child "with two heades." This dicephalous or tricephalous London child, however, was carefully probed by the surgeons; their conclusions were ambiguous. They suspected Bromley's monster "composed and put together from unnaturall and untimely births of Children or from other Animals, as Apes, Munckeys or the like." Indeed, Bromley had attempted to "delude the worlde" with "fixion and falsehood"; the handbill or sign that advertised his show[71] exhibited grave differences, in the form of "Additions," from the received record of prodigious births. Although it appears the child was closely examined, perhaps dissected, the company could not "positively affirme it proceedeth not from a woeman." Such births, they averred, had a "Body of Antiquitie" and "cannot safely receive a flatt and manifest contradiction." Whether or not the child was exhibited remains unknown; without a "flatt and manifest contradiction" to the authenticity of this monster, Bromley may well have profited from the exhibition of his embalmed curiosity.

From Herbert's and the barber-surgeons' interest in Bromley and his monster, it is clear that human exhibition caused concern. Although for the educated, skepticism and the thrill of imposture intensified rather than diminished the pleasure of seeing rarities, for the "lower sorts," who made no further use of prodigies than gossip, the political valences of exhibition were potentially incendiary. Imposters or not, monsters were seen as threatening the political stability of the commonwealth. In 1618, unlocking nature's cabinet for the benefit of the curious, Robert Basset asked "What men are very dangerous in a Common-wealth?" to which his answer was, "Those that affect novelties." Basset's sentiments echo Paré's. Arguing against illicit bone-setters, wise men and women, and folk healers, Paré is quite explicit about the dangers of imposture: "the common sort who commit themselves to . . . Impostors to be cured, doe not onely injure themselves, but also hurt the Common-wealth, and the common profit of Citizens; for whose good and justice sake a prudent Magistrate ought to deprive impostors of all freedome in a free and Christian common-weale."[72] Paré was not the only one to call for the diligent policing of imposture. The author of *A Most Straunge and True Discourse*, who, as we have seen, was careful to suggest a reading program for the reform of the lower orders, argued that in order to punish sin and control the exhibition of monsters, all "magistrates, who have authoritie to punish the same [i.e., sins], ought to be carefull, that too many offences of that kind be not redeemed by communications," lest the country be overrun by "Papists, Brownists, and others."[73] The affinity between human exhibition and politics was worrisome. "Teratoscopy," or gazing at monsters, should be thrown out with all those "*thin and curious Arts,* Capomancy, Augury, Soothsaying, Chiromancy." In 1665, John Spencer was unequivocal in his disgust: "Prodigies in general are dangerous to the state: belief in such things is, to put it mildly, disorderly." Prodigies "encourage the sudden expectation of some strange change of affairs in the state."[74]

On the whole, Bacon's and others' warnings about "frivolous impostures" were taken to heart by seventeenth-century reformers, natural philosophers, and religious authorities. The ability to discover imposture and fraud might be said to mark the difference between high and low regard for monsters. Perhaps for this very reason, virtuosi who doted unselfconsciously and uncritically on monsters and other rarities were ruthlessly satirized. Their lack of ability to discern the usefully "scientific" beneath the shapes of nature distressed—to detect, in Boyle's words, the "subtil cheats and collusions of imposters"—was pilloried by their detractors. Doubts about the virtuoso preoccupation with the rare and the strange were not only figured in satirical accounts of certain kinds of inquiry (like Butler's skepticism about the telescope in "The elephant in the moon"); they were also present in the satirical figure of the virtuoso as busybody.

Originating in the work of Theophrastus, the character of the busybody was notable for his overextended sense of urgency, inquisitiveness, and idle curiosity.[75] Joseph Hall's "Busie-bodie," for example, was preoccupied with the tales of voyages, "secret relation[s]," and "woonders." "No newes can stir but by his doore." Whereas the wise man was characterized by "plentifull observation" and a "free discourse that runnes backe to the ages past," by the fact that "his conjectures are better than others judgements," the busybody's speech was "oft broken off with a succession of long parentheses, which hee ever vowes to fill up ere the conclusion." John Earle's antiquary was "curious" enough to fill his room with "strange beasts skins" and turn it into "a kind of charnel-house of bones extraordinary."[76] In his satirical portrait of a virtuoso, Samuel Butler noted, "He is wonderfully delighted with rarities, and they continue still so to him though he has shown them a thousand times, for every new admirer that gapes upon them sets him a-gaping too."[77] The Scriblerians' *Memoirs of the Extraordinary Life, Works and Discoveries of Martinus Scriblerus* is a ruthless burlesque of pseudoscience, of sycophantic adherence to the ancients and blind faith in the moderns. Martinus Scriblerus, described as a "prodigy of science," had his rudimentary education in "Raree-shews." His father, Cornelius, is portrayed as a consummate busybody who "disdained not to treasure up [his wife's miscarried] Embryo in a Vial, among the curiosities of his family."[78] Sir Nicholas Gimcrack, a character from Thomas Shadwell's *The Virtuoso* (1676), had an afterlife in the satire of new science. In 1710 *The Tatler* printed "The will of a virtuoso"—Nicholas Gimcrack—who bequeathed "rat's testicles" and a "Whale's pizzle" to an esteemed colleague, "all my monsters, both wet and dry" to his son Charles, and disinherited his eldest son for speaking disrespectfully to his little sister, "whom I keep by me in spirits of wine."[79] The virtuoso was most often pilloried for his stubborn pursuit of useless truths, his bogus claims to utility, his excessively pedantic attitude toward the world, and his penchant for collecting rarities. Prying into the secrets of nature, just the practice that was thought to set the educated apart from the "lower sorts," was satirized in the caricatures of virtuosi.

While it was incumbent upon educated consumers of rarities to distance themselves from the iniquity of the people, the virtuoso preoccupation with gazing at *monsters* received the most incisive criticism. In the Scriblerians' *Memoirs*, Martinus Scriblerus, who, like Gimcrack, epitomized the absurdities of the experimental philosophy (including its strident materialism), encounters a living cabinet of curiosities and falls in love with part of one of the exhibits—conjoined twins named Lindamira and Indamora. True to the aesthetics of *The Spectator,* in which Addison suggests that the pleasure of the new "bestows charms on a monster and makes even the very imperfections of Nature please us,"[80] Martin is charmed with the sisters *as monsters;* for him, the problem is determining the individuality of his beloved (Lindamira) and claiming as his own someone subjected to the eyes of the vulgar. Martin professes his love for the monster "tho' she be the common Gaze of the multitude, and is follow'd about by the stupid and ignorant." He demands Lindamira, whom he eventually marries, cease submitting herself for *public* display: "Nature forms her wonders for the Wise, and such a Masterpiece she could design for none but a Philosopher. Cease then to display those beauties to the profane Vulgar." While attempting to drape his curiosity in the lineaments of science, ironically Martin is guilty of the same reckless enthusiasm and romance as the "stupid and ignorant": wishing himself "double" to match the beauty of the twins, Martin is charmed "with the gaudy ornaments of the body."[81] This episode in the *Memoirs* has been examined often in recent scholarship;[82] what is important to recognize for my argument is Martin's implication in the dynamics of curiosity he disdains in the vulgar. The Scriblerians' satirical technique involved shading the high curiosity of the virtuoso into the common curiosity of the crowd, in effect blurring the distinction between the two. In fact, the difference between educated and uneducated curiosity was more rhetorical than real, just as some natural philosophers retailed their full-blown Baconian rhetoric in order to conceal a lack of Baconian practice.

By the end of the seventeenth century, the desire to gaze at monsters and their potential importance as objects of scientific study were broadly satirized. In Margaret Cavendish's *The Description of a New World, called The Blazing World* (1666), a generic soup replete with utopian spices appended to *Observations on Experimental Natural Philosophy,* she claimed that dissecting monsters (as practiced in her representation of the Royal Society or, perhaps, the French Bureau d'Adresse) occurred "to satisfy the vain curiosities of inquisitive men." Monsters should not be preserved "except it be for novelty"; if "experimental philosophers" spend their time in such "useless inspections," they gain nothing but their labor for reward.[83] In 1700, William King was ruthless in his burlesque of the Royal Society's *Transactions* and Sir Hans Sloane. Satirizing in particular Sloane's penchant for the curious, King took the society to task for accumulating useless information about the commonplace and banalities about the rare. King accused Sloane of having "a peculiar faculty of believing almost any thing" and exhibiting a vigorous credulity in relation to monsters: "Numb. 226. [of the

Transactions] gives an Account of a Child born without a Brain, which had it lived long enough would have made an Excellent Publisher of Philosophical Transactions." As King suggested, the inclusion of monsters within the purview of scientific inquiry was suspect.[84] Observing monsters for "novelty" was attacked well into the eighteenth century. In *The Monster of Monsters* (1754), "Thomas Thumb, Esq." satirized the collective inquiry of the Royal Society by translating and exaggerating the characteristics of the virtuosi into a raucous group of ladies who argue about the relative beauty or deformity of a certain monster. Madam Chemia, who "some Years since (as is well known) discover'd that *precious Stone,* of which the Royal Society has been in quest of a long Time, to no Purpose," argued in favor of the display of the monster "because she tho't that the Publick would be hugely delighted and edified with so curious a Show." Indeed, "she said there was not a real *Virtuoso,* a true *Adept,* in all *North America,* but what would come to see it. . . . and the Populace, you know, said shee, are always fond of Novelties and strange Sights." Implicitly mooring the examination of monsters by the Royal Society to the people's love of rarities, the author taints their inquiries with the common curiosity of the vulgar. The "common and idle Stories about *Monsters* and *Prodigies* . . . amuse and please the Vulgar," but they "disgust sober and reasonable men."[85]

As the need to distance scientific observers from the idly curious deepened (since, as James Jacob has argued, establishing the new science was part of the drive for social cohesion),[86] virtuosi strove to accumulate reasons for their forays into plebian culture. Reflecting these concerns, accounts of monstrous births and human exhibition became more particular, including the names, occupations, and status of witnesses; bridging the gap between the curious (gentlemen-amateur natural philosophers) and the lower sorts, popular accounts also included similar information. Indeed, both popular ephemera, imitating the form of scientific periodicals, and learned treatises that discussed monsters were imbued with a "rhetoric of description," or a concern to anatomize discursively deformed humans and animals in spare, muted, "scientific" prose. Evidence for this change can be found in the pamphlets and single-sheet folios that give notice of preternatural humans as well as the development of description in the *Philosophical Transactions of the Royal Society,* culminating with James Parsons's detailed and lengthy account of "a preternatural Conjunction of two Female Children" in 1748.[87] As we saw with the Bromley case, there was a new concern to cite relevant teratological literature (Ambroise Paré and Jacob Rueff were perennial favorites), though such concern often faltered. In fact, the *Memoirs of Martinus Scriblerus* itself became intricated in the problems of curiosity and evidence. Grouped together with James du Plessis Paris, the *Philosophical Transactions of the Royal Society*, and the letters of Sir Hans Sloane, the *Memoirs* is cited as evidence for the existence of the Biddenden maids in Kent in the *Gentleman's Magazine* in 1770.[88]

The problem of impostors was taken up with vigor in the early eighteenth century. The case of Mary Toft the rabbit-breeder is only the most notorious. In an excerpt from *Fog's Journal* published in the *Gentlemen's Magazine* in 1733, a correspondent who might have had Toft in mind notes that in great cities "we frequently see some enterprizing Spirit start up, who lives meerly by imposing on the Publick." Inferior impostors, in fact, "draw small Sums out of Peoples Pockets, by certain little Deceits." A certain impudent fellow, for example,

> fell into a Trade of exhibiting Monsters to the People. He produced some new Monster every Year for a considerable Number of Years; and to all his Monsters gave surprizing Qualities, which they had not; and when the People complained of a Bite, he carried it off with an impudent Sneer, swearing the next Monster should make Amends for all that was past, and then he would certainly produce a worse.

This fellow employed several "Zanies" who would harangue the crowd about the "curious Curiosity" that they could view for money. True to form, this "Doctor does not hang out a Picture of his Monster, like other vulgar Projectors, but gives you an Opportunity of paying your Money before Hand."[89] For this deplorable practice "the People threatened to have him punished as an impostor." Some of the people, at least, were affronted by such blatant cozenage.

Yet it seems the crowd continued to hold the "miracles" of natural philosophy in admiration for quite some time. In 1743, for example, there were complaints among natural philosophers that "the public, the ladies and the people of quality . . . never regard natural philosophy but when it works miracles."[90] This period witnessed a marked increase in public shows; waxworks, menageries and protocircuses proliferated. Of course men and women made their own meaning out of prodigies and human display, taking away with them either a chaste and moral rebuke for their own or others' iniquity or simply a thrill felt along the pulses. Even sober exhibitions that purported to edify as well as delight were "read" in unlicensed ways: medical waxworks, for example, were often the sites of clandestine thrill-seeking, just as medical texts were read pornographically.[91] Nevertheless, until the "discovery of the people" and mid- to late-eighteenth-century treatment of folk customs as quaint, reformist sentiments prevailed among the educated. The penchant for reform, particularly in the seventeenth century, can be seen in attempts to retool popular attention to human exhibition. However, these aspirations may have been futile due not only to the tenacity with which both the lettered and unlettered clung to prodigies and freaks of nature, but also to the spectacular nature of science itself. Just as medical examination, even dissection, may be considered part of the dynamics of exhibition (as the apparatus of authority or as an attraction in itself), so too can the whole of experimental natural philosophy be considered a spectacle. Perhaps that is why Bacon interprets the fable of the Sphinx, that monstrous mythical figure, as an analogue of science. The Sphinx embodies science "joined with practice," that is, the nascent experimental science for which Bacon was the strongest advocate. Science itself "may not absurdly be termed a monster, as being by the ignorant and rude multitude always held in admiration."[92] In other words, early modern science itself was a spectacle in which human deformity had a prominent place.[93]

In the Bodyshop

As reflected in vernacular and ephemeral literature of the sixteenth, seventeenth, and eighteenth centuries, the "discomfort of Deformitie" was acute indeed. If we listen to the past, we hear two distinct, contrapuntal sounds: into the eighteenth century, voices raised against the dangers of human exhibition reached a pitch surpassed only, it seems, by an insatiable, multiform curiosity. Subject to general opprobrium and ridicule, monsters were displayed before the curious for "pleasure" and profit. By detailing several examples of public display and scrutinizing the presence of somatic fragments and "abortives put up in pickle" in early collections, I have been concerned here to provide a rudimentary history of human exhibition in England. I have also examined some of the ways in which human deformity was treated among those who possessed or pretended to a disinterested scrutiny of human and animal anomalies. For natural philosophers, the ability to see underlying causes beneath nature distressed or deformed, and to distinguish imposture from authenticity, was paramount. Yet their (and their critics') comments about the curiosity and table talk of the common sort belie any surety about the natural philosophers' own monster gazing. Indeed, in the fascination with the miniature, the rare, the double, and the singular, some of the disparities and contradictions in early modern science are laid bare. The call for reliable evidence as a basis for a history of preternatural phenomena meant a shift in the status of observers but little change in the objects of scrutiny. For the virtuosi, the common practice of gazing at monsters became a matter of testimony, evidence, and, ultimately, authority, of judicious description and the rhetoric that attended it, of developing (or arrogating) the skills that allowed one to see emergent natural forms beneath objects of scrutiny, even living human beings. Such a shift—from the "vanity" of the multitudes gaping at the latest freak to the careful accounting of the anomalous by nascent teratologists—is symptomatic of an educated attention to the body as the bearer of cultural difference. Bodies registered the friction of cultural contact, whether between old and new worlds or worlds that were considered sub- or differently human. Further, even as it was mocked, a residual faith persisted in an indexical relationship between the outside and the inside of human bodies.[94] Somatic configuration was taken as evidence of personhood; comportment was the window to the soul. Deformity, in Francis Bacon's words, was seen less as a "Signe, which is more Deceivable" and more as a "Cause, which seldome faileth of the Effect."[95] Seeing monsters at taverns, fairs, or in the street confirmed seventeenth-century men's and women's notions that what was *inside*—the character, the soul—could be accessed and assessed anatomically.

Reading deformity as a *cause* (with its requisite effects) rather than as a *sign* (requiring interpretation) secures an explanatory paradigm in which deformity figures as impetus and end. It was not until the eighteenth century, to my knowledge, that this interpretive model was challenged by a person of differing physical ability, William Hay. Hay, hunchback and member of the House of Commons, conceived of his *Deformity: An Essay* as a "finished Piece to attone for an ill-turned Person." In fact, Hay is concerned to "anatomize" himself, wishing to demonstrate that, despite his deformity, his "Heart will be found sound and untainted, and [his] Intentions honest and sincere." Anxious to counter entrenched opinion regarding human deformity, blaming Bacon for its perpetuation, Hay wishes that "Mankind . . . instead of ridiculing a distorted Person," would rather "rally the Irregularities of the Mind." Bacon had suggested that "*Deformed Persons* are commonly even with Nature: For as Nature hath done ill by them; So doe they by Nature: Being for the most part, (as the Scripture saith) void of *Naturall Affection;* And so they have their Revenge of Nature. Certainly there is a Consent between the Body and the Minde; And where Nature erreth in the One, she ventureth in the Other." Hay struggled to unravel the consent between body and mind, arguing that deformed people were irascible because they were "despised, ridiculed, and ill-treated by others." In a passage dependent on Locke, he argued that although the "Architecture" of the deformed body is wanting, it is nonetheless "habitable"; contesting the popular notion that the exterior of the body is an index of the interior, of the rational soul, Hay insisted that physical anomaly is *not* an indication of spiritual or cognitive deficiency. When he sat for a portrait, Hay wished to be drawn as he was; he had not, he noted, taken great pains to correct his "natural Defects." Hay quotes Montaigne to the effect that deformity "strikes deeper in" than mere "ill features." Since it is "more uncommon, it is more remarkable."[96] Although "Bodily deformity is visible to every Eye," Hay wrote, "the Effects of it are known to very few; intimately known to none but those, who feel them; and they generally are not inclined to reveal them." One of the "Effects" of deformity, he noted, was "Contempt in general, joined with the Ridicule of the Vulgar." As Sir Philip Sidney averred, "we laugh at deformed creatures, wherein certainly we cannot delight."[97]

Yet, in the words of one early-seventeenth-century French lawyer, defending the mother of a deformed child from disinheritance, "monstruosus homo est tamen homo," a monstrous man is nonetheless a man.[98] In his gracious and articulate essay, a work poised between defense and apologia, Hay pleaded with his peers and his detractors to scrutinize the mind rather than the body. "I believe," he wrote, "Men scarce differ so much in the Temper of their Bodies, as of their Minds."[99] Similar casuistic meditation on the many circumstances that make up a single human act led Sir Thomas Browne to comparable conclusions. Practice often runs counter to theory; we naturally know the good, he insisted, yet equally naturally pursue evil. Although we should be led by reason, we perform according to our own humors. "In briefe," he wrote, "we are all monsters."[100] Monstrosity thus describes not only a segment of humanity distracted by the discomforts of deformity, but in part the complex, composite nature of all human beings. In other words, Bacon's particular history of monsters becomes, in the form of the relationship between reason and the passions, the body and the soul, the normal and the pathological, the history of all humankind. What *is* deformity "to you all that passe by, or that come to see?" Bedford asked.[101] Deformity is a *sign*, not a *cause;* it requires interpretation.

NOTES

I would like to express my gratitude to the Centre for Reformation and Renaissance Studies, Victoria University in the University of Toronto, particularly Michael Milway; the Social Sciences and Humanities Council of Canada; and the London Goodenough Trust for support during the preparation of this paper. James Hanly patiently read an early draft as a critical nonspecialist and made very useful comments. Tamara Kaye's and Jeremy Maule's comments were invaluable. I also thank the editors and an anonymous reader at the University of Michigan Press.

1. Thomas Bedford, *A True and Certaine Relation of a Strange-Birth* (London, 1635), 15, 17, 11, 21, 18, 12–13, 19 (the pamphlet's pagination is incorrect). Bedford was evidently learned: his excursus is full of sidenotes to Latin medical literature, and, at pages 12 and 13, citing several authorities, including Sennert, he deals with the questions of baptizing monsters and whether or not conjoined twins share a soul.

2. Augustine, for example, wrote, "What pleasure can there be in looking at a mangled corpse, which must excite our horror? Yet if there is one near, people flock to see it, so as to grow sad and pale at the sight. . . . Because of this disease of curiosity monsters and anything out of the ordinary are put on show in our theatres." Noting that human deformity is highly susceptible to the attention of the curious, Augustine condemns unsavory gazing at "signs and portents," particularly when the latter are demanded "simply for the experience of seeing them" (*The Confessions of St. Augustine*, trans. Rex Warner [New York: New American Library, 1963], 10.35). See also Wendy Reid Morgan, "Constructing the Monster: Notions of the Monstrous in Classical Antiquity," Ph.D. diss., Deakin University, Australia, 1984; John Block Friedman, *The Monstrous Races in Medieval Art and Thought* (Cambridge, Mass.: Harvard University Press, 1981); Claude Kappler, *Monstres, démons et merveilles à la fin du Moyen Age* (Paris: Payot, 1980); and Dudley Wilson, *Signs and Portents: Monstrous Births from the Middle Ages to the Enlightenment* (London: Routledge, 1993).

3. A notable exception is Paul Semonin, "Monsters in the Marketplace: The Exhibition of Human Oddities in Early Modern England," in *Freakery: Cultural Spectacles of the Extraordinary Body*, ed. Rosemarie Garland Thomson (New York: New York University Press, 1996), 69–81.

4. For a sample of some of these claims, see Georges Canguilhem, "Monstrosity and the Monstrous," *Diogenes* 40 (1962): 27–42; Michael Uebel, "Unthinking the Monster: Twelfth-Century Responses to Saracen Alterity," and Jeffrey Jerome Cohen, "Monster Culture (Seven Theses)," in *Monster Theory: Reading Culture*, ed. Jeffrey Jerome Cohen (Minneapolis: University of Minnesota Press, 1966), 264–91, 3–25; and Rosemarie Garland Thomson, "Introduction: From Wonder to Error—a Genealogy of Freak Discourse in Modernity," in *Freakery*, 1–19. In a brilliant article on nineteenth-century teratology and anatomy, Evelleen Richards remarks, "Monsters have always challenged the boundaries of human identity" (377). See "A Political Anatomy of Monsters, Hopeful and Otherwise: Teratogeny, Transcendentalism, and Evolutionary Theorizing," *Isis* 85 (1994): 377–411.

5. See, for example, Rosa Braidotti, "Signs of Wonder and Traces of Doubt: On Teratology and Embodied Differences," in *Between Monsters, Goddesses, and Cyborgs: Feminist Confrontations with Science, Medicine, and Cyberspace*, ed. Nina Lykke and Rosa Braidotti (London: Zed Books, 1996), 150.

6. Although it came late to my attention, Dennis Todd's brilliant *Imagining Monsters: Miscreations of the Self in Eighteenth-Century England* (Chicago: University of Chicago Press, 1995), is free of the extremities I describe.

7. Indeed, it was *England* that was monstrous: contemporary medical treatises, books of wonders and secrets, ballads, broadsides, and chronicles testify to the apprehension that deformity and "nation" were more than incidentally related.

8. Geoffrey Goodman, *The Fall of Man, or the Corruption of Nature, Proved by the Light of Our Naturall Reason* (London, 1616), 23.

9. Thomas Browne, *Religio Medici*, in *Selected Writings*, ed. Sir Geoffrey Keynes (Chicago: University of Chicago Press, 1968), 1.15.

10. John Spencer, *A Discourse Concerning Prodigies*, 2d ed. (London, 1665), preface, sig. a5v. Spencer was attempting to counter the popularity of prodigies. There were competing views throughout the period as to whether England had been inundated with prodigies. Boyle, for example, suggested that "nature seems to do her work very weakly, or bunglingly, in the production of monsters, whose variety and numerousness is almost as great, as their deformity" (*A Free Inquiry into the Vulgarly Received Notion of Nature* [1685], in *The Works of the Honourable Robert Boyle*, ed. Thomas Birch, 6 vols. [London, 1772], 5:201). Cf. "Many times hath the Lord shewed us his wonders. . . . What a number of straunge tokens, monsterus birthes . . . hath he shewen in our land, and yet few or none regards it" (*A Most Certaine Report of a Monster Borne at Oteringham in Holdernesse* [London, 1595], sig. B1r); "There have been within these *three years and a half*, more strange, unusual and unheard-of things, then in many years before: and this is not for nothing. It were well if the true causes were considered" (*A Monstrous Birth: or A True Relation of Three Strange and Prodigious Things* [London, 1657], 4); "It has been a great happiness to this Nation, that accidents of this Nature rarely fall out among us" (*A True Relation of the Birth of a Monster Born at Exeter* [London, 1682], 2); *"There is no Person of any Age or Understanding, but must needs acknowledge that the last Forty Years has been as it were an Age of Prodigies and Wonders in these three Kingdoms"* (R. B. [Nathaniel Crouch], *The Surprizing Miracles of Nature and Art, in Two Parts* [London, 1685], sig. A2r); "Bodily deformity is very rare" (William Hay, *Deformity: an Essay*, 2d ed. [London, 1754], 13).

11. The unusual, miraculous, or monstrous was a favorite topic for popular writers. Tessa Watt notes that "some 42 publishers from 1560 to 1622 . . . produced pamphlets on miracles, monsters, witchcraft, unusual weather and sensational murders" (*Cheap Print and Popular Piety, 1550–1640* [Cambridge: Cambridge University Press, 1991], 264–65).

12. Henry Reynolds, *Mythomystes* (1633?), in *Critical Essays of the Seventeenth Century*, 5 vols. (Oxford: Clarendon Press, 1908–9), 1:154–55.

13. Thomas Sprat, *History of the Royal Society* (1667), ed. Jackson I. Cope and Harold Whitmore Jones (London: Routledge and Kegan Paul, 1959), 362.

14. Discussing seventeenth-century scientific societies, Lynn Thorndike notes, "Monsters and freaks of nature receive perhaps the most attention" (*A History of Magic and Experimental Science*, 8 vols. [New York: Columbia University Press, 1958], 8:234).

15. Richard Altick, *The Shows of London* (Cambridge, Mass.: Harvard University Press, Belknap Press, 1978). Katharine Park and Lorraine Daston have documented the popularity of monsters in early modern England and France. Although classical antiquity was fascinated with divination, prodigies, and monsters, and later Augustine lamented that "monsters and anything out of the ordinary are put on show in our theatres," Park and Daston point to the Reformation as the matrix, as it were,

of both popular and learned attention to monstrous births in the early modern period. By 1700, monsters were no longer "prodigies," disturbing, unnatural events attributed in various, often conflicting ways to the will of God; instead, monsters were "examples of medical pathology." I have suggested elsewhere that this schema is, on the whole, quite useful, but that the remarkable resonance of the deformed *human* body resisted absorption by early taxonomy or pathology. Here, by focusing on human exhibition, I wish to offer a further correction to Park and Daston's argument. See Katharine Park and Lorraine Daston, "Unnatural Conceptions: The Study of Monsters in Sixteenth- and Seventeenth-Century France and England," *Past and Present* 92 (1981): 20–54.

16. Including Holinshed, *Holinshed's Chronicles of England, Scotland and Ireland*, 6 vols. (London, 1808), 3:1063; Stowe, *The Chronicles of England, from Brute unto this Present Yeare of Christ.1580* (London, 1580), 1053; a chronicle from the collection of Stowe, *Two Chronicles from the Collections of John Stowe*, ed. Charles Lethbridge Kingsford, Camden Miscellany 12 (London: Camden Society, 1910), 26; the Grey Friars, *Chronicle of the Grey Friars of London*, ed. John Gough Nichols (London: Camden Society, 1852), 75; and the continuations of the chronicle of Robert Fabyan, *The New Chronicles of England and France, in two parts*, ed. Henry Ellis (London, 1811), 711; as well as in the diary of Henry Machyn, *The Diary of Henry Machyn, Citizen and Merchant of London, from AD 1550 to AD 1563*, ed. John Gough Nichols (London, 1848), 23. The birth was also cited in a contemporary medical treatise (published in Zurich in Latin, 1554) by Jacob Rueff, *The Expert Midwife, or An Excellent and Most Necessary Treatise of the Generation and Birth of Man* (London, 1637), 152–53.

17. *The Correspondence of Henry Oldenburg*, ed. and trans. A. Rupert Hall and Marie Boas Hall, 13 vols. (Madison: University of Wisconsin Press, 1965–86), 2:294, 277, 280, 296, 309.

18. *Holinshed's Chronicles*, 4:204. In 1564, John Barker claimed, "Within the rase, of fyve yeres space / Moche monsterous sights hath byn," while he argued that human and animal deformities were misshapen "tookens" (*The Strange News or the History of Strange Wonders* [London, 1564], sig. A5v). I should note, however, that similar claims were made about other "prodigious" periods.

19. Kathryn Brammall has noted the proliferation of the rhetoric of monstrosity in late-sixteenth-century England. See "Monstrous Metamorphosis: Nature, Morality, and the Rhetoric of Monstrosity in Tudor England," *Sixteenth Century Journal* 27, no. 1 (1996): 3–21.

20. *Strange Newes out of Kent, of a Monstrous and Mishapen Child* (London, 1609), sigs. B4r–B4v, B3v.

21. *A Wonder Woorth the Reading* (London, 1617), 8.

22. It was hoped that "the abortive and prodigious births from time to time, which many of us have bene eye witnesses of, may sufficiently summon us from sinne, and speedily awaken us from our dreames of securitie, wherein we lye carelessly sleeping" (*Strange Newes Out of Kent*, sig. A3r).

23. See Christophorus Graefius, *Disputatio Physico-Philologica de Monstris* (Lipsiae, 1660), par. 68.

24. Martin Parker, *The Two Inseparable Brothers* (London, 1637) and *A True Relation of This Strange and Wonderfull Monster* (London, 1664), both reprinted in *The Pack of Autolycus*, ed. Hyder Edward Rollins (Cambridge, Mass.: Harvard University Press, 1927), 14, 145. On Colloredo and the Waterman twins, see Stephen Pender, "'No Monsters at the Resurrection': Inside Some Conjoined Twins," in Cohen, *Monster Theory*, 143–67.

25. In a letter from Venice to the Royal Society, Jacomo Grandi, the public anatomist at Venice, noted in his examination of conjoined twin females that he "could not dissect them as [he] would, because they were deliver'd to me to embalm, and the indigent Father of them, who look'd for gain, would not let me have them but for a great Sum of money" (*Philosophical Transactions of the Royal Society* 5 [1670]: 1118).

26. *A Letter from an Eminent Merchant at Ostende, Containing an Account of a Strange and Monstrous Birth Hapned There* (London, 1682).

27. *A Monstrous Birth* (London, 1682); R. B. [Nathaniel Crouch], *The Surprizing Miracles in Nature and Art, in Two Parts* (London, 1685), 189.

28. See, for example, *Philosophical Transactions of the Royal Society*, 5 (1670): 2096–98; *Philosophical Collections* 2 (1681): 22; *Philosophical Transactions of the Royal Society* 23 (1703): 1417–18 in which Charles Ellis describes conjoined twins offered for sale (or show, it is not clear) at "Boln" for three thousand guilders, "too much for a Traveller to expend upon one thing."

29. *Philosophical Collections* 2 (1681): 21–22.

30. Robert Boyle, *Some Considerations concerning the Usefulness of Natural Experimental Philosophy* (London, 1663), 37.

31. Both quoted in Michael Hunter, "Science and Heterodoxy: An Early Modern Problem Reconsidered," in *Reappraisals of the Scientific Revolution*, ed. David C. Lindberg and Robert S. Westman (Cambridge: Cambridge University Press, 1990), 446.

32. Spencer, *A Discourse Concerning Prodigies*, preface, sig. a3r.

33. William Eamon, *Science and the Secrets of Nature: Books of Secrets in Medieval and Early Modern Culture* (Princeton: Princeton University Press, 1994), 301–18.

34. Sprat, *History of Royal Society*, 83.

35. See, for example, Pepys, *The Diary of Samuel Pepys*, ed. Henry Wheatley (London: Bell, 1938), 3:51; John Evelyn, *Numismata* (London, 1697), 277. For Evelyn's and others' gifts, see Nehemiah Grew, *Musæum Regalis Societatis or A Catalogue and Description of the Natural and Artificial Rarities belonging to the Royal Society* (London, 1681), 1–10.

36. Another man born without hands or feet, Matthew Buckinger, "used to perform before company, to whom he was exhibited, various tricks with cups and balls, corn and living birds," but he could also "shave himself with perfect ease, and do many other things equally surprising in a person so deficient, and mutilated by Nature" (James Caulfield, *Portraits, Memoirs and Characters of Remarkable Persons from the Revolution in 1688 to the End of the Reign of George II*, 4 vols. [London, 1819], 2:23–24; for other examples of human deformity, see 2:190 [a treatment of

Nathaniel St. André, the doctor who succumbed to Toft's imposture], 4:109–10). Another Restoration handbill reads: "*By His Majesty's Authority*. These are to give Notice to all Gentlemen and others, That here is newly come to this place, a *High German Woman,* that has neither Hands nor Feet; yet she performs a hundred several Things to admiration: *Viz.* She Sews, Treads the Needle, as quick as any one can with Hands; Cuts out Gloves; Writes very well, Spins as fine Thred as any Woman can do; she Charges and Discharges either Pistol or Carbine, as quick as any man can do; she makes Bone-Lace of all sorts; Several other things might be mentioned, which for brevity is omitted" (London, n.d. [ca. 1680–1700]; included in *A Collection of 77 Advertisements Related to Dwarfs, Giants, and other Monsters and Curiosities exhibited for Public Inspection,* BL Shelfmark N.Tab.2026/25 551.d.18). John Bulwer mentions in 1653 a similar case of a man born without limbs who writes, threads a needle, and deals cards with his mouth (*Anthropometamorphosis: Man Transform'd: or The Artificial Changeling* [London, 1653], 302).

37. *The Diary of Ralph Thoresby, 1677–1724,* 2 vols. (London, 1830), vol. 2, appendix; 2:229; 2:390; 2:30; 2:59. On Thoresby, see Robert Unwin, "Cabinets of Curiosities," *Historian* (U.K.) 19 (1988): 13–18.

38. There was apparently a book produced of Valerius's "postures" and writings: each print had Valerius in a certain posture ("Playing at cards and dice"') along with an inscription by Valerius himself ("In the act of managing cards and dice he does not yield in dexterity to those who play with their hands"). "It was common custom with the persons who visited Valerius, to give him some gratuity for a specimen of his writing; and, on the back of his portrait, which belonged to the late Sir William Musgrave, were four lines, written by Valerius with his toes." There were indeed other men and women who were displayed for the same skills and condition as Valerius (Matthew Buckinger and a Miss Biffin). See Caulfield, *Portraits, Memoirs and Characters,* 2:158–67, especially 159ff.; and Thoresby, *Diary,* 2:30, and his *Musaeum Thoresbyanum* (London, 1725).

39. Lorraine Daston, "Curiosity in Early Modern Science," *Word and Image* 2, no. 4 (1995): 391–404.

40. For Thoresby's peregrinations, see P. C. D. Brears, "Ralph Thoresby, a Museum Visitor in Stuart England," *Journal of the History of Collections* 1, no. 2 (1989): 213–24.

41. André Thevet, *La Cosmographie Universelle,* 2 vols. (Paris, 1575), vol. 2, fol. 941r. See also Stephen Bann, *Under the Sign: John Bargrave as Collector, Traveller, and Witness* (Ann Arbor: University of Michigan Press, 1994). For the medieval tradition, see Patrick Geary, *Furta Sacra: Thefts of Relics in the Central Middle Ages* (Princeton: Princeton University Press, 1978). To date, the most thorough work on cabinets of curiosities is found in Oliver Impey and Arthur MacGregor, eds., *The Origins of Museums: The Cabinet of Curiosities in Sixteenth- and Seventeenth-Century Europe* (Oxford: Clarendon Press, 1985); and Joy Kenseth, ed., *The Age of the Marvelous* (New Hampshire: Hood Museum of Art, Dartmouth College, 1991).

42. See Herman W. Roodenburg, "The Maternal Imagination: The Fears of Pregnant Women in Seventeenth-Century Holland," *Journal of Social History* 21 (1988): 705.

43. *The London Spy: the Vanities and Vices of the Town Exposed to View*, ed. Arthur L. Hayward (1703; London: Cassell, 1927), 51, 50. Thomas Nashe also derided the practice—"a thousand guegawes and toyes they have in their chambers, which they heape up together, with infinite expence, and are made beleeve of them that sell them, that they are rare and pretious thinges, when they have gathered them upon some dunghill" (*The Works of Thomas Nashe*, ed. Ronald B. McKerrow, 5 vols. [London: Sidgewick and Jackson, 1910], 1:183).

44. William Turner, *A Compleat History of the Most Remarkable Providences* (London, 1697), pt. 2, chap. 7, p. 8; *Philosophical Transactions of the Royal Society* 2 (1667): 481.

45. In Sir Hans Sloane's collection, later the basis of the British Museum and a site to which prominent virtuosi and tourists flocked, the holdings of "humana" (i.e., anatomical preparations and the like) increased by approximately 50 percent between 1725 and 1753 (see E. St. John Brooks, *Sir Hans Sloane: The Great Collector and His Circle* [London: Batchworth Press, 1954], 195).

46. *London in 1710: From the Travels of Zacharias Conrad Von Uffenbach*, trans. W. H. Quarrell and Margaret Mare (London: Faber and Faber, n.d.), 84–85; "These Monstrous Children were Born dead their 2 Bodies were United Together at the Breast, their four Arms Twisted Round about Both their Necks as the figure Represents them, they were both females, taken from the Original in Mr Dupuy's Cabinet of Rarities" (James Paris Du Plessis, *A Short History of Human Prodigious & Monstrous Births of Dwarfs, Sleepers, Giants, Strong Men, Hermaphrodites, Numerous Births, and Extream Old Age &c* [London, ca. 1680, BL Sloane MS. 5246], fol. 36).

47. Hay, *Deformity*, 75.

48. "About that time," Boruwlaski wrote, "I was informed that His Grace the Duke of Marlborough wished to have one of my shoes, and place it in his cabinet of among other rarities: I had had too much reason to be flattered with this nobleman's affability not to send him a pair of them immediately, to which I joined the only pair of boots I had made for me, which I had brought from Poland: His Grace was so well pleased with this mark of attention, that the next day he sent me a bank-note of 20 [pounds]" (*Memoirs du Celebre Nain [A Second Edition of the Memoirs of the Celebrated Dwarf, Joseph Boruwlaski, a Polish Gentleman]* [Birmingham, 1792], 236–37).

49. Richard Bradley, *A Philosophical Account of the Works of Nature* (London, 1721), sig. b3v.

50. One of the principal acts of the new "Fix'd Assembly" was to gather a "General Collection of all the Effects of *Arts*, and the Common, or Monstrous *Works* of *Nature*." The collection of anomalous artifacts, animals, and humans was part of the Royal Society's program (Sprat urged the collection of "*Relations* of several Monsters with their Anatomies"). Still, as Sprat noted elsewhere in the *History*, "it is an unprofitable, and unfound way of *Natural Philosophy*, to regard nothing else, but the prodigious, and extraordinary *causes*, and *effects*" (Sprat, *History of Royal Society*, 251, 199, 214–15). Sprat also claims that "the shops of *Mechanicks*, are now as full of *rarities*, as the *Cabinets* of the former *noblest Mathematicians*" (80).

51. Swift to Deane Stearne, June 10, 1708, *The Correspondence of Jonathan Swift*, ed. Harold Williams, 5 vols. (Oxford: Clarendon, 1963–65), 5:82. The twins were treated in detail in the *Philosophical Transactions of the Royal Society*. Read before the society May 23, 1751, the account includes a description of the twins' interaction at various ages, their deaths, and their anatomical structure and dissection. Helen and Judith were exhibited at the Hague and London; they died at Pressbourg in 1723. See *Philosophical Transactions of the Royal Society* 50 (1757): 311–22; and Altick, *The Shows of London*, 37.

52. See Todd, *Imagining Monsters*.

53. Henry Peacham in Thomas Coryat, *Coryat's Crudities* (1611), 2 vols. (Glasgow: MacLehose, 1905), 1:114.

54. Park and Daston, "Unnatural Conceptions," 48.

55. I. R., *A Most Straunge and True Discourse* (London, 1600), sigs. A3v–r.

56. "*M. Stubbs* in his booke entituled *The Anatomie of Abuses*, doth notably handle this point: so doth *M. Hergeste*, in his booke entituled *The right rule of Christian Chastity, M. Batmans* booke, and the *Theater of Gods Judgement &c.* The which books, I wish will all my heart, were dayly heard, & read of our amorous yonkers, & lewde huswives of the world, of Courtiers, Citizens, & Countrey people, with all other good like authors" (I. R., *Most Straunge and True Discourse*, sig. B4r). Hearing and reading tales of sin and destruction (Stephen Bateman's translation of Lycosthenes's *Prodigiorum* was called *The Doome Warning All Men to Judgemente*), for both the high and the low, for courtiers and lewd housewives, was one method for guarding against the "grosse iniquitie of the people."

57. I. R. promises "a description of all things, whereby thou mayst be fully satisfied, how, when, and where, this strange thing was done: with every other circumstance thereto belonging" (*Most Straunge and True Discourse*), sig. A4r. Unlike the popular accounts of mid–sixteenth century, the author is concerned to persuade his audience of England's defilement.

58. Francis Bacon, *The Works of Francis Bacon*, ed. James Spedding et al., 14 vols. (London, 1860) 4:110, 253, 169, 295; Joseph Glanvill, *Plus Ultra: or, The Progress and Advancement of Knowledge Since the Days of Aristotle* (London, 1668), 104.

59. Condemning superstition for turning the inductive method on its head, Bacon claims, "The Master of *Superstition* is the People; And in all *Superstition*, Wise Men follow Fooles; And Arguments are fitted to Practise, in a reversed Order" (*The Essays or Counsels, Civill and Morall*, ed. Michael Kiernan [Oxford: Clarendon Press, 1985], 54–55). In the same essay, "Of Superstition," Bacon cautions, "Care would be had, that, (as it fareth in ill Purgings) the Good be not take away, with the Bad; which commonly is done, when the People is the Reformer" (56).

60. J. S., *Teratologia: or, A Discovery of Gods Wonders* (London, 1650), 1–2; according to Nesse, who with contempt for the virtuosi presents Satan as "a *Mighty Naturalist*" ("both by his acute Observations, and almost 6000 years experience"), there are few who "understand the signs of the times" (*The Signs of the Times: Or, Wonderful Signs of Wonderful Times* [London, 1680], preface, 71, 25).

61. Simon Schaffer has noted that the "vulgar could not be trusted to know

themselves, but a privileged group was potentially capable of giving evidence." See "Self-Evidence," *Critical Inquiry* 18 (1992): 328.

62. Thomas Browne, *Pseudodoxia Epidemica* (London, 1646), 2, 26, 10, see also 8.

63. Boyle, *Some Considerations*, 6–7.

64. Robert Boyle, *Christian Virtuoso*, in *Works*, 5:532; *No Cheat, nor Meer Pretended Fortune-Teller* (London, n.d. [ca. 1680–1700]).

65. Simon Schaffer, "Natural Philosophy and Public Spectacle in the Eighteenth Century," *History of Science* 21 (1983): 2.

66. Liceti, *De Monstrorum Natura, Caussis, et Differentiis* (Padua, 1634), trans. as *De la nature, des causes, des différences des monstres* by François Houssay (Paris: Editions Hippocrate, 1937), 43.

67. *The Workes of the Famous Chirurgion Ambrose Paré*, trans. Thomas Johnson (London, 1634), 992, 994. For the provenance of such a language in England, see Thomas Harman, *A Caveat for Common Cursitors* (London, 1567) in which it is called "pedlars' French or canting" (reprinted in *The Elizabethan Underworld*, ed. A. V. Judges [London: Routledge, 1930], 64).

68. Paré, *Workes*, 995–96.

69. *The Control and Censorship of Caroline Drama: The Records of Sir Henry Herbert, Master of the Revels, 1623–73*, ed. N. W. Bawcutt (Oxford: Clarendon Press, 1996), 166.

70. Sidney Young, comp., *The Annals of the Barber-Surgeons of London* (London, 1890), 333. The letter is dated November 6, 1627.

71. In Norwich, Bromley was not permitted "to sound any Drumme or vse any other meanes to drawe company then onely the hangynge vpp of the picture of the said Child." See David Galloway, ed., *Norwich, 1540–1642*, Records of Early English Drama (Toronto: University of Toronto Press, 1984), 146–47, xxxv.

72. Robert Basset, *Curiosities; or, The Cabinet of Nature* (London, 1637), 269; Paré, *Workes*, 53.

73. I. R., *Most Straunge and True Discourse*, sigs. A3v–A4r.

74. Spencer, *A Discourse Concerning Prodigies*, preface, sigs. a2v, a4r.

75. See M. de la Bruyère, *Characters: or, The Manners of the Age* (London, 1709), 20–21. Pomian also notes that in several French dictionaries of the eighteenth century, *curieux* is a synonym for busybody (See Kryzstof Pomian, *Collectors and Curiosities: Paris and Venice, 1500–1800* [Cambridge: Polity, 1990]).

76. Joseph Hall, *Characters of Vertues and Vices* (London, 1608), 79, 81, 8–9, 81; John Earle, *Microcosmography: or, A Piece of the World Discovered in Essays and Characters* (1628; Bristol and London, 1897), 21.

77. Henry Morely, ed., *Character Writings of the Seventeenth Century* (London: Routledge, 1891), 343.

78. *Memoirs of the Extraordinary Life, Works, and Discoveries of Martinus Scriblerus*, ed. Charles Kerby-Miller (New York: Russell and Russell, 1966), 94, 107, 96.

79. *The Tatler* 216, August 26, 1710.

80. *The Spectator* 412, June 23, 1712.

81. *Memoirs of Martinus Scriblerus,* 149, 143–44. Indeed, as Dennis Todd argues, in the climactic scene of the Scriblerians' satire "the figure of the monster becomes a way simultaneously to articulate a vision of corporealized human nature and to deny it" (*Imagining Monsters,* 135).

82. Todd, *Imagining Monsters,* 126–35; Robert A. Erikson, "Situations of Identity in the *Memoirs of Martinus Scriblerus,*" *Modern Language Quarterly* 26 (1965): 388–400; and Roger D. Lund, "Martinus Scriblerus and the Search for the Seat of the Soul," *Papers in Language and Literature* 25 (1989): 135–50.

83. Margaret Cavendish, *The Description of a New World Called the Blazing World and Other Writings,* ed. Kate Lilley (London: William Pickering, 1992), 157–58.

84. William King, *The Transactioneer* (London, 1700), 55–56.

85. Thomas Thumb, Esq., *The Monster of Monsters . . . Humbly Dedicated to all the Virtuosi of New-England* (n.p., 1754), 15, 3.

86. James Jacob, "'By an Orphean Charm': Science and the Two Cultures in Seventeenth-Century England," in *Politics and Culture in Early Modern Europe: Essays in Honour of H. G. Koenigsberger,* ed. Phyllis Mack and Margaret C. Jacob (Cambridge: Cambridge University Press, 1987), 235.

87. *Philosophical Transactions of the Royal Society* 45 (1748): 526–41. Of course there are earlier accounts in the *Transactions* (22 [1701]: 992–96, for example) and elsewhere that are concerned with the same sort of accurate description of the inside and outside of preternatural bodies, but by 1748 such description superseded the popular list of historical prodigies ("In 1552, at Myddleton Stony, there was . . .") as a buttress to veracity and became the norm.

88. "Two Maiden Sisters, who grew together from the waist downwards till they were considerably advanced in years, and were so united in their affections to this parish, as to join in a bequest of the lands abovementioned. An enquiry in the parish itself will procure abundant testimony, that the reality of this prodigy has always been honoured with the highest credit; for the satisfaction of our distant and intelligent readers, we shall subjoin a few references to authors of great credit for its confirmation" (to which is added "Memoirs of Scriblerus by A. Pope") (*Gentleman's Magazine* 40 [1770]: 372).

89. *Gentlemen's Magazine* 3 (1733): 227–28.

90. *Gentleman's Magazine* 25 (1743): 193, quoted in Schaffer, "Natural Philosophy," 6.

91. See Roger Thompson, *Unfit for Modest Ears: A Study of Pornographic, Obscene, and Bawdy Works Written or Published in England in the Second Half of the Seventeenth Century* (London: Macmillan, 1979).

92. *The Wisdom of the Ancients,* ed. Henry Morley (New York: Hurst, n.d. [1609 in Latin]), 358.

93. As Barbara Maria Stafford has argued, the cabinet of curiosities, the presentation of the world as a particular *view* in which human deformity had a prominent place, was in some sense responsible for the "specularization of experience" ("Voyeur or Observer? Enlightenment Thoughts on the Dilemmas of Display," *Configurations* 1 [1992]: 122).

94. Thomas Pope Blount, for example, comments that it was "a received Opinion among the ancients that Outward Beauty, was an infallible Argument of inward Beauty; and so on the contrary, That a deformed Body was a true Index of a deformed Mind, or an ill Nature" (*Essays on Severall Subjects* [London, 1697], 217).

95. Bacon, "Of Deformity," in *Essays*, 134.

96. Hay, *Deformity*, 37, 53. Hay quotes from Bacon's "Of Physiognomy."

97. Sir Philip Sidney, *A Defense of Poetry*, ed. Jan van Dorsten (Oxford: Oxford University Press, 1966), 68.

98. Robert Robin and Simon Houdry, *Plaidoye de Maistre Robin, Advocat la Cour, avec l'Ampliation du Plaidoyé de Maistre Simon Houdry, aussi Advocat. Sur la Question, sçavoir si un enfant, qu'on pretendoit avoit esté monstre* (Paris, 1620), 44, quoted in Marie-Hélène Huet, *Monstrous Imagination* (Cambridge, Mass.: Harvard University Press, 1993), 31–33.

99. Hay, *Deformity*, 79.

100. Browne, *Religio Medici*, 1.55.62.

101. Bedford, *True and Certaine Relation*, 18.

Making a Monster: Socializing Sexuality and the Monster of 1790

Barbara M. Benedict

Monstrosity spans science, superstition, satire, and religion. Whereas medieval and Renaissance popular culture had woven these categories together,
the natural philosophers of early modern England sought to differentiate
them. At one time monstrosity had proven God's power and man's sin by
corporealizing, in violation of nature's rules, vices like lust, gluttony, and bestiality.[1] Now, it was used to explain evolution, generation, and development.
Still, the earlier penumbra of metaphorical significance persisted, especially
in printed popular culture, and no aspect more powerfully than the notion
that monsters were a warning.[2] Monsters revealed either the hidden condition or the future of mankind, biologically and/or morally. The Monster of
1790 was such a warning. He epitomizes the shift of the traditional discourse
of monstrosity to the realm of gendered relations. As several critics have explained, the fundamental cause for this shift was political.[3] In the frightened
backlash of the 1790s against earlier liberal policies, unconventional sexuality and radical politics were associated, particularly through the contro-
versial figure of the feminist Mary Wollstonecraft; as a result, examples of
aberrant or unusual sexual behavior were colored, in the eyes of conservatives, with a dangerously radical hue. Indeed, unregulated sexual behavior
was interpreted as a form of social protest or even rebellion. Women were
not the only sufferers from this sexual scrutiny: men's sexuality too underwent hostile supervision. At the height of the English reaction to the French
Revolution, when anxiety induced the regulation of political, social, moral,
intellectual, and religious life, the traditional trope of monstrosity surfaced.[4]
Challenging science in explaining deviation, it was deployed to define the unregulated part of humanity itself.

The case of Renwick Williams embodies the turn-of-the-century debate
about what made a man. Dubbed THE MONSTER, he provided the focal point

in 1790 for political, social, and especially sexual anxieties. Although he looked "normal," and thus did not fit into teratological categories, he acted in a fashion at once human and inhuman that corresponded to traditional cultural conceptions of monstrosity. By his bloody violence, he resurrected earlier definitions of monstrosity that concentrated on perceptible elements: like the hybrids, human curiosities, giants, and demons of myth and popular "science," he abused language, reason, physicality, and space. His real threat, however, seemed to lie outside the perceptible and inside the body. Whereas teratology located monstrosity corporeally, this Monster displayed an equally traditional metaphorical monstrosity that was enacted socially; his monstrosity, however, also hinted at an internal, private ontology beyond social conditioning. Despite his notoriety, he remained an invisible container of the hidden horror of mankind—indeed, specifically of men, since his crimes were considered sexual. In particular, his actions revealed what many saw as a disintegration of traditional relations between the classes and genders; this in turn seemed to warn of the collapse of civilized humanity into something beyond nature or beyond culture. In castigating Williams as the Monster, the secular institutions responsible for regulating behavior—cultural commentators, the press, the police, and the judiciary—attempted to label and control this ambigious threat to Enlightenment ideals of cultural progress. They used his crimes and trial rhetorically to sever social values from an unsocialized humanity. By excoriating the Monster for gender and class violence, they pinned normality to traditional domestic relations and the new values of sentimentality. Through negation, the Monster established humanity as publically monitored, gendered relations: socialized sexuality.

The Problem

At an hour before midnight on the evening of the Queen's birthday ball, January 18, 1790, a young man of about thirty approached Miss Anne Porter and her sister Sarah from behind, as they were returning to their father's hotel in St. James Street. Leaning over Sarah's shoulder, he uttered "abominable indecencies" to her, and when she cried to her sister, "for God's sake make haste, the wretch is behind us," hit her violently on the back of her head. The two sisters ran home, but as Sarah was ringing the bell to enter, the man struck her sister Anne with a sharp instrument in the thigh. Through her torn gown and two petticoats the surgeon discovered a stab wound ten inches long and three inches deep.[5] The Porters had been attacked by "the Monster."

They were not alone. According to the *Diary*, since May 1788, several women of "quality" had been assaulted by a man who, approaching them as they stopped at the doors of their homes, first addressed them with "shocking and indecent language," then hit them, and then watched them quietly until they gained admittance.[6] London was transfixed by the news of these assaults, and in a flurry of print evoking two centuries of definitions of monstrosity, asked how—and sometimes whether—society conditions man's nature into humanity. Sexuality, class status, nationality, political and domestic behavior, and legal regulation all intertwine to show that monstrosity at the turn of the century designated a man who, concealed under a decorous exterior, rejected public values: the hidden man, the emblem of a sexual identity impervious to social instruction.

During the decade following the French Revolution, English writers wrestled with uncertainty about the success of the Enlightenment project to rationalize human relations. This project interpreted not only human behavior, but identity or subjectivity itself, as the sign of rational and moral instincts. Like the Revolutionaries, however, the Monster destabilized this definition of mankind as rational, educable, and improvable. His acts thrust into the public consciousness the power and persistence of ancient desires that had been denied as bestial, irrational, or cultured out of existence by historical progress, suggesting that far from being conditioned into sociability, the monstrous part of humanity had merely been driven into hiding. The appearance of a man who acted out unregenerate sexual hostility aroused a panoply of responses. These responses used the social outrage touted in the newspapers to mock contemporary sanctimoniousness for a variety of purposes. In the wave of publicity following the Porters' experience, women reported attacks varying from the sinister to the ridiculous. One accused a flirtatious stranger of being the Monster because he handed her a posy of flowers whose wire pricked her finger, and he spent the night in jail.[7] Crying that he was the Monster, pickpockets roughed up and robbed a gentleman and his family.[8] Several women pretended to be attacked, and were dubbed "new kinds of MONSTERS" themselves.[9] Misogynistic humorists fed off the implicit prurience. A canard appeared that a Mrs. Smith had defended herself from Monstrous attack with a borrowed pistol, shooting "the wretch" in the neck.[10] Cartoonists joined in by portraying not only Mrs. Smith, but the Monster feeding off women's buttocks, and a variety of "copper bottoms" as protection for women, some shaped like saucepans enveloping each buttock, others like undergarments. These responses indicate that people, especially women, were unclear and uncomfortable about the standards governing sexual behavior and relations. What was courting and what assault? Monstrosity was the name of the distinction, but this monstrosity seemed

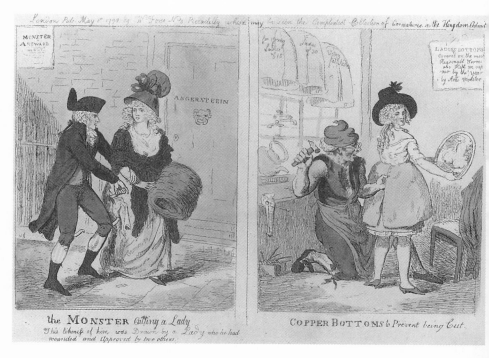

Fig. 10. Isaac Cruikshank, *The Monster Cutting a Lady and Copper Bottoms to Prevent Being Cut* (London, May 1, 1790). The first engraving, brightly colored in the original, depicts the victim as an expensively dressed beauty, and the Monster as a gentleman getting away with the villainy beneath the very description of him published by Mr. Angerstein; the second plate, a mock advertisement, portrays the crimes as opportunities for fashionable purchases, while it exploits the sexual exposure of the incidents by showing the purchaser's breasts. (Courtesy of the Print Collection, Lewis Walpole Library, Yale University.)

very like masculinity itself. The real distinction seemed to lie only in the publicity of this masculinity: when bruited on the social stage, the impulse to stab a woman in her private parts was deplored.

The connection between the implicit violence of male sexuality and monstrosity clearly occurred to contemporary Londoners. Men felt threatened. One wrote,

> The MONSTER, Is now a mischief of more than his common magnitude. Inhuman himself, the villainy is visited upon all who are of the same sex. Alike

the source of apprehension, terror and flight . . . It is really distressing to walk our streets towards evening. Every woman we meet regards us with distrust, shrinks sideline from our touch, and expects a poignard to pierce what gallantry and manhood consider as sacred.[11]

This monstrosity usurps civilized sexual relations, exposing men as predators. Just as people with bestial features reveal human brutality in conventional teratology, this Monster makes evident the hidden appetites of men.

Women, however, could be blamed for men's monstrosity, in both teratology and broader culture. Accusations appeared that women's "groundless Apprehensions" had created a monster from a madman, implying that sex denied drove men insane.[12] Some writers, echoing periodicals of the last forty years, attributed the Monster to new domestic values that had dismantled the traditional customs placing women under the "protection" of their husbands.[13] Humphry Henpeck explains the "Men-Monsters" as a gang of frustrated husbands trying "to keep of their wives at home," but he warns them that they will long for the domestic peace of an empty house when the wives rail at their confinement.[14] Another, named Benedict, reproaching the philanthropic merchant John Julius Angerstein for offering a fifty-pound reward for the Monster's capture, writes,

> Good ANGERSTEIN,
>   Be not so keen,
> For Women still will roam:—
>   Nor wound nor death,
>   'Till stopp'd their breath—
> Can keep our Wives at HOME.[15]

Like the traditional belief that "monsters" literally embodied their mother's corrupt imaginations, such attacks attribute monstrous sexuality to female perversion.[16] In this cultural formation, women make monsters by their own sexuality: it is their unregulated appetites that defeat the Enlightenment ideal of social progress.

This attack on women alludes to a traditional discourse blaming man's fall on women's original sin of sexual curiosity, a curiosity that makes them monstrous. On the meretricious report that a Mrs. R. Walpole had escaped injury when the Monster stabbed the apple in her pocket instead of her body, one poetaster penned:

> The Apple was, in days of yore,
>   As Agent to the Devil,
> When Eve was tempted to explore

> The Sense of Good and Evil.
> But present Chronicles can give
> An instance quite uncommon,
> How that which ruin'd mother Eve,
> Hath sav'd a modern Woman.[17]

Through the biblical allusion the writer links Mrs. Walpole's sexual experience to sexual purity, implying that modern women have fallen so far and so
willingly that they are impervious to sexual attack. Moreover, this victim's
name refers to the past prime minister Robert Walpole, ridiculed widely in
print—even in Jonathan Swift's *Gulliver's Travels* (1726)—for ignoring his
wife's flagrant infidelity, and also ridicules Horace Walpole, foremost of the
critics of Angerstein's gesture.[18] Here, the image of tempted Eve symbolizes
a modern female corruption that matches the Monster's sexuality. Whether
male or female, sexuality itself emerges as the monstrous trait, a trait concealed but not controlled by modern manners.

The correlation of monstrosity and sexuality raised questions about
whether any social relations were adequately regulated, either within society or within the self. Middle- and upper-class people worried that the Monster's behavior signaled social regression. Repeatedly, the journalistic reports
exclaim against the irrationality and brutality of assaulting the "fair" sex,
deploring the stabbings as examples of "Cruelty." At stake were not only
manners, but the economic enterprises of sentimentalism. Some saw the attacks as a "parallel atrocity" to slavery: at the "Desire of Several Ladies," a
debate was held in May in Westminster Forum on "Which is the greater Disgrace to Humanity, the Ruffian who drags the Female African from her Family, her Kindred, and her Native Country, or the Monster who has lately
wounded and terrified many Ladies in this Metropolis?"[19] Sentimental behavior—the moral regard for gentleness, courtesy, emotional expressiveness,
and sensitivity, especially to women—had become a commercial enterprise
by the end of the century.[20] Even while its ideology sheltered nostalgic values, it could be used to sell fashionable literature, art, clothes, decorative and
domestic objects, travel, spa cures, and a host of other consumable luxuries.
Moreover, sentimentalism signaled social progress: the gentling of humanity
in obedience to reason and to the emotionally fueled morality that Shaftesbury, Francis Hutcheson, Adam Ferguson, David Hume, and others had argued was innate.[21] Such reasonable gentling facilitated trade relations. The
Monster violated these values, intimating a slip back to savagery. He was a
monstrum of cultural failure.

This failure extended beyond sexual and racial relations. The Monster violated not only sentimental values, naturalized through thirty years of printed

culture, but also those between the classes. Historically, accusations of un-controlled sexuality have often been flung by one class at another to differ-entiate culture, equated with control, from nature, identified as human fail-ings in need of control. For example, such Renaissance texts as Shakespeare's *As You Like It* characterize laborers as lusty—indeed lust as labor itself in Touchstone—while nobles are politic. In the more cynical Restoration, when reaction against metaphysical reasoning prompted a view of man's nature as irrepressibly sensual, dramas like Wycherley's *The Country Wife* and Etherege's *Man of Mode* depict an elite who control their behavior so skill-fully that they can use refined culture to serve their insatiable sexual natures. In the late eighteenth century, when periodicals, novels, and conduct books bristled with warnings to middle-class women to beware of predatory aris-tocrats, the channeling of desire into sentimental delicacy signaled internal-ized culture, a kind of inner class that distinguished the rising bourgeoisie.[22] The Monster's evident resistance to such channeling or indoctrination sug-gested parallel rejections of the sentimental negotiations of class relations. His acts induced the fear, sharpened to painful immediacy by the Revolution and ensuing Terror, that the rash of stabbings revealed social unrest. When the attacks spread further into London, people began to believe that "there is more than ONE *of those* WRETCHES infest[ing] the streets."[23] One victim's husband deduced "a gang of these Monsters . . . [who] communicate with one another," and another writer fumed against a "diabolical gang" of "monsters in the shape of men."[24] Men opposed sensibility, humanity, and gallantry to the behavior of "a Nest of unnatural banditti."[25] In construing a gang, domestic or foreign, these writers extend monstrosity to an alterna-tive society, a conspiracy against the state. They make the denial of senti-mental sexual, class, and political relations the monstrous act of a saboteur or traitor. In doing so, they resurrect satirical characterizations, stretching from the Renaissance to the modern period, of political and religious oppo-nents as monsters. This late-century manifestation of political monstrosity, however, remained ominously invisible, and so beyond the regulation of law, force, or culture.

If some feared that this monstrosity would undermine the rule of law, oth-ers feared that it had already done so. Accusations express the distrust Lon-doners felt about the policing authority, a paid force in the 1750s but still unsystematized.[26] In the aftermath of the French Revolution, many people preferred to believe in police corruption rather than incompetence, for cor-ruption paradoxically reaffirmed the power of the legal system by locating the problem not in the absence or inadequacy of policing but in its perver-sion. One letter reproached the constabulary for failing to show "that SKILL, which on less important occasions has manifested itself to bring culprits to justice," adding that their alarmed "delicacy" seems to be preventing them from pursuing the "train of leading circumstances" they possess to arrest the "unnatural villain."[27] The following day, "Sift" declared that "the MONSTER is known to the *Runners of Bow-Street,*" and that their "unwillingness to bring him to justice" indicates that they are awaiting a "reward." Two days later, another letter reiterated current "strictures on the *supineness* of the *Bow-street Runners.*"[28] Sampson Wright was forced to deny refusing to arrest "a gentleman of some rank in life" in the newspapers.[29] Many people believed that Wright and his police force were concealing the true perpetrator because he had privilege: he was a nobleman. Like the rumors dogging the hunt for Jack the Ripper in the following century, fin de siècle gossip explained the Monster's sexual perversity as the sadism of a fin de race scion. The marquis de Sade himself was just becoming a public example of the elite elision between pleasure and pain, and sympathizers with the French revolutionaries were tracing his debauched tastes to his class. In a society reeling under the impact of merchants with new wealth from the colonies buying their way into the traditional aristocracy, blue-blooded nobility represented simultaneously unmonitored power and personal impotence.[30] The Monster exhibited both.

Moreover, monstrous manners seemed gentlemanly. The Monster's quiet approach seemed courteous before he struck with verbal and physical violence. One victim, Mrs. Smith, claimed she recognized him at Robert's Auction, letters characterize him as "genteel looking," and descriptions of him emphasize his fashionable dress:

> He appears to be . . . of a middle size, rather thin made . . . of a pale Complexion, large Nose, [and] light brown Hair, tied in a Queue, cut short and frizzled low at the Sides; is sometimes *dressed* in *black,* and sometimes in a shabby *blue* Coat, sometimes wears *Straw coloured* Breeches, with half Boots, *laced up before;* sometimes wears a *cocked* Hat, and at other Times a *round* Hat, with a very high Top, and generally carries a *Wangee* Cane in his Hand.[31]

In the press, the weapon was identified as a sword stick, the devolution of a dueling sword and another sign of class. Indeed, Elizabeth Davis was astonished at her attack because "she had been told 'he only cut the nobility, and she was but a washerwoman.'"[32] The Monster was billed as gentry, tyrannizing like the pope or the French king over the people. The notion that the Monster could manipulate the system produced rage. Like the abuse of the public space for private pleasure, it was a sign of the tyranny that traditionally marked the monster.[33]

The pressure for an arrest proving the triumph of public over monstrous private interest was mounting. Indeed, the public-spirited merchant, Anger-stein, besides offering a fifty-pound reward for the Monster's arrest and another fifty pounds for his conviction, advised servants to monitor their masters:

> ALL Servants are recommended to take Notice if any Man has staid at home without apparent cause, within these few Days, during Day light. All Wash-erwomen and Servants should take Notice of any Blood on a Man's Hand-kerchief or Linen . . . All Servants should examine if any Man carries sharp Weapons about him, and if there is any Blood thereon, particularly Tucks; and Maid Servants are to be told that a Tuck is generally at the Head of a Stick, which comes out by a sudden Jerk. All CUTLERS are desired to watch if any Man answering the above Description is desirous of having his Weapon of attack very sharp.[34]

Another man urges the police to attend "on a business of so dark and mys-terious a nature" even "to ANONYMOUS" information. Such Stalinesque pub-lic vigilance authorizes the working classes, as representatives of "normal" morality and sexual behavior, to inspect the property of their employers and to report on their behavior. The abnormaliy is located within the private space of the domestic and the human interior.

Not only does this inspection reverse the moral authority of the classes, but it also collapses the separation of spheres. It redefines domestic privacy, an arena becoming increasingly feminized and sentimentalized, as a realm of public morality. Men were put on notice: were they aberrant, or were they citizens of the moral majority? Addressing "the Bow-Street Justices" in the *Morning Herald*, one writer, anxious to prove his probity, asseverates that

> there is no MAN, when he reflects on the motives that have excited your zeal . . . but must applaud your activity, and approve of your conduct;—therefore the slightest suspicion AUTHORISES you . . . to have any person, no matter how exalted his rank, brought before you . . . —I confess I have been among those who were taken to the Office on suspicion; and so far from conceiving myself insulted, I think you are intitled to my best thanks, as an individual, for us-ing such efforts to discover so unaccountable and sanguinary a ruffian.[35]

This resident of St. James Street asserts his "individual" morality by joining the consensus. Again, "Sift" proclaims that he "cannot think so poorly of the gallantry of the nation as to believe, that any of the Officers who may detect the Ruffian would not be immediately made *independent* by a volun-try [sic] subscription from the Public." Citizens proved their citizenship by differentiating themselves from the Monster, even at a financial cost. In re-action to the contemporary concealment of private relations, these responses define monstrosity as a social isolation beyond the boundaries of private and public.

So strongly did men desire to demonstrate their social conformity in opposition to the Monster that they initiated neighborhood efforts to police London.[36] After an attack on a local woman, a group of fifteen men on May 7 in the Percy Coffee House formed an "ASSOCIATION for the Prevention of similar *Assaults*," dedicated to ensuring the safety of their district.[37] They signed a contract or "Subscription" vowing

> nightly [to] patrole the streets of the South Division of the St. Pancras from half an hour before Sunset till Eleven at Night for the Public Safety and especially to guard that Sex which a Monster or Monsters in opposition to the Dictates of Nature and Humanity have dared to assault and wound with wanton and savage Cruelty.[38]

Envisioning that "the Monster or Monsters will either be quickly driven from their horrid and unnatural acts" or arrested, each man paid 2s. 6d. for a three-month period. The price of policing "Nature" and "Humanity" was high. However, the Monster's unchecked sexual violence was usurping male power, and these men were determined to regain control of the urban and cultural space by reinscribing the difference between humane masculinity and monstrosity.[39]

This charge of usurpation conventionally characterizes monstrosity, as does the rhetoric of "unnatural" and "bloody." In the cultural history of monstrosity, these terms are closely related. As I have argued elsewhere, monstrosity is a violation of social identity: whereas oddly formed people do this by incorporating other bodies, bestial or human, into their own, metaphorical monsters do it by co-opting public property, be this material or cultural. Thus, the traditional crimes designating monstrosity are ingratitude, which is a social alienation often portrayed as hypocrisy, and bloodlust, appetite grown gigantic and hazardous to others.[40] Both were regarded as abuses of a human nature defined by a social norm of desire, and the woman-stabber of 1790 exhibited both. Drawing blood from quantities of women, he snaked through London in the guise of a gentleman, manifesting the doubleness of the hypocrite and the power of the tyrant. Indeed, one squib locates his political, domestic, and economic monstrosity in tyranny:

> the MONSTER . . . is dressed in a Scarlet Coat, wears a prodigious Cockade, and bears in every respect a Striking Likeness to that much respected Character
> PHILIP THYCKNESS, Esq.
> He has already frightened a Number of Women and Children; made several desperate attempts upon different Noblemen; and, has attempted to cut up his own Children.

Since his last arrival in London, he has assumed the name of Lieutenant Governor GALLSTONE; and, as it is strongly suspected that his present Journey to Town, is in Order to devour all Editions of Newspapers, Booksellers, Engravers and Publishers of Satiric Prints, and every other Person who has dared to arraign his Conduct, the Public are cautioned to be on their Guard.[41]

Monstrous in his violation of the bonds of family and society, in his voracious appetite—here, for print—and in his military tyranny that stifles the press, he models the usurpation of public liberty that marks the traditional monster in early modern English culture.[42] Nonetheless, this satire refigures the Monster as a public threat in conventional terms by emphasizing his grotesque visibility, whereas the danger of the "real" Monster lay in his unconventional invisibility.

The Monster co-opted another public value that bordered private and social communication: language. By his verbal "indecencies," he violated the sanctioned use of language, as he did the general understanding of intimacy. Moreover, although his verbal crimes remained unlegalized, they evoked a further contemporary definition of monstrosity. In advertising and teratology, the ability to speak a language defined humanity—if also the deviation from it.[43] In a similar fashion, the Monster's idiosyncratic use of linguistic formulas echoed yet violated the standards of social intercourse. Moreover, the Monster was identified partly by his irregular address in greeting the Porters by uttering, "Oh ho! Are you there?" In the trial, Judge Buller emphasized this as a sign of guilt: "The familiar manner—'O ho!['] in which the assassin addressed Miss Porter . . . certainly indicated a previous intimacy. It was not the manner of a stranger; and yet [he had] no intimacy with Mr. Porter's family. To what cause then must we impute this strange manner of address—'O ho!'" (Jenkins, *Full Account*, 29–30). In rationalizing this ejaculation as the expression of a previous relationship, Buller rejects the possibility that language might be used, if not antisocially, asocially. He denies that this verbal recognition of the Porters might bespeak a kind of knowledge unlicensed by society—a general and gendered intimacy with women that entirely ignores sentiment and individuality. Yet the public emphasized the Monster's language as much as his stabbing. By his words, the Monster took over not only public communication, but intimate relations.

The "commonly called" Monster also exhibited disproportionate desires that impinged on others' property: the female body.[44] He struck repeatedly, showing a gargantuan appetite, and he drew blood, rather than finding more usual satisfactions from women. Such a taste indicated an aspect of human nature that had escaped control and grown imbalanced or out of proportion, and for cultural monitors of the late eighteenth century, balance and proportionality were the very proofs of order and rationality. In teratology as in art, eighteenth-century writers diagnosed monstrosity as an aberration from the classical values of regularity and unity.[45] Furthermore, commentators also found this Enlightenment monster "unaccountable" for committing a crime with no "reason." He never robbed his victims, nor did he attack their chastity. As Mr. Piggott, the prosecutor in the Monster's trial, declaimed, "In almost every crime we can trace a motive for committing it, but in the present case, what could induce the prisoner to such barbarous and cruel depredations; no motive to induce him, no revenge to be satisfied."[46] Furthermore, "the Prisoner betrayed a degree of folly, which is impossible for reason, or for reasonable minds, to account for" by looking at Miss Porter "till she ascended the whole flight of steps, and went into her father's house; so that he gave her the fullest opportunity of discovering who he was" (Hodgson, *Trial at Large*, 7). Since no one could—or would—name a motive, his act seemed to reveal the inhuman in human nature, the part of mankind that deviated from divine rationality. For purposes of legal indictment, however, a crime had to be named. When a suspect was finally arrested, he was charged not with an attack on the person, but with a crime against property.

The Solution

On Sunday June 13, 1790, Mr. John Coleman, a fishmonger, and the Miss Porters were strolling in St. James's Park when a man approached them, exclaimed "Oh ho! Are you there?" and uttered "indecent," "highly gross and improper" language to them (Jenkins, *Full Account*, 10, 13–14). When Miss Anne Porter and her sister Sarah identified him as the Monster who had attacked them six months earlier, Mr. Coleman gave chase, from a discreet distance, through the streets of London. Although he lost sight of the Monster for a few blocks, he fortunately spotted someone who looked like him, and followed his man closely as he knocked at the doors of certain houses, looking nervously at Coleman behind him. Eventually, emboldened by the man's evident concern at being pursued, Coleman pushed into one of the houses after him, and demanded "satisfaction" for his "having insulted some ladies that were in his company" (16). The man demanded the cause, but eventually he furnished his name and address as Mr. Renwick Williams of No. 52 Jermyn Street. Coleman insisted that he accompany him for the Miss Porters' identification, and Williams agreed. As Jenkins recounts,

> When the prisoner [Williams] went into Mr. Porter's house and entering the parlour with the witness [Coleman], the ladies (Ann[e] and Sarah) who were

there, cried out "Good God that's the wretch," and fainted away, upon this the prisoner seemed astonished and said he hoped they did not suspected [*sic*] him for the *Monster*. Upon their positively answering in the affirmative he made no further notice. (17)

Amid a frenzy of publicity, Williams was rapidly brought to trial.

But what was his crime? In his opening statement, the prosecutor Piggott charged him "with a crime the most disgraceful which can possibly taint the character of man: his object, to insult the fairest, the most amiable, the most beautiful part of the creation, with language gross, obscene, and horrible" (L. Williams, *Trial of Renwick Williams*, 4). But bad language to women was not a legal infraction, and the attack merely a common law misdemeanor, carrying a maximum penalty of two years and a fine.[47] This was not enough to assuage a public resenting "enormities" beyond the human scale (L. Williams 9). Hence, Renwick Williams was charged under the Coventry Act. Passed into law in 1720 but never before used, this act was intended to punish disaffected weavers who were protesting their loss of trade by despoiling the fashionable muslins of the gentry in the streets. The act made a deliberate attack on clothing into a felony carrying seven years imprisonment.[48]

The trial lasted only eight hours. Most of it was spent in proving Williams's sexuality. Eschewing explanation for the acts, Williams's defense provided the alibi that he had been working the night in question, making artificial flowers for the queen's ball, but relied on demonstrations of the normality of his sexual relations. Repeatedly Williams was shown to be gallant toward women. Jenkins records him saying, "The female sex . . . was always in his eyes, the most admirable and lovely. . . . therefore he had no cause" for these crimes, and "Seventeen witnesses were called to the prisoner's character, some of whom were very handsome women [who] all gave him a most excellent character for good-nature, humanity, and kindness to the fair sex in particular."[49] His employer, Mr. Michell, and his household of a sister and three female servants asseverated his character as "the best," "good-natured," "kind," "civil . . . to women" (21, 23). Neither misogyny nor frustration could be said to drive him.

But these testimonials turned sour. Michell and his sister were French immigrants who spoke no English, and were therefore politically suspect in 1790. Mr. Michell's nationality and linguistic limitation compromised his authority. In his summation to the jury, Judge Buller undermined his testimony first for lack of candor, and then for lack of accuracy. Noting, "Where Jervoise and Michell disagree [concerning when Williams remained in the house], the former's accounts, being fair, seem to justify his relation. The accounts of the latter have not that candid appearance. . . . it may be observed, that the principal evidences are foreigners; that, without an evil intention, they are more liable than others, to mistakes" (Jenkins, *Full Account*, 30–31). Michell's nationality is seen to explain his deficiencies: he might be lying to protect a rebel against property, as his Revolutionary brethen would, or he might just be a muddle-headed foreigner who couldn't understand English principles.

Moreover, many of the women defending Williams occupied a class deemed lower than those he attacked: their social standing undermined their testimonial authority. Jenkins reports that several were "young women, whose appearance . . . did not bespeak them of the highest class, but rather of the inferior sort" (26). In contrast, when Piggott interrogated Miss Martha Porter during the trial by asking, "did he behave as a gentleman ought?" she replied, "No; his expressions were dreadful; his manner horrid" (15). Williams, later recognizing this bias, angrily defending his women witnesses despite their dress, unpainted faces, and inability to "declaim the fashionable cause of the day."[50] Williams himself belonged to the working classes; as a servant to a Frenchman catering to the frivolous tastes of the court, he stood in a position ominously parallel to that of the Revolutionaries across the channel. Indeed, the formal charge against Williams was that

> with force and arms . . . [he] in a certain public street, unlawfully, willfully, maliciously, and feloniously, did make an assault on Ann Porter, spinster, with an intent to tear, spoil, cut, and deface her garments and cloaths, to wit, one silk cloak value 10s.. A silk petticoat value 5s. one other petticoat value 5s. her property, part of the apparel which she had on her person, against the form of the statute, and against the King's peace, &c.[51]

By using the Coventry Act, prosecutors implied a comparison between Williams and the angry workers of 1720: both had committed crimes against their social superiors' property. In the light of the panic about monstrous gangs that preceded the trial, the charge that Williams had defaced property cast a political penumbra over the stabbings. His crimes became strikes simultaneously against gender and class.

Finally, Williams exhibited socially hazardous sexuality—a monstrous appetite. The court ridiculed his relations with women, so that the more he demonstrated a prowess contradictory to monstrosity, the less respect he won. As the trial reports document, "Thomas Wiliams [sic], of St. James's Street, had known him six years, and was perfectly astonished at the accusation. He always tbought [sic] he *liked the ladies too well!* . . . Sarah Seward said she had known him four years . . . that his behavior to her had been *manly [loud laugh];* that he had saved her life!" (Jenkins, *Full Account;* 27). While such claims hint that Williams received sexual favors and therefore would not be driven by frustration, they also document a sexual appetite conceived as voracious—a sexual appetite exhibited as much by Williams's women friends as by himself. If the Monster exhibited one kind of sexuality that injured the public, Williams exhibited another: both were unregulated and disproportionate. Such license at a time when sociability and morality were tightening in response to the Revolution could not go unpunished.[52] The combination of panicked xenophobia, class prejudice, and sexual jealousy was too potent. Williams was found guilty.

The press had been the first to monsterize the stabber. To his victims, he was a "Wretch," but to journalists, a "Monster," and that designation clung. Moreover, the press profited from this monstrosity, as it always did. In *The Trial at Large of Rhynwick Williams,* E. Hodgson, generally more sympathetic to Williams than the other journalists, records that, when Williams was identified, he did not exclaim against being "the *Monster,*" as Jenkins reported, but said, "'Good God! They do not take me for the person about whom there has been so many Publications'" (22). Hodgson's version highlights the press's part in constructing the Monster, and Williams himself, in his opening statement of defense, reproached "the standing cry . . . against him; scandalous paragraphs and injurious reports were multiplied against him" (L. Williams, *Trial of Renwick Williams,* 10).[53] By constructing a villain beyond humanity, the press stimulated a public commentary and appetite for news that profited them. Part of this profit arose from the differentiation of isolated, asocial monstrosity from the cooperative sociability of normal humanity, a sociability manifested in print.

Legal institutions, nonetheless, confirmed the Monster's status by the application of a law against social protest that echoed contemporary constructions of monstrosity as a social threat. So did society at large, for monstrosity on show could also be a social opportunity. Throughout the early modern period, advertisements of human curiosities had guaranteed their value by the testimonials of the privileged: royalty and scientific authorities like the members of the Royal Society.[54] Some of these "monsters" or "demonstrations" made social mobility itself the marvel. For example, the "Painted Prince," a tattooed African king, showed the enslavement of a ruler, providing revolutionary as well as colonial frissons for the audience.[55] At the same time, legless dancers, handless artists, giants, dwarfs, and physically unusual people rose in society by purveying their bodies to become invited guests at fine houses.[56] Traditionally, dwarfs had been the playthings of kings, permitted rare freedom, like King Lear's fool, and still people with special talents, like Mary Toft, mother of seventeen and a half rabbits, or the English Sampson, who proved his strength "before the KING," could find

Fig. 11. William Dent, *A Representation of Rynwick alias Renwick Williams, commonly called THE MONSTER* (July 12, 1790). This triptych engraving emphasizes the Monster's duplicity as he traverses the streets "in DISGUISE" yet appears respectable when "on TRIAL." (Courtesy of the Print Collection, Lewis Walpole Library, Yale University.)

fame and fortune from royalty.[57] Curiosity thus provided social advancement for observers and observed alike. Yet despite the rage for monsters, curiosity and monster mongering, like monstrosity itself, still drew strong criticism as an abuse of public resources for private pleasure.[58] Williams's trial brought both of these cultural traditions to the fore. Jenkins reports, "The Court was more crowded than ever was known" (32). People from all ranks attended, even the nobility, and people of Williams's own class, in this apparently democratic, social space for the curious, watched the wonder of Williams.[59] His sudden notoriety made him the most fashionable curiosity; at the same time, he represented unregulated desires that all the observers renounced by participating in his condemnation.

Politically, legally, and psychologically, the Monster's motive remained troublesome. Piggott was mystified: "In the commission of almost every human crime, we may trace a motive. But what shall I say to the present case: no visible inducement, no purpose to answer, no revenge to satisfy, no injury to be redressed—Beauty and Virtue falling by the assassin's hand—in vain must we look for the object and the end. Yet has this man *female* relations!" (L. Williams, *Trial of Renwick Williams,* 9). His act showed ingratitude, the monstrous rejection of the identity conferred by female family. Even Williams's defense counsel, Mr. Knowlys, saw the crime as beyond reason and therefore nature:

> It is an unpleasant task to call your minds to a scene so new in the annals of mankind; a scene so unaccountable: a scene so unnatural to the honour of human nature would not have been believed ever to have existed. . . . we are trying the prisoner at the bar for this unnatural, unaccountable, and until now, unknown offence. . . . Indeed, this case affords a melancholy lesson to our nature, and teaches us not to be too consistent of the impossibility of any event on the principle of its appearing to us to be out of nature; for it must appear unaccountable to us, that any human being, unless impelled by some impulse which cannot be explained, should have committed an act to which no hope of reward, no inclination of revenge, excited by a real or supposed injury, no idea of concealing an atrocious offence, nor any natural propensity which had hitherto been supposed to actuate a human creature, could have urged him. . . . Thus acting apparently and visibly without a motive for the commission of the deed, the prisoner at the bar has made a wanton, wilful, cruel, and inhuman attack on the most beautiful, the most innocent, the most lovely, and perhaps, I shall not trespass upon the truth when I say the best work of Nature. (Hodgson, *Trial at Large,* 6)

The acts are characterized as motiveless and therefore irrational, unnatural, and inhuman.

Indeed, even the legally constructed motive of destruction of property could not stand.[60] Although Judge Buller suggested to the jury that an attack on the body presupposed an intentional attack on the clothes, citing a case in which intentionality had been reconstructed from evidence of violence, the deployment of a political statute for Williams in so highly public a forum was too dangerous.[61] Needing the most careful and strongest legal protection for the case, Judge Buller referred it to the Twelve Judges of England, a very unusual move, and they determined that Williams would have to be retried. He was, but nonetheless, despite the abler defense counsel Theophilus Swift, convicted like lightning in four hours on three misdemeanors, each carrying a penalty of two years in prison, plus a four-hundred-pound fine.[62] Williams could never pay such an amount. In effect, he was imprisoned for life.[63] In the wake of his general ostracization, he bitterly attacked what his lawyer had identified as class bias: if "in any cause

Fig. 12. James Gillray, *Swearing to the Cutting Monster: or a Scene in Bow Street* (London, May 20, 1790). In this example, Williams is endowed with a monstrous head and mouth, signifying appetite, but his expression reveals dismay as the fashionably dressed Anne Porter exposes herself to condemn him before a fat-faced observer, a leering counselor whose swollen lips approach her bottom, and a clerk biting his pen as he gazes, transfixed. (Courtesy of the Print Collection, Lewis Walpole Library, Yale University.)

made a topick of public and private conversation, rich and powerful individuals are found to be officiously (though unnecessarily) exerting themselves to procure a Verdict, and establish a claim to popular approbation for supporting ambitious views. I ask, whose character, liberty, and life, shall *not* be in danger?" (R. Williams, *An Appeal*, 15). He further noted that Coleman had been motivated by the reward, a point that undermined the rhetoric of public good and revealed the real motive of private greed.[64] Some agreed. A query about the trial, and sympathetic accounts of Williams's Welsh upbringing, good education, and employment history appeared in the papers.[65] Gillray and other caricaturists portrayed the trial as a feast of sexual prurience dominated by faintly Semitic judges and lascivious nobility, in which the monstrosity is transferred from the hapless prisoner to the gawking crowd (fig. 12). But by attacking the legal system, the public's motives, and class relations, Williams became the Monster indeed. He disappeared into Newgate.

Conclusion

Just as teratology was being systematized into evolutionary theory, so definitions of humanity shifted from one kind of biological realm to another. Indeed, the blurring of the line between physical abnormality and human development may have added impetus to this shift. If physical aberrations resembled stages of human development, humanity as a moral value itself seemed in doubt, especially after the French Revolution. The English needed a definition that naturalized social quiescence and conformity. The definition of humanity as sentimental sexual relations did just this by locating humanity, not in biology, but in behavior. Sexuality was key in this definition, for it was the realm in which masculine, brutal impulses could be seen to be cultured into spiritual, cooperative action. The physical nature of humanity is not so much the body as an object of science, but the body as a vehicle of will in society—the body in relationship to other bodies in culture. This relationship was figured as sentimental.

The Monster, as he was "commonly called," sharpened this new definition of humanity by violating it. Like the metaphorical and physical monsters of the previous two hundred years of print, he had huge, bloody appetites, demonstrated hidden and evil nature, and possessed the power to terrify thousands. Ungrateful, despite his genteel demeanor, to his "female relations," he carried a concealed tuck, proving his kindness duplicitous, and revealing him to be the quintessential modern monster, the hypocrite. By approaching women in the manner of courteous gallantry and then stabbing them, he co-opted sentimental, public freedoms for private gratification, the trait of all metaphorical monsters. He used language, physicality, and the urban arena for his own purposes. In escaping justice for so long and abusing public space, he exhibited the monstrous tyranny that British liberty rejected. His verbal abuse signaled his abuse of human nature, defined by language itself.

As the trial emphasized, however, the Monster's animus lay specifically against women. His was not bloodlust in the abstract, but gender-based bloodlust: he was the *monstrum* of social degeneration, and he provoked the first instance of a trial prosecuting a hate crime against women. His crimes demonstrated an unregenerate sexuality which, in turn, suggested that human nature, especially masculine nature, merely concealed its monstrosity, but never cast it off. At the period when England was most anxious to insist on a sentimental definition of humanity, the existence of the Monster invalidated the ethic of transparency, in which all motives, as aspects of humans' fundamentally virtuous morality, should lie open for public inspection. Instead, enveloped in a contrary and ancient ethic of hidden hatreds, he seemed to snatch sexuality from refined culture and return it to base nature, and thus to recommend repressive regulation. The phenomenon of the Monster crystallized contemporary concerns about how to negotiate privacy and transparency, the license for sexual freedom and the need for social control. Even while certain responses indicate resistance to the new privatization of domesticity that sentimental relations fostered, most of London fretted to expose the invisible sin in humanity by locating it, and labeling it Monstrosity, in the figure of Renwick Williams. In contriving the ostracization of the Monster, English regulatory institutions rejected the frightening possibilities that human nature was evil, unregenerate, and could never be controlled except through force, and reasserted the dominance of sentimental values, exercised by a benign government.

Ironically, however, it was Renwick Williams's very sociability and innocuousness that doomed him to become the Monster. Employed by a Frenchman, a maker of artificial flowers, he symbolized foreign corruption and the effete manners that could conceal monstrous appetite. His manner and history proved him a gigolo, rather than a predator, but it was, indeed, his very gentleness, his apparent conformity to sentimental social rules, that made him so sinister, for they revealed that within even the kindest of cultivated gentlemen a Monster can lurk. Whether read as a working-class revolutionary, an urban bourgeois, or an effete aristocrat, he suggested to contemporary Londoners that, despite cultural progress, sexuality can never be controlled. In being condemned by so obdurate a court and public, like Dreyfus a century later, however, he served to refute this possibility. His condemnation confirmed the unity of the regulating institutions of society and the regulated society, the power of the law, and the dominance of sentimental values over regressive brutality. By putting the Monster away, fin de siècle English society sought to cleanse itself of aberrant sexuality, and reassert a sentimental definition of desire:

> Now the naughty Monster's fast
> Beauty stands no more aghast:

At the terrifying word,
Milk of nature turned to curd.
. . . .
Let Woman then securely walk,
Let Woman then securely talk,
And find in man a kind protector
An advocate and sure director;
From every dart unwounded move,
Except alone the dart of Love.[66]

Renwick Williams was the victim of the panic in England surrounding social values and behavior in the last decade of the eighteenth century. He was
in the wrong place at the wrong time for his own good, but he was a gift
from heaven for the government, police, judiciary, and press. Although he
exhibited none of the bloodthirsty aggression of the "real" woman-stabber,
he represented an equivalent kind of political danger: not violence but excessive pleasure, not tyranny but a charm that could also sway crowds. Despite the differences between his soft-spoken, flower-fluffing sweetness and
the brutal sexual anger of the Monster, contemporaries easily elided his kind
of ambiguous sexuality with Monstrous sexual deviation. Indeed, in its proximity to femininity, Williams's masculinity was conceived as just as ominous
as the perverted masculinity of the woman-stabber. Both offered models of
relationships between the genders that slid off the map of regulated social
norms. Thus, Williams became the symbol of a threat that London society
itched to condemn publically and confine permanently: the threat of revolution. His occupation, his class, and especially his character as a ladies' man
fitted him for the part of the Monster, worked to identify sexual liberty with
blood violence, and made both seem hazards to middle-class English society.
In shutting him away, England symbolically reasserted governmental control
not only over the public streets, public behavior, and its citizens' bodies, but
even over the anarchic urges within those bodies themselves. Desire itself was
socialized.

NOTES

1. See Marie-Hélène Huet, *Monstrous Imagination* (Cambridge: Harvard University Press, 1993), 6; Evelleen Richards, "A Political Anatomy of Monsters, Hopeful and Otherwise: Teratology, Transcendentalism, and Evolutionary Theorizing,"
Isis 85, no. 3 (1994): 377–411; Katherine Park and Lorraine J. Daston, "Unnatural

Conceptions: The Study of Monsters in Sixteenth- and Seventeenth-Century France and England," *Past and Present* 92 (1981): 21–54.

2. See *Inventing Human Science: Eighteenth-Century Domains,* ed. Christopher Fox, Roy Porter, and Robert Wokler (Berkeley and Los Angeles: University of California Press, 1995), esp. Wokler's "Anthropology and Conjectural History," 31–52. Roger Chartier, among others, has explicated the two-way dissemination of "high" and "low" culture in *The Order of Books: Readers, Authors, and Libraries in Europe between the Fourteenth and the Eighteenth Centuries,* trans. Lydia G. Cochrane (Cambridge: Polity Press, 1994). I explore the cross-pollination of empirical theory and popular culture in my "Reading Faces: Physiognomy and Epistemology in Late Eighteenth-Century Sentimental Novels," *Studies in Philology* 92, no. 3 (1995): 311–28.

3. See Darryl Jones, "Frekes, Monsters and the Ladies: Attitudes to Female Sexuality in the 1790s," *Literature and History,* 3d ser., 4, No. 2 (1995): 1–24. Basing his account on the sensationalized responses of Mrs. Thrale, Jones erroneously blames Williams for "vaginal mutilation," but he ably demonstrates that the final decade of the eighteenth century identified "sexual deviancy with political anarchy" (2). See the fuller account of this in Claudia L. Johnson, *Jane Austen: Women, Politics, and the Novel* (Chicago: University of Chicago Press, 1988), 14–16, and *Equivocal Beings: Politics, Gender, and Sentimentality in the 1790s* (Chicago: University of Chicago Press, 1995), which argues that contemporary sentimentalism "unsettles customary definitions of gender and sexuality both *between* and *within* the sexes, problematizing both femininity as well as other versions of masculinity" (17).

4. See Michael Foucault, *Madness and Civilization: A History of Insanity in the Age of Reason,* trans. Richard Howard (New York: Vintage, 1985) and *Discipline and Punish: The Birth of the Prison,* trans. Alan Sheridan (New York: Random House, 1979). For analyses of fin de siècle anxiety, see Ronald Paulson, *Representations of Revolution (1789–1820)* (New Haven: Yale University Press, 1983); Marilyn Butler, *Romantics, Rebels, and Reactionaries: English Literature and Its Background, 1760–1830* (Oxford: Oxford University Press, 1981); and Johnson, *Equivocal Beings.*

5. All surviving accounts of the trial of Renwick Williams, including newspaper descriptions and the legal record, reiterate these details. See 1790 Case 239, "The King vs. Rhenwick Williams": 366–70, reprinted in Thomas Leach, *Reports of the Estimable Thomas Leach: Cases in Crown Law Determined by the 12 Judges of the Court of the King's Bench from 1730 to 1815,* 4th ed. (London: J. Butterworth et al., 1815): 1:529–36. My thanks to the solicitors Russell Bywater and Rhiannon Lewis, and the intern John Longwell, of Dawson Cornwell Associates in London. References to the trial are drawn from the three published versions: A FULL ACCOUNT OF THE TRIAL OF RENWICK WILLIAMS, commonly called the MONSTER, at the Old Bailey, On Thursday the 8th of July Taken in Short-Hand by Nathan. Jenkins (London: J. Smith, 1790), BL 1508/723; THE TRIAL OF RENWICK WILLIAMS, (Commonly called The MONSTER) at the OLD BAILEY, on Thursday the 8th of July 1790, Before JUDGE BULLER, AND A MIDDLESEX JURY, For assaulting and wounding Miss Ann Porter. Taken in Short-Hand by L. WILLIAMS, Esquire (London: D. Brewman, 1790), BL 6495.g.34;

and *THE TRIAL AT LARGE OF RHYNWICK WILLIAMS*, at *The Old Bailey, July 8ᵗʰ. 1790, Before JUDGE BULLER, For maliciously and feloniously making an Assault on MISS ANN PORTER, and cutting her Cloak, Gown, Stays, Petticoat, and Shift; with the Pleadings of the Counsel, and Judge Buller's excellent Charge to the Jury, verbatim. By E. Hodgson, Short-hand Writer to the Old Bailey* (London: R. Butters, 1790), BL 1419.k.1. For convenience, these accounts will be cited in the text by the recorder's surname and the short title.

6. This article, titled "Monsters," cites an attack on Mrs. Smith in May 1788, on Mrs. Godfrey of Charlotte Street and a female companion in May 1789, and on Mrs. Blaney of Bury Street in March 1790; see *Diary*, May 1, 1790. The specific victims are in the trial named as Ann Frost, Sarah Davis, Sarah Godrey, Mary Forster, Elizabeth Baughan, Frances Baughan, and Ann [*sic*] Porter (Williams, 3).

7. *Oracle*, June 10, 1790; the circumstances suggest that the police were especially harsh because the man was clearly picking up the woman for a romantic encounter, but one, hysterical, report claims she was cut beneath the eye "and horribly disfigured" (*Morning Herald* June 17, 1790).

8. *World*, May 11, 1790.

9. *World*, May 15, 1790.

10. This tale is reported in the *Diary*, May 14, 1790, and refuted in the *World* the same day, lambasting fabricators of false reports as "a new kind of MONSTER"—presumably for abusing the public.

11. *Oracle*, May 15, 1790.

12. *Morning Herald*, July 12, 1790.

13. Beginning with Addison and Steele's spectacularly popular *Spectator* (1711–12, 1714), periodicals had commented extensively on changing social values, and as the century wore on, the discourse had grown increasingly minatory, conservative, and nostalgic. See, for example, Colman and Thornton's *Connoisseur* (1754–56), and Mackenzie's *Mirror* (1779–80) and *Lounger* (1785–87). See Kathryn Shevelow's *Women and Print Culture: The Construction of Femininity in the Early Periodical* (London: Routledge, 1989); Barbara M. Benedict's *Framing Feeling: Sentiment and Style in English Prose Fiction, 1745–1800* (New York: AMS Press, 1994), esp. 92–171; Robert D. Mayo's *The English Novel in the Magazines, 1740–1815* (Evanston Ill.: Northwestern University Press, 1962); and James Raven's *Judging New Wealth: Popular Publishing and Responses to Commerce in England, 1750–1800* (Oxford: Clarendon Press, 1992).

14. *Diary*, May 31, 1790.

15. *World*, June 17, 1790.

16. Huet, *Monstrous Imagination;* Dennis Todd, *Imagining Monsters: Miscreations of Self in Eighteenth-Century England* (Chicago: University of Chicago Press, 1995), esp. 218.

17. *World*, April 2, 1790.

18. Jones, "Frekes, Monsters, and Ladies," 2–3.

19. Proclamation, No. 45AA; advertised in the *Gentleman's Journal*, May 4, 1790.

20. See Janet Todd, *Sensibility: An Introduction* (London: Methuen, 1986); also

G. J. Barker-Benfield, *The Culture of Sensibility: Sex and Society in Eighteenth-Century Britain* (Chicago: University of Chicago Press, 1992), and John Mullan, *Sentiment and Sociability: The Language of Feeling in the Eighteenth Century* (Oxford: Clarendon Press, 1988).

21. See Neil McKendrick, John Brewer, and J. H. Plumb, *The Birth of a Consumer Society: The Commercialization of Eighteenth-Century England* (Bloomington: Indiana University Press, 1982); also Ann Bermingham and John Brewer, eds., *The Consumption of Culture: Image, Object, Text* (London: Routledge, 1995). In "Consumptive Communities: Commodifying Nature at Eighteenth-Century Spas," I argue that even the nature-worship sentimentalism promoted was packaged as a consumer item (*Eighteenth-Century: Theory and Interpretation* 36 [1995]: 203–19). See also John Dwyer's "Clio and Ethics: Practical Morality in Enlightened Scotland," *Eighteenth-Century: Theory and Interpretation* 30 (1989): 45–72.

22. In "Sentimentality as Performance: Shaftesbury, Sterne, and the Theatrics of Virtue," Robert Markley argues that sentimentality was seen as demonstrating in the bourgeoisie an internalized nobility in late-eighteenth-century texts; see *The New Eighteenth Century: Theory, Politics, English Literature*, ed. Felicity Nussbaum and Laura Brown (New York: Methuen, 1987), 210–30.

23. Pall-Mall Handbill, May 7, 1790; see also the *Morning Herald*, April 10, 1790, signed G. Simpson.

24. Dr. Smith, *Diary*, April 14, 1790; *Oracle*, May 11, 1790.

25. *Morning Herald*, June 17, 1790.

26. In fact, this case must have propelled the systematization of the constabulary in 1792.

27. *Morning Herald*, April 8, 1790.

28. *Morning Herald*, April 8, 1790, April 10, 1790.

29. *Morning Herald*, April 10, 1790, signed Sampson Wright and N. Bond.

30. See Roy Porter, *English Society in the Eighteenth Century* (Harmondsworth: Penguin, 1982); Olwen Hufton, *Europe: Privilege and Protest, 1730–1789* (Ithaca: Cornell University Press, 1980); and E. P. Thompson, *The Making of the English Working Class* (New York: Vintage, 1963).

31. *Morning Herald*, April 10, 1790; handbill issued by Mr. Angerstein on Thursday, April 29, 1790, and posted at the Public-Office, Bow Street (printed by J. Moore, No. 134, Drury Lane, 1790). This is no. 44AA of Sarah S. Banks's collection of monsterabilia on Williams, compiled from her father Joseph Banks's papers, in the British Library volume L.R. 301.h.3. For further descriptions of his dress, see Angerstein's subsequent handbill for May 7, 1790 (printed for J. Moore), no. 45AA.

32. *World*, June 17, 1790.

33. See Frederick John Stopp, *Monsters and Hieroglyphs: Broadsheets and Emblem Books in Sixteenth-Century Germany*, the Sandars Lectures, 1975 (Cambridge: Cambridge University Press, 1975); many early modern satires, religious and political, correlate tyranny and monstrosity.

34. This reward followed a published hint from Dr. Davis.

35. Signed April 7, printed the *Morning Herald*, April 8, 1790.

36. Such efforts were promoted by the press: the *World* of May 3, 1790, pro-

posed two "stout Patroles, well armed" to assist "those tottering pillars, the Watchmen," on each street for six months.

37. Public proclamation headed "St. Pancras May 7 1790" (John's Street, Goodge Street, Tottenham Court Road: Bartlett and Co., Printers), no. 46AA.

38. Manuscript Subscription, no. 47AA.

39. Johnson analyzes the ambiguity surrounding masculinity in the literature of the 1790s in *Equivocal Beings*.

40. See Barbara M. Benedict, "European Monsters through English Eyes: Eighteenth-Century Cultural Icons," *Anglistik*, no. 1, (forthcoming fall, 1999).

41. Handbill no. 48AA.

42. Napoleon garners precisely the same satire during the next twenty years.

43. In *An Essay concerning Human Understanding*, John Locke differentiates reasonable man from imitative creatures like parrots by their ability to speak in languages; see II.27, sects. 9–10. Christopher Fox mentions this paradigm in his introduction to Fox, Porter, and Wokler, *Inventing Human Science*, 6, 23–24 n. 38.

44. In "A Night at the Opera: The Body, Class, and Art in *Evelina* and Frances Burney's *Early Diaries*," Beth Kowaleski-Wallace diagnoses the class distinctions between transcendent art and body-bound spectacle to analyze the ways in which the female body was a contested area of authority in the late eighteenth century (in *History, Gender, and Eighteenth-Century Literature*, ed. Beth Fowkes Tobin [Athens: University of Georgia Press, 1994], 140–58); for a wide range of analyses of the cultural treatments of the body, see also *Body and Text in the Eighteenth Century*, ed. Veronica Kelly and Dorothea von Mücke (Stanford: Stanford University Press, 1994).

45. See Barbara Maria Stafford's *Body Criticism: Imagining the Unseen in Enlightenment Art and Medicine* (Cambridge: MIT Press, 1991).

46. Jenkins, *Full Account*, 4. As the hastiest and briefest of the accounts, it was probably the first to be published, while the more elaborate version of the court reporter, E. Hodgson, has more details. Regardless, Jenkins' seems best to represent the public understanding of the trial. I have noted significant differences between them in the text.

47. The ability to speak in languages had been used to prove the humanity of physically misshapen "monsters" throughout the eighteenth century; Williams's intimate exclamation, "O ho! It is you, is it?" which Judge Buller interpreted as proving a previous relationship between Williams and the Porters, resurrects this idea that language simultaneously documents humanity and monstrosity.

48. Statute 23, section 11, anno 6 Georgii I reads, "That if any person or persons shall, at any time or times, from and after the 24th of June, in the year of our Lord 1720, wilfully and maliciously assault any person or persons in the public streets or highways, with an intent to tear, cut, burn, or deface, or shall tear, spoil, cut, burn, or deface the garments or cloaths of such person or persons, that then all and every person or persons so offending, being thereof lawfully convicted, shall be, and be adjudged to be guilty of *felony*, &c." Both the newspapers and the judge reiterate the precise terms of this act. See *Statutes at Large from the First Year of the Reign of George the First to the Third Year of the Reign of George the Second* (London: Mark Baskett et al., 1668–1815), v.

49. Jenkins, *Full Account*, 20, 28. Other accounts change this number, depending on how they interpret the witnesses' testimony—L.Williams cites fourteen—but no evidence appeared disputing Renwick Williams's sexual interests. Under cross-examination by Mr. Knowles, Williams's defense attorney, even Coleman admitted, "He behaved somewhat like an innocent man" (Jenkins, *Full Account*, 19).

50. R. Williams, *An Appeal to the Public* (London: R. Williams, 1790), 20.

51. Hodgson, *The Trial at Large*, 5; L. Williams's account of the trial also records that the Monster had injured costly property: "Miss Porter's dress was produced; the gown, of silk, had a very long rent in it; as had the shift" (6). The legal account of the trial specifies the silk gown, a silk petticoat, two linen shifts and "one pair of stays of the value of six shillings" (1 Leach 530).

52. For the social regulation of sexuality, see Michel Foucault, *The History of Sexuality*, vol. 1, trans. Robert Hurley (New York: Random, 1978) and *The Use of Pleasure*, trans. Robert Hurley (New York: Random, 1985); also Eve Kosofsky Sedgwick, *Between Men: English Literature and Male Homosocial Desire* (New York: Columbia University Press, 1985) and *Epistemology of the Closet* (Berkeley and Los Angeles: University of California Press, 1990); and Thomas Laqueur, *Making Sex: Body and Gender from the Greeks to Freud* (Cambridge: Harvard University Press, 1990).

53. Hodgson reports Williams saying, "but while I revere the law of my country, which presumes every man to be innocent till proven guilty, yet I must reprobate the cruelty with which the Public Prints have abounded, in the most scandalous paragraphs, containing malicious exaggerations of the charges preferred so much to my prejudice, that I already lie under premature conviction, by almost an universal voice" (25).

54. See, for example, the advertisements in the four-volume collection of handbills, newspaper clips, and advertisements, titled *Collectanea*, compiled by Daniel Lysons in the British Library. See also Richard D. Altick, *The Shows of London* (Cambridge: Harvard University Press, Belknap Press, 1978).

55. See *A Collection of Advertisement* (BL N. Tab. 2026/25), no. 651.d.10 (2). See also "The tall *Black*, called the Indian-King," another example of European perfidy (no. 24).

56. See C. J. S. Thompson, *The Mystery and Lore of Monsters. With Accounts of Some Giants, Dwarfs, and Prodigies* (London: WIlliams and Norgate, 1930).

57. See Dennis Todd's account of the Toft fraud in *Imagining Monsters; A Collection of Advertisements*, N. Tab. 2026/25, no. 29.

58. Most of this criticism was based on Biblical exhortations against the "lust of the eyes," and the "Athenian itch," but anxiety about the public uses of curious inquiry gathers added impetus after the publication of Bacon's *Advancement of Learning* (1604). See Jerry Weinberger, *Science, Faith, and Politics: Francis Bacon and the Utopian Roots of the Modern Age* (Ithaca: Cornell University Press, 1985), 283–84. Sermons and disquisitions against curiosity are legion: see, for example, William Newton's *Essay against Unnecessary Curiosity in Matters of Religion* (London: S. Billingsley, 1725).

59. The *Morning Herald* reports that the duke of York, Prince William of Glou-

cester, Lord Beauchamp, Lord Essex, and many other nobles attended, with the duke of Cumberland on the bench (June 17, 1790).

60. For a historical review of the problem of negotiating public, political, and legal definitions of justice, and an analysis of the political attitude toward property, see Douglas Hay, "Property, Authority, and the Criminal Law," in *Albion's Fatal Tree: Crime and Society in Eighteenth-Century England* (New York: Random House, 1975), 17–63.

61. See *Cook and Woodburn*, using the Coventry Act (statutes 22 and 23, Car. II. C. 1). In this case, the defendants argued that they intended to kill Mr. Crispe, not to maim him, and thus could not be indicted for maiming, but the judge, Lord King, suggested to the jury that the means for murdering were maiming, so if the defendants were guilty of the former, they must have intended the latter. They were executed. Buller persuaded Williams's jury, however, of the pertinence of the act, by arguing, "There was a wound given with an instrument not calculated altogether for the purpose of affecting the body, such for instance, as *piercing* or *stabbing* by making a hole. Here was an actual cutting, and the wound was of considerable length; so was the rent in the cloaths. It remained, therefore, with the Jury to decide, whether, as both body and cloaths were cut, he who intended the end did not at the same time intend the means" (*Full Account,* 31).

62. The jury took fifteen minutes. Three witnesses, including Anne Porter, each identified Williams as the Monster, although only the Porters had so identified him at the first trial: Mary Davis, and the two Baughan sisters.

63. A poetaster and a liberal polemicist, Swift wrote a defense of Williams, called *The Monster at Large; or the Innocence of Rhynwick Williams Vindicated* (London: J. Ridgway, 1790), comprising an attack on class prejudice, and several poetic works, including a squib on college life called *Prison Pindarics, or a New Year's Gift from Newgate* (Dublin: T. Burne, 1795).

64. Although Miss Porter refused the reward, Coleman's attitude is less (or more) clear. He certainly received an extra 134 pounds from a private "Subscription" taken at Lloyd's Coffee House on May 11, 1790. Viscount Beauchamp was among the donors.

65. See *Diary,* July 27, 1790; also the *World,* July 12, 1790 and July 17.

66. W.H., *New Lady's Magazine* (London: Alex Hogg, 1790), 384, ll. 1–4, 37–44. This poem follows a five-page account of the Monster's trial, embellished with engravings.

Monstrous Knowledge: Representing the National Body in Eighteenth-Century Ireland

Joel Reed

If we take our cue from the *OED*, the mere *topic* of "defect" seems to be unsettling, even vertiginous, since we find there that the word means "the fact of falling short," and once meant "a falling away from" a party or cause, as if a well-fixed "order of things," the standard by which the defect is measured, or a political system of allegiances, is a tall, vertical fabrication. This image is not so far from the truth, for "defects" can take their meaning in relation to hierarchical taxonomic or social codes that systematically arrange things and people into classes. The heights to which these classificatory standards climb require a degree of epistemic and political stability that was difficult to establish in a seventeenth- and eighteenth-century period shaken by revolutions in politics and information. In fact, Samuel Johnson demonstrated in 1755 that instability constitutes even the word *defect,* for it points both to social conventions of understanding, as when Johnson defines the term as a "fault; mistake; error," as well as to an asocial or ahistorical flaw, "any natural imperfection."[1] In this essay I consider this defect or instability in the concept of defect, by looking at its relation to standards of both natural categorization and the construction of social groups. More specifically, I address here a set of eighteenth-century Irish texts that are "defective" in that, though seeking systematically to define natural and national spaces, in fact, to define national identity by delineating the natural world, they instead continuously "fall away" from the standards of both, reveling in forms of each that lie outside of systems of classification, those imperfections or aberrations that would have been identified as "monsters," in Johnson's definition of "out of the common order of nature," or in Robert Boyle's sense of being "preternatural" or "contrary to nature."[2] These texts reveal the historical "insufficiency" (as Johnson also defines *defect*) of these natural and national systems, suggesting that, rather than falling away from the standard, defective bodies and monstrous nationalisms are the norm.

My consideration will focus on a series of texts by Dr. Charles Smith, the "Natural, Civil, Ecclesiastical, Historical, and Topographical" surveys of Down, Waterford, Cork, and Kerry, that he first published in the 1740s and 1750s "with the Approbation of the [Dublin] Physico-Historical Society" and for which "not only the Honour, but the real Interest of our Country are the Objects of its View."[3] Through rationalism, Smith seeks to harmonize the discordant or monstrous form of knowing the world present in these texts.[4] This "monstrous" form is duplicated within the closing chapter of each text, "Of Remarkable Persons born in this County," about which Smith writes "as natural historians have taken care in their writings to note the birth places of men, famous either for arts or arms, piety or munificence, which having been sometimes neglected, has become doubtful, and has raised disputes between cities and countries for the honour of their birth. . . . I shall present the Reader with a few, whose names will afford no small honour to this county, and also of some others who have been remarkable in their life time in other respects."[5] What interests me about these figures is what makes them both "remarkable" and "honour[able]," and what they are doing in texts that are themselves generically multivalent: natural, civil, and above all, national histories. In representing those who are "remarkable . . . in other respects," or, as we will see, the monstrous, with the "honorable," Smith's texts disrupt our late-twentieth-century ways of viewing defects. By using the defective or imperfect as the standard, Smith's books reveal the unformed character of interlinked concepts—not only those of the qualitative "remarkable" and "honorable," but also physiological concepts of monstrosity, gender, and life itself, as well as concepts of political and institutional organization, such as those of the nation and the academy; rather than "fall away" from an ideal national identity, these figures help Smith call it into being.

Studying these concepts in their formative stages, rather than after they have calcified into definitions taken for granted today, shows that at their heart lies ambivalence both in the "science" or taxonomies with which the nation is represented, and in the subjects of that nation. Of the need to treat in its own terms the discursive multiplicity of early natural history or "life sciences," rather than reduce these studies to our own disciplinary or epistemological constraints, Georges Canguilhem writes that "a congenital clubfoot, a sexual inversion, a diabetic, a schizophrenic, pose innumerable questions which, in the end, refer to the whole of anatomical, embryological, physiological and psychological research. . . . [T]his problem must not be broken up [because] the chances for clarifying it are greater if it is considered *en bloc.*"[6] Any attempt to represent or "know" those who seem to be natural exceptions, the "defects" who fall short of some standard, or the monstrous who are "out of the common order of nature," inevitably links with a multiplicity of representational strategies and discourses. In the eighteenth century, when "science" remained quite close to theological and political epistemes, attempts to reduce the world to a classificatory schema result instead in processes of multiplication and accretion, splitting, bifurcation, and mediation, which affect not only the representation of natural history, but also that of the other topics that concern Smith's texts: the nation and its subjects. By examining en bloc, without diminishing to a single master code or standard, both the "civil" history presented in these works and the figures who populate their "topographical" surveys, we will see that beneath the skin of national identity lies an uncertain nature.

The role of natural history is central to these interconnected conceptual formations, for, as Michel Foucault suggests, this early "science" was less formalized, less philosophically elevated than fields such as optics or physics, and instead "much more dependent on external processes (economic stimulations or institutional supports)."[7] As I first discuss in this essay, the science of Smith's texts is overdetermined by the Dublin Physico-Historical Society's institutional relationship with the Royal Society of London, a relationship itself overdetermined by national connections—and conflicts—between Ireland and England. We will see, however, that the two poles of this national context are triangulated by that of an intermediary group, the Protestant Anglo-Irish who composed the Physico-Historical Society. After our examination moves from Smith's explicit consideration of heroic or otherwise "honorable" figures and toward a catalog of the physically "remarkable," we will find that these institutional and national forces make themselves felt in epistemological and classificatory instability. Rather than find their place within any particular standards, the figures of Smith's texts lie *in between* them, neither purely remarkable nor honorable, national nor colonial, perfect nor defective, scientifically studied objects nor fantastic projections.

Though the Physico-Historical Society was short-lived, and only one other text in addition to Smith's appears to have been explicitly affiliated with it, the repeated reprinting of Smith's works helped legitimate the group and raise its visibility.[8] Some thirty years after the Society folded, Robert Burrowes finds there a foundation for nationalist research, and includes it as a precedent to the more successful Royal Irish Academy: "To attain purposes of so great national utility as this Academy proposes to itself, the patriotism of the inhabitants of this kingdom has made many efforts, which though not entirely effectual, have yet given a well-founded hope, that when circumstances more favourable should arise such endeavours might be attended with success."[9] The role of the Dublin group in a patriotic research tradition, however, is not as clear-cut as the Irish Academy, or even as Smith, would have their readers believe. Just as the hyphen between its "physical" and "historical" work both separates and brings into contact two forms of knowledge, the Society's institutional position is nationally ambivalent, aligned at times with Britain, and at others with Ireland against colonial Britain and Europe, though even in these moments an internal split between a general Irish identity and a particularly Protestant defensiveness makes itself visible.

Lacking an Irish scientific academy with which to align itself, Smith looks to London and dedicates the book on Down to Sir Hans Sloane, past president of the Royal Society: "The only end aimed at is the Approbation and Encouragement of You, and other learned Enquirers, who may see by this Essay, that the Nature and State of IRELAND, is no less worth inquiring into, than other Countries" (iv). Here we can sense not only Irish pride, but also national insecurity, both expressed and absolved in this appeal to British cultural authority. Approval from Sloane and the Royal Society marks a point of contact between the London and Dublin groups at which they identify Ireland as "worthy" of unprejudiced study that would "take off the Veil that has long lain upon this Country, and for removing those Mistakes and Misrepresentations, that have been handed down from remote Times, and are yet admitted to Truths" (vi). Underwriting the Physico-Historical Society's work is the acknowledgment that scientific investigation—both its object and mode—has been nationally determined, and Smith's hope is that "mistakes and misrepresentations" of the type he cites from Guy Miege's *Present State of Ireland,* "that the People are uncivilized, rude, barbarous" (vi), would be corrected through Sloane's more disinterested epistemological method.[10] Smith suggests that a natural historiography permeated by stereotypes is too couched in a "national style" of knowing, rather than in the internationalism or universalism he finds in the Royal Society's mode of inquiry.[11] He therefore, and somewhat paradoxically, argues that the universalist route to knowing Ireland is through a British, or colonial, methodology mediated by the Dublin Physico-Historical Society.

But in the middle of the eighteenth century, to mediate Ireland and the British designated a position no less ambivalent than that of the duality of a "Physico-Historical" society: that of the Protestant Anglo-Irish. Throughout the "Protestant Ascendency" in Ireland, Anglo-Irish like William Molyneux, founder in 1683 of the Dublin Philosophical Society and author of the ur-text of Irish nationalism, *The Case of Ireland's being bound by acts of Parliament in England* (1698), argued for increased political independence for Ireland, but for a specifically Protestant nation, one in which strong distinctions would be drawn—and legally enforced—between itself and the native Catholics.[12] These distinctions, however, were not always as clear to the British as they were to the Irish, and this categorical instability leads to another, more subjective or personal affect: the insecurity that mingled with Smith's proud claim that "IRELAND, is no less worth inquiring into, than other Countries." This tension between a national self-identification and a desire for colonial approval echoes that of Jonathan Swift, another Anglo-Irish patriot, who strongly voiced a nationalistic anomie or resentment at the prejudice of "mistakes and misrepresentations" when he noted that "what we call the Irish Brogue is no sooner discovered, than it makes the deliverer, in the last degree, ridiculous and despised. . . . [T]he bad consequence of this opinion affects those among us who are not the least liable to such reproaches, further than the misfortune of being born in Ireland, although of English parents."[13] Swift feels strongly that what to him is a clearly evident distinction of birth is misrecognized by others, as a common accent masks or makes ambivalent the difference between Anglo-Irish and Irish Catholic, a peculiarity internal to the Irish nation. At another time, he emphasizes and reinforces that difference by expressing his desire to "reduce this uncultivated people from that idle, savage, beastly, thievish manner of life, in which they continue sunk."[14] In Swift's texts, a proper view of things corrects misrepresentation or misrecognition by showing that the Anglo-Irish, though striving to become a politically separate nation from Great Britain, are subjectively linked and common to the British, and separate from their neighbors the Irish Catholics. The Anglo-Irish, then, both played and rejected the mediating role their hyphenated name suggests, for they would seek to inscribe both similitude and radical difference, universal interests with the British and particular uniqueness from the natives whom British colonial policy suppressed, even as in the political realm they claimed that particularism for their own "nation."

This web of national interests obscures Smith's apparently clear rejection of the prejudices of "mistakes and misrepresentation." Guy Miege's stereotyping of the Irish as "uncivilized, rude, barbarous" looks like Swift's own characterizations of them as "uncultivated . . . savage, beastly," and it resembles some of the statements in Smith's book on Down as well. In his introduction to that text Smith presents the sources of his civil history: "we had also Recourse to the Publick Records, and Libraries" (xii), finding there "the *Original Depositions* of the *detestable Massacres* made on the Protestants of this Kingdom in the Rebellion of 1641" (xii). Though at odds with supposedly disinterested scientific practice, this reference to the Irish Rebellion of 1641 reinforces Smith's dedication to the Royal Society and to Anglo-Protestant culture. In insisting that his material about the "massacres" comes from the firsthand accounts of "original depositions," Smith forges an epistemological link with the British group by emphasizing that his sources were themselves witnesses. Steven Shapin and Simon Schaffer write that, more important to early science than empirical evidence was the public performance of experiments before as many witnesses as possible: "If knowledge was to be empirically based, as Boyle and other English experimentalists insisted it should, then its experimental foundations had to be *witnessed.*"[15] Strategies for increasing the pool of "witnesses" included having as large an audience as possible for experimental performance and replication, but also the literary creation of "virtual witnessing."[16]

While Smith does not religiously follow the Royal Society's stylistic prescriptions for the creation of a virtual-witnessing effect, he dramatically emphasizes, in keeping with Boyle's and other's declarations of the Royal Society's methods, the *experience* of the history they recount, by including in his text both a broad statistical overview of the rebellion and specific anecdotes of its effects: "there were 40 or 50000 Protestants murthered before they suspected themselves to be in any Danger. . . . We have . . . for the present Purpose . . . set forth in this Tract, several Instances of the Barbarities of the *Irish* committed on the Protestants in this single County, and find their Numbers specified to be near 3000" (*Down*, xii). The author signals that the "disputes between cities and countries" he uses to justify the chapters "Of remarkable Persons" are overdetermined by the religious struggles that are omnipresent in questions of Irish nationalism and that split Irish identity. Here, in fact, the Anglo-Irish are identified only as Protestants, a *supra*national label that distinguishes them from the hostile, "barbarous," and more exclusively presented Irish nationals. This supranational self-identification reinforces the strategic alliance with the British by asserting their universal interests in defending Protestantism, while nonetheless contributing to Anglo-Irish nationalism. To emphasize the abstraction of universalist ideologies, Smith compiles a set of martyrs, anonymous dead whose significance lies precisely in their irreducibility to particular individuals. In so doing, he contributes early links to a chain of nationalist historiographers such as Jules Michelet, who, in the words of Benedict Anderson, "exemplifies the national imagining being born, for he was the first self-consciously to write *on behalf* of the dead," and Fernand Braudel, who gathers so many dead as part of the French national biography that Anderson refers to his "remorselessly accumulating cemeteries" from which are snatched "exemplary suicides, poignant martyrdoms, assassinations, executions, wars, and holocausts."[17] The anonymous contents of Braudel's and Smith's cemeteries erase the individual identities of the nation's subjects, remembering these subjects instead as a corporate corpse, as a national body whose death is the lifeblood of the future, or monumentalizing them in a textual tomb of the unknowns; as Ernest Gellner writes, nationalism "is the establishment of an anonymous, impersonal society, with mutually substitutable individuals."[18] The numbers of dead, then, are what counts, not the details of these people's lives, nor even, as one would find in John Foxe's *Acts and Monuments* (1563), a text central to the creation of a Protestant-English nationalism, the details of their deaths.[19]

We would be remiss, however, in understanding Smith's martyrs *only* in terms of the links Anderson and Gellner draw between nationalism and anonymity; Anderson makes a point of designating the Tomb of the Unknown Soldier a feature of *modern* nationalism, while for Gellner, nationalism itself is a modern phenomenon, and against those standards, the forms of nationalism promoted in Smith's texts would be monstrous indeed. For contrasting with the Protestant martyrs' anonymity is the biographical detail in his chapters on "Remarkable Persons." In a sense, recounting the origins and family backgrounds of these people is another means of "virtual witnessing," of presenting to an audience enough evidence to convince them of the factuality or even naturalness of the events or figures on display—despite the social construction of biographical conventions.[20] The brief biographies of the remarkable persons monumentalize national culture in the bodies of particular individuals, while maintaining the empiricist epistemology these texts seek to institutionalize.

At another level these chapters contrast with the discussion of the martyrs, for, at least initially, they evenhandedly represent both Catholic and Protestant accomplishments. *The Antient and Present State of the County and City of Waterford* includes among its local heroes Peter Lumbard, "the son of a merchant in Waterford, and educated, for a time, at Westminster, under the learned Cambden . . . [and] made provost of the cathedral of Cambray, afterwards titular archbishop of Armagh, and domestic prelate and assistant to the Pope," and "Thomas Strange, a native of Waterford, . . . a franciscan friar," as well as Roger Boyle, the Protestant "earl of Orrery, fifth son of Richard Boyle, first earl of Cork . . . born at Lismore, in this county, April 25, 1621," Boyle's brother Robert Boyle, the fellow of the Royal Society, and the playwright William Congreve.[21] In *The Antient and Present State of the*

County of Kerry we find the abbot of St. Brandon, the son of Finlog, who "presided over 3000 monks" and "related several monstrous stories, or . . . *apochryphal dreams*" (412). Less luminous local heroes are also noted: "I have in my survey met with some good latin scholars who did not understand the english tongue; particularly one *Peter Kelley.* . . . Neither is the genius of the commonalty confined to this kind of learning alone, for I saw a poor man near *Black-Stones,* who had a tolerable notion of calculating . . . altho he had never been taught to read English" (418). The *Antient and Present State of the County and City of Cork* contains a similarly eclectic group of national heroes, such as George Rye, "the only son of *Christopher Rye,* an Alderman of *Cork,* and of Mrs. *Anne Evans.* . . . He had studied natural philosophy and physick for his own curiosity," and the doctor Maurice O'Connel.[22] *Cork,* however, also includes various colonial heroes such as Edward Barry, M.D., "Fellow of the Royal Society, and his Majesty's Physician General to the army in Ireland" (422), or Sir Richard Cox, noted for being honored in 1697 by the Protestants of Bandon for exposing "the cruelties and impostures of the papists" (417), for his Williamite *Aphorisms, proving . . . the necessity of making the Prince of* Orange *King,* and for being nominated in 1693 "one of the commisioners for the forfeitures" (417), who would distribute land appropriated from those opposing the Williamite cause. Though Smith fails to mention it, Cox also wrote *An essay for the conversion of the Irish shewing that 'tis their duty and interest to become Protestants* (1698) and the anti-Catholic *Hibernia anglicana* (1689). Also included in the book on Cork are "three others, who were eminent Commanders in the *British* navy, whom this county gave birth to" (422).

Smith's nationalist surveys are populated, then, with either Catholics and Anglo-Irish noted for their learning, or with Anglo-Irish colonial heroes. The only Catholic nationalist mentioned is Cnogher O. Mahoney, who wrote a text in 1645 exhorting the "*Irish* to persist in their Rebellion, and to continue the Massacre of those *Hereticks,* the *English . . . to extirpate the* English, *their Manners and Religion out of the Kingdom,*" and illustrates the "monstrous Instances of Cruelties" visited upon the Protestant martyrs (*Down,* xiv). Mahoney is himself a monster in Smith's text, a deviant among the remarkable or patriotic subjects whom Smith proudly presents. Yet the infamy Mahoney represents for Smith suggests that as examples of national history, these texts are themselves monstrous, for they promote not the universal goals of unity and cohesion to which nationalism explicitly directs itself, but rather the divisive ones of the exclusion and conquest of an internal other. These texts exemplify not a "bad" form of nationalism, but demonstrate instead how "the notion of nationalism," in the words of

Etienne Balibar, "is constantly dividing."[23] Smith wrote his texts to correct the "Mistakes and Misrepresentations" of imperial ones such as Miege's *Present State of Ireland,* Edmund Spenser's *View of the Present State of Ireland* (1596), or Gerard Boate's *Irelands Naturall History* (1652), works in which tales of Irish Catholic "barbarism" intermingle with complaints about the unhealthy environment and proposals for military intervention. Yet Smith ended up writing a different, more indigenous form of imperial-national text, one in which a "civil history" is founded on uncivil war, and a gathering of late national heroes becomes a triumphalist display. Rather than "correct" the mistakes of these imperial texts, Smith's texts justify imperial militarism by means of the distinction between the honorable figures worth praising and studying and the infamous or monstrously cruel.

These texts' varied, and at times competing, institutional and national affiliations leave their mark in a decentered gathering of national martyrs, heroes and antiheroes, which shows that, for the Anglo-Irish, national honor was itself a concept in formation.[24] The series of bifurcations that we have been tracing, in which particularism forks off of universalism, national self-promotion becomes deference to colonial authorities, and hostility erupts from civility, demonstrates that concepts of honor or nationality admit little of the epistemic stability requisite for a fixed standard. In turning to the "scientific" half of the chapters on "Remarkable Persons," where Smith replaces notable figures with those who are esteemed not for their deeds, but "by some accident, or other particular affection of their bodies" (*Cork,* 423), or by being "remarkable for their great age" (427), we find that a natural survey is no more secure than a national one. Smith's figures follow the system of "Queries recommended to the *Curious,* to enable them to make proper Enquiries in their respective Neighbourhoods" that he appends to the introduction of the book on Down, a complicated set of fourteen investigative categories containing seventy-two subsets and at least as many questions within those; the figures derive in part from scientific reports first published in the Royal Society of London's *Philosophical Transactions.* Despite the fetishistic order of this system and Smith's respectable sources, its results demonstrate that, at its moment of documentation and classification, knowledge is essentially ungovernable, monstrously "out of order" as superstitions or anecdotes mix with observation and fact and pertinent data mingles with irrelevant aside. As "remarkable persons" slip from national civil and not-so-civil history to national history as natural history, they reveal the instability within the governing epistemological categories of the life sciences that distinguish life from death, define sex and gender, and discern the human form itself.

Section 9 of Smith's "Queries . . . to the Curious," "*Men* and *Women*," groups questions about extreme age, uncommon disease, and unusual accidents, including "Unusual Sizes in Defect or Increase" as well as those "In their Deaths or Graves" (*Down*, xviii). The catalog of people notable for their longevity reflects a fascination with those who can fend off death, including John Richardson, aged 112 years, and Daniel Keaghly, from the parish "*Inchegeelagh*, a very mountainous tract," who is 103. About both of these centenarians Smith claims "I saw him," thereby playing the role of a witness (*Cork*, 427). The detail about Inchegeelach is also significant to Smith, who presents longevity as a result of national topography: "Mountainous countries have been always remarkable for the longevity of the inhabitants" (*Waterford*, 375), though, if "Doctor *Lyne* an *Irish* Physician" is an example, fresh air too may be a means of extending life, for, though he died at 85, "for 50 years together nobody died out of his house," which was "built in an odd manner, every window had another opposite to it. . . . [These windows] were continually kept open without any defence against the weather" (*Cork*, 429). Local longevity *could* be seen as a source of national pride or as evidence of national virility, but that does not seem to be Smith's point, as the hodgepodge of explanations suggests. Adding about Zachariah Fives, who died when he was 112, that "his flesh was very hard and gristly" (*Cork*, 428), an aside of little explanatory relevance, strengthens the sense that Smith is randomly gathering information, rather than processing his data or ordering it unequivocally to "correct" the earlier natural histories of Ireland. In fact, along with the people of "extreme age" who would demonstrate the healthfulness and productivity of the Irish environment, there are those in Smith's texts whose sudden grayness suggests premature aging, such as "Michael Ronayne [who] turned gray in a night's time, his hair being of a dark brown before the change" (*Waterford*, 376); Ronayne testifies that these texts are uncertain about the limits of life or the signs that display it. The story of John Goodman's mother brings this point home: she "was interred while she lay in a trance; having been buried in a vault, which she found means to open, she walked home; and this Mr. *Goodman* was born sometime after" (*Cork*, 428). Mrs. Goodman fits in the category of "Reviviscence," those who return to life from death, though Smith suggests that she was never actually dead, only "in a trance," the misrecognition of which led to her entombment.

Smith is silent about whether we should consider Mrs. Goodman's pregnancy, and the subsequent birth of John, as a miraculous result of her entombment, and provides no other details of his family. Like Christ, Goodman apparently has no material father, though in his case it is his mother who miraculously or wondrously awakes from death. The shift in this tale from natural to supernatural or sacred history is mirrored in the questions about "unusual accidents" in "death or graves" that Smith directs the "Curious" to ask about "Preservation from Putrefaction" (*Down*, xviii), queries that give credence to the relics, those preserved saintly body parts, gathered and revered by Catholics throughout Europe. These moments in Smith's texts are part of a broader Protestant appropriation of the monstrous that reinscribed them from a popular tradition into miraculous signs of the unknowability of divine power.[25] At the same time, the voyeuristic appeal that would have accompanied such preserved or "revivified" figures in a carnival or street fair is not far from Smith's presentation; that the audience for his "queries" *are* the "Curious" links his project of gathering or collecting information to that of the collections early modern virtuosi maintained and displayed in their curio cabinets. The sexual or perhaps fetishistic nature of this voyeurism becomes clear as Smith's natural history crosses a further epistemological line: his example of a hermaphrodite who transgresses sexual and gender distinctions. Smith frames the anecdote of the hermaphrodite by covering both theological and scientific bases, as its source is an article the bishop of Clogher wrote for the Royal Society's *Philosophical Transactions.* In response to the bishop's charity, a man from Inishonan "shewed him a curiosity, which was that of his breasts, with which he affirmed he had given suck to a child of his own: His wife, he said, died when the child was about 2 months old; the child crying exceedingly while it was in bed with him, he gave it his breast to suck, only with an expectation to keep it quiet; but, behold, he found that the child in time extracted milk, and he affirmed, that he had milk afterwards to rear the child. His breasts were very large for a man, and his nipple larger than is common in women" (*Cork*, 423). The scene of this man baring his woman's breasts to a bishop is, perhaps, as "remarkable" as the "curious" event depicted here, where a man's attempt to nurse his child results in a physiological transformation. Yet, despite its beginning as a "curiosity," the final descriptive sentence of the passage returns this miraculous and wonderful sexual scene back to the rhetoric of science and its strategies of "virtual witnessing," as does, even more, the supporting footnote in the text, which presents "other instances of the same kind," delivered "with such circumstances, as may create a belief of the truth of it," despite the fact that the note emphasizes a man's ability to will his breasts into producing milk by "intense and continual thought" (*Cork*, 423).

The man from Inishonan's sex- and gender-bending supports Londa Schiebinger's claim that by the middle of the eighteenth century, anatomists sought new explanations for sexual difference.[26] Smith's text is caught between explanatory standards, as it represents a theologian's report to a scientific society as an empirically recorded "curiosity." Smith combines this search for an essential sexuality with one for the limits of the human form itself in the instance of Ann Jackson, an Anglo-Irish girl with horns, or at least excessive warts, who had been reported by Dr. St. George Ash as "the *Horny Girl*" in the *Philosophical Transactions*.[27] Smith copies most of the case study from the Royal Society publication and follows Ash in ending the description of Jackson's pathology with the observation that "she eat and drank heartily, slept soundly, and performed all the offices of nature like other healthy people, except that she had not the evacuation proper to her sex" (*Waterford*, 371), though he neglects to include Ash's statement that "the owner of this Monster would not be perswaded to let us take the figure thereof."[28] By excising Ash's sixty-year-old reference to Jackson as a "monster," and by omitting Ash's frustration at being unable to present visual evidence of Jackson's existence and graphically provide the *Transactions*' readers with a kind of secondhand voyeurism, Smith may be signaling a discursive advance in medical reports. The disinterested results of his queries are far from the seventeenth-century accounts and displays of monsters, even those within the *Philosophical Transactions*, that sensationalized them as wondrous curiosities. At the same time, as we have seen, this "advance" (if indeed it is one), is uneven or nonsynchronous at best, present as it is alongside the curious case of the man from Inishonan. Smith fails to resolve this uncertainty, but rather bullies it into exactitude by using "proper" in his description of Ann Jackson. Designating menstruation a sign of "proper" womanhood is a disciplinary move, signaling not only what is "natural" but what is "correct." Here, the dual valence of "order" may be relevant, for Smith's taxonomic queries arrange the data he finds, classifying them while also commanding them to conform or fit into his conceptual structure. The monstrous ignore those commands, acting improperly or out of order and violating the decorum with which scientific institutions, and apparently their objects of study, are supposed to comport themselves.[29] So, the hermaphrodite and Ann Jackson violate norms of sex, gender, and the human, both behaving and appearing improperly, and therefore conforming to Johnson's definition of the monstrous as being "out of the common order." Without mincing words, in another place Smith writes of a "monstrous birth: The head was much deformed, it had four arms and four legs, two rumps and but one body" (*Cork*, 427). Recording these "Unusual Accidents" allows the Anglo-Irish Smith to discipline an unruly Irish nature, even one that infects other Anglo-Irish, while his ordered examination can nonetheless contribute to Ireland's honor, a split purpose in keeping with the uncertain sense of honor or nation that permeates this text.[30]

Perhaps the most dramatic of Smith's collection of people "remarkable by some accident, or other particular affection of their bodies" is William Clark, who suffered from a type of osteopathology that led his bones to fuse together. Clark's narrative condenses many of the features we have been considering, revealing not only formal but also epistemic multiplicity. It opens with a biographical sketch, noting Clark's origins ("the son of *John Clark*, a soldier in Sir *Richard Aldworth's* company, was born in Newmarket in this county, in 1677" [*Cork,* 423]) and presenting a series of anecdotes that illustrate his worsening condition from birth through adulthood (423–24). In places, Smith narrates with a particular scientistic detachment, as in his description of the autopsy that followed Clark's death:

> A bone grows from the back of his head, which shoots down towards his back, and passes by the vertebræ of the neck about an inch distance; this bone unites to the vertebræ of the back, and the scapula of the left shoulder, from whence it disengages itself again, and continues distinct, till it divides into two, towards the small of the back, and fixes itself into the hip bones behind. (*Cork,* 425)

Nonetheless, Smith mediates, or even aestheticizes, the cool indifference of his reporting style—emphasized on the next page in the reference to Clark's "dissection" (426)—when he writes that "the posture into which he is fixed, sometime before his death, is somewhat like that of the *Venus* of *Medicis*" (425), and in the illustration that accompanies the entry on Clark. Depicting an animated skeleton who stands upright with a grin permanently fused on his face, the image perfectly conforms to the convention of *contrapposto,* in which the human form, its weight unevenly distributed, stands in an exaggerated curve that creates an ideal of the beautiful. The convention, developed out of attempts to represent the body as animated and fluid rather than stiff and unmoving, is in exact opposition to Clark's predicament, as is the ultimate, horrible affect of this figure in opposition to its beautiful legacy.[31] Continuing the aestheticization he began, but shifting it in the direction of the sublime, Smith suggests that Clark's form is beyond words, "as difficult a task" to represent "as to describe *Calypso's* grotto" (426). The sublime excess of Clark's form, a structure in which "nature seems to have sported herself" (425), must account for the wonder Smith feels, despite his scientistic distance, when confronted by this "surprizing" and "curious" skeleton. Perhaps to compensate for this loss of control, Smith calls again for the disciplining of nature, complaining that "there is scarce one bone in the whole of

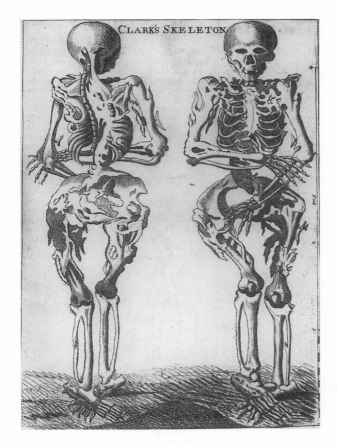

Fig. 13. Charles Smith, *The Antient and Present State of the County and City of Cork* (Dublin, 1750). (Reprinted by permission of the William Andrews Clark Memorial Library, University of California, Los Angeles.)

it's [*sic*] proper natural form," in a return to that moral language of propriety and order he earlier used in his discussion of Ann Jackson.

William Clark is remarkable not only for the body that Smith's narrative draws for him, but for the ways his narrative concentrates the disparate features of these texts, not least of which is their combination within a single chapter of monstrous figures and those gathered as national treasures for their actions or learning. Yet, seeing the monsters as anomalous misses the point—in these texts the honorable persons are misplaced, the afterthoughts or playful sports that uncontrollably figure at the end of his natural histories. Noting his debt to English institutional models, Smith writes that his texts will conclude "(according to the Hon. Mr. *Robert Boyle* and Dr. *Plott's* Method of Enquiry) with Observations on Men and Women, as to their extreme Age, unusual Accidents at their Birth, and uncommon Sizes in Defect or Increase. To which we shall annex an Account of Men eminent for their useful Inventions, Learning or Promotions" (*Down*, 251). The monstrous national products have priority here over eminent ones; interest in "honorable" people is completely missing from the "Queries recommended to the *Curious*" Smith includes in the book on Down, as they are from Robert Plot's *Enquiries To be propounded to the most Ingenious of each County in my Travels through England and Wales, in order to their History of Nature and Arts,* where researchers are directed to uncover precisely the hermaphroditic, long-lived, or revived monsters on whom Smith focuses.[32] The pantheon of honorable men is an "annex" to the gallery of freaks, or, we could say that these figures donate a supplement of eminence, adding the national spirit to the natural body, and in so doing perhaps replacing nature with nation.

But the architecture of Smith's "annex" is not as well designed as that; the logic of the supplement operates neither as a process of accumulation, nor synthesis, nor negation, but rather directs our attention to the spaces opened between the bifurcations and forks in Smith's texts, the cracks in the foundation of his structure, and a more fundamental instability in its attempts to dissect and represent Ireland. The national determinations of Smith's epistemological model, in which Royal Society of London documents and guides formed the basis of collection and representation of Irish data, complicate the "disputes" between countries that Smith evoked as occasioning his chapters on remarkable persons, much as the nationally overdetermined situation of the Anglo-Irish complicates Smith's Irish national political history. The Royal Society, as did the Dublin Physico-Historical Society, proclaimed nationalistic goals and sources for its scientific inquiries. The first official history and manifesto of the group declared that "Nature will reveal more of its secrets to the English, than to others; because it has already furnished them with a Genius so well proportioned, for the receiving, and retaining its mysteries."[33] If the Royal Society model roots scientific epistemology in an English "genius," where does that leave the Anglo-Irish scientist? William Molyneux, who preceded Smith in the creation of Anglo-Irish national identity, similarly preceded him in this form of scientific national ambivalence: in 1683 he founded the Dublin Philosophical Society, a precursor of the Physico-Historical Society, claiming the glory of his discoveries for "our city and nation."[34] At the same time, Molyneux was *also* a fellow of the Royal Society and dedicated one of his books on optics, *Dioptrica Nova* (1692), to the group with the words, "I cannot omit expressing my Sence of that excellent Method of Experimental Philosophy, which now, by your Example and Incouragement, does so universally prevail, and is so highly advanced all over *Europe,* and other Parts of the World."[35]

Molyneux's contemporary Robert Boyle complicates the identity of Irish natural history even further. As we have seen, Smith includes Boyle among the eminent men from Waterford (364), and as one of the sources of his methodology. Working in theological, ethical, philosophical, alchemical, and scientific discourses that themselves reveal multiple affiliations, Boyle's texts are very much in keeping with the epistemological instability between historical, scientific, and nationalist writings that we have been tracing, and accordingly reveal a similar inability to maintain a systematic "Method of Enquiry."[36] At the heart of this method may be Boyle's work on the philosophy and theology of science, *A Free Enquiry into the Vulgarly Received Notion of Nature* (1686), where, rather than the certainty about the natural world one expects from the ideals of taxonomy and classification represented in Smith's "Queries," one sees instead that such classification is bound to be defective. In this text, Boyle tries to define the concept of nature itself, but finds an indeterminate category, for

> the ambiguity of the word is so great . . . and it is even by learned men frequently employed to signify such different things that . . . it were very unsafe to venture a giving a definition of it, and perhaps it were very impossible to give any that would not be liable to censure. I shall not therefore here presume to define a thing of which I have not found a stated and settled notion so far agreed on.[37]

Boyle's book argues not that no definition of *nature* exists, but rather that the surplus of definitions cancel themselves out. The term is made empty through its excess.

Without knowing what nature *is,* Boyle defines it by what it is *not,* arguing that it is neither ordered nor principled and suggesting that it is indistinct from superstition or folk knowledge. After noting that "big-bellied women have been made to miscarry by the smell of an extinguished candle," Boyle claims that "nature is, in these cases, very far from being so prudent and careful as men are wont to fancy her, since by an odour . . . she is put into such unruly transports" (77). Smith too presents an image of an unruly nature when he complains that nature "seems to have sported herself" (*Cork,* 425) in William Clark's skeleton, but for Boyle this sport or unruliness is met by male fantasies about nature's prudence. This conspiracy of unreason prevents us from determining or understanding nature itself. Boyle, in fact, is even harsher in his condemnation of nature, and of claims that it has a reasonable purpose, when he argues that "nature seems to do her work very

weakly or bunglingly in the production of monsters, whose variety and numerousness is almost as great as their deformity or their irregularity" (78),
and tells of other instances of "nature, widely missing her mark" (114),
though, like Smith, he suggests a disciplinary desire in his accusation that nature takes "improper and oftentimes hurtful courses" (78) in producing these
figures. These "monsters" or "aberrations" (119) become the rule for Boyle,
a demonstration of our fundamental incapacity to understand something
that "is so dark and odd a thing, that it is hard to know what to make of it"
(60), except that the "limitations" of our understanding are part of God's
plan (73–76).

So, rather than a method for knowing and representing nature, in his *Free
Enquiry* Boyle concludes that it is instead one of God's mysteries, and that
categories and systems for defining it result in failure. This skeptical text suggests that Boyle is an odd figure with which Smith should identify himself,
just as Boyle's genealogy frustrates Smith's attempts to identify him among
those who would bring honor to Ireland. Boyle's father has been called a
"robber baron of heroic stature" who used "his position to defraud Irish
landowners . . . of their existing titles and to pass title to himself" and expel
"the Irish tenants and replace them with more pliable and profitable English
settlers"; his exploits were so extreme as to attract the hostility of not only
the Catholic but also of the Anglo-Irish.[38] Perhaps due in part to this family history, Boyle himself eschewed the types of national identifications
Molyneux—and Smith—proclaimed, though he made for himself, in the
words of Steven Shapin, "a very particular identity," monstrously composed,
we might say, of three bodies: "the philosopher, the Christian, and the
gentleman."[39]

Boyle's form of particularity, however, was not uniquely in his possession,
for it is in many ways typical of the Anglo-Irish scientist, who needed to defend an interstitial nationality, while seeking to contribute to and articulate
an international project of universal knowledge. The eighteenth-century institution of science within societies and academies brought these tensions between national particularity and universal epistemology into relief by highlighting a "neutral" process of information gathering that is at the same time
an act of epistemological—and actual—colonialism. These Anglo-Irish
helped establish "metropolitan science . . . a way of doing science, based on
learned societies, small groups of cultivators, certain conventions of discourse and certain theoretical priorities," while they *also* furthered the work
of colonial science, "identified with fact gathering," with "the work of theoretical synthesis . . . tak[ing] place elsewhere."[40] National glorification
through local, natural history falls prey in Smith's texts to an episteme that

leaves the nation caught in the trap of representing itself as it is represented in the metropolitan core. The case of Ann Jackson, the "Horny Girl" whose narrative Smith takes from one published seventy years before in the Royal Society's *Philosophical Transactions,* only emphasizes this process; within the *Transactions,* Ann's narrative is denationalized and decontextualized, sandwiched between a report by Boyle on "a strangely Self-moving Liquor," and an "Account of the Aqueduct near Versailles." By reprinting this narrative, Smith is repatriating Ann's monstrous Anglo-Irish corpse, though his nearly verbatim quotation of the *Transactions* account, rather than bringing an Anglo-Irish subject back home, may instead export metropolitan forms of science and representation to Dublin. Understated criticism of the Society within the narrative of William Clark, in which Smith justifies his lengthy discussion because "some relations already published in the Philosoph. Transact. of this skeleton are far from being accurate, nor is the history of his life given there more just" (*Cork,* 426), only reveals the tensions within the "very particular identity" of texts that nonetheless repeatedly proclaim Smith's colonial desire that his *Antient and Present State*s will encourage "foreigners to settle among us" (*Waterford,* ix; see also *Kerry,* ix).

Even disregarding the nationalistic tensions Smith's sources place on his Irish natural history, we find a second fissure running through his taxonomic queries. For Bacon and the Baconian fellows of the Royal Society, the monstrous was an interstitial category, dividing the natural from the artificial, though not quite either of these.[41] At the same time, in various collections and cabinets of the seventeenth and eighteenth centuries, the monsters or freaks held especially prominent places. They were both the fissure that runs through distinctions such as natural and artificial, and the point of their contact. As Elizabeth Grosz writes, "freaks exist outside and in defiance of the structure of binary oppositions that govern our basic concepts and modes of self-definition. . . . They imperil the very definitions we rely on to classify humans, identities, and sexes—our most fundamental categories of self-definition and boundaries dividing self from otherness."[42] The monsters Smith musters collectively cross a series of borders, each of which differently demarcates the space of human essence: the old man who breast-fed his child demonstrates the failure of even so "natural" a distinction as male and female, just as the monstrous birth, William Clark, or Ann Jackson crosses the line separating the nonhuman from the human. The centenarians or the woman who walked from her burial vault only to later give birth shows that somehow death itself is indistinct, as does the image of Clark, a dead man represented as an animated skeleton. These figures show the very limits of the scientific taxonomy into which they are written. While the "Queries recommended to the *Curious*" and Plot's *Enquiries to the most Ingenious* provide proper places within which nationalized nature can be represented, these systems still cannot guarantee a knowledge of their subject. Smith both acknowledges and seeks to correct the epistemic failure of a natural taxonomy that hinges on the unnatural and unclassifiable in his disdain for Jackson's and Clark's improper bodies.

Nature's unwillingness to remain in its categories returns us to those no less problematic categories of the honorable and the remarkable, and their implications for Smith's brand of national promotion. Though the "remarkable" monsters do not bring "honor" to Ireland, their study does. Smith's overarching point is that Ireland is simply "worth" studying by representing, objectifying, or classifying its virtues and wonders, even when its wonders defy classification. In this context, the fact that most of those remarkable persons were dead contributes to this process of national objectification, laying out the national body like a corpse on a dissecting table. What the national heroes and national monsters have in common is that their representation here contributes a sense of uniqueness, or of particularity, to the nation; they allow the nation to claim an identity completely separate from that of other nations, and this uniqueness is itself a source of pride. The family backgrounds Smith provides for these figures further emphasize their individuality—they are real people, born in particular places at particular times, yet who nonetheless collectively merge into a national body that has *its* own particularity. The presence of tombs of unknown soldiers in probably *every* modern nation suggests the reverse, the universality of anonymity: the Unknown Soldier could be any national citizen, or any transnational subject. It may be that early modern Ireland needed more to assert its unique identity against the hegemony of Britain—though if this is so, this identity was split by the hyphen within the Anglo-Irish with whom Smith identified— and hence the unique monster was as important as the original genius, even if, as Plot's *Enquiries* and other sources suggest, monsters populated Britain as well. I am tempted to suggest that the Anglo-Irish monsters that bring so much doubt to categories of humanity, sex, and even life, must represent a sublimated anxiety about the identity of the Anglo-Irish themselves, subjects who live in the space between two known, though no less arbitrary, categories. Yet I am more intrigued by one of Jeffrey Jerome Cohen's theses on "monster culture," that "the monster threatens to destroy not just individual members of a society, but the very cultural apparatus through which individuality is constituted and allowed."[43] In threatening categories of individuality by revealing the process of their conceptual formation, Smith's unique monsters paradoxically help figure forth a collective subject. Later national cemeteries would allow only the eminent into their grounds, while "accidental" or "defective" monsters are kept in jars more appropriate to the curio cabinets of scientists and doctors, where they become lost in the arcana of medical history. Yet the national heroes also become lost, in misremembered national mythology, where they are absorbed into a more universalizing and absolutely fictive national character. Confronting these figures may help us remember the monstrosity of nations themselves, that they are like the two-headed beasts in sideshows, for they turn one face to the ideals of universalism and self-determination, while simultaneously turning another to exclusive particularisms.

NOTES

I presented a different version of this material on a panel at the meeting of the American Society for Eighteenth-Century Studies in 1997, "The Corpse as Spectacle"; my thanks to the panel's organizer, Lorna Clymer, to the audience for helpful comments and questions, and to Susan Edmunds, Helen Deutsch, Felicity Nussbaum, and especially Katie Hauser for comments on earlier drafts.

1. Samuel Johnson, *A Dictionary of the English Language* (London, 1755).

2. Robert Boyle, *A Free Enquiry into the Vulgarly Received Notion of Nature* (1686), ed. Edward B. Davis and Michael Hunter (Cambridge: Cambridge University Press, 1996), 109, 40.

3. Charles Smith, *The Antient and Present State of the County Down. Containing a Chorographical Description, with the Natural and Civil History of the Same* (Dublin, 1744), xiv.

4. Cf. Barbara Maria Stafford's consideration of monstrous and grotesque confusion within a range of physiological, philosophical, and artistic texts in *Body Criticism: Imagining the Unseen in Enlightenment Art and Medicine* (Cambridge, Mass.: MIT Press, 1991), 211–79.

5. Charles Smith, *The Antient and Present State of the County and City of Waterford: being a natural, civil, ecclesiastical, historical and topographical description thereof. . . . Published with the approbation of the Physico-Historical Society* (Dublin, 1746), 359.

6. Georges Canguilhem, *The Normal and the Pathological,* trans. Carolyn R. Fawcett (1978; reprint, New York: Zone Books, 1989), 33.

7. Michel Foucault, introduction to Canguilhem, *Normal and Pathological,* 13.

8. Smith notes in his dedication to *The Antient and Present State of the County of Kerry. Being a Natural, Civil, Ecclesiastical, Historical, and Topographical Description Thereof* (Dublin, 1756) that the Physico-Historical Society's "meetings have been . . . long discontinued," so, as the 1744 book on Down included the first public announcement of their meetings and bylaws, the group could not have lasted much longer than ten years. For another text published in connection with the society, see

W. R. Chetwood, *A tour through Ireland. In several entertaining letters. . . . Humbly inscribed to the Physico-Historical Society* (Dublin, 1746). The antiquarian work of Walter Harris, who may have collaborated with Smith on the book on county Down, shares in the spirit of the texts produced "with the approbation of the Physico-Historical Society"; see his *Hibernica: or, some antient pieces relating to Ireland* (Dublin, 1747) and *The History and Antiquities of the City of Dublin* (Dublin, 1766). Smith's survey of Down was reprinted in 1757; the second of his four works, *The Antient and Present State of the County and City of Waterford*, was first published in 1746, then brought out in an expanded edition in 1773, and reprinted twice in 1774; *The Antient and Present State of the County and City of Cork* was first published in 1750 and again in an expanded edition in 1774, while the final text of the series, *The Antient and Present State of the County of Kerry* (1756), was also expanded and twice printed in 1774.

9. Robert Burrowes, preface to *The Transactions of the Royal Irish Academy* (Dublin, 1787), xiii–xiv.

10. Smith paraphrases Guy Miege, *The Present State of Great Britain, and Ireland, in Three Parts*, 8th ed. (London, 1738), pt. 3, chap. 2, "Of the Antiquity, Inhabitants, Air, Soil, &c. of *Ireland*," 3–8.

11. On what we might call national epistemology, see Nathan Reingold, "The Peculiarities of the Americans; or, Are There National Styles in the Sciences?" *Science in Context* 4 (1991): 347–66.

12. For a broad introduction to the Protestant Ascendancy, see T. W. Moody and W. E. Vaughn, eds., *A New History of Ireland*, vol. 4 (Oxford: Clarendon Press, 1986). Writing about the effects of the penal laws that persecuted the eighteenth-century Irish Catholics, J. C. Beckett observes that they "placed the catholic majority in a markedly inferior position and both protected and demonstrated the dominant status of the protestants. It was they who constituted the 'political nation'" (*New History of Ireland*, 4:xliv). For a quick summary of the laws' reach during the period in which Smith and Harris were writing, see J. L. McCracken, "The Social Structure and Social Life, 1714–60," in *New History of Ireland*, 4:37–39.

13. Swift, "On Barbarous Denominations in Ireland" (n.d.), in *The Prose Works of Jonathan Swift*, ed. Herbert Davis (Oxford: Basil Blackwell, 1957), 4:281.

14. Swift, "Answer to Several Letters from Unknown Hands" (1729), in *Prose Works*, 12:89.

15. Steven Shapin and Simon Schaffer, *Leviathan and the Air-Pump: Hobbes, Boyle, and the Experimental Life* (Princeton: Princeton University Press, 1985), 56.

16. Shapin and Schaffer, *Leviathan and the Air-Pump*, 60–65.

17. Benedict Anderson, *Imagined Communities: Reflections on the Origin and Spread of Nationalism* (1983; rev. ed., London: Verso, 1991), 197, 206.

18. Ernest Gellner, *Nations and Nationalism* (Ithaca: Cornell University Press, 1983), 57.

19. For a strong argument relating Foxe's text to early English nationalism, see William Haller, *The Elect Nation: The Meaning and Relevance of Foxe's "Book of Martyrs"* (New York: Harper, 1963); for a more nuanced view, see Richard Helger-

son, *Forms of Nationhood: The Elizabethan Writing of England* (Chicago: University of Chicago Press, 1992), 254–68.

20. See William H. Epstein, *Recognizing Biography* (Philadelphia: University of Pennsylvania Press, 1987), 34–51, on relations between conventions of empirical observation and biographical writing. Steven Shapin links the study of science to biographical writing as well: "No genre is better established in the history of science and ideas than that of individual biography" (*A Social History of Truth: Civility and Science in Seventeenth-Century England* [Chicago: University of Chicago Press, 1994], 127).

21. Charles Smith, *The Antient and Present State of the County and City of Waterford. Containing a Natural, Civil, Ecclesiastical, Historical and Topographical Description Thereof* (Dublin, 1773), Lumbard, 361; Strange, 362; Richard Boyle, 363; Robert Boyle, 364; Congreve, 374–75. Subsequent references are to this edition.

22. Charles Smith, *The Antient and Present State of the County and City of Cork. Containing a Natural, Civil, Ecclesiastical, Historical and Topographical Description Thereof* (Dublin, 1774), 422.

23. Etienne Balibar, "Racism and Nationalism," in Balibar and Immanuel Wallerstein, *Race, Nation, Class: Ambiguous Identities* (London: Verso, 1991), 47.

24. We may expect no less than this instability of "honor," a moral or ethical category as slippery in the eighteenth century as "virtue"; cf. Michael McKeon, *The Origins of the English Novel, 1600–1740* (Baltimore: Johns Hopkins University Press, 1987); and J. G. A. Pocock, *Virtue, Commerce, and History* (Cambridge: Cambridge University Press, 1985).

25. See Paul Semonin, "Monsters in the Marketplace: The Exhibition of Human Oddities in Early Modern England," in *Freakery: Cultural Spectacles of the Extraordinary Body,* ed. Rosemarie Garland Thomson (New York: New York University Press, 1996), 69–81.

26. Londa Schiebinger, *The Mind Has No Sex: Women in the Origins of Modern Science* (Cambridge, Mass.: Harvard University Press, 1989), 189–213.

27. "*A Letter from Mr* St George Ash, Sec. *of the* Dublin Society, *to one of the* Secretaries *of the* Royal Society; *concerning a* Girl *in* Ireland, *who has several* Horns *growing on her Body,*" *Philosophical Transactions* 176 (November 26, 1685): 1202.

28. St. George Ash, "A Letter," 1202.

29. Steven Shapin's *Social History of Truth* explores the role of civility and politeness in scientific culture.

30. Smith's predecessor in political natural history, Gerard Boate, criticizes an earlier generation of Anglo-Irish for "going native," or succumbing to a process of cultural infection, and thereby losing territory conquered under Henry II: "through the degenerating of a great many from time to time, who joining themselves with the Irish, took upon them their wild fashions and their language, the English in length of time came to be so much weakened, that at last nothing remained to them of the whole Kingdome, worth the speaking of" (*Irelands Naturall History* [London, 1652], 7).

31. Cf. "contrapposto," in Ralph Mayer, *A Dictionary of Art Terms and Techniques* (New York: Thomas Crowell, 1969).

32. Robert Plot, *Enquiries To be propounded to the most Ingenious of each County in my Travels through England and Wales, in order to their History of Nature and Arts* (Oxford, 1679?). Plot asks his researchers, "Know you of any *strange accidents* that have befallen *Men* or *Women?* Of any *Hermaphrodites?* Men or Women *extreamly alike? . . .* of Men of *extream age . . .* of any reputed *dead* that have strangely come to *life* again?"

33. Thomas Sprat, *The History of the Royal Society* (London, 1667), 114–15.

34. Molyneux, quoted in K. Theodore Hoppen, *The Common Scientist in the Seventeenth Century, a Study of the Dublin Philosophical Society, 1683–1708* (London: Routledge and Kegan Paul, 1970), 91.

35. William Molyneux, *Dioptrica Nova. A Treatise of Dioptricks, in Two Parts. Wherein the Various Effects and Appearances of Spherick Glasses, both Convex and Concave, Single and Combined, in Telescopes and Microscopes, Together with Their Usefulness in many Concerns of Humane Life, are Explained* (London, 1692), sig. Ar.

36. For the range of Boyle's discursive activities, see Rose-Mary Sargent, *The Diffident Naturalist: Robert Boyle and the Philosophy of Experiment* (Chicago: University of Chicago Press, 1995); Jan W. Wojcik, *Robert Boyle and the Limits of Reason* (Cambridge: Cambridge University Press, 1997); and the essays in Michael Hunter, ed., *Robert Boyle Reconsidered* (Cambridge: Cambridge University Press, 1994).

37. Boyle, *Free Enquiry*, 105. Subsequent references are given in the text.

38. Shapin, *Social History of Truth*, 132–33.

39. Shapin, *Social History of Truth*, 191.

40. Roy MacLeod, "On Visiting the 'Moving Metropolis': Reflections on the Architecture of Imperial Science," in *Scientific Colonialism: A Cross Cultural Comparison*, ed. Nathan Reingold and Marc Rothenberg (Washington, D.C.: Smithsonian Institution Press, 1987), 220–21.

41. On Bacon and the monstrous, see Semonin, "Monsters in the Marketplace."

42. Elizabeth Grosz, "Intolerable Ambiguity: Freaks as/at the Limit," in Thomson, *Freakery*, 57.

43. Jeffrey Jerome Cohen, "Monster Culture (Seven Theses)," in *Monster Theory: Reading Culture*, ed. Cohen (Minneapolis: University of Minnesota Press, 1996), 12.

The Author as Monster: The Case of Dr. Johnson

Helen Deutsch

In the eyes of his contemporaries, Samuel Johnson was both a monument and a monster. He was, in other words, the image of an author. At once subject and object, printed voice and aberrant spectacle, the Dr. Johnson who longed for what he praised in his elegy to his friend, the unlettered surgeon Robert Levet, as "the power of art without the show," embodied literary authority as a paradox for his age. The immortal Johnson whose distinctive style of writing and speaking lives on in English literature classrooms across the country as a signature for certainty, enacted in his mortal person a series of apparently compulsive movements, mutterings, and rituals that in different ways to different viewers compromised agency itself. Dubbed by contemporaries both Great Cham and Caliban of Literature, the spectacle of Johnson's body in perpetual motion was inextricably linked during his own time to a distinctively fixed literary style.[1] This essay works to uncover the historical logic of a link that Johnsonians of our own day have tended to ignore, a link that in its own time took the form of the vanity of authorial wishes.

For eighteenth-century England the case of Johnson—and by "case" I mean at once "body" and "example"—united style with substance, text with body, universal truth with the individual writer, posing paradoxes that attempted to make personal agency and interiority legible on the body of the author. My purpose here is not merely to reinforce an enduring impression of Johnson's immeasurable greatness, nor to write a familiar narrative (one critiqued by Lennard J. Davis in this volume) of a powerful mind heroically overcoming a defective body. Rather, this essay contemplates Johnson's singularity as representative of a late-eighteenth-century chapter in the Western formulation of the mind-body problem during which mind and body, through the complex workings of sensibility, are both inextricably interconnected and inscribed in each other's image. Neither the once-sacred body of the king, nor the incorruptible body of the saint, nor the malleable body of the actor, the unique body of the eighteenth-century author figures the ineffable and embattled substance of individuality and intention.[2] I begin with a meditation on the relation between the seemingly meaningless repetition of Johnson's tics and the meaningful repetition of his literary style, paying special attention to his use of that most condensed of vehicles for paradox, the heroic couplet (inherited from another authorial monster, Alexander Pope) in one of his most thematically representative texts, *The Vanity of Human Wishes*. I then consider Johnson as an embodied figure of such "vanity," by pondering eighteenth-century definitions of and speculations about those "convulsive starts and odd gesticulations"[3] that so fascinated audiences in polite drawing rooms and that have recently been diagnosed as a twentieth-century medical version of mind-body interconnection, Tourette's syndrome. What follows, in short, reflects on the ways in which Johnson's physical particularity turned authorship into a performance, an enactment of agency by a body in motion that made monstrosity exemplary.

The Ends of Style

> Years foll'wing Years, steal something ev'ry day,
> At last they steal us from our selves away;
> In one our Frolicks, one Amusements end,
> In one a Mistress drops, in one a Friend:
> This subtle Thief of Life, this paltry Time,
> What will it leave me, if it snatch my Rhyme?
> If ev'ry Wheel of that unweary'd Mill
> That turn'd ten thousand Verses, now stands still.[4]

One of the first readers to link Alexander Pope's body of work to his physical corpus was Samuel Johnson, whose mercilessly detailed description of Pope's shrunken form in his *Life of Pope* seems determined to reanchor Pope's polished art in the writer's aberrant body. There Johnson's account of Pope's "petty peculiarities" reduces his most important predecessor as a professional author to a helplessly feminized "person well known not to have been formed by the nicest model," a person deformed, in fact, by excessive literary effort, a fleshly allegory for the vanity of authorial wishes.[5] Johnson's scrutiny of Pope's body points us toward an eighteenth-century reading of authorship as visibly and aberrantly embodied personification, a figure that Pope himself exploited to his own advantage. Pope's literary career was modeled on deformity's ambiguity; shaping, and shaped by, the "monstrous contingency" of modern authorship. Throughout this poet's life of literary imitation, deformity guaranteed him a marked and marred originality. As I have argued in *Resemblance and Disgrace: Alexander Pope and the Deformation of Culture,* for Pope, deformity and form made the ultimate couplet, a couplet that, as this section tries to show, Johnson both resisted and rewrote.[6] My ongoing work investigates the connections between physical difference, authorship, and literary form in eighteenth-century British culture by examining individual authorial cases while interrogating the idea and the ideology of the exemplary case itself. What follows is a necessarily short venture into a continuing project.[7]

This brief excerpt from Pope's imitation of Horace's second epistle of the second book with which this section begins condenses a literary tradition into a metronome of loss and finally into a contemplation of death. The evocation of time's predation through the couplet's hierarchy of pauses—all but the second and penultimate line relying heavily on caesuras, the second couplet's emphasis on "one" like the relentless ticking of a cosmic clock—culminates in a semiapostrophe to time's force that echoes a host of predecessors from Pope himself, to Dryden, to Milton, to Montaigne, before turning to a startlingly original moment of emotional self-revelation: "what will it leave me, if it snatch my rhyme?" That blunt monosyllabic question with its emphasis on the violence of "snatch," as stark as the line that preceded it is musically overdetermined, is then rephrased, paradoxically, as the poet's contemplation of himself as machine devoid of affect and of agency, "that unwearied mill / that turn'd ten thousand verses," and, finally, devoid of life imagined as the power to write, "Now stands still."

What can these lines, with their exceptional lyrical power in a poetry more often satiric or didactic than plaintive, reveal about Pope's control over and submission to the couplet form? What can they begin to tell us about the relationship of literary style to the body of the author? How does poetic form possess, even figure, those who create by its means? How, to invert the question, is style a kind of embodiment of meaning at once inimitable and imitated? How then, does Samuel Johnson, in part through his own idiosyncratic use of the couplet, inherit and transform his predecessor's work as monarch of letters into his own ambivalent brand of embodied literary authority? The curious fact that the two most prominent men of letters in eighteenth-century England were so strikingly physically visible in such different ways was at once coincidental—who could have predicted Pope's tuberculosis of the spine or Johnson's nervous tics?—and overdetermined.

These two authorial bodies were as much framed by cultural modes of

vision as they were arbiters of cultural production; for both writers, style depended on embodied particulars and, like the body itself, at once signified
and limited individuality and agency. For Pope at this moment, style at once
subsumes and threatens to erase the self: the silent answer to the multivalent
question "what will it leave me?" as subject and object waver in the balance,
is "nothing."

Yet this contemplation of the end is the English poem's incentive to continue. Pope uses the couplet at this moment, in a remarkably compressed example of a career of literary imitation, to revive his literary predecessors with
dazzling virtuosity. But the couplet logic of this passage balances such general resurrection with a kind of personal death, rendering the poet a personification of poetic form itself, a couplet machine. The ensuing prospect
of inspiration's absence, of standing still, allows Pope a moment of what we
could call the couplet sublime, a sublime at once dynamic and mathematical
in its possible erasure of the self and its personal end to potentially infinite
repetition. In keeping with the logic of the sublime, however, the thought of
self-extinction is recuperated as self-affirmation. Rather than end, Pope
transforms his version of Horace's decorous sacrifice of lyric poetry for a life
of philosophy into an affirmation of all poetry as satire and his own identity
as heroic satirist. Horace submits himself to the rules of propriety: "It is time
for you to go," the Latin version ends, "lest, having drunk too much, a more
properly playful age should laugh and push you out of their way." But Pope
submits propriety—the "grace and ease" of writing that he had celebrated
in the youthful *Essay on Criticism*—to satire's strict scrutiny, leaving himself
permanently on the stage of satire, not form's servant but its judge.

> Walk sober off; before a sprightlier Age
> Comes titt'ring on, and shoves you from the stage:
> Leave such to trifle with more grace and ease,
> Whom Folly pleases, and whose Follies please.
> (324–27)

For Johnson, the couplet after Pope, and with it the genre of literary imitation, are both forms of monstrosity. Johnson had dismissed Pope's mas-
terpieces of self-fashioning, the Horatian poems, in *The Life of Pope* as "uncouth and parti-colored; neither original nor translated, neither ancient nor
modern,"[8] in much the same way that contemporary lampooners, Mary
Wortley Montagu and John Hervey first among them, had dismissed both
Pope himself and his imitations as at once "resemblance and disgrace" of human and classical originals.[9] Yet Johnson also mourned, however melan-
cholically, Pope's earlier witty age when it "was worth while being a dunce"

and accompanied that pronouncement with the boast that it was his own imitation of Juvenal's third satire, *London,* that caused Pope himself to inquire the author and opine that "he will soon be *déterré.*"[10]

Johnson's emulatory respect for Pope is haunted by a powerful desire to expose the emptiness of his predecessor's artifice; authorial art is the greatest vanity. In his *Life of Pope,* for example, he observes of Pope's grotto with a modicum of contempt, "as some men try to be proud of their defects, he extracted an ornament from an inconvenience, and vanity produced a grotto where necessity enforced a passage."[11] The biographer's studied disavowal, his reduction to "vanity," in the coupletlike balance of this sentence's satire of the very key to Pope's authority—the transformation of natural lack into aesthetic power—demonstrates his drive to undo that authority, to reduce Pope's art to its origins in defect.

Pope's seamless paradoxes of couplet form embody for Johnson a prospect of art without "end," without closure or moral purpose. The vanity of such couplet art expands by analogy, constituting not just the self but the divinely ordered world, culminating in the *Essay on Man*'s "All Nature is but Art Unknown to thee," and Soame Jenyns's smug defense of that poem's proclamation of "Whatever IS is RIGHT." In his relentlessly logical refutation of Jenyns's *A Free Enquiry into the Nature and Origin of Evil,* with the same excruciating detail with which he would later describe Pope's body, Johnson rejects what he reads as Jenyns's and Pope's endorsement of a great chain of being in which all endings are happy, thereby exposing the impossibility of intelligible order: "In the scale, wherever it begins or ends, are infinite vacuities. . . . So that, as far as we can judge, there may be room in the vacuity between any two steps of the scale or between any two points of the cone of being, for infinite exertion of infinite power."[12] Johnson's description of Jenyns's and Pope's universe could also be read as a formal appreciation of the power of the couplet to create a seemingly infinite variety through the repetitions of two lines, a paradoxical openness to the couplet's closure. Having thus done away with the possibility of an infinite repetition that for him amounts to aesthetic cruelty, Johnson asserts another sort of end: "The only end of writing is to enable the readers better to enjoy life, or better to endure it; and how will either of those be put more in our power by him who tells us that we are puppets, of which some creature not much wiser than ourselves manages the wires?" (536).

The couplet in this view becomes an empty means with which to confront and control emptiness. Unable to stomach Pope's ability to pause from life in order to extend the domain of letters, Johnson bases his own authority on his instructions to the aspiring scholar in the *Vanity,* to "pause a while from letters to be wise."[13] When Johnson fully appropriates the couplet in *The Vanity of Human Wishes,* he rejects the monstrosity of Pope's spectacularly visible self-authorization, his refusal to leave the stage of writing, through a transformation of form itself. The *Vanity's* form demonstrates that the author of perfect art must be brought back to the body, and reminds every author that he is authored by another.[14]

If Pope's indelibly marked deformity allowed him to embody imitative originality for a public newly obsessed with the author's person and literary property, Johnson's "tricks," "antics," "convulsions," and "gesticulations," as we shall see, put authority on display by turning it to perpetual motion without apparent end, as if determined by the rhythms of the couplet itself. So distinctive is this style's analogical linkage of gesture to thought to conversation to printed word that it becomes an icon for imitators from Garrick to Boswell to contemporary Johnsonians. Boswell wished that Johnson's "bow-wow way" could be "preserved as music is written," and Hannah More, "umpire in a trial of skill between Garrick and Boswell, which could most nearly imitate Dr. Johnson's manner, . . . gave it for Boswell in familiar conversation, and for Garrick in reciting poetry," which the latter did, according to Boswell's description of one couplet performance, "with ludicrous exaggeration . . . with pauses and half-whistlings interjected, looking downwards all the time, and, while pronouncing the four last words, absolutely touching the ground with a kind of contorted gesticulation." Even Johnson's seesawing—"his head," one female observer remarked, "swung seconds"— seemed a kind of bodily mimicry of the couplet; while William Cooke's observation of his "rolling about his head, as if snuffing up his recollection," before breaking out into twenty lines of Juvenal's tenth satire (the source for the *Vanity*) in the original Latin marks a similar purpose to a seemingly meaningless act.[15] And his mode of composition of the *Vanity,* ordering the rhythms of potentially obsessive thoughts into the regularity of the couplet form almost without writing's mediation, elucidates Johnson's characteristic opening of the couplet into larger blocks than Pope's: Boswell marvels at the "fervent rapidity" with which the poem was written, remarking that Johnson "composed seventy lines of it in one day, without putting one of them upon paper till they were finished."[16]

The *Vanity's* rejection of satire, which Johnson's choice of Juvenal as model after Pope's Horace would seem to belie, its enactment of what Walter Jackson Bate called satire manqué, the continually "active balance" with which it undoes and expands its own impulses to judge (its brutality to Swift, who "expires a Driv'ler and a Show" [318], is as much a result of that impulse as of its failure),[17] its near-obsessive reliance upon personification and abstraction, its resistance to narrative in the form of endless repetition of the same end to every attempt at self-signification, its disembodied preoccupation with the visible and with the destructive power of objectification, and its final abandonment of agency and closure in the form of a prayer, demonstrate the same Johnsonian couplet of meaningful and meaningless repetition. From the perspective of the *Vanity's* melancholic reduction of all human attempts at distinction to the same meaningless end, the perpetual motions of Johnson's tics, much like Pope's image of himself as an unwearied couplet-mill, render the great author a kind of personification of self-destructive intention. In all his oddity, peculiarity, and particularity, Johnson the man becomes an exemplary character precisely because of his resistance to perfect form. The detritus, the scattered waste of the synecdochal signs of fame that fill the *Vanity,* and the satirist's thwarted and at times angry voice ("But hear his Death, ye Blockheads, hear and sleep" [174]), all evidence the death-ridden inevitability of particular embodiment, which Johnson sees through and mourns in the *Vanity* and which brought him to life.[18] The personifications of the *Vanity,* in this regard, have a curiously contagious effect, threatening to reduce even the disembodied author to a rhetorical and physical figure.[19]

The Johnsonian penchant for personification, while extreme, and noted by many of his critics as characteristic of his style,[20] was far from unique. The proliferation of personification in the eighteenth-century, as Steven Knapp has shown, signaled a larger cultural anxiety about the animating power of enthusiastic agency and its excess; the trope's rhetorical contagion threatened absurdity, or worse, solipsistic fanaticism.[21] When Johnson criticizes Milton's licentious use of allegory in the personification of Sin and Death in *Paradise Lost,* for example, he is also implicitly censuring a Miltonic authority nearly Satanic in its excess.

Johnson's personifications in the *Vanity* are by contrast strictly rhetorical. They govern a poem about the futility of action by the power of their own limitations. In reading them, Chester Chapin claims, "the impulse toward visualization . . . is rather a hindrance than a help."[22] But by the sheer weight of their stasis, these figures become curiously animate, possessing as much "metaphorical force" as the verbs that they rule, bringing even grammatical relations to life: "Where then shall Hope and Fear their Objects find?" (343). Chapin characterizes these vivified abstractions as couplets in miniature, balancing moral truth and individual examples in "verbal reflection of a particular moral paradox."[23]

From this perspective we can read the opening lines of the *Vanity,* a poem in which the human agents are as empty of meaning as the rhetorical ones, as ticlike in its compulsion to repeat—"let Observation with extensive View, / Survey Mankind from *China* to *Peru*." At once controlled and excessive, the grandeur of this evocation of a universality at once abstract and spatial, its magisterial surrender of agency by an imperative to Observation that erases any particular observer, and its elaboration of a simple action into a series of ornate repetitions, all typify the Johnsonian style in the simultaneous undermining and evocation of meaningful purpose. Coleridge paraphrased the line with acute annoyance, "Mere bombast and tautology as if to say 'Let observation with extensive observation observe mankind extensively.'"[24]

Similarly, just as nervous tics have been described as the bodily hieroglyphics of a personal narrative whose origins have atrophied into mere mechanics,[25] so the hypercondensed careers in *The Vanity* serve only to point morals and adorn tales. Just as the dynamic fluidity of fictional agents in Milton threatens contagion to ostensibly "real" agents, so the Johnsonian personification's yoking of "live" metaphors to dead abstractions[26] infects the poem's historical subjects and renders them personified characters, "moral paradoxes" in a plotless, redundant story. It is the personifications who act, "Hope and Fear, Desire and Hate" who "O'erspread with Snares the clouded Maze of Fate" (5–6), while the poem's persons, no matter how active, seem by contrast curiously passive. Wolsey and Marlborough are particular examples no more nor less vivid than the unnamed "young Enthusiast" (136), whose quest for scholarly fame moved Johnson to tears in the reading of it. Names in the poem often serve as encapsulated history, the narrative impulse truncated to a single word. This poem, to which only a prayer can put an arbitrary end,[27] by "pierc[ing] each Scene with Philosophic Eye" (64) reframes both history and its authors as spectacle.

The *Vanity* makes us aware of the inadequacy of its own attempts at order, even though such attempts are as insatiable in their own way as those of the ambitious, greedy subjects it portrays. Even the anonymous bearer of a reasonable wish in the poem's context—the wish for a life without narrative, the progression of "An Age that melts with unperceiv'd Decay, / And glides in modest Innocence away" (293–94), a potentially endless life as unconscious subject and invisible object—is consumed by the poem's relentless need to close:

> Year chases Year, Decay pursues Decay,
> Still drops some Joy from with'ring Life away;
> New Forms arise, and diff'rent Views engage,
> Superfluous lags the Vet'ran on the Stage,

> Till pitying Nature signs the last Release,
> And bids afflicted Worth retire to Peace.
> (305–10)

Johnson rewrites even the humble life that replaces ambitious solipsism with what he would similarly praise in his elegy to Robert Levet as the "narrow round" of social virtue, the submission to an inhumanly regular process of inevitable loss that makes its end—Nature's signing of a "last Release" from life refigured as debt—like the end of the poem itself, a devoutly-to-be-wished escape from selfhood. The passage with which we began, Pope's poignantly personal identification with, and refusal to abandon, the couplet form, is directly alluded to here, but Pope's satiric end is collapscd into its beginning, and individual authorship generalized into the inevitable progression of general art and shifting perspective: "New Forms arise and different Views engage." Johnson transforms Pope's heroic refusal to stand still into a universal desire for an end to life's infinite gradations of loss. Both Pope's original appropriation of imitation's stage with deformity's trademark, and Johnson's impersonal subjection of individuality on that same stage to a divine author's ends, form particular couplets of mind and body, of the disembodied power of art with the embodied particulars of spectacle and show. Both authors are monstrous characters and national monuments in the eighteenth-century theater of authorship.

Couplets

> Let Observation with extensive View,
> Survey Mankind, from *China* to *Peru.*

What can Johnson's particular use of the couplet form in poetry, a form in which he was distinguished but not prolific, tell us about a style that was predominantly defined in prose? If we frame the paradoxes of *The Vanity of Human Wishes* with contemporary criticisms of Johnson's style at the end of his career, his highly compressed couplets seem to bear the same relation to his prose that his prose—in its excessive artfulness, its ornate Latinity, its elaborate balance of abstractions, and its (to some) monstrous hybridity—bears to the plain style that many of his critics favored, and that Johnson himself bears to the general idea of authorship. Making explicit the thematic preoccupations that haunt Johnson's work throughout his career, *The Vanity* demonstrates in exceptionally concentrated form how style for Johnson is itself an empty performance, a defamiliarization of mimesis that advertises its own artifice, rendering itself a vain spectacle.

Johnson's vivification of abstraction in his prose is both a formal problem and a philosophical and epistemological project. Formally the question concerns the utility of particular detail for conveying general truth: how to make meaning most effective, persuasive, and emphatic without numbering the streaks of the tulip? Philosophically (and thematically) the dilemma involves the effectiveness of exemplarity itself: how to distinguish one's own sentiments from general truth, how to cut a figure in the world, without coming to the same vain end?[28] Johnson's desire to delight a large audience through instruction thus is undermined by an awareness of that or any desire's futility. If we begin with an awareness of how the genre of literary imitation intensified the questions of authorship and originality that preoccupied both Johnson and his audience, *The Vanity* can be read as the exemplary form of Johnson's public prose, the mournful strain that haunts its sonorous distinction.

By uncovering the structural homology that links Johnson's poetic style to his nervous tics we make visible his paradoxical relationship to originality, to authorship, and to agency. By taking on the couplet form and the imitation of Roman satire, Johnson lets himself be partially determined by his most formidable satiric neoclassical predecessor, Alexander Pope, in the act of writing his own distinction. Style thus appears to be both a kind of compulsion, and a singularity vulnerable to imitation, suspended, like tics and habits, between volition and its lack. Such paradigmatic authority invites readers to disavow its particular origins in ambivalence about self-assertion: this most celebrated of talkers, whose "language was so accurate, and his sentences so neatly constructed, that his conversation might have been all printed without any correction," never spoke in public until he was spoken to;[29] this most prolific of authors famously insisted that "no man but a blockhead ever wrote, except for money."[30] In all its emulable substance, distinctive literary style generates itself out of the void that the *Vanity* repetitively evokes in commemorative erasure of all attempts at personal distinction, out of an ambivalent response to the poet's own authorial self-consciousness and ambition.

In the potentially self-effacing poetry of classical imitation Johnson's labors were unmistakably his own and irrefutably opaque. David Garrick echoed many criticisms of Johnson's difficult prose when he complained that the *Vanity* was "as hard as Greek."[31] The first section of this essay contrasted Johnson with Pope in order to consider what was distinctive about Johnson's use of the couplet form. I would now like to consider how

Garrick's jest resonates with other critical accounts of Johnson's prose that saw him as monstrous in his distinction. Archibald Campbell's Lexiphanes and Charles Churchill's Pomposo[32] begin a series of parodies and criticisms of Johnson's "hard words," ornate and excessively Latinate language, that persists after his death. William Cadogan, in his marginalia to Boswell's *Life*, remarks, "His Brutality and thy Folly, Bozzy, were ever, I believe, very prominent & *con*spicuous & his Style i.e. the construction & form of his sentences was easy & *per*spicuous—they were without difficulty analysed, but without his Dictionary not to be understood."[33] Cadogan's contrast of the clear visibility of the great man's "brutality" with the easy opacity of his prose links embodied presence to the printed word by emptying style of substance.[34]

William Burrowes astutely identifies Johnson's penchant for Latin phrases as a kind of poetification of prose, and similarly focuses on the seductively audible, rather than visual or clearly comprehensible, nature of Johnson's distinction in print: "The first of these reasons for substituting, in place of a received familiar English word, a remote philosophical one, such as are most of Johnson's Latin abstract substantives, is its being more pleasing to the ear. But this can only be deemed sufficient by those who would submit sense to sound, and for the sake of being admired by some, would be content not to be understood by others."[35] For Burrowes, Johnson's catering to the ear is a cultivation of deliberate obscurity; his style thus becomes an accumulation of "confirmed and prevailing habits," and a dangerous imperial project, "new-raised colonies disdaining an association with the natives, and threatening the final destruction of our language" (30–31). Johnson's style in this account is monstrous, confounding the distinction between poetry and prose, overly singular in its willful exclusion of women and unlearned readers in its attempts at erudition (29),[36] and, like any great style based on "peculiarities" (29), contagious: "many . . . from admiration of his general excellence are led at last involuntarily to resemble him" (42), just as Burrowes often seems, either voluntarily or involuntarily, to be imitating Johnson himself.[37] Stylistic ambition makes Johnson not manly but deviant and indecipherable; just as, "determined to deviate from the English language," Johnson in his "antipathy to the French," becomes not more English but rather a Latinate hybrid (40). In his refusal of Frenchness but incorporation of the foreign matter that informs Frenchness—Latinity—into English, Johnson resists while promoting the coherence of the English national body and lays bare the process of exchange the English language ought to aestheticize and conceal.[38]

These responses to Johnson's prose take on new meaning in light of Neil

Saccamano's reading of Joseph Addison's use of the concept of false wit in the *Spectator* to delineate proper agency as the proper embodiment of language.[39] False wit, in this account, made visible when language's agency, the authority of the verbal frame itself, becomes apparent, tortures language figured as body. The figure of the body is a kind of narcissistic projection, as I read it, of cultural fantasies of agency, wholeness, coherent limits, individuality, and iterability that false wit disrupts. The paradox that Addison in particular, and Augustan writers more generally, continually confront is the interrelation of nature and art, which this essay has figured as Johnson's particular exemplification of the mind-body problem. Both Addison's fantasy of self-regulating nature, and Johnson's efforts at self-evident exemplary truths, are haunted by an awareness that the singular is difficult to distinguish from artifice, mimesis, and monstrosity.

The critical language about Johnson's stylistic deformity, in this context, renders the author not as an *agent* of false wit but somehow an object of it. Johnson's prose displays itself as a body deformed by art (deformed bodies may be unnatural—made not born), a monstrous blend of poetry and prose, art and artlessness. As an author, Johnson embodies the paradox of repeatable singularity, almost as though he stands for the untranslatable power of language itself, and the ways in which language compromises any author's control.

James Thomson Callender's *Deformities of Doctor Johnson* (1782) is one of many texts to demonstrate style's basis in personal, embodied peculiarity and habit. In Johnson's particular case, style's link to the body has a degrading force. Callender's title page epigraph from *Rambler* 176 aptly quotes Johnson's judgment that "*baiting* an AUTHOR . . . is more lawful than the sport of teizing other *animals*, because for the most part HE comes voluntarily to the stake."[40] Here that which elevates an author above an animal, his will, is that which renders him less than human. John Courtenay in *A Poetical Review of the Literary and Moral Character of the Late Samuel Johnson* (1786), attempting to distinguish the literary from the moral when considering Johnson as an example (a project with which Johnson himself, for whom character was always exemplary, allegorical, and enlivened by its peculiarities, would have been in sympathy),[41] creates in couplets a kind of metacouplet that balances Johnson's moral "foibles" with his stylistic "peculiarities":

> In solemn pomp, with pedantry combin'd,
> He vents the morbid sadness of his mind;
> In scientifick phrase affects to smile,
> Formed on Brown's turgid Latin-English style.[42]

While laboring to distinguish the man from the author, Courtenay's couplet logic unites moral foible with prose peculiarity in the language of defect. Most shocking is a comparison of Johnson's fear of death to that of Maecenas, which balances pagan superstition with failed Christian heroism:

> A coward wish, long stigmatiz'd by fame,
> Devotes Maecenas to eternal shame;
> Religious Johnson, future life to gain,
> Would ev'n submit to everlasting pain:
> How clear, how strong, such kindred colours paint
> The Roman epicure and Christian saint!

Courtenay goes on to comment that Maecenas, "had he liv'd in more enlighten'd times," would have trembled at the 1680 comet, or Mary Toft's mock births. In a note to this passage, Maecenas's words haunt Johnson's deathbed declaration with a vision of deformity:

> Let me but live, the fam'd Maecenas cries,
> Lame of both hands, and lame in feet and thighs;
> Hump-back'd, and toothless;—all convuls'd with pain,
> Ev'n on the cross,—so precious life remain.[43]

The eponymous patron of the arts is united with the exemplary author who defied aristocratic patronage in the fear of death and the language of deformity that makes the self a spectacle. Courtenay's comparison unites not only pagan and Christian but also monster and man, nobleman and slave (for only slaves die on the cross), and finally subject and object, moralizing and internalizing the language of deformity as it articulates an inner fear. Defect is no longer associated explicitly with Johnson's body but rather with what is implied to be, as the Roman and the Englishman blur, his superstition and credulity, his unenlightened affinity for monsters and divine signs. Just such a hybrid being, in its Christianization of a Roman text, and in its fear of an end, is Johnson's *Vanity of Human Wishes;* just such a monster is Johnson himself.

Re-viewing

The Victorian image of Boswell's Johnson is the culmination of a nation's sustained gaze at the author as grotesque tableau, a gaze become by the nineteenth century almost childishly sentimental:

In the foreground is that strange figure which is as familiar to us as the figures of those among whom we have been brought up, the gigantic body, the huge massy face, seamed with the scars of disease, the brown coat, the black worsted stockings, the grey wig with the scorched foretop, the dirty hands, the nails bitten and pared to the quick. We see the eyes and mouth moving with convulsive twitches; we see the heavy form rolling; we hear it puffing; and then comes the "Why, sir!" and the "What then, sir?" and the "No, sir;" and the "You don't see your way through the question, sir!"

What a singular destiny has been that of this remarkable man! To be re-garded in his own age as a classic, and in ours as a companion! To receive from his contemporaries that full homage which men of genius in general re-ceived only from posterity! To be more intimately known to posterity than other men are known to their contemporaries! That kind of fame which is commonly the most transient is, in his case, the most durable. The reputation of those writings, which he probably expected to be immortal, is every day fading; while those peculiarities of manner and that careless table-talk the memory of which, he probably thought, would die with him, are likely to be remembered as long as the English language is spoken in any quarter of the globe.[44]

While Lord Macaulay's vision is based on Boswell's *Life of Johnson* (1791), what follows will remind us that Boswell's "flemish painting" of a biogra-phy, while perhaps the most careful in its use of personal detail,[45] was far from unique in its close attention to Johnson's bodily particularity. John Wol-cot among many others complained of those biographers, particularly Boswell and Hester Thrale, who, following Johnson's own example in *The Lives of the Poets,*

> Blest! . . . his philosophic phiz can *take,*
> *Catch* ev'n his *weaknesses*—his NODDLE's shake.[46]

Macaulay's response to Boswell, his lingering close-ups on bodily details, doc-ument the durable transience the *Life* has most successfully constructed from such careful scrutiny of Johnson's peculiarities. "I have *Johnsonised* the land;" Boswell declares, "and I trust they will not only *talk,* but *think* Johnson."[47]

Boswell's hope that his biography will transform the theatrical mimicry of "talking" Johnson into the internalized identification of "thinking" John-son hints at a tension between the unique oddity of Johnson's physical pres-ence and the universal wisdom and imitable expression of his words. "It is certain," Boswell writes of the *Rambler* in particular and Johnson's style in general, "that his example has given a general elevation to the language of his country, for many of our best writers have approached very near to him; and, from the influence which he has had upon our composition, scarcely any thing is written now that is not better expressed than was usual before he appeared to lead the national taste."[48] This tension between exemplary authoritative style and singular defect is also a connection, a connection that is a constant subtext, we might even say the subconscious, of the *Life*. When we bring the British fascination with Johnson's body back into view in its panoply of representations, we set it against his monumental authorial person and exemplary voice; in the process we are compelled to see the latter in the former's image.[49]

Properly "Johnsonised," both Boswell and Macaulay assert a national "we" based on a vision at once intimately personal and collective, an author-turned-character's immortal fame, remembered as long as the English language (linked in Macaulay's account to the terrain of the British empire) endures, built from eccentrically embodied trifles. Possessed of a style irresistibly imitable yet incapable of impersonation,[50] of a body at once super- and subhuman marked by its excesses and lacks,[51] neither completely manly, nor properly gentlemanly, Johnson comes to mirror the nation's imagination of itself as language in an unruly balance of universal transparency and aberrant detail.[52]

The disembodied counterpart of Macaulay's familiar recognition of Johnson is described by Boswell in an account of reading the great man's prose:

> What I read now elevated my mind wonderfully. I know not if I can explain what I have felt, but I think the high test of great writing is when we do not consider the writer, and say, "Here Mr. Johnson has done nobly"; but when what we read does so fill and expand our mind that the writer is admired by us instantaneously as being directly impressing us, as the soul of that writing, so that for a while we forget his personality, and, by a reflex operation, perceive that it is Mr. Johnson who is speaking to us.[53]

While Macaulay transforms Boswell's book into a vision of Johnson's body, Boswell's experience of Johnson's text perceives not the author's "person" but his "soul," not an image of the great man but the writer's unmistakable "voice." Boswell's recognition of Johnson, and his shift, paralleling Macaulay's, from "I" to "we," is contingent upon the reader's failure "to consider the writer"; only when the author has been completely forgotten can he be remembered, ghostlike, by an involuntary "reflex operation." As Boswell's reading self is momentarily fused with what it reads in a kind of textual sublime, the recollection of reading becomes a description of hearing: to fail to consider Johnson the writer is to be in the presence of the speaking voice itself.

After considering Johnson's moral flaws, John Courtenay remarks:

> But who to blaze his frailties feels delight,
> When the great author rises to our sight?
> When the pure tenour of his life we view,
> Himself the bright exemplar that he drew?
> Whose works console the good, instruct the wise,
> And teach the soul to claim her kindred skies.[54]

In this case, once personal frailties have been reviewed they are rejected so that the author is completely fused with the man, the "tenour of his life" made identical to "his works." "Johnson" like Pope's Longinus in his *Essay on Criticism*, "is himself the great Sublime he draws." To read him is to envision the author himself as exemplary.[55]

Defining

> Since the eighteenth century the word *tic* has faced the perils of definition many a time, and has as often all but succumbed.
> —Henry Meige and E. Feindel, *Tics and Their Treatment* (1902)

The word *tic,* a locus classicus for the mind-body link,[56] is a French import to English, brought into medical discourse (its first usage in the *OED* is from an 1824 medical journal) from the lower reaches of "popular expression" in order to resolve "the perils of definition" of bodily motions without proper names. The preface to Meige and Feindel's classic and groundbreaking 1902 study, *Tics and Their Treatment,* the first in the wake of Charcot and Gilles de la Tourette to theorize extensively the nature of tics, pays special attention to the "justice" the two have done to the word *tic* itself, remarking,

> If popular expression sometimes confounds where experts distinguish, in revenge it is frequently so apt that it forces itself into the vocabulary of the scientist. In the case under consideration Greek and Latin are at fault. The meaning of the word tic is so precise that a better adaptation of a name to an idea, or of an idea to a name, is scarcely conceivable, while the fact of its occurrence in so many languages points to a certain specificity in its definition.[57]

From the perspective of this essay's preoccupation with style and its link to embodiment, the simple word *tic* thus can seem to be a kind of lexicographical cure, a mark of scientific objective precision, in contrast to the deliberate and ornate Latinity of the Johnsonian style of the *Rambler.* These twentieth-century medical efforts to define it properly have their roots in eighteenth-century literary and medical ambiguities.

The opening sentence of *Tics and Their Treatment* is definitive in its understanding of the history of a set of nervous symptoms as primarily a linguistic problem. These doctors rescue the word *tic* from etymological ambiguity and almost inevitable misunderstanding. Such salvation from "the perils of definition," a phrase almost Johnsonian in its near personification of an abstraction, would set proper limits for the word "tic" itself and the body in motion it delineates: "our work will not be superfluous," their preface concludes, "if we succeed in allotting to the word a definite position in medical terminology, or if any information we have amassed prove of service to future observers."[58] For these authors, tics, unlike the involuntary spasms with which they are often confused, manifest a degenerate disease of the will, and can be treated by discipline: "the man who tics has both the debility and impulsiveness of the child. . . . He does not know how to will; he wills too much or too little, too quickly, too restrictedly."[59] If "tic was a psychical disease in a physical guise,"[60] proper diagnosis became a form of seeing through the body, an unmasking of physical gesture that relied upon proper linguistic terminology. Clearly defined words would therefore lead to properly observed, properly diagnosed, and ultimately properly controlled bodies.

In Johnson's own time, his erratic movements, when not diagnosed as wholly involuntary convulsions, chorea, spasms, or "devil's jig," are described in words that echo or submerge the French term: *gesticulation, antic,* or *trick*.[61] If we turn to those definitions in Johnson's dictionary, and in physician Robert James's *Medicinal Dictionary* (1742–45), to which Johnson was an important contributor,[62] we can see that over a century before Meige and Feindel's fixing of proper verbal categories, the body in motion posed problems of naming, interpretation, and etymology that collapsed words with what they were intended to represent. Observed in action, Johnson's movements jeopardized the limits between body and mind, and between intention and its lack. In their definition—in their translation into representative or exemplary status—such motions threatened linguistic categories, collapsing definitional or diagnostic objectivity with subjective ambiguities of agency, the linguistic equivalent of Meige and Feindel's "disease of the will."

Johnson's dictionary defines *gesticulate* as "to play antick tricks; to shew postures," and thus as intentional, theatrical (a "shewing" of the body in display), and deceptive. If we turn to the adjective *antick*, etymologically linked to "antient, as things out of use appear old" and thus to social constructions of novelty and fashion, defined as "Odd; ridiculously wild; buffoon in gesticulation," Johnson's choice of example emphasizes the word's sense of masquerade, and with it the undermining of authority inherent in such excessive performance:

> "What! dares the slave
> come hither cover'd with an *antick* face,
> And fleer and scorn at our solemnity?"
>   Shakespeare

With a fluidity of agency that makes noun and verb forms difficult to distinguish, whether metaphorically linked to death (a connection that will bear further investigation) and parodying royal authority, or splitting a speaking self deceived by the "wild disguise" of its own words,[63] *antick* in Johnson's illustrations undermines authenticity, authority, and uniform identity.[64] The ambiguities of *trick*, first defined as "sly fraud," moving through "dexterous artifice," "vicious practice," to "a juggle; an antick; any thing done to cheat jocosely, or to divert," and ending with the seemingly innocuous "A practice; a manner; a habit," further demonstrate the potential moral "perils" underlying what in this definition has become the very stuff of personal distinction and effective representation. As the language of moral disapprobation diminishes, the language of intention narrows (culminating in the exculpatory "to cheat jocosely," or "to divert") and finally, with "habit," virtually disappears.

If we turn to James's *Medicinal Dictionary* and first examine the definition for Boswell's diagnosis of Johnson, Saint Vitus' dance, also known as chorea minor, the similarities are striking:

> *Sydenham* says, that St. Vitus's Dance is a kind of Convulsion, which principally attacks Children of both Sexes, from ten to fourteen Years of Age. It first shews itself by a certain Lameness, or rather Unsteadiness of one of the Legs, which the Patient draws after him like an Idiot; and afterwards affects the Hand on the same Side, which, being brought to the Breast, or any other Part, can by no means be held in the same Posture for a Moment, but is distorted, or snatched by a kind of Convulsion, into a different Posture and Place, notwithstanding all possible Efforts to the contrary. If a Glass of Liquor be put into the Hand to drink, before the Patient can get it to his Mouth, he uses a thousand odd Gestures; for, not being able to carry it in a straight Line thereto, because his Hand is drawn different Ways by the Convulsion, as soon as it has reached his Lips, he throws it suddenly into his Mouth, and drinks it very hastily, *as if he only meant to divert the Spectators.*[65]

Here "odd" gestures are voluntary efforts to battle involuntary convulsions that are misread and perhaps determined by "the spectators" as antics (in Johnson's definition), as comic performance. Even when the body in question is defined as unable to control its gestures, the metaphor of performance, here consciously employed in an effort of description, seems unavoidable.

The term in James's dictionary that bridges the discourses of objective description and theatrical metaphor is *gesticulatio,* defined as "a species of gymnastics, consisting in a spontaneous Agitation of the Parts, and throwing the Body into different Postures, much like Actors on the Stage. Gesticulation, says *Oribasius,* is a middle kind of Exercise, between dancing and Mock-fighting, but more like the latter, and is useful for the same Intentions (see UMBRATILIS PUGNA); but it is more adapted to Children, Women, and aged Persons, and those of Weak and thin Bodies." The association with effeminacy inherent in the Saint Vitus' dance definition is clarified here,[66] while the theatrical ambiguity of agency remains in "spontaneous," which could mean either willingly (its literal sense) or without obvious cause.

But theatricality in this case becomes not only metaphor but also cure. The definition of *umbratilis pugna* further elucidates the "use" of such posturing, "a species of Gymnastics, in which the Patient fights with Head and Heels, or boxes and wrestles with a Shadow." Here the parodic element in gesticulation is not linked, as it was in Johnson's dictionary, to the subversive power of illusion and deceit but rather to the therapeutic effects of a self-consciously theatrical performance that advertises its own futility. Fredric Bogel, quoting Roland Barthes's essay on wrestling in explication of Bertrand Bronson's famous characterization of Johnson Agonistes, has used just such a metaphor to describe Johnson's version of ironically assumed, performative authority: "[He gives] to his manner of fighting the kind of vehemence and precision found in a great scholastic disputation, in which *what is at stake is at once the triumph of pride and the formal concern with truth.*"[67] The connections Bogel draws in his discussion between Johnson's self-asserting pride and self-effacing concern with truth, between self-evident artless content and pure artificial form, are given new resonance when we consider the gestures, at once theatrical and unintentional, that characterized and divided Johnson in the flesh.

Diagnosing

> Between tic and chorea there is an abyss.
> —Jean-Martin Charcot, quoted in *A System of*
> *Medicine, by Many Writers* (1905)

"What could have induced him to practise such extraordinary gestures who can divine! his head, his hands and his feet often in motion at the same time."[68] Frances Reynolds was not alone in asking the question; Johnson's tics put both body and mind on display, creating an audience of interpreters. Frances Burney was one of many to describe the spectacle Johnson made in company:

> he has naturally a noble figure; tall, stout, grand and authoritative: but he stoops horribly, his back is quite round: his mouth is continually opening and shutting, as if he were chewing something; he has a singular method of twirling his fingers, and twisting his hands: his vast body is in constant agitation, see-sawing backwards and forwards: his feet are never a moment quiet; and his whole great person looked often as if it were going to roll itself, quite voluntarily, from his chair to the floor.[69]

Burney juxtaposed what seems to be an involuntary distortion of a "naturally" noble figure by stooping and "constant agitation," with the vision of a body with a will of its own, leaving the great mind at its mercy.

Boswell's account, a passage uneasily sectioned off from the flow of his narrative, enacts a similar series of contradictory impulses toward interpretation, moving from minute and random singularities to the positing of meaning and intention through a metaphor that reinforces Johnson's superiority in conversation:

> That the most minute singularities which belonged to him, and made very observable parts of his appearance and manner, may not be omitted, it is requisite to mention, that while talking or even musing as he sat in his chair, he commonly held his head to one side towards his right shoulder, and shook it in a tremulous manner, moving his body backwards and forwards, and rubbing his left knee in the same direction, with the palm of his hand. In the intervals of articulating he made various sounds with his mouth, sometimes as if ruminating, or what is called chewing the cud, sometimes giving a half whistle, sometimes making his tongue play backwards from the roof of his mouth, as if clucking like a hen, and sometimes protruding it against his upper gums in front, as if pronouncing quickly under his breath, *too, too, too*: all this accompanied sometimes with a thoughtful look, but more frequently with a smile. Generally when he had concluded a period, in the course of a dispute, by which time he was a good deal exhausted by violence and vociferation, he used to blow out his breath like a Whale. This I suppose was a relief to his lungs; and seemed in him to be a contemptuous mode of expression, as if he had made the arguments of his opponent fly like chaff before the wind.

Boswell ends his description of Johnson's movements with an aesthetic justification:

> I am fully aware how very obvious an occasion I here give for the sneering jocularity of such as have no relish of an exact likeness; which, to render complete, he who draws it must not disdain the slightest strokes. But if witlings

should be inclined to attack this account, let them have the candour to quote what I have offered in my defence.[70]

Here the curious gaze is not an end in itself but a means toward effective mimesis, and the opacity of bodily detail in Boswell leads to a transparent understanding of Johnson's monumental greatness.

Johnson himself attributed his repetitive movements to "bad habit" and coupled the self-diagnosis with an admonition to the young woman bold enough to inquire about their cause, "do you, my dear, take care to guard against bad habits."[71] Meige and Feindel posit the need for such mindfulness by defining tics as thoughts that imperceptibly turn to gesture, the line between them as difficult to draw as it is to define the domain of "habit" in mind or body: "As one thinks, so does one tic."[72] The paradoxes with which doctors and patients alike in the past two centuries have described nervous tics are structured like a series of couplets: physical enshrinements of psychic detail, grotesque caricatures of everyday acts, voluntary capitulations to an almost irresistible force, immediate habits.[73] It is significant too, in this regard, that medical scholarship on Tourette's syndrome, unable to resolve the question of whether or not tics were voluntary, began with the Rousseauian "Confessions of a Victim to Tic," and has come full circle to reconsider patients' first-person accounts of their experiences.[74] This disease, with which Johnson has been recently and frequently diagnosed, through its challenging of clear limits between body and mind, and through its affinities with mimesis (tics often begin with an irresistible desire to mimic someone else's strange gestures), displays an abyss between intention and its lack.[75] Such an abyss at once posits and undermines intention, origin, and order.

The embattled history of scholarship on Tourette's reinforces the power of Johnson's example to compromise our ability to distinguish between tics, symptoms, habits, and compulsions. What difference is there between a physical and psychological tic, between a bodily compulsion and a mental obsession? Johnson's public evincing of psychological turmoil by praying in public in silent mutters and audible whispers, his recitation at moments of conversational absence of poetic contemplations of death, "ay, but to die and go we know not where," his perpetual resolves to overcome his compulsion to resolve, that is, his "scruples," make an answer impossible.[76] How does a tic differ from a symptom? Here what his contemporaries referred to as convulsions, gesticulations, the devil's jig, his head shakings, and seesawings, which made him roll rather than walk, come to mind. But such purposelessness can have its purpose: seesawing, like a bodily mimicry of the couplet, appeared to aid him, Frances Reynolds notices, in the memorization of

Fig. 14. James Heath, *Samuel Johnson*, after the 1756 portrait by Sir Joshua Reynolds. Reynolds gave the original to Boswell, who had the engraving made as the frontispiece to the first edition of the *Life of Johnson* (1791). Note that Johnson is shown with his head tilted toward the right shoulder, a pose that is visible in his earliest known portrait (believed to be painted around 1736), and that is termed in medical discourse a "tonic" or attitudinal tic based on habitual pose rather than motion. (Reproduced by permission of the Huntington Library, San Marino, California.)

poetry.[77] How does a nervous tic differ from a habit? We might think here of Johnson's need to touch every post he passed on the road, or his elaborate whirlings and twistings at doorways, his "gigantick straddles" on the street, his rapt attention to the precise positioning of his feet in polite drawing rooms.[78] Johnson's "air of great satisfaction"[79] at the successful completion of such rituals might also lead us to ask, along with James's dictionary, whether a tic is a performance, and if so whether that performance is voluntary or involuntary and for an audience real or imagined. If as one early medical authority states, "the victims of tic are thankful for solitude as the only way of escaping observation," what are we to make of Johnson's need for that audience, his lifelong fear of solitude, his perpetual desire to "escape from himself,"[80] or, his authorial persona's magisterial command of impersonal observation?

In the accounts of contemporaries, Johnson's tics at once warded off and figured anxieties about repetition, representation, mastery, and meaning that preoccupied and shaped his habits of mind. In a more general historical sense, such questions of agency and intention preoccupied both eighteenth-century authors negotiating their role in a newly professionalized and commodified print culture, and eighteenth-century doctors imagining a nervous system that would prove the body to be more than a machine. If Robert Whytt's "sentient principle" enlivened earlier mechanistic models of the body with divine intention, how to make sense of Johnson's seemingly purposeless tics?[81] Michel Foucault invokes a vision of corporeal intention gone chaotically indecipherable when he describes Whytt's pathologization of the mysterious female body, a body at once physically and morally weaker than the male, a body in excessive sympathy with itself.[82] When we consider the gendered equivalence in the taxonomy of nervous disease of male hypochondria and female hysteria, Johnson's case in particular, and that of the man of letters in general, takes on added mystery. How might the public figure of the moral arbiter Johnson be aligned in contemporary imaginations with such a pathologically private body? And how might such a body, debilitated by its nervous secrets, be made heroically representative of a literary culture? Indeed, *nervous* in late-eighteenth-century usage has ambiguously gendered meanings, conveying both physical effeminacy and, when applied to a literary style such as Johnson's, sinewy, muscular masculinity.[83] One answer to such a question relies on contemporary accounts of Johnson's conversation, one of the most salient testing grounds for what we might call the embodiment of style.

If a diagnosis of Tourette's allows us to see tics as purposeful and purposeless, habitual and symptomatic, mental and physical, it also brings us surprisingly close to Joshua Reynolds's penetrating view, that such gestures were "not involuntary" in Johnson's case, but rather were the product of solitary reverie turned to spectacle in company. Johnson's tics, Reynolds argued, "proceeded from a habit which he had indulged himself in, of accompanying his thoughts with certain untoward actions, and those actions always appeared to me as if they were meant to reprobate some part of his past conduct." These actions occurred in moments of absence from conversation and were cured by a return to it.[84] Reynolds was one of many to puzzle over the contrasts between Johnson in person and in public, Johnson in private, and Johnson in his published work, and in so doing to remark the striking opposition of his passionate need to talk for victory in public and his earnest submission to the rules of virtue and truth in intimate tête-à-tête and, especially, in print. "In mixed company," Reynolds observed, "he fought on every occasion as if his whole reputation depended upon the victory of the minute, and he fought with all the weapons. If he was foiled in argument he had recourse to abuse and rudeness."[85] The tension that Boswell feels compelled to excuse in his closing commemoration of Johnson would be for Reynolds the central point of any biography he might produce: "what appears extraordinary," writes Reynolds of the author of *The Vanity of Human Wishes*, "is that a man who so well saw, himself, the folly of this ambition of shining, of speaking, or of acting always according to the character [he] imagined [he] possessed in the world, should produce himself the greatest example of a contrary conduct."[86]

In person Johnson neglects to watch himself by watching an idea of himself too fixedly: by acting "always according to [his] character," he becomes a spectacle of an uncontrollable rage for authority. While in print his authority is based on a skeptical questioning of personal agency, his conversational style, like mock epic, transforms the "loose sparkle of thoughtless wit" into a performance of aggressive self-assertion.[87] In print such a style bases its originality in the iterability of the Latinate paraphrase, asserts what it undermines in controlled repetition, wards off chaos by degrees, and turns toward the agency of others for resolution—in the form of imagined sympathetic and judgmental readers at the end of the *Life of Savage*, or public opinion in the acceptance of Tate's ending to *King Lear*, or celestial wisdom at the close of *The Vanity of Human Wishes*, a comfort that *Rasselas* abandons in a "conclusion in which nothing is concluded." In person, by contrast, print's solitary struggle against singularity in the eye of posterity becomes an agonistic drama for a polite company, an enactment that, like the tics that accompanied it, is repetition with a difference, not authority but its antic staging.

Johnson's conversation, as Reynolds describes it, transforms ambitious intention into something automatic: the "continual practice" of shining in conversation "made that a habit which was at first an exertion." In this account, the "habit" of "speaking his best,"[88] cures the unconscious repetition of the nervous tic with the conscious repetition, what Boswell and Reynolds call the labor, of the Johnsonian style.[89] We can see this process in action when

Boswell observes Johnson, who "seemed to take a pleasure in speaking his own style," rephrasing himself into Johnsonese: "It has not wit enough to keep it sweet," becomes "it has not vitality enough to preserve it from putrefaction."[90] Or consider Johnson's unintentional pun on "the woman had a bottom of good sense," rephrased with prideful resolve at the mirth of the company, as Boswell describes it:

> to assume and exercise despotick power, [he] glanced sternly around, and called out in a strong tone, "Where's the merriment?" Then collecting himself, and looking aweful, to make us feel how he could impose restraint, and as it were searching his mind for a still more ludicrous word, he slowly pronounced, "I say the *woman* was *fundamentally* sensible;" as if he had said, hear this now, and laugh if you dare. We all sat composed as at a funeral.[91]

Here the sheer force of authority on display in the translation into Johnsonese of a pun that remains a pun, silences the group's amusement at the master's inability to control his language. Such authority asserts itself through self-conscious rehearsal and makes itself strange through repetition.[92]

Conversation thus brings a melancholy mind otherwise painfully preoccupied with itself, and from which "the great business of his life . . . was to escape," into safety by bringing it into view.[93] Conversation is convulsion transformed by the "cure" of company into the performance of distinction:

> For every person who knew him must have observed that the moment he was left out of the conversation, whether from his deafness or from whatever cause, but a few minutes without speaking or listening, his mind appeared to be preparing itself. He fell into a reverie accompanied with strange antic gestures; but this he never did when his mind was engaged by the conversation. [These were] therefore improperly called . . . convulsions, which imply involuntary contortions; whereas, a word addressed to him, his attention was recovered. Sometimes, indeed, it would be near a minute before he would give an answer, looking as if he laboured to bring his mind to bear on the question.[94]

In Reynolds's account tics, such as Johnson's compulsive prayer and recitation, signal the "reverie" of self-absorption. But while such actions can signify an indecipherable inwardness that demands the audience's diagnosis, at a word from the company they are made legible as "preparation" for reentering the conversational fray.[95] The performance of style in the mock-heroic battle of conversation, in which Johnson holds forth in perfection fit for print according to his character,[96] thus becomes a kind of salutary habit, a meaningful repetition that orders the potential incoherence of self-enclosure and alleviates both the fear—and the lack—of an end.

By excluding Johnson's nervous tics from a consideration of his conversation, we ally ourselves with Hogarth, who, in the midst of a talk with Samuel Richardson,

> perceived a person standing at a window in the room, shaking his head, and rolling himself about in a strange ridiculous manner. He concluded that he was an ideot, whom his relations had put under the care of Mr. Richardson, as a very good man. To his great surprize, however, this figure stalked forwards to where he and Mr. Richardson were sitting, and all at once took up the argument, . . . he displayed such a power of eloquence, that Hogarth looked at him with astonishment, and actually imagined that this ideot had been at the moment inspired.[97]

Johnson's verbal mastery here becomes the subject of "display" to the artist's eye, a shockingly visible figure against the ground of his bodily incongruity.

Yet Hogarth's vision has something in common, I uneasily admit, with my efforts to think body and mind together in Johnson's case. In the context of Boswell's *Life,* this vision of the great man is profoundly disorienting, since here the objectifying eye scrutinizes not the physical antics of a known genius but rather Johnson's defining and usually disembodied trait, his eloquence. To label Johnson an "inspired ideot" is to make his speech, rather than his tics, the product of another. My point in thus shifting our perspective is not to argue for the body's agency, its essentialized determination of literary form; rather, such a reframing, like the uneasy balances that the couplet form and Johnson's concretized abstractions in both poetry and prose enact, reveals the illusory nature of any attempt to define and identify agency. If the aberrant body and disembodied voice are read as inextricably related, the fragility and theatricality of Johnson's authority is left visibly in the balance. Hogarth's vision of a Johnson made momentarily strange to us demonstrates how, in diagnosing Johnson with a difference, mind and body are always inseparable, and the power of art always asserts itself against a background of spectacle and show.

NOTES

1. While Johnsonian critics have rightfully and somewhat defensively observed that Johnson's style varied significantly from work to work, the necessity of such a claim itself indicates that few eighteenth-century voices were more distinctive, more consistent, or more frequently parodied than Johnson's. See, for example, the still definitive W. K. Wimsatt, *The Prose Style of Samuel Johnson* (1941; reprint, New Haven: Yale University Press, 1972), esp. chap. 5, "Consistency of Johnson's Style,"

and *Philosophic Words: A Study of Style and Meaning in the "Rambler" and "Dictionary" of Samuel Johnson* (New Haven: Yale University Press, 1948); as well as William Vesterman, *The Stylistic Life of Samuel Johnson* (New Brunswick: Rutgers University Press, 1977); and James Boswell's "exhibiting specimens of various sorts of imitations of Johnson's style," both emulative and parodic, at the close of the *Life of Johnson*, ed. George Birkbeck Hill, rev. L. F. Powell, 6 vols. (Oxford: Clarendon Press, 1934–50), 4:385–92.

2. For a related argument on the early modern author as representative figure that focuses on self-marketing rather than embodiment, see Michael McKeon, "Writer as Hero: Novelistic Prefigurations and the Emergence of Literary Biography," in *Contesting the Subject*, ed. William Epstein (West Lafayette, Ind.: Purdue University Press, 1991), 17–41.

3. The phrase is Lucy Porter's, upon first meeting Johnson (Boswell, *Life of Johnson*, 1:95).

4. Alexander Pope, *The Second Epistle of the Second Book of Horace Imitated*, 72–79, in *The Poems of Alexander Pope*, ed. John Butt et al., 11 vols. (London: Methuen, 1939–69), vol. 4.

5. Samuel Johnson, *Life of Pope*, in *Selected Poetry and Prose*, ed. Frank Brady and W. K. Wimsatt (Berkeley and Los Angeles: University of California Press, 1977), 532, 531.

6. The phrase "monstrous contingency" is coined by David Saunders and Ian Hunter in "Lessons from the 'Literary': How to Historicize Authorship," *Critical Inquiry* 17 (spring 1991): 485. See also Helen Deutsch, *Resemblance and Disgrace: Alexander Pope and the Deformation of Culture* (Cambridge: Harvard University Press, 1996), 1–39.

7. See Helen Deutsch, "Symptomatic Correspondences: The Author's Case in Eighteenth-Century Britain," *Cultural Critique* 42 (fall 1999): 40–103.

8. Johnson, *Life of Pope*, 557.

9. [Lady Mary Wortley Montagu,] *Verses Address'd to the Imitator of the First Satire of the Second Book of Horace. By a Lady* (London, 1733).

10. Boswell, *Life of Johnson*, 2:84–85.

11. Johnson, *Life of Pope*, 503.

12. *Samuel Johnson*, ed. Donald Greene (Oxford: Oxford University Press, 1984), 526.

13. Samuel Johnson, *The Vanity of Human Wishes*, l. 158, in *Samuel Johnson: The Complete English Poems*, ed. J. D. Fleeman (New Haven and London: Yale University Press, 1982).

14. Johnson powerfully concludes the review of Jenyns with a different sort of "end": "the only end of literature is to enable readers better to enjoy life or better to endure it" (536).

15. Letitia Hawkins, in *Johnsonian Miscellanies*, ed. George Birkbeck Hill, 2 vols. (Oxford: Clarendon Press, 1897), 2:142; Frances Reynolds, in Hill, *Miscellanies*, 2:254, observes Johnson "seesawing" while he reads in order to better memorize poetry; Boswell's description of Garrick and More's comment in *Life of Johnson*, 2:326; Cooke, in *Dr. Johnson: Interviews and Recollections*, ed. Norman Page

(London: Macmillan, 1987), 27 (hereafter cited as *Interviews and Recollections*), or Hill, *Miscellanies*, 2:167.

16. Boswell, *Life of Johnson*, 1:192, 2:15. Thomas Percy, in Page, *Interviews and Recollections*, remarks that he "has often heard [Johnson] humming and forming periods, in low whispers to himself, when shallow observers thought he was muttering prayers, etc" (29). Here Johnson's tic of talking to himself in public is revealed as composition. For alternative interpretations of this mannerism, see also Hill, *Miscellanies*, 2:257 (struggling with "mental evil"), and 273 (repeating past conversation).

17. See Jonathan Lamb, "Blocked Observation: Tautology and Paradox in *The Vanity of Human Wishes*," in *Cutting Edges: Postmodern Critical Essays on Eighteenth-Century Satire*, ed. James E. Gill (Knoxville: University of Tennessee Press, 1995), 335–46.

18. See Thomas Reinert, *Regulating Confusion: Samuel Johnson and the Crowd* (Durham, N.C.: Duke University Press, 1996), 75–88, for the synecdochal character of objects and agents in the poem. For an analysis of line 174 that unpacks Johnson's satiric sentimentality, see Lamb, "Blocked Observation," 339–40.

19. On the rhetorical contagion of personifications, see Paul de Man, *The Rhetoric of Romanticism* (New York: Columbia University Press, 1984), 78.

20. See, for example, Robert Burrowes, *Essay on the Stile of Doctor Samuel Johnson* (1787; reprint, Los Angeles: Clark Library, 1984): "even in Johnson's hands this ornament has become too luxuriant, when affections, instead of being personified, are absolutely humanized" (45).

21. Steven Knapp, *Personification and the Sublime: Milton to Coleridge* (Cambridge: Harvard University Press, 1985).

22. Chester Chapin, *Personification in Eighteenth Century English Poetry* (1954; reprint, New York: Crown Press, 1955), 112.

23. Chapin, *Personification*, 113.

24. Samuel Taylor Coleridge, *The Collected Works of Samuel Taylor Coleridge*, vol. 5, pt. 1, *Lectures 1808–1819 on Literature*, ed. R. A. Foakes (Princeton: Princeton University Press, 1987), 292.

25. Oliver Sacks, *An Anthropologist on Mars* (New York: Alfred A. Knopf, 1995), 81.

26. See Christopher Ricks, "Samuel Johnson: Dead Metaphors and 'Impending Death,'" in *The Force of Poetry* (Oxford: Oxford University Press, 1984), 80–88.

27. Robert DeMaria Jr., *The Life of Samuel Johnson* (London: Blackwell, 1993), 139, argues that the Christian ending to the English imitation was added to appeal to a wider audience and to sell more copies of the poem.

28. For Johnson's contemplation of the futility of exemplarity, see Reinert, *Regulating Confusion*, particularly 75–121.

29. Boswell, *Life of Johnson*, 4:236, 3:307. For Johnson's conversation's relation to print norms, see Alvin Kernan, *Printing Technology, Letters and Samuel Johnson* (Princeton: Princeton University Press, 1987), 205–6.

30. Boswell, *Life of Johnson*, 3:19.

31. Boswell, *Life of Johnson*, 1:194. Garrick contrasts the "lively and easy" *Lon-*

don, written "when Johnson lived much with the Herveys," to the difficulty of *Vanity,* written in relative retirement.

32. See Churchill's poem *The Ghost* (1762), parodying Johnson's rumored credulity in the story of the Cock-Lane ghost, discussed in Boswell, *Life of Johnson,* 1:406.

33. Linda R. Payne, "An Annotated *Life of Johnson:* Dr. William Cadogan on 'Bozzy' and His 'Bear,'" *Collections* 2 (1987): 12. I thank David Brewer for this reference.

34. For a similar critique of Johnson's conversational style, consisting of mere "surly tone of voice, and scholastic phrase," see William Temple in Page, *Interviews and Recollections,* 24.

35. Burrowes, *Essay on the Stile,* 34.

36. See also Archibald Campbell, repeating Swift's advice, on the necessity of imagining female and laboring readers in *Lexiphanes: a dialogue* (London, 1767), 143–45.

37. See, for example, the continuation of Burrowes's discussion of the *Rambler* (*Essay on the Stile,* 31), an ambiguous act of imitation that may or may not be conscious and that persists throughout Burrowes's text.

38. For an argument that focuses on the Scottishness of many critics of Johnson's style in a battle for the Englishness of English, see Janet Sorenson, "Mapping the British Lexicon: Johnson's *Dictionary* and National Identity," in *Language, Culture, and the Grammar of Empire in 18th-Century British Writing* (Cambridge: Cambridge University Press, forthcoming).

39. Neil Saccamano, "Wit's Breaks," in *Body and Text in the Eighteenth Century,* ed. Veronica Kelly and Dorothea von Mücke (Stanford: Stanford University Press, 1994), 45–67.

40. James Thomson Callender, *Deformities of Dr. Samuel Johnson. Selected from his Works,* 2d ed. (1782; reprint, New York: Garland Press, 1974), title page.

41. On the allegorical nature of character in Johnson, even in his *Lives of the Poets,* and on the enlivening function of physical detail, see Reinert, *Regulating Confusion,* 105 and 177n. 13.

42. John Courtenay, *Poetical Review of the Literary and Moral Character of the Late Samuel Johnson* (1786; reprint, Los Angeles: Clark Library, 1969), 13.

43. Courtenay, *Poetical Review,* 8–9.

44. Thomas Babington, Lord Macaulay, "Samuel Johnson" (1831), in *Critical and Historical Essays,* ed. Hugh Trevor-Roper (New York: McGraw-Hill, 1965), 115.

45. On Boswell's innovations in the use of physical detail, particularly in the context of his rescuing of Johnson from the indiscriminate use of such particularity by Hester Thrale and John Hawkins, see Ralph Rader, "Literary Form in Factual Narrative: The Example of Boswell's *Johnson,*" in *Boswell's "Life of Johnson": New Questions, New Answers,* ed. John A. Vance (Athens: University of Georgia Press, 1985), 25–52; Felicity A. Nussbaum, "Boswell's Treatment of Johnson's Temper: 'A Warm West-Indian Climate,'" *Studies in English Literature* 70 (1974): 421–33, and Nussbaum, *The Autobiographical Subject* (Baltimore: Johns Hopkins University Press, 1989), 103–26.

46. John Wolcot (Peter Pindar), *Bozzy and Piozzi, or, The British Biographers. A Town Eclogue* (1786), 10th ed. (London, 1788). For similar complaints, see O M Brack Jr. and Robert E. Kelley, eds., *The Early Biographies of Samuel Johnson* (Iowa City: University of Iowa Press, 1974), 223. A review in 1786 of Thrale's *Anecdotes* in the *Monthly Review* (reprinted in *Contemporary Criticism of Dr. Samuel Johnson*, ed. John Ker Spital [New York: E. P. Dutton, 1923], 11) criticizes both Thrale and Johnson himself in his *Life of Pope* for abuse of personal detail.

47. Boswell, *Life of Johnson*, 1:13.

48. Boswell, *Life of Johnson*, 1:222.

49. I owe to Julia Epstein the beginning of my thinking about the contrast between Johnson's monumentality and his disability (*Altered Conditions: Disease, Medicine, and Storytelling* [New York and London: Routledge, 1995], 66–67).

50. Frances Burney and Frances Reynolds characterize Johnson by his bodily lack. Burney in her memoir of her musicologist father makes deafness central to Johnson's character, and follows Johnson's description of himself: "All animated nature loves music, except myself!" (Page, *Interviews and Recollections*, 50). Reynolds explains Johnson's unpolished "want of politeness," with reference to "the disqualifying influence of blindness and deafness" and "corporeal defects" (Hill, *Miscellanies*, 2:276, 299). The debate such accounts provoke over the actual extent of these deficiencies continues to be considerable. Contemporaries similarly debated whether Johnson was physically deformed or exceptionally well endowed. William Cooke encapsulates both extremes: "in respect to person, he was rather of the *heroic* stature, being above the middle size; but, though strong, broad, and muscular, his parts were slovenly put together" (Brack and Kelley, *Early Biographies*, 125).

51. On the contagious imitability of Johnson's style, see Boswell, *Life of Johnson*, 4:385–92; Burrowes, *Essay on the Stile*, 42. On his inability to take on the voices of others, see Boswell, *Life of Johnson*, 2:231; see also Burrowes, *Essay on the Stile*, 32; Campbell, *Lexiphanes;* and James Northcote, in Page, *Interviews and Recollections*, 45.

52. While Naomi Schor argues in *Reading in Detail* (New York: Methuen, 1987), that attention to detail constitutes a feminine aesthetic, here the detail paradoxically undermines and asserts masculinity. The important distinction here is between the cultural construction of the feminine and the cultural power of male feminization. For Johnson's impossible project in the *Dictionary* of representing a national language riven with internal difference, see Sorenson, "Mapping the British Lexicon."

53. *Boswell: The Ominous Years, 1774–1776*, ed. Frederick A. Pottle and Charles Ryskamp (New York: McGraw-Hill, 1963), 80.

54. Courtenay, *A Poetical Review*, 11.

55. On the sublime's collapsing of author into text, see Neil Hertz, "A Reading of Longinus," in *The End of the Line* (New York: Columbia University Press, 1985), 1–20.

56. I owe this phrase to Jayne Lewis.

57. Henry Meige and E. Feindel, *Tics and Their Treatment*, trans. S. A. K. Wilson (New York: William Wood and Co., 1907), v–vi.

58. Meige and Feindel, *Tics and Their Treatment*, xiv.

59. Meige and Feindel, *Tics and Their Treatment,* 80.

60. Meige and Feindel, *Tics and Their Treatment,* 74.

61. For the gamut of these phrases, see Boswell, *Life of Johnson,* 1:144.

62. For the extent of Johnson's contributions, see O M Brack Jr. and Thomas Kaminsky, "Johnson, James, and the Medicinal Dictionary," *Modern Philology* 81, no. 4 (May 1984): 378–400.

63. Samuel Johnson, *Dictionary of the English Language,* 3d ed. (London, 1765).

64. For an argument that links the word *antick* to an ancient popular and comic conception of the grotesque body, see Paul Semonin, "Monsters in the Marketplace: The Exhibition of Human Oddities in Early Modern England," in *Freakery: Cultural Spectacles of the Extraordinary Body,* ed. Rosemarie Garland Thomson (New York: New York University Press, 1996), 69–81.

65. Definition for "Chorea Sancti Viti," in Robert James, *A Medicinal Dictionary,* 3 vols. (London, 1743–45; my emphasis). When Boswell quotes Sydenham's definition of the disease, he omits the reference to children (*Life of Johnson,* 1:143–44).

66. In Robert Hooper's *Lexicon Medicum; or, Medical Dictionary,* ed. Klein Grant, 8th ed. (London, 1848), the cause of Saint Vitus' dance is attributed to "an irritability of the nervous system, chiefly dependent upon debility," and aggravated by the "general irritation that pervades the system" at puberty, making females "in weakly habits" particularly liable to the disease (379).

67. Bogel, "Johnson and Authority," 204.

68. Frances Reynolds, in Hill, *Miscellanies,* 2:274.

69. Frances Burney, *Memoirs of Doctor Burney,* 3 vols. (London, 1832), 2:91. For an earlier (1777) and less idealized version of this passage, see Chauncey Brewster Tinker, ed., *Dr. Johnson & Fanny Burney* (New York: Moffat, Yard and Co., 1911), 2.

70. Boswell, *Life of Johnson,* 1:485–86.

71. Boswell, *Life of Johnson,* 4:183, note 2.

72. Meige and Feindel, *Tics and Their Treatment,* 82.

73. The term "enshrinement" is used by an unidentified woman with Tourette's to describe the unique psychic archival character of the syndrome's symptoms, noted by Sacks in *An Anthropologist on Mars,* 81. Meige and Feindel in *Tics and Their Treatment* repeatedly use the latter three descriptions.

74. The first chapter of *Tics and Their Treatment* is "Confessions," a document praised by Sacks. See also Joseph Bliss's first-person narrative, "Sensory Experiences of Gilles de la Tourette Syndrome," ed. Donald J. Cohen, M.D. and Daniel X. Freedman, M.D., *Archives of General Psychiatry* 37 (December 1980): 1343–47.

75. See Meige and Feindel, *Tics and Their Treatment,* especially "Confessions," 1–24; Thomas Clifford Allbutt, *A System of Medicine by Many Writers,* 9 vols. (New York: MacMillan, 1905–11), 7:875. For the persistence of the urge to imitate as a symptom of Tourette's and inherent in tic formation, see Ruth Dowling Bruun and Bertel Bruun, *A Mind of Its Own: Tourette's Syndrome: A Story and a Guide* (New York: Oxford University Press, 1994); and Sacks, *An Anthropologist on Mars,* 89, who links the Touretter's tics to caricature. For diagnoses of Johnson with Tourette's,

see Bruun and Bruun, *Mind of Its Own*, which notes that the syndrome is sometimes accompanied by excessive religiosity and a drive toward self-punishment (156–57); Lawrence C. McHenry Jr., "Samuel Johnson's Tics and Gesticulations," *Journal of the History of Medicine and Allied Sciences* 22 (April 1967): 152–68; Epstein, *Altered Conditions*, 64–67; for a diagnosis of tic see Allbutt, *System of Medicine*, 7:885; and for a skeptical overview, John Wiltshire, *Samuel Johnson in the Medical World* (Cambridge: Cambridge University Press, 1991), 24–34.

76. Boswell, *Life of Johnson*, 4:399–400, note 6. For a compelling analysis of Johnson's scruples that links them to his obsessive-compulsive turn of mind (itself linked by medical thinkers to Tourette's) and to his distrust of satire, see Walter Jackson Bate, *Samuel Johnson* (New York: Harcourt Brace Jovanovich, 1977), 380–81, 493–97.

77. Hill, *Miscellanies*, 2:254.

78. Hill, *Miscellanies*, 2:275.

79. Hill, *Miscellanies*, 2:275.

80. Allbutt, *System of Medicine*, 7:877; Boswell, *Life of Johnson*, 1:144–45; Thrale in Hill, *Miscellanies*, 1:219, 231; and Joshua Reynolds, in Hill, *Miscellanies*, 2:221.

81. Christopher Lawrence argues that Whytt's "principal contention was that the body's responses are purposeful and not the result of blind mechanism" ("The Nervous System and Society in the Scottish Enlightenment," in *Natural Order: Historical Studies of Scientific Culture*, ed. Barry Barnes and Steven Shapin [Beverly Hills, Calif.: Sage, 1979], 25).

82. Michel Foucault, *Madness and Civilization*, trans. Richard Howard (New York: Vintage, 1988), 153–54.

83. I owe this insight to Robert Folkenflik.

84. Quoted in Boswell, *Life of Johnson*, 1:144; see also Hill, *Miscellanies*, 2:222.

85. Hill, *Miscellanies*, 2:228.

86. Hill, *Miscellanies*, 2:228.

87. Johnson, *Rambler 89, The Yale Edition of the Works of Samuel Johnson*, ed. John H. Middendorf et al., 16 vols. (New Haven: Yale University Press, 1958–90), 4:108. On Johnson's skepticism about authority, see Bogel, "Johnson and Authority"; and Reinert, *Regulating Confusion*.

88. Hill, *Miscellanies*, 2:222, 221.

89. Many accounts of Tourette's, including Allbutt, *System of Medicine*, Meige and Feindel, *Tics and Their Treatment*, and Bruun and Bruun, *Mind of Its Own*, note the ways in which people with Tourette's adopt "voluntary" tics in order to "mask the involuntary movements" (Allbutt, *System of Medicine*, 877).

90. Boswell, *Life of Johnson*, 4:320.

91. Boswell, *Life of Johnson*, 4:99.

92. What Bogel reads as a simultaneity, I read as a temporal sequence of *repetition*, an important distinction for my argument about the habitual ticlike nature of Johnson's conversation. See Bogel, "Johnson and Authority," on "the copresence of genuine authority and the histrionic affectation of authority . . . that makes this episode so revealing" (204).

93. Joshua Reynolds states: "The great business of his life (he said) was to escape from himself; this disposition he considered as the disease of his mind, which nothing cured but company" (Boswell, *Life of Johnson*, 1:144–45).

94. Hill, *Miscellanies*, 2:222.

95. For Joshua Reynolds's depiction of Johnson's gesticulations as a kind of oratory, see, in this volume, Davis, "Dr. Johnson, Amelia, and the Discourse of Disability in the Eighteenth Century," fig. 1.

96. "Everything he says is as *correct* as a *second edition:* 'tis almost impossible to argue with him, he is so sententious and so knowing" (Ozias Humphry qtd. in Page, *Interviews and Recollections*, 31).

97. Boswell, *Life of Johnson*, 1:145–47.

PART 3 Imperfections

Lady Mary Wortley Montagu and the "Glass Revers'd" of Female Old Age

Jill Campbell

Old age presents us with cases of what Horace Walpole at one point calls "acquired deformities." That is, the deformities brought by old age do not conform to an understanding of deformity as essential and categorical. If old people may be seen as monsters, they are made such by time and did not begin that way. One group of old people, however, may be said to have always been monstrous in at least one sense: *some* people are not only old but female.[1] At the age of sixty-nine, Lady Mary Wortley Montagu complained that "the most despicable creatures alive" are "Old women."[2] Late-eighteenth-century collections of "remarkable persons" group the extremely aged of both sexes with "deformed persons" and convicts, but it is old women that they hold up as examples of the physically freakish. In the first half of this essay, I review a range of ways that the eighteenth century conceptualized the process of aging in both men and women. The difficulties of conceiving that process, we shall find, are denied or displaced in certain favorite images and narratives of the woman whose "face," whose human self, is lost altogether with illness or age. Thus, in a number of the works we will consider, broad concerns about human identity in time are vented in men's gleefully horrified rejection of the figure of the aging woman. We can think of the "'glass revers'd' of female old age" that appears in my title as the inverted mirror-image that aging women present to men concerned with their own identities' implication in time.[3]

What do women themselves see in that mirror? In the second half of this essay, when I turn to the case of a particular historical woman, Lady Mary Wortley Montagu, I will consider first her male contemporaries' insistence on the corruption and incoherence of her aging body and then Lady Mary's own meditations, over the course of forty years, on female age. If this progression allows us to compare views of female aging from the "outside" and from the "inside"—as something that happens to the "Other" and to one's self—it will also reveal how deeply aging may challenge the assumed relation between these perspectives on the self.

In its original context, the phrase "glass revers'd" in my title refers to a woman's rejection of the mirror image of her own altered face. In "Satturday," the twenty-seven-year-old Lady Mary, herself recently scarred by smallpox, depicts Flavia's sudden loss, through smallpox, of her youthful beauty. Encountering a face in the mirror that she declares "a frightfull Spectre to my selfe unknown," Flavia desperately averts the mirror: "A Glass revers'd in her right hand she bore; / For now she shunn'd the Face she sought before."[4] Though Flavia's scarring by disease has been rapid, Lady Mary and her contemporaries repeatedly equate that scarring with the more gradual loss of beauty to age, and Flavia shares her alienation from the reflection of her own face with many aging women. "When we look at the image of our own future provided by the old," Simone de Beauvoir remarks, "we do not believe it: an absurd inner voice whispers that *that* will never happen to us—when *that* happens it will no longer be ourselves that it happens to"; "Within me it is the Other—that is to say the person I am for the outsider—who is old: and that Other is myself."[5] De Beauvoir's comments connect the problem I observed above—the difficulty of conceiving of selfhood as temporal, as something that is sustained and changes in time—with another kind of problem: the difficulty of understanding selfhood as at once an internal entity and something that is perceived and represented from the outside. Defined by her appearance, the beautiful woman's "self" always was "Other—that is to say the person I am for the outsider"; age or disease breaks the apparently integral relation between the experience of self and the image in the mirror. Indeed, the trauma of aging is again and again represented as a break in the assumed relation between a human subject and her appearance to herself and others: with age, a familiar self may confront itself as "Other."

In her later years Lady Mary claims to have simply rejected that confrontation by putting all mirrors aside. In 1757, at the age of sixty-eight, Lady Mary reports to her daughter, "It is eleven Year since I have seen my Figure in a Glass. The last Refflection I saw there was so disagreable, I resolv'd to spare my selfe such mortifications for the Future, and shall continue that resolution to my Live's end. To indulge all pleasing Amusements and avoid all Images that give Disgust is in my opinion the best method to attain of confirm Health."[6] In this declaration of a philosophy at once stoic and epicurean, Lady Mary claims not simply to have averted the glass but to have banished it altogether. She refuses the external image of her face and body that a mirror's reflection could offer, and chooses to know that body only as it can be experienced from the inside, as more or less healthy and comfortable: to "avoid all Images that give Disgust," she declares, including images of oneself, is "the best method to attain of confirm Health."

At a point in her life halfway between her composition of "Satturday" and of this letter, however, Lady Mary expressed a more ambivalent response to the external image of one's changing self found in a mirror or a portrait when she sent a painting of her youthful self to her younger lover. In the poem that accompanied the portrait, which begins, "This once was me," Lady Mary expresses a wish that her aging present body could be merged with the painted image of a younger self contained in the portrait, so as to prove more pleasing to the object of her desire. In the complicated, shifting relations this poem constructs among Lady Mary herself, the painted image of her younger self, and her beloved,[7] the fact of aging and the discontinuities in self that it entails are cast largely as a problem in the relation between a living self, or selfhood as lived, and the external representation of it. This rather particular version of the problem of aging and of the threats it poses to the coherence of personal identity occurs, in different forms, in many of the works we will consider. "This once was me" provides a particularly complex and dynamic rendering of the vexed relation between the outside and the inside of a self existing in time. In the sublime avowals of the poem's close, the loss of personal coherence wrought by age also extends the possibility of a release from the rigid bounds of socially sanctioned identity—and the opportunity to claim a beloved "other" as part of one's essential self.

Although essays in both *The Tatler* and *The Spectator* assert that "you cannot fall on a better Subject, than that of the Art of growing old,"[8] the subject of growing old, or of aging more generally, is afforded little sustained attention or real conceptual refinement in the essays, poems, biographies, and visual arts of the long eighteenth century. When the process of aging or aged persons appear in those works, they are often treated with a crude quantitative model that reckons up or computes the effects of aging, positing personal identity as a static entity to which elements are added or subtracted in the course of time. Thus, optimistic accounts of aging treat it as a process of accretion, and satiric or tragic ones treat it as ineluctable course of loss and diminution, while more mixed accounts suggest an equation balancing gain against loss. When the bishop of St. Asaph sought Dr. Johnson's opinions about aging, he asked him "if an old man does not lose faster than he gets";

encountering Johnson's resistance to any notion of the inevitable depredations of time, the bishop concludes that Johnson's wish for aging might be summarized in the Greek epigram: "I grow in learning as I grow in years."[9]

The visual arts frequently answer the bishop's question about a man's "getting" or losing with age through the visible index of a subject's gain or loss of fleshly weight. Commissioned portraits of both male and female sitters in their fifties, sixties, and later years most frequently register a sitter's age with the studied inclusion of a fleshy but firm curve of skin between the chin and neck, often displayed through a profile or three-quarter angling of the head (figs. 15 and 16). This fleshy throat or "dewlap" seems, in the portraits of Reynolds, Gainsborough, and others, almost an iconographic convention for indicating the gains—the dignity and prosperity—of middle or later age.[10] Positioned near the face, the dewlap annexes those gains to personal identity rather than locating them in the expanding stomach or buttocks, which might suggest that a sitter was merely becoming more corporeal as well as corpulent with time; positioned close to but not within the face, the dewlap also does not threaten the essential elements of personal identity encoded in the features of the face.[11] These portraits rarely record boniness, stoopedness, wrinkles, creases, or crow's-feet as marks of age in

Fig. 15. Sir Joshua Reynolds, *Anne, Countess of Albemarle* (portrayed at about age fifty-six; ca. 1759). (Courtesy of the National Gallery, London. Copyright © National Gallery, London.)

Fig. 16. Sir Joshua Reynolds, *James Boswell* (portrayed at age forty-five; 1785). (Courtesy of the National Portrait Gallery, London.)

the sitters who commissioned them;[12] neither do they often (to my eyes) convey a sense of distinctive beauties, virtues, or authority gained through age. Age is acknowledged in them in the well-fed pouch of flesh beneath the face, and sometimes in a modest increase in the heaviness and complacent set of the face itself. In conversation pieces depicting several generations of a family, the faces of the oldest generation sometimes appear slightly larger than those of the younger adults as well as children in the group—as if the grandparents had continued very gradually to grow.

In the wickedly savage depictions of older people in eighteenth-century caricatures and satiric prints, on the other hand, to grow older is to be stripped of flesh as well as of dignity and personal character. Whereas the subjects of commissioned portraits become modestly plumper in the face and throat as they age, the subjects of more irreverent visual forms either develop grotesquely fat protuberances around their middles or—more often—become so gaunt that their faces dwindle to caricature and their bodies to skeletons. Late-century satires of the affectations or amorousness of older people characteristically contrast the rich amplitude of their dress and headdress with bony faces, in which the shrinking away of flesh has left nose and chin grotesquely prominent. In *Age and Folly, or the Beauties* (1776), the aging coquette's pointed nose and chin nearly meet; in one frame of Cruikshank's

Ladies Wigs! (1798), an elderly woman happily contemplates herself in the mirror as she lifts an extravagant wig above her hairless and bony head, exclaiming, "Now for the Natural ringlets—Mr. Friz assures me I shall look like an Angel" (fig. 17).[13] When artists depict aging as a process in which the face's flesh collapses, leaving one or a few features disproportionately prominent, they suggest that, with time, naturalistic portrayal of an aging face will converge on the conventions of caricature. In the bottom panel of Hogarth's *Characters Caricaturas* (1743), the features of the faces to the left, exemplifying "characters," become bonier and more pronounced as they pass into "caricaturas." As an aging face degenerates into living caricature, personal identity becomes risibly schematic.

Some images of the period also play on the notion that to grow thin in old age is to have one's body and identity reduced to the visibly, merely anatomical. For example, in the early-nineteenth-century aquatint *Rare Specimens of Comparative Craniology: An Old Maid's Skull Phrenologised,* the head of an "old maid" offers itself up both as caricature and as scientific specimen; a phrenologist measures that sharply featured, hairless and wigless

Fig. 17. Isaac Cruikshank and George Moutard Woodward, detail from *Ladies Wigs!* (1798). (Courtesy of the Print Collection, Lewis Walpole Library, Yale University.)

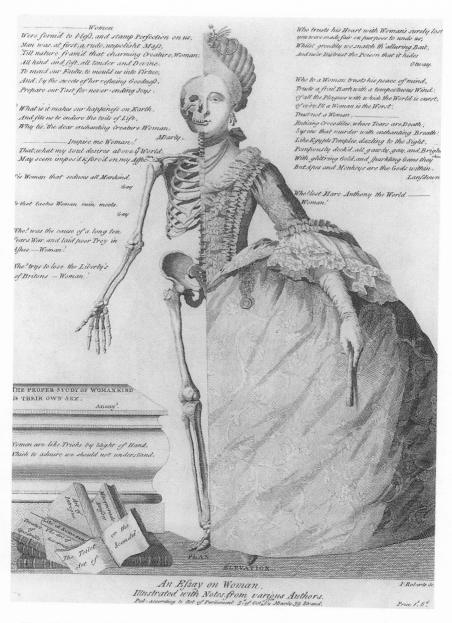

Fig. 18. James Roberts, *An Essay on Woman* (1769). (Courtesy of the Print Collection, Lewis Walpole Library, Yale University.)

head with ruler and compass.[14] In Reynolds's *Macbeth and the Witches* (1786–89; engraved 1802), a throne made of bones and a pair of actual skulls, floating just above the old witches' faces, emphasize the frighteningly skeletal quality of those faces themselves. To grow thin in old age, these works imply, is not only to lose the complexity, substance, and depth of "real" individual identity as one's face is reduced to caricature, but also to become a walking reminder of the grave on which one teeters, as one's body approaches the skeletal. The popular rendering of "Life and Death Contrasted" offers a graphic memento mori in a human figure divided vertically, one half's fashionable youth joined down the middle to an assemblage of bones;[15] representations of the elderly as barely fleshed skeletons suggest that old age forms the elided bridge between such images' starkly contrasted two halves (fig. 18). An early-nineteenth-century nonsatiric work, Charles Bell's *Essays on the Anatomy of Expression,* insists on this association when it instructs the would-be artist that to depict an aged face, one must register an accelerating series of physiological losses. Beneath his description of this process—"the teeth and adventitious part of the jaws being gone, the chin and nose approach, and the mouth is too small for the tongue; the lips fall in, and the speech is inarticulate"—Bell silently places a drawing of a skull (fig. 19). Only on the next page does Bell then offer the sketch of the aging face of a living person generated by his narrative of loss, shrinking, and decline; that sketch, significantly, is one of an old woman rather than of a man (fig. 20).[16]

Eighteenth-century portraitists in fact found a number of ways to indicate that in the course of their adult lives, older male sitters had gained more than the weight visible at their throats, while techniques for suggesting that older female sitters might have done so were much more limited. As Richard Wen-

Fig. 19. Skull, from Charles Bell, "Of the Distinction of Character in Different Ages," *Essays on the Anatomy of Expression in Painting* (1806). (Courtesy of Yale University Library.)

Fig. 20. Old woman, from Charles Bell, "Of the Distinction of Character in Different Ages," *Essays on the Anatomy of Expression in Painting* (1806). (Courtesy of Yale University Library.)

dorf observes, in the remarkable series of self-portraits that Reynolds painted between the ages of twenty-three and fifty-seven, Reynolds gradually adds element after element (a large book, doctoral robes, a black cap, a roll of paper with an inscription) that emblematizes his increasing accomplishment and authority, until "this careful accretion of elements" culminates in the self-portrait Reynolds painted for the Royal Academy in 1780, which incorporates all these elements, adds a bust of Michelangelo, and suggests, through Reynolds's posture, "the assurance, the authority, and the control that now characterize the Academy's first President." Brilliant as he was at thus suggesting the cumulative gains a sitter (himself, or another) had achieved with age, Reynolds also experimented boldly with including references to the infirmities or impairment of faculties an older sitter might suffer. An equally remarkable group of self-portraits represents the artist's own increasing age in terms of the diminution of his faculties: the self-portrait of 1775 shows Reynolds with one hand cocked behind his left ear, as he strains to hear; that of 1788 presents him in spectacles; and another of 1788 depicts him peering short-sightedly, his mouth somewhat open, his wig stiff.[17] Reynolds extended his experiment in representing the physical limitations of a sitter to his friend Samuel Johnson, who appears in a 1775 portrait short-sightedly holding a book close to his nose. According to Hester Thrale,

Johnson in fact objected to this portrayal, declaring that "'he would not be known by posterity for his *defects* only, let Sir Joshua do his worst.'" When Thrale responded that Reynolds had at least afforded himself the same treatment in the portrait in which he depicts himself straining to hear, Johnson grumbled, "'He may paint himself as deaf if he chuses . . . but I will not be *blinking Sam*.'"[18] Johnson complains that Reynolds's portrayal of him has flattened his character out to the one attribute of his short-sightedness, reducing him to "blinking Sam"; he might well wish that Reynolds would instead use the techniques of portraiture to indicate the knowledge, the authority, the fame that "Dr." Johnson had by that point in his life achieved. For women, no such knowledge, authority, or fame could be achieved with time or duly registered in portraiture; instead, only a physical loss of one particular kind—the loss of a beautiful appearance—might be tactfully suppressed (in commissioned portraiture) or maliciously heightened and moralized (in caricature or satiric works).

Johnson's own essay on old age in *The Rambler* opens with the assertion that age involves all "in one common distress," but, like other essayists, he eventually suggests that "old age" has a different duration as well as a different meaning for women and for men.

> [T]hough age be to every order of human beings sufficiently terrible, it is particularly to be dreaded by fine ladies, who have had no other end or ambition, than to fill up the day and the night, with dress, diversions and flattery, and who having made no acquaintance with knowledge, or with business, have constantly caught all their ideas from the current prattle of the hour, and been indebted for all their happiness to compliments and treats. With these ladies, age begins early, and very often lasts long; it begins when their beauty fades, when their mirth loses its sprightliness, and their motion its ease. From that time all which gave them joy vanishes from about them.[19]

In this account, "fine ladies" can reap no cumulative benefits from the passage of years, as they merely "fill up the day and the night" with trivial concerns, "catching" all their ideas from the constantly changing stream of "current prattle." As they have "no acquaintance with knowledge, or with business," time can bring them no profit of learning or even of wealth.[20] These ladies exist only moment to moment, their identities uninflected by time—except for one catastrophic alteration brought inevitably, and early, when their essential characteristics (beauty, sprightliness, ease) are stripped from them by the sudden onset of "age." Johnson notes that although age thus sets in early for women, depriving them both of joy and of any purpose in life, women often nonetheless (inconveniently, defying all logic) live on, so that female age may indeed "last long." This long period of female adult life, after the loss of beauty and youth, is referred to in *The Tatler* as "that State I have often heard you call an After-life";[21] loss of the beauty that defined a young woman's essential identity constitutes such a sharp break in her life course that her earlier self might as well be declared dead, while her new self is ghostly because it has no place in the material social world.

This frequently reiterated view of a woman's life course offers little conceptualization of personal identity's accommodation of time: instead it insists that identity remains essential and static (a young woman *is*, in the common parlance, "a Beauty") until a sudden snap of discontinuity occurs and she enters a new, perhaps long, but undifferentiated period of the "afterlife" of female "age" (an old age that may encompass her late twenties, her eighties, and everything in between). As flat and minimally dynamic as this charting of identity in time may be, it is frequently made to stand in for any more general characterization of human identity's inflection by time. Johnson heads *Rambler* 69's general discussion of age with an epigraph about the loss of beauty ("The dreaded wrinkles when poor Helen spy'd, / Ah! why this second rape?—with tears she cry'd"), and eighteenth-century literature again and again exclaims over the sobering fact of beauty's transience. In these exclamations, the psalmist's spiritual reminder to all mankind—"As for man, his days are as grass: as a flower of the field, so he flourisheth. / For the wind passeth over it, and it is gone"—is recast as a more specific comment on the perishability of women's social value: "For beauty is a fleeting flow'r: / Then how can wisdom e'er confide / In beauty's momentary pride?"[22] The loss of beauty is indeed treated as "momentary" in these reflections; its passing is imagined to be almost instantaneous ("The Beauty grows wrinkled while we are yet gazing on her"; "every thing presses on—while thou art twisting that lock,—see! it grows grey").[23] This favorite eighteenth-century reflection not only confines time's effects to the female half of mankind but also concentrates those effects in a single moment (often, in particular, a moment of male observation)—denying, in a strange way, the temporal nature of their unfolding.[24]

By focusing so insistently on beauty as that which is lost in time, eighteenth-century writers also avoid addressing the many other ways that the human body and "self" might complexly, uneasily interact in the course of time. Although the passage of time (in the sustaining of consciousness) is essential to the definition of "self" so influentially offered by Locke, he seems simply to rule out alterations in the body over time as having any effect on that self. "'Tis necessary for me to be as I am"; he declares, "GOD and Nature has made me so: But there is nothing I have, is essential to me. An Accident, or Disease, may very much alter my Colour, or Shape; A Fever, or

Fall, may take away my Reason, or Memory, or both"; and, earlier, "Thus we see the *Substance,* whereof *personal self* consisted at one time, may be varied at another, without the change of personal *Identity:* There being no Question about the same Person, though the Limbs, which but now were a part of it, be cut off."[25] According to the periodical literature of the eighteenth century, former beauties, physically transformed by illness or age, cannot share Locke's confidence that they are nonetheless the same "persons."[26] In one of the many essays dealing with the loss of beauty that follows smallpox, "Parthenissa," recently beautiful but now "disfigured with Scars," writes in to lament,

> 'say what you can to one who has survived her self, and knows not how to Act in a new Being. . . . Consider the Woman I was did not dye of Old Age, but I was taken off in the Prime of my Youth, and according to the Course of Nature may have Forty Years After-Life to come. I have nothing of my self left which I like, but that
>
> I am, SIR,
Your most Humble Servant,
Parthenissa.'

The Spectator does not argue with Parthenissa's sense that with her youthful beauty she has lost her very self so that her persistence in the world constitutes a mere "After-Life." Instead, he encourages her to accept this loss philosophically and with style, citing for her the example of another smallpox sufferer who charmed her lover with this witty billet:

> SIR,
> 'If you flattered me before I had this terrible Malady, pray come and see me now: But if you sincerely liked me, stay away; for I am not the same
> Corinna'[27]

The physical "defects" brought by age or infirmity to Reynolds and Johnson are impairments of their faculties of perception, and Locke in fact worries at points in the *Essay concerning Human Understanding* (despite the confidence of the assertions just quoted) that such impairments might eventually draw into question the continuing existence of an essential self.[28] The self definitively lost by women through disease or age depends not on physical faculties of perception but on physical appearance.[29] For them, the problem of the self's dependence on a body that may change over time is located on the surface of that body, or (more precisely) in the impression made by that body on the eyes of others. Thus, the effects of a brief, life-threatening disease and the effects of the passage of years are rendered identical, if both destroy a woman's socially valued appearance. Parthenissa expresses this view above; "Euphemia," the philosophical friend of "Victoria," a smallpox victim whose case is considered in *The Rambler,* insists on the same equation when she denies Victoria sympathy, saying, "You have only lost early what the laws of nature forbid you to keep long."[30] Thus, the periodical essayists (and others) return repeatedly to the story of "that dreadful malady which has so often put a sudden end to the tyranny of beauty."[31] That story supplies a specific narrative topos within which beauty's loss may be understood as nearly instantaneous; it thereby interprets the effects of time on identity in terms of a condensed, *almost* nontemporal tableau. It insists that such effects are a specifically female problem, and it presses to an extreme the notion that the female self in fact adheres in appearance—as if that "self" *were* its representation through the body, or its image in the mirror.

One of the *Spectator's* ruminations on smallpox and beauty takes the form of a fanciful dream in which Fidelio, a man who has been metamorphosed into a mirror, narrates Narcissa's sickness and scarring. The narrative of the young beauty's trauma is apparently so familiar that it need be sketched only quickly, but the fanciful choice of a man/mirror as narrator heightens the essay's commentary on a beauty's relation to her mirror image. Fidelio's transformation into a mirror of glass occurs after the recuperating Narcissa has run "with transport to her Darling," only to be met with his shock and fear at "so loathsome a Spectacle." She steps back, "swollen with Rage" at his response, but it is only when he comments that "her ill-timed Passion had increased her Ugliness," that she snatches a bodkin and stabs him to the heart. "Dying I preserved my Sincerity," recalls Fidelio, "and express'd the Truth, though in broken Words; and by reproachful Grimaces to the last I mimick'd the Deformity of my Murderess."[32] While her favorite companion is transformed into the "smooth, polish'd, and bright" surface of a looking glass, Narcissa's own body grotesquely confirms that it already constitutes a mirror of her mind: her "Ugliness," and even her "Deformity" (replicated by Fidelio in "Grimaces"), become the effects of her passions rather than traces of a bodily disease. At the same time, the state of Narcissa's mind depends entirely on what she discovers in the mirror about the state of her body, which has suddenly and arbitrarily been altered by the happenstance of a contagious disease. In this confusing scenario, Narcissa's body is at once a mere representation of the state of her mind and prior to it;[33] the reflected image of her body that appears in the mirror redundantly reproduces what is itself already an image, but the mirror image still (circularly) serves as the medium by which the mind, the "self," is in turn fundamentally changed by its body's alteration.

This convoluted set of relations among self, body, and mirror is so central to eighteenth-century accounts of women's passage through time that when Locke compares a soul that retains nothing from its course of thought to "a Looking-glass, which constantly receives variety of Images, or *Ideas*, but retains none," one might easily identify that soul as belonging to one of Johnson's fine ladies who merely "fill up the day and night" with passing concerns and catch "all their ideas from the current prattle of the hour."[34] The looking glass, in Locke's language, retains "no footsteps" or imprints from the past; its image is synchronic; in that way it may serve as a trope for women's failure to gain from time. Yet a mirror image, as periodical essays insistently remind us, may be altered either suddenly or slowly by catastrophic disease or the depredations of age. Fidelio's conflation of Narcissa's scars with the marks of "deformity" wrought in her face by passion points to an opposite, though still damning, account of women's failures in time. If we accept the *Spectator*'s equation of the loss of beauty to smallpox and the loss of beauty with age, we might speculate that Narcissa's story condenses the way that her face might be scarred in fact by its very responsiveness to time—that is, by the physical impression made by its reiterated representation of features of her character or inner "self."

Ideally, in the writings of this period, the body and particularly the face are to offer representations of the inner self to the observing world;[35] and yet for the body or face to be marked, cumulatively, by the traces of inner feelings or thoughts is to pass first into caricature and then into the more egregious distortions of "deformity." Lady Mary Wortley Montagu makes an analogy between the transformation of the mind and the descent of the face into caricature as they age; she remarks (at the age of sixty-nine), "Time has the same Effect on the mind as on the Face; the predominant Passion and the strongest Feature become more Conspicuous from the others' retiring. The various views of Life are abandonn'd from want of Abillity to persue them, as the fine Complexion is lost in wrinkles; but as surely as a large Nose grows larger and a wide mouth wider, the tender child in your Nursery will be a tender old Woman."[36] In his chapter "Of the Face," Hogarth extends the relation between the aging mind and face beyond analogy to causality, although he hastens to note the deliberate or accidental factors that may prevent the mind from appearing clearly in the face.

> With regard to character and expression; we have daily many instances which confirm the common received opinion, that the face is the index of the mind. . . . the frequent aukward movements of the muscles of the fool's face, tho' ever so handsom, is apt in time to leave such traces up and down it, as will distinguish a defect of mind upon examination. . . .
> It is by the natural and unaffected movements of the muscles, caused by the passions of the mind, that every man's character would in some measure

be written in his face, by that time he arrives at forty years of age, were it not for certain accidents which often, tho' not always prevent it. For the ill-natur'd man, by frequently frowning, and pouting out the muscles of his mouth, doth in time bring those parts to a constant state of the appearance of ill-nature, which might have been prevented by the constant affectation of a smile; and so of the other passions.[37]

Thus every face either is a mask of hypocrisy (a deliberate misrepresentation of its possessor's mind) or is damaged by the repeated marks of his or her characteristic passions upon it—for, as Hogarth laments, "It is strange that nature hath afforded us so many lines and shapes to indicate the deficiencies and blemishes of the mind, whilst there are none at all that point out the perfections of it beyond the appearance of common sense and placidity." Hogarth concludes his chapter on the face with this visual analysis of the inevitable destruction of its beauty over time (fig. 21):

after this time [after the age of thirty], as the alterations grow more and more visible, we perceive the sweet simplicity of many rounding parts of the face, begin to break into dented shapes, with more sudden turns about the muscles, occasioned by their many repeated movements; as also by dividing the broad parts, and thereby taking off the large sweeps of the serpentine lines. . . . Something of what is here meant between the two ages of thirty and fifty [117 and 118, plate 2 bottom], and what further havock time continues to make after the age of fifty, is too remarkable to need describing: the strokes and cuts he then lays on are plain enough.[38]

Faced with this inevitably damaging relation between the mind and the body in the course of time (as with the indissoluble association between age and physical ugliness),[39] some eighteenth-century moralists urge women to imagine themselves as gradually exchanging features of their bodies for spiritual or mental attributes over time, as if they could incrementally transfer their existences from the realm of the physical to that of the immaterial. The countess dowager of Carlisle exhorts her female readers, "Let each year, which shall steal a charm or a grace, the companions of your youth, add a virtue in return"; the Reverend Timothy Rogers as well as moral writers such as Steele and Johnson exhort their readers to "substitute" some spiritual or moral attribute—"the Grace of God," the "durable and valuable excellencies" of the mind, "Good-Nature"—for the physical charms that vanish with time.[40] In this vision, at best, a woman's prolonged "old age" might be termed an "afterlife" in the laudatory sense that she evolves into a more and more strictly spiritual entity in the course of it.[41] In this vision, however, the persistence of the woman's aging body itself becomes a scandal and a horror, the very fact of it an appalling transgression. Thus, in *The Whole Duty*

Fig. 21. William Hogarth, detail from plate 2 of *The Analysis of Beauty* (second state), referred to in "Of the Face" (1753). (Courtesy of the Print Collection, Lewis Walpole Library, Yale University.)

of Woman, an old widow who marries a young man is a "dead carcass," to which his "living body" is loathsomely tied.[42] As we have seen, the more irreverent forms of visual art picture the "afterlife" of female age as the grotesquely comic animation of a corpse: in them, an old woman's head appears as a speaking skull and her body as a living—and often lascivious—skeleton.

Eighteenth-century writings and visual commentaries on old age often focus on the risible or reprehensible incongruities of the aged person's pursuit of youthful vanities or desires,[43] and this notion of incongruity—the mixing of categories and the violation of proper decorums—is emphasized in several of the accounts of the aging Lady Mary that we will examine below. The level of horror attached to Lady Mary's incongruities of dress or behavior derives, however, not from some specifics of her transgressive dress or behavior but from the basic contradiction I have just described. She epitomizes for her male viewers the horrific persistence of the female body after it has been declared socially dead at the end of its reign of beauty. The social illogic of its material persistence defines it as inherently monstrous or deformed. For that body even to continue to dress itself becomes potentially peculiar; for it to remain a sexual entity is positively scandalous. In a 1746 tract, the personal experience of the "True Penitent" who pens the polemic ultimately "demonstrates" the danger of marrying old women by attesting to their insatiable sexual appetites, which make such unions "monstrous Violations of the great Laws of Nature." In James Caulfield's *Portraits, Memoirs, and Characters of Remarkable Persons,* Margaret Patten, included in the collection for her remarkable achievement of "the very advanced age of one hundred and forty-three years," titillates and astonishes her interlocutor by responding to his question, "at what period of life a woman's amorous propensities ceased? . . . that to be satisfied in that particular he must consult an older woman than herself."[44]

The advertisement to Caulfield's collection explains that he includes under the rubric of "Remarkable Persons" criminals, "instances of the deviation of nature, such as giants, dwarfs, strong men, personal deformity, &c.," and "those persons who have lived to an extraordinary age," as well as "empirics and quacks, buffoons, prize-fighters, and adventurers" (v–vi; see also 1). Caulfield is not alone in casually grouping together very old people and people with extraordinary physical "deformities." Class 12 of the Reverend James Granger's influential taxonomical system in *A Biographical History of England, from Egbert the Great to the Revolution: consisting of Characters disposed in different Classes, and adapted to a Methodical Catalogue of Engraved British Heads* (first published 1769) consists of "Persons of both

Sexes, chiefly of the lowest Order of the People, remarkable from only one Circumstance in their Lives; namely such as lived to a great Age, deformed Persons, Convicts, &c." (An earlier work assumed a similar grouping when it offered *A Short History of Human Prodigies and Monstrous Births, of Dwarfs, Sleepers, Giants, Strong Men, Hermaphrodites, Numerous Births, and Extream Old Age &c.*)[45] Although the old people whose portraits appear in these works are of course exceptionally, even phenomenally, old, their appearance in these volumes among traitors, tricksters, giants, dwarfs, the deaf and dumb, and men with no arms or legs suggests that even the more ordinarily aged belong (in a more everyday way) among the criminal and the physically abnormal. To approach old age is to pass into the category of the uncategorizable: the monstrous, the "outré," the deformed.

Significantly, it is in Caulfield's and Granger's female examples of extremely advanced age that both visual portrait and accompanying account emphasize physical decay, defect, and repulsive appearance. While Granger's Henry Jenkins, who "lived to the surprising age of 169," exhibits a remarkable memory for the historical events of the past 140 years and is linked by implication to the long-lived biblical patriarchs, Granger's "Mother Louse, an old woman in a ruff," is ridiculed for her antiquated dress, associated by her name with parasites and filth, and placed alongside a woman who grew excrescences on her head like horns, another aged woman, and an infamous whore.[46] Caulfield, too, in discussing aged men, expresses wonder at all the historical events that their memories must encompass; he also admires the "patriarchal appearance" that their "silvered locks and flowing beard[s]" must bestow, exciting feelings of "veneration and respect." The aged "Blind Granny," on the other hand, horrifies spectators by licking her blind eye with her phenomenally long tongue; and Margaret Patten (mentioned above) is exhibited in a crude print that emphasizes her sagging jowls and furrowed brow, her underbite, her wrinkled visage, and her old-fashioned clothes (fig. 22).[47] These aged women also, suggestively, appear among female cross-dressers and women who adopt male vocations, as if their age may, like the assumption of male clothes or occupation, sensationally compromise their sex.

As she is not (in Granger's phrase) "of the lowest order of the People," Lady Mary Wortley Montagu does not appear among the criminals, deformed people, eccentrics, and geriatrics whose images and brief histories are collected by Caulfield and Granger. Vivid verbal portraits of her by her contemporaries, however, emphasize the freakishness and horror of her aging female body in terms that resonate with the continuum we have traced across her period's definitions of age—as loss, as caricature, as living death, as a deformity that sets in over time. These portraits of Lady Mary characteristi-

Fig. 22. James Caulfield, engraving of Margaret Patten, *Portraits, Memoirs, and Characters of Remarkable Persons* (1820 ed.). (Courtesy of Yale University Library.)

cally lay great weight on the idiosyncrasy, the "slovenliness," and the incoherence of her dress. They also implicitly or explicitly suggest that her face and body display the devastating effects of an immense sexual appetite that has persisted, monstrously, into her middle and old age. I will use the example of Lady Mary to explore in more detail how an eighteenth-century understanding of the prolonged old age of a former beauty enters into the "character" of one woman. That character is constructed as an emblematic image, to moralizing or titillating effect, by her male contemporaries. It also must be formulated, narrated, and experienced by Lady Mary herself as a dynamic entity that is sustained, changed, and recovered over time.

A passage in the Marquis of Halifax's very popular conduct book, *The Lady's New-Years-Gift*, begins to suggest some of the emblematic import of the criticisms of Lady Mary's dress that are lodged so insistently as she grows older. In this passage, Halifax briefly turns his attention from the main subject of his book—the proper behavior of a young woman before marriage and in the early years of marriage—to consider what happens to women later. Halifax does not discuss appropriate and inappropriate dress for the aging woman, but rather uses the imagery of dress metaphorically to argue for certain decorums in her behavior. He combines this imagery with the language of deformity and monstrosity to describe the danger to a woman of growing old in the wrong way, ending his chapter on "Behaviour and Conversation" with the admonition:

> I will add one *Advice* to conclude this head, which is, that you will let every seven years make some alteration in you towards the *Graver* side, and not be like *Girls* of Fifty, who resolve to be always *Young*, what ever *Time* with his Iron Teeth hath determined to the contrary; unnatural things carry a *Deformity* in them never to be *Disguised*; the *Liveliness* of *Youth* in a riper Age, looketh like a *new patch* upon an *old Gown;* so that a *Gay Matron*, a chearful *old Fool* may be reasonably put into the List of the *Tamer* kind of *Monsters*. . . . It is good to be early in your Caution, to avoid any thing that cometh within distance of such despicable Patterns.[48]

Halifax's invective implicitly defines all that is ridiculous, unnatural, deformed, or monstrous about the women he describes as effects of incongruity and contradiction. Proceeding from the relatively simple oxymoron that identifies the type—"*Girls* of Fifty"—the rhythm and momentum of the passage create the impression that the emphatic phrases that follow are similarly straightforward oxymorons; the adjectives "gay" and "chearful" are treated sneeringly as obvious antonyms to "Matron" and "old." At the same time, these contradictory creatures are flattened to mere caricatures of human personality, easily "put into" the category of "the *Tamer* kind of *Monsters*" and finally reduced to the status of "despicable Patterns" for the reader's instruction.

In the middle of the passage, Halifax provides a simile to help us envision the lesson represented by such patterns. The youthful qualities that aging women resolve to retain "looketh," he suggests, "like a *new patch* upon an *old Gown*." This brief but pivotal image performs several functions: it renders what is inherently a diachronic process (the women's improper responses to aging) as a synchronic, visual image, and it does so by metaphorically equating the women themselves with the appearance of their (or someone's) clothing, moving the location of their identities outward beyond the surface of their bodies to the clothing they wear. Halifax thus participates in the tendency that we have observed to formulate the effects of time on female identity as a visual, nontemporal image or tableau; but, in doing so, he seems to push the temporal order of past and present, old and new, beyond simultaneity to inversion. The new patch that looks so ridiculous on that "old Gown" that is a fifty-year-old woman's self is from *her* point of view an old and familiar patch—some aspect of her younger self, such as her "Liveliness," that she makes the mistake of trying to retain. It is this effort to preserve parts of an existing, internal self-image that creates the incongruity of an extraneous, superficial "new Patch" applied to the costume of the social self. Time thus renders Halifax's aging women discontinuous or incoherent in identity whether they change or try to remain the same; they are deformed "Monsters" that cannot live long. Indeed, in a related passage on affectation, Halifax insists on the ephemerality of beauties' reign by shortening their life span to a few months: "They may be compared to *Flies,* that have pretty shining *Wings* for two or three hot Months, but the first cold Weather maketh an end of them; so the *latter Season* of these *fluttering Creatures* is dismal."[49]

Pope's famous satiric portrait of Sappho in *Epistle to a Lady,* like Halifax's more generalized portrait of the "gay Matron," uses visual imagery both to render time static and to exaggerate the speed of its passage for the aging woman. Like Halifax, Pope uses an image of incoherent dress to evoke the distastefulness of a middle-aged woman seeking fashionable entertainment. He does not invoke this image as a simile, however, but as a supposedly literal, though symbolically significant, description of the actual dress of a particular woman, Lady Mary Wortley Montagu. The passage in which this portrait appears develops an analogy between the ill-agreement of parts of Rufa's self and the ill-agreement of parts of Sappho's; it of course supports the epistle's general thesis that women are characterized only by self-contradiction.

> Rufa, whose eye quick-glancing o'er the Park,
> Attracts each light gay meteor of a Spark,
> Agrees as ill with Rufa studying Locke,
> As Sappho's diamonds with her dirty smock,
> Or Sappho at her toilet's greasy task,
> With Sappho fragrant at an ev'ning Mask:
> So morning Insects that in muck begun,
> Shine, buzz, and fly-blow in the setting-sun.[50]

The passage moves from an inconsistency manifested over time—Rufa's different behavior at different times—to an inconsistency in self-presentation at one moment—"Sappho's diamonds with her dirty smock"—and then back to an inconsistency that unfolds over time—the difference between Sappho at her toilet's greasy task and Sappho fragrant at an evening's mask. This final instance of ill-agreement with one's self over time incorporates, however, the sense of a synchronic incoherence suggested in the line preceding: by implication, Sappho's fragrance in the evening only conceals the layer of dirt and grease so obvious in the morning. By this point in the passage, the moral failing of women's internal inconsistencies has become so profoundly associated both with their passage through time and with bodily corruption that Sappho can be summarily consigned to the fate of Halifax's flies. The course of her life is even more accelerated, however, than that of Halifax's vain beauties: having begun in muck, she becomes the equivalent of an insect whose life cycle spans the movement from dawn to dusk.

Laura Brown has argued that Pope's relentless detailing of the self-contradictoriness of the women in *Epistle to a Lady* provides an outlet for the troubling instabilities and unknowabilities that are neither resolved nor acknowledged in Pope's account of male character in his first moral epistle, *To Cobham;*[51] we might also observe that Pope's sometimes hysterical rendering of women's vulnerability to time takes the place of any more general acknowledgment of humanity's mutable and mortal state. In Clarissa's annoyingly didactic speech to Belinda in *The Rape of the Lock,* for example, she dwells on the inevitable prospect of aging, and specifically on the prospect of changes in a woman's physical appearance, in a way Sarpedon does not in the address to Glaucus on which Clarissa's speech is modeled. Waxing philosophical, Clarissa urges Belinda to consider:

> since, alas! frail Beauty must decay,
> Curl'd or uncurl'd, since Locks will turn to grey,
> Since painted, or not painted, all shall fade,
> And she who scorns a Man, must die a Maid;
> What then remains, but well our Pow'r to use,
> And keep good Humour still whate'er we lose?
> (5.25–30)

Presumably, men's locks, curled or uncurled, will also turn to gray, but *The Rape of the Lock* is not concerned with that fact. (Men are not included, apparently, in the "all" who inevitably "shall fade.") Indeed, if we are to take the poem's fanciful epic machinery seriously, we might wonder whether men grow old and die in the world of this poem at all. Although the spirits of various kinds that inhabit the poem take both male and female forms, they were all, Ariel explains, women of one or another character in their mortal states. Obsessed with the fleetingness of female beauty and even of female life, the poem does not suggest any need for a provision of an afterlife for the mortal men that its fading women must marry, or "die Maids." Instead, it concentrates on impressing the ephemerality of their own physical attributes upon women, at least half-seriously recommending (like the authors discussed above) that they seek to exchange those attributes for immaterial ones, such as "Good Humour," as they age.

Like the Sappho of Pope's *Epistle to a Lady*, the Lady Mary that appears repeatedly in Horace Walpole's letters over the course of twenty years is the very embodiment of an incoherence so extreme that it threatens to crumble into mere dirt. Often, Walpole dwells on the supposedly insatiable sexual appetites of Lady Mary and associates those appetites with what he calls her "acquired deformities." In fact, he invents this phrase when complaining about another woman who affronts and frightens him with her sexual aggressions: he reports to Lord Lincoln that a singer in the opera has "a mind" to attract him and has appeared in his box, uninvited and unwelcome, for she is appallingly "short, crooked, humpbacked, shrill, painted and stinking, in short she has all the acquired deformities of Lady Mary, added to considerable ones of nature."[52] When Walpole refers to Lady Mary's vagina as "an ocean [with] neither side nor bottom" or exclaims over her "poxed, foul, malicious, black blood!"[53] he implicitly invokes the association between female sexual desire and physical deformity that Felicity Nussbaum has taught us to observe.[54] He also expresses the horrified surprise we have noted elsewhere that an aging woman would persist in possessing a body at all, much less a sexual one. Walpole finds the idea of Lady Mary's sexual desire, and even of her physiological possession of a reproductive system, increasingly freakish as she reaches middle and older age. In 1741 (when Lady Mary was fifty-two), he claims to have learned that she has displeased the owner of her lodging at Florence by "spoil[ing] his bed with her flowers"—that is, her menstrual blood—and then quotes Virgil's *Georgics* on an ever-flowing stream to express his view that Lady Mary is a kind of freak of nature in her physiology as well as character. In the same year, he composes a poem addressed to Lady Mary's post chaise, in which he refers to Lady Mary as "The Queen of Lust," apostrophizes the chaise, "O chaise, who art condemn'd to carry / The rotten hide of Lady Mary," and concludes with the wish that the chaise not "jumble off with jolts and blows, / The half she yet retains of nose!"[55] In this climactic vision of Lady Mary's face, Walpole exaggerates to the point of parody the familiar model of aging as loss; the joke here is that a particularly radical loss makes visible the corruption wrought by a lifetime of "lust."

When Lady Mary returned to England in 1762 after a more than twenty-year self-imposed exile in Europe, Walpole eagerly rushed to visit her so that he could report immediately and in vivid detail to his male correspondents on the new level her physical grotesqueries had reached. Indeed, he assured George Montagu,

> Lady Mary Wortley is arrived; I have seen her; I think her avarice, her dirt, and her vivacity are all increased. Her dress, like her languages, is a galimatias of several countries; the groundwork, rags; and the embroidery, nastiness. She wears no cap, no handkerchief, no gown, no petticoat, no shoes. An old

black laced hood represents the first, the fur of a horseman's coat, which replaces the third, serves for the second; a dimity petticoat is deputy and officiates for the fourth, and slippers act the part of the last.[56]

Like Pope in his portrait of Lady Mary as Sappho, and like Halifax in his more generalized portrait of an inappropriately vivacious aging woman, Walpole here invokes the monstrosity of wildly incoherent dress. In this case, Lady Mary's heterogeneous dress visually represents her accumulation of disparate experiences in foreign countries abroad, and Walpole likens that dress to the babel of various languages he elsewhere says she "imperfectly" speaks.[57] In the middle of Walpole's account, Lady Mary's dress threatens to descend, however, from heterogeneity into nullity: its "groundwork," we are told, is mere rags, and then Walpole reiterates the word *no* in canceling a whole catalog of common articles of clothes: "she wears no cap, no handkerchief, no gown, no petticoat, no shoes." Having stripped Lady Mary of all the components of ordinary dress, Walpole then replaces those articles with the mere representation of such, odd substitutes that poorly stand in, respectively, for each of the five missing articles, from an old black laced hood that "represents" a cap to a pair of slippers that merely "act the part" of shoes. In this formulation, various heavy, dirty, highly material objects are wittily imagined as the mere representations of the missing articles of conventional clothing, and are somehow linked to the verbal medley of different languages Lady Mary incoherently speaks.[58]

When Lady Mary composed "Saturday," the last of her six "town eclogues," in 1716 (before her falling-out with Pope), she wrote about her own physical deformity rather than about that of another. Having survived a bout with smallpox in 1715 that left her without eyelashes, and with a deeply pitted skin, Lady Mary "always said," according to her granddaughter, that "she meant the Flavia of her sixth Town-Eclogue for herself, having expressed in that poem what her own sensations were while slowly recovering under the apprehension of being totally disfigured."[59] If so, she "expresses" her own "sensations" in this poem in a distanced and patently conventional, even satirical, style. Though most of the poem consists of Flavia's long monologue, the opening lines present her in the third person as part of a dramatic tableau, and the monologue that follows emphasizes her vanity and histrionic self-pity in a way reminiscent of the poems of Pope or Gay (indeed, Lady Mary's eclogues were initiated in collaboration with those poets).[60] If the style and circumstances of the poem's composition raise questions about Lady Mary's placement "inside" or "outside" the scarred woman's suffering, the poem turns out to pose Flavia's problem precisely in terms of the troubled placement of her sense of self. While "Satturday" ad-

dresses a young woman's sudden loss of beauty through disease, its position among the eclogues immediately following "Friday," in which Lydia
laments her "old age" at thirty-five, links Flavia's trauma to the familiar scenario of the aging beauty who discovers she has herself become that despised
"Other"—an old woman. Abruptly changed in outward appearance, Flavia
finds herself desperately confused about where she should now locate her
sense of self. Turning her eyes to a portrait of her unscarred self, she laments,
"That Picture, which with Pride I us'd to show, / The lost ressemblance but
upbraids me now" (ll. 45–46). In Flavia's formulation, "the lost ressemblance" between herself and the portrait becomes an animated agent; some
expressive self (her lost past self? a self constituted by the distance between
her past and present selves?) "upbraids" her from the portrait's frame.

Before this loss, Flavia recalls, her beauties in fact came most fully into
being when reflected back at her through the closed, self-confirming circuit
of her face and its external image in the glass. That circuit has been broken,
and her own face now confronts her with the image of a ghastly and unfamiliar "other," a specter-self that cannot replace the *real* self she recalls:

> How am I chang'd! Alas, how am I grown
> A frightfull Spectre to my selfe unknown!
> Where's my Complexion, where the radiant bloom
> That promis'd Happyness for Years to come?
> Then, with what Pleasure I this Face survey'd!
> To look once more, my Visits oft delay'd!
> Charm'd with the veiw, a fresher red would rise,
> And a new Life shot sparkling from my Eyes.
> Ah Faithless Glass, my wonted bloom restore!
> Alas, I rave! that bloom is now no more!
>   (ll. 5–14)

The glass of course all too faithfully reflects the image of her present self;
what it is "faithless" to is the old face for whom Flavia continues to speak.
For that reason, when we first see Flavia in the poem's opening lines, while
she still holds the glass, she has turned it sharply away.

> The wretched Flavia, on her Couch reclin'd,
> Thus breath'd the Anguish of a wounded mind.
> A Glass revers'd in her right hand she bore;
> For now she shunn'd the Face she sought before.
>   (ll. 1–4)

The averted or "reversed" position of the glass not only directs its reflective surface away from Flavia's face, breaking the circle of narcissistic self-

confirmation the mirror used to provide, but also represents a reversal in her characteristic actions, a pivot that Lady Mary's formal structuring of the line captures well: "For now she shunn'd the Face she sought before." Within the taut crux of the glass's reversal, then, Lady Mary compresses both diachronic and synchronic views of Flavia's situation; the possibility of a self in *motion* waits to spring out of the static, emblematic representation it offers of a woman's sudden alteration. Though Flavia never becomes that self in motion within the poem's bounds, she has ceased (for the moment) to seek an image of herself in its reflection in the mirror. Briefly contemplating the visual image of her old "self" in the portrait she used proudly to display, Flavia struggles to imagine that external image altering (as she has) with time: "Far from my Sight that killing Picture bear," she cries, "The Face disfigure, or the Canvas tear!" (ll. 43–44).[61]

Writing in her own person, largely in letters to her sister Lady Mar, in the decade following the composition of this poem, Lady Mary often dwells on the more gradual incursions upon her former beauty made by the process of growing "old." "For my own part," she writes Lady Mar in 1724, when she is thirty-five, "I have some Cotterys where wit and pleasure reign, and I should not fail to amuse my selfe tolerably enough but for the Damn'd, damn'd Quality of growing older and older every day, and my present Joys are made imperfect by fears of the Future." A month later, she again expresses pleasure in the company of "des Amis choisies," and exclaims,

> if Life could be allways what it is, I beleive I have so much Humility in my temper, I could be contented without any thing better this two or three hundred year, but alas!
>
> Dullness and wrinkles and disease must come,
> And Age and Death's irrevocable Doom.[62]

Preoccupied with aging in these letters, Lady Mary nonetheless insists in them on her own undiminished, or even increasing vitality, countering the fear of "dullness and wrinkles" with descriptions of her pleasure in riding astride, rebutting Lady Mar's own complaints about being "an old Woman," and locating her daily pleasure and pride in the "Cotterys" of witty female friends she enjoys.[63] She also comments repeatedly that she has become a mere "Spectatress" to the busy world of London life, wondering that others choose to continue as ignominious spectacles on "stage," where "time and infirmities" may disable one "from making a tolerable figure."[64] Trying to raise the spirits of the melancholic Lady Mar, she highly recommends a self-aware embrace of the pleasures of self-deluding "Vanity"—as if one could be at once Flavia and the satiric poet who sees through the pettiness of her concerns.[65] Underlying all the responses to aging in the letters to Lady Mar is the emotional premise of this voluminous correspondence itself: the feeling affirmation of her sister as a beloved second self, a kind of "mirror" to the writing self beyond that found in the looking glass.[66]

> For my own part, I have no concern there or any where but hearty prayers that what relates to my selfe may ever be exactly as it is now. The Mutability of Sublunary things is the only melancholy Refflection I have to make on my own Account. I am in perfect Health and hear it said I look better than ever I did in my Life, which is one of those Lyes one is allways glad to hear. However, in this dear minute, in this golden Now, I am tenderly touch'd at your Misfortunes, and can never call my selfe quite happy till you are so.[67]

In a poem written ten years later, in 1736, Lady Mary has a very different occasion to meditate upon the disappearance of her youthful charms. Apparently, this poem was composed to accompany a portrait of her younger self that she sent to Francesco Algarotti, the Venetian man about half her age whom she would eventually pursue across the channel and over the Alps into Italy.[68] Although Lady Mary begins the poem by lamenting her "lost ressemblance" to the portrait she sends, her voice seems to assume its location in an older self—that older self is not regarded as an "Other," as a "frightfull Spectre to my selfe unknown"—and the poem (like the letters to Lady Mar) ultimately invests the speaker's sense of "self" in her relation to her addressee rather than in any version of her past or present appearance. Language is the medium by which the self is thus suspended in the space between writer and recipient, and the language of the poem dizzily conflates both past and present selves and self and other.

"This once was me," Lady Mary begins, as if her younger self *was* the painted portrait rather than merely being depicted in it. At the same time (as the meter of the line encourages us to hear), "*once* was" firmly emphasizes, from the start, the awareness that the portrait no longer *is* anything she would claim as "me." In the lines that follow, Lady Mary's younger self is recalled not only as a face in a portrait but also as the writer of poetic lines.

> This once was me, thus my complexion fair,
> My cheek thus blooming, and thus curl'd my Hair,
> This picture which with pride I us'd to show
> The lost ressemblance but upbraids me now,
> Yet all these charms I only would renew
> To make a mistrisse less unworthy you.
>
> (ll. 1–6)

Reusing a couplet from her poem of 1716—the one describing Flavia's portrait in "Satturday," here returning almost word for word in lines 3–4—Lady Mary might be said to bind together past and present selves, incorporating words of a younger self directly into the utterance of the moment, even as she wistfully implies the impossibility of incorporating the lost physical charms of the blooming girl into the older woman. The context of the couplet has changed from the sudden loss of beauty through smallpox to its gradual loss through aging; the adaptability of the lines reinforces the link constructed by the proximity of "Friday" to "Satturday" (and by the *Spectator* essays we considered), but the change in what follows them also suggests a difference: Flavia responded to the "lost ressemblance" with a desperate fantasy of aggression against the portrait's affront, while the aging speaker only wishes she could derive something from the portrait's image to put it to present use.

The reiteration of the lines composed twenty years earlier does not, in fact, insist upon any point of strict identity between the speaker's younger and older selves. First, the reused lines have to do precisely with traumatic breaks in the continuity of self; it is those breaks that provide the recurrent occasion that seems to bind together a life. Second, the lines here pass from an original context in which they were spoken by a third-person character, Flavia, within a self-consciously conventional and even ironized genre, the "town eclogue," into a first-person, lyrical vehicle for ostensibly authentic, autobiographical expression. They thus confuse the boundary between simple self-expression and the depiction of a character from the "outside." In any case, the poet makes explicit her largely instrumental interest in her own younger self in the last couplet of the poem's first stanza when she comments, "Yet all these charms I only would renew / To make a mistrisse less unworthy you." Her allegiance is to her present love object rather than to her younger self, and she wishes she could pillage that younger self for its physical attractions in order to achieve union with *him* and not with it.

In the two Ovidian allusions with which Lady Mary supports her wish for a renewal of her charms in the poem's second stanza, the relations among her present self, the painted image of her younger self, and the beloved become even more complex:

> 'Tis said, the Gods by ardent Vows are gain'd,
> Iphis her wish (however wild) obtain'd,
> Pygmalion warm'd to Life his Ivory maid,
> Will no kind power restore my charms decaid?
> (ll. 7–10)

In the second and more familiar of the two allusions, Algarotti may seem to play the "Ivory maid" to Lady Mary's impassioned Pygmalion; the crossing of genders such a reading requires accords both with the preceding allusion to Iphis and with the many inversions of gender positions in the letters between Lady Mary, who was the aggressive pursuer in this relationship, and the bisexual Algarotti.[69] As the final line of the stanza makes clear, however, what this ardent petitioner pleads for is not that an unresponsive representation of a love object, a statue of a beloved other, be brought to life so that it may return the petitioner's desire, but rather that a representation of her own past self be brought to life in order to re-endow her with its lost charms, that she may inspire desire in another. Apparently, the wish to merge past and present selves is as "wild" as a wish to bring a statue to life or to be transformed from woman to man; the recovery of youthful appearance is here associated not with the static preservation of an essential self but rather with the risky and sublime possibilities of radical transformation. Conjuring a metamorphic ideal of the feeling self, the Ovidian allusions of the stanza imply the possibility of an identification of the self with the beloved through the ambiguities of their application. More explicitly, they serve to emphasize the gap between the present self and a lost, past self, existing now only in the form of a representation.

In the final stanza of the poem, Lady Mary suggests that that past self perhaps always existed only as a representation, or as an unfeeling object of the crowd's admiring and desiring gaze. If that image no longer exists to exert its power, a new kind of self has come into being to take its place, one capable of ardent feeling and desire:

> With useless Beauty my first Youth was crown'd,
> In all my Conquests I no pleasure found,
> The croud I shunn'd, nor of Applause was vain
> And Felt no pity for a Lover's pain.
> The pangs of passion coldly I despise
> And view'd with scorn the ravage of my Eyes.
> Now that contempt too dearly is repaid,
> Th'impetuous Fire does my whole Soul invade.
> O more than Madness!—with compassion View
> A Heart could only be enflam'd by You.
>   (ll. 11–20)

By the end of the poem, the poet no longer asks the addressee to contemplate a permanent image of a beautiful face and, implicitly, to love her because she once possessed that face; instead, she ends by holding herself out as a face-less object of love:

> with compassion View
> A Heart could only be enflam'd by You.
> In that Lov'd Form there does at once unite
> All that can raise Esteem, or give delight,
> A Heart like mine is not below your care,
> Artless and Honest, tender and sincere,
> Where no mean thought has ever found a place
> Look on my Heart, and you'll forget my Face.
> (ll. 19–26)

As she elsewhere banishes mirrors with their alienating reflections of her own face, Lady Mary here ultimately banishes not only the portrait she plans to send but the real image of her own face, as seen from the outside. For a moment, she suggests an escape from the structure she delineates in this stanza, by which one is either an unfeeling object of desire or an unwanted feeler of it. Perhaps her desire itself could become the object of desire, she suggests, even if that entails the erasure of her own face. This fantasy takes the expected losses of aging to an extreme—Lady Mary imagines her face disappearing altogether. At the same time, she radically revises the exchange between physical and immaterial attributes recommended, for instance, by the countess of Carlisle ("Let each year, which shall steal a charm or a grace, the companions of your youth, add a virtue in return"). In Lady Mary's version, the consuming erotic desires of a feeling heart, not "virtues," are what replace the banalities of a beautiful face.

This strange last line to a love poem—"Look on my Heart, and you'll forget my Face"—contains a conscious or unconscious echo of a famous line in another poem. At the beginning of canto 2 of "The Rape of the Lock," describing Belinda's dazzling beauty, Pope comments,

> If to her share some Female Errors fall,
> Look on her Face, and you'll forget 'em all.
> (ll. 17–18)

Pope's Belinda is just what Lady Mary describes her own lost, former self to have been—her beauty exercises the same powers over the crowd, and the crowd's admiration meets with the same cold indifference from her. But Lady Mary's echo of Pope's equivocal compliment of Belinda sharply inverts it in applying its language to her older rather than younger self—not, "Look on her face, and you'll forget her moral nature, with its possible failings," but,

"Look on my Heart, in all its artless sincerity, and you'll forget my Face." If the echo aggressively revises Pope's emphasis in evaluating women, it also, however, admits him into the intimate space of the poet's passionate address to her love. Whereas the echo of "Satturday" in lines 3–4 briefly merges the voices of the older Lady Mary and of her younger self, this echo in the poem's final line seems to merge the voice of the older Lady Mary and of an alien and even antagonistic other, the satiric poet who by this time had adduced Lady Mary in her diamonds and dirty smock as a prime example of the monstrosity of female incoherence. These two instances of verbal echo are not so different as they might seem, however, since Lady Mary (as we have noted) composed "Satturday" and her other town eclogues in collaboration with Pope, and Pope even transcribed these poems lovingly into his own hand. Although the strange, sublime ending of this poem provides a utopian glimpse of a feeling self with no face—no outside to be seen—at all, it nonetheless can provide that "glimpse" only in the language of vision ("Look on my Heart . . ."). This poem does not transcend the aging self's double existence as an internal experience and as an external image, perceived and rendered by others, as it passes through time. Instead, it speaks to that experience in vertiginously dynamic terms.

One of the privileges of old age, "This Once Was Me" implies, is a release from the obligation to be a static and integrated "self" in the eyes of the world—to "be" either the portrait of a beautiful young woman referred to in the poem's opening line or the bodily image it portrays. If to age, terrifyingly, is to become "the Other," perhaps that other may encompass more than the caricature of an aging face found in the looking glass. This process may include the verbal incorporation of the misogynist Pope, but also, more redemptively, the wished-for absorption of the "lov'd Form" of the beloved other into the speaker's self. In the loose syntax of the poem's final eight lines, the poet both acts out the erasure of her own face and confuses that face and her heart with the loved form of her addressee.[70] Frightening as this in some ways is, the passion it enacts seems to promise certain pleasures in the very deformities of an aging woman's desires.

NOTES

1. See, for instance, the view described in a mid-eighteenth-century essay that women are "neither more or less than *Monsters*" (*Female Rights Vindicated*, cited by Nussbaum in this volume).

2. Letter to Sir James Steuart, November 14, 1758, *The Complete Letters of*

Lady Mary Wortley Montagu, ed. Robert Halsband (New York: Oxford University Press, 1965–67), 3:189.

In an essay on the Enlightenment interest in "prolongevity" as a "corollary of progress," Marie Mulvey Roberts comments briefly on the differential gendering of old age, noting, "though the elderly could be objects of buffoonery for rambunctious wits, it was old women who tended to be singled out for specific derision" ("'A Physic against Death': Eternal Life and the Enlightenment—Gender and Gerontology," in *Literature and Medicine during the Eighteenth Century,* ed. Marie Mulvey Roberts and Roy Porter [New York: Routledge, 1993], 158–64).

3. Observing that "the image of the mirror dominates western literary representations of the aged body," Kathleen Woodward explores the dynamics of distancing and denial that allow the individual to reject the "mirror image" of his own aging self provided by the faces and bodies of his contemporaries ("The Mirror Stage of Old Age . . . Marcel Proust's *The Past Recaptured*," *Aging and Its Discontents: Freud and Other Fictions* [Bloomington: Indiana University Press, 1991], 53–72). Woodward does not focus specifically, as I do, on the place of gender in these dynamics of distancing and denial.

4. Lady Mary Wortley Montagu, "Satturday," the sixth "town eclogue," in *Essays and Poems and "Simplicity," a Comedy,* ed. Robert Halsband and Isobel Grundy (New York: Oxford University Press, 1993), ll. 3–6. All passages from Lady Mary's poems are cited from this edition; line numbers of citations are provided parenthetically in the text.

5. Simone de Beauvoir, *Old Age,* trans. Patrick O'Brian (London: André Deutsch and Weidenfeld and Nicolson, 1972), 5, 284.

6. Letter to Lady Bute, October 8, 1757, *Letters of Lady Mary,* 3:135–36. As Woodward notes, de Beauvoir "chronicles countless instances from the historical record" of aging men and women's disgust with their mirror images, including several who simply refuse to see themselves in the mirror ("Mirror Stage," 65–66).

7. In "'Make What You Will of Me': Lady Mary and Erotic Desire" (manuscript in preparation), I discuss this poem in the context of the triangulated structures that characterize Lady Mary's renderings of erotic desire from her youth onward. Often, those structures involve three (or more) parties in an erotic relationship, but they also appear as characteristic rhetorical and imaginative features of Lady Mary's expressions of desire.

8. *Spectator* 260, December 28, 1711, letter from "Jack Afterday," attributed to Steele, in *The Spectator,* ed. Donald F. Bond (New York: Oxford University Press, 1965), 2:511. See also *The Tatler* 266, December 21, 1710, in *The Tatler,* ed. Donald F. Bond (New York: Oxford University Press, 1987), 3:342–46.

9. James Boswell, *Life of Johnson,* ed. G. B. Hill, rev. L. F. Powell, 6 vols. (Oxford: Clarendon Press, 1934–50), 3:254–55, April 9, 1778. Boswell comments in an aside that at the time of this conversation, Johnson was "now in his seventieth year."

10. In addition to the paintings reproduced in figures 15 and 16, examples in the portraits of Reynolds include those of the Reverend Samuel Reynolds (probably painted posthumously); George Clive with his family (probably painted when he was in his forties); the "Contessa" della Rena; *David Garrick in the Character of Kiteley*

and *Garrick between Tragedy and Comedy* (painted when he was in his forties and early fifties); Giuseppe Baretti (at fifty-four); Sir William Chambers (at fifty-seven); Mary, countess of Bute (at about sixty); and Joshua Sharpe. I have used the catalog commentary in Nicholas Penny, ed., *Reynolds* (New York: Harry N. Abrams, 1986), for notes on these paintings.

For other uses of a "dewlap" in the conventional manner I have described, see, for example, Gainsborough's portrait of Sir Benjamin Truman and his self-portrait of circa 1787; Sir James Thornhill's portrayal of himself in *George I and His Family* (1722–24); and John Opie's portrait of Mrs. Mary Delaney, painted when she was eighty-two. The latter portrait is discussed by Marcia Pointon, who comments that "portraits of women of advanced age are not common" (*Hanging the Head: Portraiture and Social Formation in Eighteenth-Century England* [New Haven: Yale University Press, 1993], 34–36, pl. 54).

11. On the eighteenth century's focus on the face as the privileged location of personal identity, see Deidre Shauna Lynch, *The Economy of Character: Novels, Market Culture, and the Business of Inner Meaning* (Chicago: University of Chicago Press, 1998), 30–35.

12. Interesting exceptions are the portrait by George Beare of "an elderly lady and a young girl," painted in 1747 (Yale Center for British Art), and Reynolds's portrait of Mary, countess of Bute (ca. 1780). Both Beare and Reynolds balance unusually graphic depictions of the subject's age with an image of youth (a young girl, a lively young dog) placed in close association with the subject, as if to indicate that youthful vitality remains part of her social presence.

13. For other examples, see *An Old Ewe Drest Lamb Fashion* and *Lady Drudger Going to Ranelagh* (1772). I am grateful to Joan Sussler, curator of the print collection at the Lewis Walpole Library (Farmington, Connecticut), for her expert assistance in choosing these prints.

14. The science of phrenology, satirized in the etching, itself reduces mental and personal character to anatomical features. The work (by E. F. Lambert, ca. 1820s) appears in *English Caricature 1620 to the Present: Caricaturists and Satirists, Their Art, Their Purpose and Influence* (London: Victoria and Albert Museum, 1984), no. 24, pl. 9. An earlier etching, James Gillray's *Female Curiosity* (1778), provides a perverse turn on this association between gaunt agedness and the anatomical. In this etching, the bony, leering face of an elderly woman appears just above the slanted mirror she holds to her chest, in which are reflected the plump buttocks and private parts of a younger woman; the "anatomical" here becomes a lascivious interest the old woman pursues as well as something she involuntarily embodies (*English Caricature*, no. 62, pl. 28).

15. I reproduce a 1769 version of this image entitled simply *An Essay on Woman;* new impressions from the plate seem to have been issued in later years. A pair of more elaborate, watercolor versions of the image by Robert Dighton, entitled *Death and Life Contrasted, or An Essay on Man* and *Life and Death Contrasted, or An Essay on Woman* (ca. 1784), are reproduced in *English Caricature*, pls. 10 and 11. The paintings form a symmetrical pair, with the man's left half a skeleton, while the woman's right is. One might argue that the artist treats the inevitable movement

between life and death differently in the two sexes, partly through the usual movement of the eye from left to right and partly through the different poetic selections engraved on the monuments in the two images.

16. Charles Bell, *Essays on the Anatomy of Expression in Painting* (London, 1806), 28–29.

17. Richard Wendorf, *Sir Joshua Reynolds: The Painter in Society* (Cambridge: Harvard University Press, 1996), 38–45. Art historians have also analyzed the use of landscape prospects in outdoor portraits to suggest sitters' possession of landed property and social stature.

18. Quoted in Wendorf, *Sir Joshua Reynolds*, 44. See also the related portrait by Reynolds of Giuseppe Baretti.

19. *The Rambler* 69, November 13, 1750, in *The Yale Edition of The Works of Samuel Johnson*, ed. W. J. Bate and Albrecht B. Strauss (New Haven: Yale University Press, 1969), 3:363–67.

20. In his *Serious Call to a Devout and Holy Life* (1808; first published 1728), William Law sternly drives this general observation home through a numerical accounting of how "Flavia," the vain beauty, has "disposed of" her time in her first thirty years (chap. 7, 88).

21. Bickerstaff introduces his friend's story about a visit to two widows with the comment that, as "the Ambition of the Fair Sex" is "confined to advantagious Marriages, or shining in the Eyes of men, their Parts were over sooner," and they embark early on this social "After-life" (*Tatler* no. 266, 3:342–43).

22. Psalm 103; epigraph to *Rambler* no. 130, June 15, 1751 (freely translated from Seneca, Hippolytus), 4:326. For similar reflections offered in a pious vein, see, for example, Timothy Rogers's funeral discourse *The Character of a Good Woman, Both in a Single and Marry'd State* (London, 1697), 87–88; and for the same commonplaces rendered in an irreverent and humorous vein, see airs 6, 12, and 29 of *The Beggar's Opera*.

23. *Spectator* 260, 2:511; *Tristram Shandy* (New York: Odyssey Press, 1940), 610–11. The second quotation appears in an address to Jenny, in which Tristram seems to me in fact to move beyond his tendency to locate time's effects primarily in the female body.

24. Although she does not treat the frequent gendering of this opposition between observer and observed, Veronica Kelly provides a brilliant account of the way this opposition structures accounts of the self's deformation or evacuation in time in "Locke's Eyes, Swift's Spectacles," in *Body and Text in the Eighteenth Century*, ed. Veronica Kelly and Dorothea von Mücke (Stanford, Calif.: Stanford University Press, 1995), 68–85. I am indebted to Kelly's suggestive reflections on aging in this essay.

25. *An Essay concerning Human Understanding*, ed. Peter H. Nidditch (New York: Oxford University Press, 1975), III.vi.4 and II.xxvii.11, pp. 440 and 337; see also II.xxvii.17, p. 341. I am grateful to Blakey Vermeule for her suggestions about Locke's references to identity, the body, and time.

26. Lynch reminds us that eighteenth-century culture "made *person* both a word for someone's physical appearance and a word for someone" (*The Economy of Character*, 38).

27. *Spectator* 306 (Steele), February 20, 1712, 3:101–2.

28. See, for example, *Essay concerning Human Understanding*, II.ix.14 and II.x.5, and Kelly's discussion of these sections in "Locke's Eyes, Swift's Spectacles," 77–79.

29. A contemporary book on aging by the psychotherapist Elissa Melamed, *Mirror, Mirror: The Terror of Not Being Young* (New York: Simon and Schuster, 1983), confirms what we would expect—that the stigma of aging for women is still focused on questions of appearance, while for men it is focused on issues of "performance" (69–90).

30. *Rambler* 133 (continuation of no. 130), June 25, 1751, 4:344–45.

31. *Rambler* 130, 4:330. Smallpox did in fact pose one of the greatest threats to the health of eighteenth-century English men and women; it was responsible for about 10 percent of all deaths and killed an estimated 60 million Europeans between 1700 and 1800 (G. B. Risse, "Medicine in the Age of Enlightenment," in *Medicine in Society*, ed. A. Wear [Cambridge: Cambridge University Press, 1992], 189). Essayists' interest in it therefore might not seem disproportionate. They concentrate, however, quite disproportionately on the plight of the young female "beauty" left scarred by the disease; they do not tell stories about the blindness the illness could inflict, about the death of smallpox victims or the grief of their survivors, or even about the unsightly scarring of male sufferers from the disease.

32. *Spectator* 392 (Steele), May 30, 1712, 3:470–73.

33. In sneering judgments on female character in this period, one often encounters the suggestion that a woman's mood or state of mind (or even the apparent elements of her distinctive "character") may be determined by the trivial ups and downs of her physical appearance. See, for example, the portrait of "soft" Silia in Pope's *Epistle to a Lady* who suddenly "storms" and "raves" because of "a Pimple on her nose" (ll. 29–37), and the closely related portrait in Law's *Serious Call* of Flavia, for whom the "rising of a pimple" is a dire matter (87).

34. *Essay concerning Human Understanding*, II.i.15, p. 112, discussed by Kelly in "Locke's Eyes, Swift's Spectacles," 81–82. For a book-length survey devoted to the centrality of the "mirror" in conceptions of female identity (mostly in nineteenth- and twentieth-century texts), see Jenijoy La Belle, *Herself Beheld: The Literature of the Looking Glass* (Ithaca: Cornell University Press, 1988). Chapter 4, "The Glass of Time," explores the role of the mirror in accounts of women's changing identities in time.

35. Lynch refers to this simple view of the body and face as she introduces a complex account of the eighteenth century's more troubled views of them. She comments that "the body was discursive, a telltale transcript of the identity it housed. . . . Writers of the first part of the eighteenth century seem eager to understand faces less as natural facts and more as signs, prototypical reading matter" (*The Economy of Character*, 30).

36. Letter to Lady Bute, September 5, 1758, *Letters of Lady Mary*, 3:174. See also, in a related vein, Boswell's comment that in Reynolds's final self-portrait (at age sixty-five), the features are "rather too largely and strongly limned" and yet "are most exactly portrayed" (quoted in Wendorf, *Sir Joshua Reynolds*, 45).

37. William Hogarth, "Of the Face," in *The Analysis of Beauty*, ed. Ronald Paulson (New Haven: Yale University Press, 1997), 95–96.

38. Hogarth, "Of the Face," 99, 101.

39. On the inevitability of this association see, for example, *The Folly, Sin, and Danger of Marrying Widows and Old Women in General, Demonstrated; and earnestly addres'd to the Batchelors of Great Britain, By a True Penitent* (London, 1746), 7; and Lady Mary Wortley Montagu's own pithy comment: "Age and ugliness are as inseparable as heat and Fire, and I think it all one in what shape one's Figure grows disagreable" (letter to Lady Bute, December 24, 1750, *Letters of Lady Mary*, 2:473).

40. Isabella Howard, countess dowager of Carlisle, *Thoughts in the Form of Maxims, Addressed to Young Ladies on their First Establishment in the World* (London, 1789), 129, and see also the maxims immediately following, 129–30; Rogers, *Character of Good Woman*, 87; *Rambler* 133, 4:345; *Spectator* 306, 3:104.

41. In the mid–twentieth century, Simone de Beauvoir echoes this notion in her description of her own aging self: "In spite of everything, it's strange not to be a body any more" (*Force of Circumstance*, trans. Richard Howard [New York: G. P. Putnam's Sons, 1965], 657).

42. [William Kenrick], *The Whole Duty of Woman. By a Lady. Written at the Desire of a Noble Lord* (London, 1753), sec. 23, "Widowhood," 85–86.

43. For some examples of the many reflections on this theme, see Rogers, *Character of a Good Woman*, 89; *Tatler* 266; *Spectator* 260 and 496, September 29, 1712, 4:258–60; *Rambler* 50, September 8, 1750, 3:272; Kenrick, *Whole Duty of Woman*, sec. 19, "Virginity," 66–67; and the examples from Fielding's and Matthew Lewis's novels discussed in Roberts, "A Physic against Death," 160–62.

For some examples in the visual arts, see *Age and Folly, or the Beauties* and *Ladies Wigs!* discussed above, and the satiric prints mentioned in note 13.

44. *Folly, Sin, and Danger* (7, 12ff.); James Caulfield, *Portraits, Memoirs, and Characters of Remarkable Persons, From the Revolution in 1688 to the End of the Reign of George II* (London, 1819–20), 4:143–45.

45. Compiled by James Paris du Plessis (ca. 1733). I derive this reference from Felicity A. Nussbaum, *Torrid Zones: Maternity, Sexuality, and Empire in Eighteenth-Century English Narratives* (Baltimore: Johns Hopkins University Press, 1995), figs. 6 and 7.

46. James Granger, *A Biographical History of England, from Egbert the Great to the Revolution: consisting of Characters disposed in different Classes, and adapted to a Methodical Catalogue of Engraved British Heads* (1769), 3d ed. (London, 1779), 4:212 and 216–19. Pointon briefly discusses Granger's entry on Mother Louse, and she makes the point I have incorporated here, that Mother Louse is the "bearer of a name suggesting a parasitic existence in a medium of filth" (*Hanging the Head*, 93–94, pl. 112).

47. See Caulfield, *Portraits, Memoirs, and Characters*, 1:103 (Blind Granny), 4:143 (Margaret Patten), 4:223 (James Turner), and 4:248–51 (William Walker).

48. Sir George Savile, marquis of Halifax, *The Lady's New-Years-Gift, or Advice to a Daughter* (Kensington: Cayme Press, 1927), 46–47; see also 12 and 59–60.

49. From Halifax's chapter "Vanity and Affectations," *Lady's New-Years-Gift*, 59–60.

50. *To a Lady. Of the Characters of Women*, in *The Poems of Alexander Pope*, ed. John Butt (New Haven: Yale University Press, 1963), ll. 21–28.

51. Laura Brown, *Alexander Pope* (New York: Basil Blackwell, 1985), 94–107; see also Kristina Straub, *Divided Fictions: Fanny Burney and Feminine Strategy* (Lexington: University Press of Kentucky, 1987), 31–45, 66–69, 77. For another example of Pope's treatment of the theme of beauty's ephemerality, see *Epistle to Mr. Jervas*.

52. April 18, 1741 NS, *The Yale Edition of Horace Walpole's Correspondence*, ed. W. S. Lewis et al. (New Haven: Yale University Press, 1937–83), 30:14–15.

53. Letter written in Florence to Lord Lincoln, January 31, 1741 NS, *Walpole's Correspondence*, 30:10–11.

54. Felicity Nussbaum, "Feminotopias: The Seraglio, the Homoerotic, and the Pleasures of 'Deformity,'" *Torrid Zones*, 135–62. For a pithy expression of Walpole's insistence on Lady Mary's gargantuan sexual appetites (as well as her miserliness), see his postscript to a letter to George Montagu at the very end of Lady Mary's life, upon hearing a mistaken report that she had returned to England: "P. S. Lady Mary Wortley Montagu is arrived. If you could meet with ever a large prick very cheap, you would make your court to her by it" (October 8, 1761, *Walpole's Correspondence*, 9:338).

Note that Walpole specifically links physical deformity to sexual license in the adjective "poxed" describing Lady Mary's "black blood"; like Pope's reference in the "First Satire of the Second Book of Horace" to the danger that one might be "P—x'd" by Lady Mary's "Love," Walpole ambiguously evokes venereal disease as well as smallpox with the term (Joseph Lew observed Pope's exploitation of this ambiguity in "Lady Mary's Nose," paper presented to the Annual Meeting of the Modern Language Association, Toronto, 1993).

55. Letter to Lord Lincoln, January 3, 1741 NS, *Walpole's Correspondence*, 30:8; "To the Postchaise that carries Lady Mary Wortley Montagu (Wrote at Touloun 1741)," *Walpole's Correspondence*, 14:246–47.

56. February 2, 1762, *Walpole's Correspondence*, 10:5.

57. Letter to Sir Horace Mann, January 29, 1762, *Walpole's Correspondence*, 22:3.

58. In the attack on Alexander Pope that she coauthored with Lord Hervey thirty years earlier, Lady Mary had herself developed much more aggressively than Walpole here does an association between deformity and the collapse of the physical body into merely representational status, describing Pope's body as a mere "Sign-Post Likeness of the noble Race" and asserting that it (like the mark of Cain) offers an "Emblem" of his "crooked Mind" ("Verses Address'd to the Imitator of the First Satire of the Second Book of Horace" [London, 1733], l. 14, ll. 109–12). Helen Deutsch derives the title phrase of her book, *Resemblance and Disgrace: Alexander Pope and the Deformation of Culture* (Cambridge: Harvard University Press, 1996), from the "signpost" passage in this poem, and she discusses the phrase directly at several points (10, 22–23).

59. Robert Halsband, *The Life of Lady Mary Wortley Montagu* (New York: Oxford University Press, 1956), 51–52; Lady Louisa Stuart, "Biographical Anecdotes of Lady M. W. Montagu," in Lady Mary Wortley Montagu, *Essays and Poems*, 35. Isobel Grundy's important new biography, *Lady Mary Wortley Montagu: Comet of the Enlightenment* (New York: Oxford University Press, 1999), was not available in time to consult in the preparation of this essay.

60. See Grundy's preface (x–xii) and headnote to the "Eclogues" in Lady Mary Wortley Montagu, *Essays and Poems*. On the significant differences between Gay's and Lady Mary's versions of "Friday," see Ann Messenger, "Town Eclogues: Lady Mary Wortley Montagu and John Gay," in *His and Hers: Essays in Restoration and Eighteenth-Century Literature* (Lexington: University Press of Kentucky, 1986), 84–107.

61. I am indebted to students in my undergraduate seminar "Women Writers from the Restoration to Romanticism," 1995 and 1997, for the development of my understanding of this poem. They spoke and wrote feelingly about its complex resonances for them.

62. Letter of December 1724, *Letters of Lady Mary*, 2:44; letter to Lady Mar, January 1725, 2:45.

63. On her riding and stag hunting, see letters sent in July and August 1725 and November 1726, *Letters of Lady Mary*, 2:53–55 and 71. For her response to Lady Mar's own complaints about age, see a letter of May 1727, 2:76. Her pleasure in her female friends is a frequent theme in this period.

64. See letters of circa March 20, 1725, March 1727, July 1727, and (to Lady Pomfret) October 1738, *Letters of Lady Mary*, 2:48, 72–73, 82, 125–26.

65. In October 1727 she describes, with a virtually Walpolean relish, the "Delightfull Spectacle" at Coronation Day of the magnificently embellished, fat, and wrinkled old countess of Orkney, and then comments, "In General I could not perceive but the Old were as well pleas'd as the Young, and I (who dread growing Wise more than any thing in the World) was overjoy'd to observe one can never outlive one's Vanity" (*Letters of Lady Mary*, 2:85–86; see also 2:44–45).

66. In an earlier version of her "The Mirror Stage of Old Age," Woodward speculates that "the mirror stage of old age may precipitate the loss of the imaginary, with the result that identification becomes a real and perhaps impossible problem that can only be 'solved' on a personal level . . . by blindness, by repression" (*Memory and Desire: Aging—Literature—Psychoanalysis*, ed. Woodward and Murray M. Schwartz [Bloomington: Indiana University Press, 1986], 110); she omits this pessimistic speculation from the revised essay in *Aging and Its Discontents*. I am interested in the especially intense identifications (familial, social, and erotic) that appear alongside experiences of alienation within Lady Mary's repertoire of responses to age.

67. Letter of May 1726, *Letters of Lady Mary*, 2:65–66.

68. Grundy dates the poem December 1736, based on an apparent reference to it in a letter from that month. This poem was discovered in manuscript and published by Grundy in "'New' Verse by Lady Mary Wortley Montagu," *Bodleian Library Record* 10 (1981): 237–49, as well as in *Essays and Poems* (1993), appendix I. Halsband discusses Lady Mary's relations with Algarotti in *The Life of Lady Mary*

Wortley Montagu; he also summarizes there (291–92) the history of the manuscripts of her letters to Algarotti, which were first published in his edition of her complete letters (1966).

69. In her footnote to lines 8–9, Grundy glosses the allusion as likening Lady Mary to Pygmalion and Algarotti to the female statue. For examples of gender inversions in Lady Mary's letters to Algarotti, see the letters of 1736 and 1739 in which she compares Algarotti to the Blessed Virgin, or describes herself as playing Don Quixote to his Dulcinea. I discuss these passages in "Make What You Will."

70. In discussing this poem with audiences at visiting lectures, I have encountered disagreement among readers about the primary reference of "lov'd Form" in l. 21, suggesting real syntactic slippage and ambiguity of reference there. I would like to thank the audiences at visiting lectures at University of North Carolina and University of Oregon, as well as at the Clark Library session "Deformity, Monstrosity, and Gender," for their many perceptive comments on specific lines in the poem. Participants at the Clark Library session drew out, in particular, the visual aspects of the poem's final appeal.

"Perfect" Flowers, Monstrous Women: Eighteenth-Century Botany and the Modern Gendered Subject

Elizabeth Heckendorn Cook

At the end of the eighteenth century, flowers stood at the intersection of nature and culture, marking the convergence of scientific, moral, and aesthetic discourses. As such, they mediated a crucial aspect of emerging modern subjectivity: the relation between sexed bodies and gendered identities, which, in part precisely because of developments in botanical knowledge, it was no longer possible to understand as seamless. In particular, because of their long association with the feminine, flowers now challenged fundamental cultural assumptions about female sexuality and femininity.

The late-seventeenth-century microscopic and experimental confirmation of plant sexuality, in combination with eighteenth-century investigations of phytodynamism (plant mobility), most significantly of the mobility of female sexual organs in plants, had had the effect of decoupling what could be defined as "natural," that is, physiological structures and their reproductive functions, from what then had to be recognized as cultural and therefore as contingent, even as potentially arbitrary, that is, gender affiliations, or the enacting of social scripts and codes. The descriptive sexual categories assigned to plants (male, female, and hermaphrodite) could perhaps be construed as natural and universal across genera and species, although in 1735 Linnaeus, whose taxonomy of plant sexual organs organized botany for fifty years, had to invent the category "cryptogamia" (secret marriage) for plants with no discernible sexual organs. But as subsequent studies of plant reproduction showed, these sexual categories were clearly distinct from normative gendered behaviors (active masculinity, passive femininity) that were, it began to appear, specific only to humans, and perhaps only to that subgroup of humans identified as Anglo-Europeans.[1]

Despite the fact that under the microscope most aspects of plant sexuality seemed by human standards monstrous, Linnaeus's botanical writings sought to realign nature and culture through a relentless analogizing of plant propagation and human heterosexual monogamy, even in cases where the reproductive mechanisms being charted were strikingly alien to animal physiology. This gendering of plant sexuality resonates with a widespread preoccupation with sexual identities and practices, with gender definitions, and with the relations between these that is evident throughout the long eighteenth century. In this sense, the history of botany supports Thomas Laqueur's claim about the eighteenth-century invention of sexual "incommensurability" "as a new foundation for gender"—but with a twist.[2] Laqueur writes that in this period "the framework in which the natural and the social could be clearly distinguished came into being" (154), but eighteenth-century botanical literature reverses Laqueur's emphasis, functioning as a sort of rearguard action zone in which various strategies were deployed to insist on the continued linkage of the natural and the social, of sexuality and gender codes. Much writing on botany became something like an exercise in damage control.

The first section of this essay examines the responses of late-eighteenth-century botanical literature to the differentiation of the "natural" (meaning physiological structures and their reproductive functions) from the social (gender conventions) implicit in botanical research. These responses ranged from flat denial to ingenious recuperative exercises. On the one hand, the "antisexualists" dismissed both plant sexual reproduction and Linnaeus's eroticization of botany as scientifically inaccurate and morally corrupting, especially for women, in whom the examination of plants' sexual parts and behaviors might awaken a monstrously unfeminine sexual appetite. On the other hand, the "sexualists," amateur enthusiasts and protoscientists, rejected the charge of Linnaean corruption, often in ways that left intact the gendered model of feminine purity that it implied.

In the second and third sections I turn to Erasmus Darwin's writings on girls' education and on botany as examples of what I have called damage control. Unlike Linnaeus and his followers, Darwin attempts to cordon off the feminine from the female, emphasizing their distinctiveness, in ways that strip the feminine of sexuality. Simultaneously he seeks to contain female autonomy, figured as monstrous sexual appetite, in support of what I will argue is a disciplinary program designed to shore up the gendered hierarchies of the existing social order. The second section, examining the paradoxes of contemporary ideologies of feminine character, argues that as long as femininity was defined as a kind of quasi-allegorical suspendedness, the pedagogical task of forming a feminine character was by definition impossible. In his *Plan for the Conduct of Female Education in Boarding Schools* (1797), while arguing for the importance of a characterological authenticity anchored in the body, Darwin nonetheless prescribes disciplining the female body and its involuntary motions into a responsive femininity that should become a girl's "second nature." A more dramatic disjunction between the female and the feminine structures appears in Darwin's 1789 poetic anomaly, *The Loves of the Plants,* which I will argue is deeply internally divided as a result of its attempt to isolate feminine character from female nature. This division results in a programmatic incoherence between his poetics, including a gendered aesthetic of readerly suspendedness or absorption, and scientific discourses of sexuality. In the context of botany, despite Darwin's best efforts, the female and the feminine prove both indivisible and irreconcilable.

Flowers: A Cultural History of Botany

The Linnaean taxonomy that came to dominate botany in the second half of the eighteenth century was based on the arrangements of sexual organs in plants. In earlier centuries, it had been hypothesized that some plants reproduced sexually; an example cited from Pliny onward was a pair of male and female palms, one at Otranto, one at Brindisi, whose "love" was consummated by the winds. Sexual union, however, was by no means considered the universal mechanism of plant propagation. Nor were there consistent efforts to identify structural or functional analogies between plant and animal sexual organs.[3] For example, far from identifying the pollen-bearing stamen with the penis, some early botanists dismissed it as entirely irrelevant to propagation; indeed the seventeenth-century taxonomist Tournefort associated pollen with excrement and thus saw the stamen as cloacal rather than phallic. But by the mid-eighteenth century, after the wide dissemination of Linnaeus's works (in England, around midcentury), most botanists and amateur enthusiasts came to accept the sexual reproduction of plants, along with Linnaeus's gendering of plant sexuality. At first, the confirmation that plants possess female and male reproductive organs led to the assumption that the prescriptions and hierarchies of human gender codes of masculinity and femininity were grounded in sexual differences between male and female that were universal, fundamental, and natural. Linnaeus's own willful elision in his botanical writings of distinctions between sexual categories and gender identities set the tone and the terms for his followers: in his writings, male sexual structures identify masculine entities such as suitors, bridegrooms, and husbands; female sexual structures identify feminine entities such as virgins, wives, and concubines or harlots. His own design for the frontispiece of the anthropomorphically titled *Praeludia sponsaliorum plantarum* (1730) illustrates a prototypically gendered botanical union: two distinct individuals, one an active male, the other a passive female (fig. 23).

Linnaeus's inclination to heterosexualize plant propagation was powerful enough to assimilate even the inconvenient fact that most plants, rather than being male or female, are sexually hermaphroditic ("perfect," to use the contemporary English term, meaning that they bear male and female reproductive organs within the same flower structure). Rather than imagining a third gender identity to match this third sexual category, Linnaeus simply miniaturized the paradigmatic heterosexual encounter between male and female and located it within the flower, as in the eroticized passage below from the *Praeludia,* which fervidly develops an analogy between botanical propagation and heterosexual marriage:[4]

> In spring, when the bright sun comes nearer to our zenith, he awakens in all bodies the life that has lain stifled during the chill winter. . . . Words cannot express the joy that the sun brings to all living things. Now the black-cock and the capercailzie begin to frolic, the fish to sport. Every animal feels the sexual urge. Yes, Love comes even to the plants. Males and females, even the hermaphrodites, hold their nuptials . . . showing by their sexual organs which are males, which females, which hermaphrodites. . . .
>
> The actual petals of a flower contribute nothing to generation, serving only as the bridal bed which the great Creator has so gloriously prepared, adorned with such precious bed-curtains, and perfumed with so many sweet scents in order that the bridegroom and bride may therein celebrate their nuptials with the greater solemnity. When the bed has thus been made ready, then is the time for the bridegroom to embrace his beloved bride and offer her his gifts.[5]

In this passage, the initial allusions to a physiologically determined hermaphroditism evanesce into the allegorical illustration that follows: hermaphroditic autofertilization "anthropomorphs" into a heterosexual wedding-night scene. As botany filtered out of the herbarium and the gentleman-amateur's library into the parlor and schoolroom, this model of plant sexuality dominated its popular reception.

The same compulsion to heterosexualize and gender botanical reproduction is evident in Linnaeus's fieldwork and in the implications of his system of binomial nomenclature. In his diary of a 1732 voyage to Lapland,

Fig. 23. Frontispiece to *Praeludia sponsaliorum plantarum* (1730). Courtesy of the Manuscript and Music Department, Uppsala University Library.)

Linnaeus describes his decision to give a certain plant the Latin classification *andromeda polifolia*. He composes a self-consciously Ovidian portrait of the plant as the virginal and victimized Andromeda:

> I noticed that she was blood-red before flowering, but that as soon as she blooms her petals become flesh-colored. I doubt whether any artist could rival these charms in a portrait of a young girl, or adorn her cheeks with such beauties as are here and to which no cosmetics have lent their aid. As I looked at her I was reminded of Andromeda as described by the poets, and the more I thought about her the more affinity she seemed to have with the plant; indeed, had Ovid set out to describe the plant mystically he could not have caught a better likeness. . . . Her beauty is preserved only so long as she remains a virgin (as often happens with women also)—i.e., until she is fertilized, which will not now be long as she is a bride. She is anchored far out in the water, set always on a little tuft in the marsh and fast tied as if on a rock in the middle of the sea. The water comes up to her knees, above her roots, and she is always surrounded by poisonous dragons and beasts—i.e., evil

toads and frogs—which drench her with water when they mate in the spring. She stands and bows her head in grief. Then her little clusters of flowers with their rosy cheeks droop and grow ever paler and paler.[6]

This discursive anthropomorphization of *andromeda polifolia* is given tabular graphic form in the little sketch that accompanies it in the diary (fig. 24). As Alan Bewell notes of this passage, Linnaeus "treats the sexuality of the marsh andromeda as if it were the same thing as the specific conception of female sexuality conveyed by the Andromeda myth—that of ideal innocence threatened by bestiality. . . . To see the plant properly . . . requires a special kind of double vision, which allows us to see both plant and female as one, passing easily from one to the other."[7] Bewell goes on to claim that "plant sexuality seemed to provide botanists with a means of entering visually into the innocent sexuality of an Edenic world, of recovering the unfallen Eve in an unfallen pastoral world as yet unaffected by the 'poisonous dragons and beasts' of human sexuality" (179). Although Bewell emphasizes that such botanical fantasies offer access to "ideal innocence" for the botanist, Linnaeus's "double vision" of the plant-woman depends on the evocation of a perversely eroticized menace: the botanist's recovery of the pastoral is certainly not shared by the feminized and sexualized object of investigation. Linnaeus's preoccupation with the blood-red color of the plant's "cheeks" before it blooms and "is fertilized" alludes to the blush of the virginal young girl that, as Ruth Bernard Yeazell has suggested, was read as signaling, ambiguously, her foreknowledge of, even her desire for, her sexual destiny, so that she is "always already" sexualized.[8] Above all, the passage makes clear Linnaeus's investment in a mythology of feminine virginity—specifically, in an ideal of femininity corresponding to the period of a girl's life just before sexual initiation, emblematized by the blush.

In the decades following his Lapland journey, Linnaeus developed a binomial nomenclature that again emphasized not only the sexual basis but also the gendering of botanical terminology. The names of the twenty-four classes of plants end in *-andria*, from the Greek word for husband, and the secondary divisions, the orders, end in *-gynia*, from the word for wife. Thus the primary taxonomic distinction of Linnaean botany is based on the number, proportions, and locations of the stamens, the male sex organs of the flower; subdivisions are based on the female organs. Eighteenth-century botany was founded on the modes of sexual union of plants—how they reproduce—rather than strictly on their formal physiological structures.[9] Linnaeus implicitly presents conjugal love between monogamous husband and wife as normative, even though only one class out of twenty-four, the *Monandria,* with one stamen and one pistil, could very plausibly suggest a

Fig. 24. Sketch from Linnaeus's diary of his Lapland journey (1731). (Reprinted by permission of the Linnean Society of London.)

human romantic dyad.[10] From the point of view of an established patriarchal social order, then, the centrality of plant sexuality to botany might make it seem a risqué study, especially for young ladies. But as botanical literature, following the lead of Linnaeus, continued to map the reproductive strategies and mechanisms of plants onto the Anglo-European social ideal of heterosexual monogamy, the study of botany did not in any sense threaten the existing social order itself. Instead, botany seemed neatly to affirm the gender hierarchy on which that order depended.

As Ann Shteir has pointed out, the allegorical figure of Flora suggests that notions of femininity were "always already" imbricated in the scientific discipline of botany. Shteir offers a detailed history of how botany became part of the social construction of middle- and upper-class femininity in the second half of the eighteenth century. Leisured women and girls collected plants, pressed them, and learned enough Latin to read botany handbooks. Sometimes, especially if a father, brother, or husband were involved in botanical study, women could write (or ghostwrite) botany handbooks, often targeted at children, and do botanical illustrations to support themselves and their families.[11] The prestige of female botanical activities was assured by the enthusiasm of royal ladies: Princess Augusta, her son George III, and his queen

Charlotte patronized the botanic garden at Kew, and Charlotte and her daughters were known to spend many hours on botanical studies, a royal mandate for female botanizing that was widely remarked in contemporary print material dedicated to the construction of the polite lady.[12]

However, as I will show, this domestication and feminization of the social practices of botany required effacing or suppressing what botany actually made evident: the radical dissociation of sexual categories (to which a specimen could be assigned based upon the observation of physical structures) from what we today call gender identity (the more or less consistent performance of cultural scripts). Precisely because botanical observation made explicit the artificiality of human gender conventions, much botanical literature compulsively tried to resuture "sex" and "gender," making the former look more like the latter. Following Linnaeus, botanical literature sought to establish an ideologically assimilable narrative that covered over the inconsistencies of botanical sexes and sexuality with normative human gender models.

But as further botanical discoveries were confirmed, the Linnaean analogical model could not change the fact that botanical reproduction rarely parallels human heterosexual monogamy. For example, once the primary mode of plant propagation was generally accepted to be sexual, botanists' attention turned to phytodynamism, that is, vegetal mobility.[13] Botanists became increasingly concerned to explain how and why plant parts moved: leaves, roots, stems, petals, and, especially, sexual organs. If the three botanical sexes necessarily highlighted the artificiality of a dichotomous human gender taxonomy of masculinity and femininity (in that the majority of plants—twenty of Linnaeus's twenty-four classes—are hermaphroditic) and thus provoked anxiety, even more challenging to a belief in the naturalness and cross-species universality of gender identities was the observation that in perfect or hermaphroditic flowers, the female sexual organs often play a decidedly active role in fertilization. In short, far from affirming as universal and natural the human gender conventions of male activity and female passivity, almost every aspect of the sexual reproduction of plants instead offered a series of appalling counterexamples.

This fact was not lost on Linnaeus's contemporaries, who divided themselves up as "sexualists"—those who supported Linnaeus's sexually based taxonomy—and "antisexualists"—those who rejected the centrality of sexuality to plant identity. Among the antisexualists were botanists who found the binomial nomenclature inferior to the more extended taxonomic descriptions of earlier scientists such as John Ray or Tournefort; also educators and clerics who found the focus on the organs and mechanics of sexual reproduction grossly immoral. Historians of science have gathered some of the more colorful of these responses. For example, in 1737 Johann Siegesbeck dismissed Linnaean taxonomy on the grounds that God would not permit such "loathsome harlotry" in the plant kingdom.[14] Later in the century, Charles Alston, professor of medicine and botany at Edinburgh, insisted with Tournefort that pollen was "excrementitious and noxious," and had nothing to do with fecundity. The sexual system had brought about "an intire deformation of botany," producing plant descriptions that were "too smutty for British ears."[15] William Smellie argued against plant sexuality from the relative absence of botanical monsters: the promiscuous broadcast of pollen would surely have resulted in interspecies miscegenation. Since, he insisted, many animals reproduced without sexual intercourse, there was not sufficient positive evidence to show that plants enjoy "all the endearments of love." Furthermore, Smellie condemned Linnaeus's writing on aesthetic grounds: his metaphors were worse than those of the most "obscene romance writer."[16] In 1808, the Reverend Samuel Goodenough, his pen dripping with righteous sarcasm, wrote to the founder of the Linnaean society that "a literal translation of the first principles of Linnaean botany is enough to shock female modesty. It is possible that many virtuous students might not be able to make out the similitude of [such a botanical term as] *Clitoria*."[17]

The most notorious expression of "antisexualism" is to be found in Richard Polwhele's poem *The Unsex'd Females* (1798), which presents Mary Wollstonecraft as a kind of whoremonger general and Linnaean botany as the first step toward the brothel. Polwhele is fascinated and appalled by the torrid *jouissance* that botany offers to girls, who

> With bliss botanic as their bosoms heave,
> Still pluck forbidden fruit, with mother Eve,
> For puberty in sighing florets pant,
> Or point the prostitution of a plant;
> Dissect its organ of unhallow'd lust,
> And fondly gaze the titillating dust.[18]

What follows, clearly intended as the clincher, is a parodic vignette imitating Darwin's *Loves of the Plants*, in which Wollstonecraft, to cure her unrequited love for Fuseli, voluptuously succumbs to Imlay in a bower of myrtle and *Collinsonia* (the latter included specifically because Darwin describes their mode of reproduction as "adulterous"). A storm ensues, "the floral arch-work withers o'er their heads," and "Whirlwinds the paramours asunder tear," plunging them into Miltonic despair (here in a gloating footnote Polwhele details Wollstonecraft's two suicide attempts). In the closing lines of the poem, her abject corpse becomes an apotropaic guide to virtue, itself figured by female authors who, unlike Wollstonecraft, refrain from advocating plain speaking about sex, whether in plants or people.[19]

A few pro-Linnaean enthusiasts addressed the moral issues raised by antisexualists by challenging the gendered assumptions that underlay them, including the model of a virginal femininity vulnerable to contamination that was shared by antisexualists and Linnaeans alike. This ultimately more radical reading redefined femininity as consistent with scientific competence. Anna Seward, Darwin's memoirist, wrote that the Linnaean terms "can only be unfit for the perusal of such females as still believe the legend of their nursery, that children are dug out of a parsley-bed; who have never been at church, or looked into a Bible—and are totally ignorant that, in the present state of the world, two sexes are necessary to the production of animals." Pleasance Smith, wife of a Linnaean Society president, argued that botanical sexuality in no way threatened conventional codes of femininity but rather reinforced them: "If nature may be admired and inquired into at all by women, surely vegetable nature is remote from indelicacy, and it is much more likely to dispose the mind both innocently and religiously than the paltry pursuits to which so many are doomed."[20]

What this sketch of the battle over plant sexuality suggests is that Linnaean taxonomy became so central to botany and botanical practices in the eighteenth century not only because it was pragmatically user-friendly. At a deeper level, its implication that sexuality is a crucial if anxiety-charged component of identity, in humans as in plants, resonated with contemporary obsessions about sex and gender and how the two were related. The sexualist/antisexualist quarrels are part of the history of definitions of "femininity" and "femaleness" and of the construction of women as modern gendered subjects that emerged from how relations between these two were understood.

Faces

The next two sections of this essay take the writings of Erasmus Darwin on pedagogy and botany as guides to one way in which later-eighteenth-century British society negotiated the complex relations between what they thought of as femaleness (a physiologically determined category in which sexual appetites and practices were broadly implicated) and femininity (a set of gendered practices and behaviors that, among other things, proscribed or severely limited sexual appetites and practices). Femaleness and femininity are linked in Darwin's interest in and anxiety about what he calls "involuntary motions" in both plants and humans, for such motions reveal the extent to which sexual bodies fail to match ideally gendered models of character.

The *Plan for the Conduct of Female Education in Boarding Schools* is simultaneously a general treatise and a promotional brochure for an actual institution, a boarding school run by Darwin's two illegitimate children, the Misses Parker.[21] As bastard daughters, with a social status that was ambiguous at best, these women suggest part of what is at stake in the question of female sexual desire as that which exceeds the boundaries of normative gender codes of femininity. Darwin's writing on female education implicitly acknowledges that the indices of femininity do not naturally inhere in the female body; instead, the body must be trained to exhibit them in the hope that they will become something like "second nature."

According to the *Plan*, the education of girls is a delicate balance between preserving certain spontaneous bodily impulses or "involuntary motions" while disciplining others. The term "involuntary motions" is one of a jumble of forty chapter headings of the *Plan*, including not only the usual academic, aesthetic, and moral accomplishments thought desirable in young ladies (music, dancing, compassion, veracity, embroidery) but also categories that concern bodily regimens (posture, cold baths, care of the shape, dumbbell exercises, new milk). The chapter "Involuntary Motions" follows chapters titled "Lisping," "Stammering," and "Squinting," and precedes one on "Swell'd Fingers, and Kibed Hands." Clearly, the phrase is associated with a range of minor somatic grotesqueries of which the well-bred female body must be purged.[22]

Along with these undesirable involuntary motions, Darwin, like Linnaeus and many other eighteenth-century writers, is also deeply interested in the phenomenon of blushing, which he takes to be the primary somatic marker of feminine purity. As an incontrovertible sign, the blush speaks to a physiognomic semiotics that also structured much of late-seventeenth-century and early-eighteenth-century taxonomy. Marcia Pointon has connected a contemporary concern for portraiture with "the differentiation of faces for the proper ordering of society," citing Hogarth and other caricaturists as important in this regard, and notes that John Ray, the seventeenth-century English taxonomist, wrote about the face as signifier of such sociotypical traits as criminality and immorality (an interest echoed in Lavater's late descriptions of the physiognomy of social deviants).[23] These discourses of the face were attempts to stabilize and regulate facial signifiers, to prevent what we could punningly call *impersonation*—an artificial construction of character that entails the radical dissociation of exterior appearance from one's "real" self.

However, by midcentury both physiognomic taxonomy and the character it purported to reveal had come to be seen as more complicated. Deidre Lynch has argued that from the mid-eighteenth century, the definition of "character" literally undergoes a critical change. A metadiscourse of marking in literary, theatrical, and aesthetic criticism leads to new ways of representing and indeed of producing subjectivity, challenging the earlier coherence of the various registers of the word "character." In the works of Fielding, Hogarth, and Reynolds, and in debates over Garrick's "naturalistic" acting style, based on the remarkable plasticity or "ductility" of his countenance, "character" was redefined so that it now stood in opposition to "caricature," signaling something beyond a mere aggregate of discrete signs of difference.[24] Character had become subjectivity, we might say: what Peter de Bolla, writing on oratorical handbooks, calls "an excess . . . in relation to the body and the body's representations."[25]

In the second half of the century, then, the face had become a semiotic battle-zone. In one camp were aligned those who believed that the languages of the body spoke involuntarily and therefore always truthfully. In another were those who understood the face as a socially constructed site. True, the face is unique to the individual, concentrating the signs of self-distinction, but it is also public, the part of the body that is available to everybody. Furthermore, it can be trained and disciplined, thus setting up the conditions for deception, misreading, and impersonation. As Lynch points out, the novelistic character secures its claim to deep authenticity precisely by not matching the representations of it that are circulated among others; this is true above all for the misread and misrepresented blushes of the heroine.[26]

These overlapping models of how character is represented and apprehended may help explain why the *Plan* offers such an internally inconsistent reading of, specifically, the subjectivity of girls. Neither de Bolla nor Lynch consider the special case of representations of girls; a female Garrick, if we can imagine such a thing, would have produced a very different debate. In *Hanging the Head*, Marcia Pointon does take up the question of representations of girls and young women. She reminds us that modern portraiture works by balancing traditional pictorial conventions with the singularity and uniqueness of the individual represented. But this balance is achieved differently along a spectrum that ranges from least to most individualized: from infants through girls and young women on to boys (represented as more individually distinct because as potential heirs they are genealogically significant) and up to adult males, whose individuality is most fully documented.[27] The young girl, who is located at something like the zero degree of subjectivity, is by definition supposed to be in no way singular, unique, or individual: this explains why, when Arabella, the romance-saturated heroine of Lennox's *Female Quixote,* invites other young females to tell her their "adventures" or their "history," they angrily insist that they haven't had any. Like the blush described by Yeazell, the girl should be only a representation of her own suspendedness: as Girlhood, she personifies her own future, that is, her sexual destiny. Thus portraits of girls, like those of children (and those of flowers) hover on the edge of an allegorized universality. For the artist to individuate the girl—to deviate from the generalizable—would be to represent a deviant, a caricature, perhaps even a monster.[28]

As in portraiture, so in pedagogy: eighteenth-century theorists of education faced the same paradox of feminine character. In the context of what we might call an ideology of the *suspendedness* of femininity, what can it mean to form a girl's character? Pedagogical theory, like portraiture, must seek to ground character in the older theory of the stabilizing semiosis of the face and body. But Darwin's *Plan* reveals the futility of attempts to embody feminine character. To produce the feminine subjectivity he desires, Darwin tries to reconcile a complex and sometimes contradictory set of readings of the female body's "involuntary motions." On the one hand: the female body speaks its truths through such involuntary (and therefore necessarily "authentic") somatic eruptions as the facial blush. Therefore, Darwin advises that the impulse to blush not be dulled by public exposure: for example, in the chapter "Musick and Dancing," he notes that excessively rigorous training detracts from the natural elegance and gracefulness of the female body: "It is perhaps more desirable, that young ladies should play, sing, and dance, only so well as to amuse themselves and their friends, than to practice those arts in so eminent a degree as to astonish the public; because . . . as they consist in an exhibition of the person, they are liable to be attended with vanity, and to extinguish the blush of youthful timidity; which is in young ladies the most powerful of their exterior charms."[29] Again, amateur theatricals are forbidden, lest "the acquisition of bolder action, and a more elevated voice, should annihilate that retiring modesty, and blushing embarrassment, to which young ladies owe one of their most powerful external charms" (32). Thus the limits of feminine formation are marked by an involuntary bodily response that must be preserved.

On the other hand, the face is a site of feminine self-fashioning. If the female face sometimes appears in Darwin's *Plan* as a transparent veil, at other moments it becomes a flexible opaque surface, a screen sharing the plasticity of Garrick's countenance: it can be molded, shaped, impressed, twisted, indeed warped. This facial malleability, radically inconsistent with the model of the transparent countenance, is repeatedly invoked to support Darwin's strongest argument for female boarding schools. Since the pleasures of social intercourse (including those of companionate marriage) depend on the responsive countenance, girls should be trained as ideal interlocutors. Under the heading "Conversation," Darwin writes,

> The art of pleasing in conversation seems to consist in two things; one of them to hear well; and the other to speak well. The perpetual appearance of attention, and the varying expression of the countenance of the hearer to the sentiments or passions of the speaker, is a principal charm in conversation. . . . Those, who have been educated at schools, and have learnt the knowledge of physiognomy from their playfellows in their early years, understand the pleasurable or painful feelings of all with whom they converse, often even before their words are finished; and, *by thus immediately conforming the expression of their own features to the sensations of the speaker*, become the interesting and animated companions above described. (63–64; emphasis added)

However, this physiognomic exercise, uncoupling signifier from signified, carries with it a moral danger of which Darwin is well aware. In the chapter "Address," he recalls Machiavelli's account of Castruccio Castricani, who, Garrick-like in his facial ductility, "could assume such openess of countenance; that though he was known to be a man practised in every kind of fraud and treachery, yet in a few minutes he gained the confidence of all, whom he conversed with; they went away satisfied of his good will towards them, and were betrayed to their ruin" (61). Darwin attempts to stabilize the potentially fraudulent semiosis of the plastic countenance by claiming that even Castricani's power to deceive must have originated in authenticity: "This conciliating manner . . . probably proceeded originally from friendliness and openess of heart, with cheerful benevolence; and . . . in those, who have in process of time become bad characters, the appearance of those virtues has remained, after the reality of them has vanished" (61–62).

Despite the dangers implicit in this account of impersonation, Darwin remains committed to prescribing this exercise to girls: "What then is the method, by which this inchantment of countenance can be taught? certainly by instilling cheerfulness and benevolence in to the minds of young ladies early in life, and at the same time an animation of countenance in expressing them; and *though this pleasurable animation be at first only copied, it will in time have the appearance of being natural;* and will contribute to produce by association the very cheerfulness and benevolence, which it at first only imitated" (62; emphasis added). In this daisy chain of nature and imitation, if boarding-school practice makes perfect, the physiognomic technology that makes the girl an animated mirror of the other will become a desirable involuntary motion like the blush. But this "second nature" is culturally constructed: gendered character is made, not born, and once this is acknowledged, one might well imagine not only a female Garrick but a female Castricani, one whose "impersonation" of femininity, like that of a "perfect" flower, conceals a monstrous female sexuality.

Bodies

In the *Plan*, Darwin promotes his poem *The Botanic Garden*, of which *The Loves of the Plants* is the second part, by way of a significant *occupatio:* "I forebear to mention the *Botanic Garden*, as some ladies have intimated to me, that the loves of the plants are described in too glowing colors; but as the descriptions are in general of female forms in graceful attitudes, the objection is less forceable in respect to female readers" (38). The comment is patently disingenuous, for many passages in *The Loves of the Plants* are not only "glowing" but by late-eighteenth-century standards positively lurid. Precisely for this reason, the poem is instructive for the female reader. In its preoccupation with phytodynamism, specifically with the mobility of female reproductive organs, *The Loves of the Plants*, like *The Plan*, manifests an attempt to distinguish nature from culture in support of a subtextual disciplinary program. In the context of botany, however, the female and the feminine prove paradoxically both indivisible and irreconcilable.

Formally, the *Loves of the Plants* is a strange assemblage: it is made up of four cantos of conventionally elegant Augustan couplets, with prefatory material (frontispiece, advertisement, preface, table of the Linnaean classes, and proem), massive footnotes, three prose Interludes, plates and engravings, an appendix, and separate indexes by plant name and by incidents and personifications. While some or all of these were standard features of contemporary didactic poems, the proliferation of parts here and their interrelations and contradictions strike the reader as at least eccentric, verging on the anomalous and indeed, in the scientific sense, the monstrous. The cantos describe the methods of sexual reproduction of the twenty-four Linnaean classes of plants, personified in miniature narratives or vignettes of human courtship and marriage; these are recited by the Muse of Botany to a group of nymphs and gnomes over the course of a day. The footnotes are written in the lucid, anecdotal prose characteristic of contemporary natural-history writing. The "Interludes" record an ongoing dialogue on poetics and aesthetics between a Poet and a Bookseller. Last but not least, the appendix reprints a traveler's prose account of the poisonous Javanese upas tree from the *Gentlemen's Magazine*. Each of these formally distinct elements is engaged, implicitly or explicitly, with the ideological project of the poem: clearly distinguishing the feminine from the female and containing the female when it threatens to take on a monstrous life of its own.

The formally bifurcated structure of the work, which quarantines off the scientific footnotes from the romantic vignettes, can perhaps be read as Darwin's frontline strategy: the hierarchical ordering of gender and sexuality. The two are, as it were, assigned to separate zones, typographically differentiated: the upper portion of the page, with its visually distinctive arrangement of marginal and interlinear spaces and its larger type, is, at least initially, reserved for an idealized femininity; the female is relegated to the lower zones, to the cramped and solid print of the footnotes. This quarantining is particularly important where vignette and footnote offer wildly different accounts of a plant. Consider the *Collinsonia,* which exemplifies Linnaeus's class Diandria (two males, one female); we have already encountered this wayward plant in Polwhele's fantasy. The couplets present the reproductive mode of this plant as a version of pastoral:

> Two brother swains, of Collin's gentle name,
> The same their features, and their forms the same,
> With rival love for fair Collinia sigh,
> Knit the dark brow, and roll the unsteady eye.
> With sweet concern the pitying beauty mourns,
> And sooths with smiles the jealous pair by turns.[30]

Of course, the propagation of *Collinsonia* requires more than soothing smiles, as the footnote to these lines makes clear. But after all, *Collinsonia's* promiscuity is perhaps less disturbing than the sexually active role of its female organs. In the footnote, Darwin writes, "I have lately observed a very singular circumstance in this flower; the two males stand widely diverging from each other, and the female bends herself into contact first with one of them, and after some time leaves this, and applies herself to the other." The note goes on to cite other examples of the active involvement of female organs in reproduction.

The disjunction between vignette and notes appears again in the description of *Genista* (ten males, one female), again emphasizing phytodynamism in the female sexual organs. The couplets present a romantic, even courtly image of modest female hesitation: "Sweet blooms Genista in the myrtle shade, / And ten fond brothers woo the haughty maid" (I.57–58). The footnote, in contrast, offers a vivid description of female sexual agency: "In the *Spartium Scoparium,* or common-broom, I have lately observed a curious circumstance; the males of stamens are in two sets. . . . the upper set does not arrive at their maturity so soon as the lower, and the stigma, or head of the female, is produced amongst the upper or immature set; but as soon as the pistil grows tall enough to burst open the . . . hood of the flower, it bends itself round in an instant, like a French horn, and inserts its head, or stigma, amongst the lower or mature set of males" (note to I.57). It is clear why such observations must be cordoned off in footnotes: this vividly animated female French horn could never be accommodated in the shady groves of pastoral courtship.

As similar examples accumulate, readers find themselves engaged in a kind of dizzying epistemological balancing act. In individual cases, the separate registers of the feminine and the female remain more or less stabilized against one another, but the cumulative effect becomes peculiar indeed. The pastoral romance narratives of the couplets are, as it were, ruthlessly deconstructed in the footnotes (especially if we regard these notes as the locus of accurate empirical "scientific" observation); on the other hand, the vignettes' relentless anthropomorphization of plant sexuality begins to color our reading of the accounts in the notes, and we slip into attributing agency to the "involuntary motions" of the plant organs described there.[31] Neither representational order is powerful or flexible enough to accommodate, absorb, or cancel out the other; while they are mutually exclusive, they both remain operative and indeed mutually constitutive throughout the text.

This destabilizing oscillation is consistent with Darwin's analysis of how poetry ought to work. In the "First Interlude," the Poet describes the hallucinatory effects of graphic and rhetorical representations:

> When by the art of the Painter or Poet a train of ideas is suggested to our imaginations, which interests us so much by the pain or pleasure it affords, that we cease to attend to the irritations of common objects, and cease also to use any voluntary efforts to compare these interesting trains of ideas with our previous knowledge of things, a compleat reverie is produced: during which time, however short, if it be but for a moment, the objects themselves appear to exist before us. This I think has been called by an ingenious critic [Kames] "the ideal presence" of such objects. (55)

Darwin's own poem works in precisely this way: the personifications of the vignettes combined with the emphasis on sexuality of the footnotes produce "a compleat reverie," indeed a hallucination, of female sexual agency. What Darwin may not have bargained for is that the very power of the vision disrupts the quarantining strategy implicit in the formal separation of poetic fancy from prose footnotes, a strategy that seems designed to support or protect an ideal femininity.

Looking at the division of couplets from notes, one might draw the opposite conclusion about the poem's attitude toward sexuality and gender: that in fact the very presence of the footnotes recording the activity of female sex organs is evidence of Darwin's desire to subvert the conventions of femininity conjured up in the couplets.[32] However, the poem develops a second strategy for containing female sexual agency that undermines the emancipatory reading of the text: a network of classical misogynist tropes familiar in Augustan satire, particularly in the poetry of Alexander Pope.[33] Darwin's "Proem" appeals explicitly to Ovid's *Metamorphoses* as his poem's model, but implicitly, in its description of what is to follow as "diverse little pictures suspended over the chimney of a lady's dressing room," it invokes the portrait gallery of Pope's *Epistle to a Lady* and the dressing table of *The Rape of the Lock*. The poem's opening allusion to the "Beaux and Beauties [that] crowd the gaudy groves, / And woo and win their vegetable loves" and its Rosicrucian "machinery" of sylphs and gnomes also echo Pope. If, as Ellen Pollak and others have argued, Pope's poems were central to the Augustan framing of feminine character, then Darwin's Popean references reinforce the disciplinary subtext of his botanical vignettes.[34]

The cantos deploy an elaborate series of references to either unfortunate or transgressive and morally monstrous women from mythology, literature, and history: Pope's Belinda and Eloisa are accompanied by Medea, Circe, Arachne, Dejanira, Desdemona, Ninon de l'Enclos, and Thalestris. Both sorts of monitory allusion undermine the idea of female autonomy: in his representations of the merely unfortunate, Darwin portrays women, often bereaved mothers, as victims and surrogates; his invocations of the monstrous offer examples of female sexual agency that are usually spectacularly punished.

In the category of victims, women are above all passive, constrained even in relation to their own bodies. For example, the laurel (one female, twenty male) is represented by a Pythian priestess attended by twenty priests; she "speaks in thunder from her golden throne / With words unwill'd, and wisdom not her own" (III.39–50). This image of a woman possessed is followed by a meditation on sleep as the "abolition of all voluntary power, both over our muscular motions and our ideas" (note to III.74) in which Darwin evokes the troubled female figure of Fuseli's painting *The Nightmare*, here suggestively characterized as a "love-wilder'd Maid" who is racked by involuntary shudders of horror:

> Back o'er her pillow sinks her blushing head,
> Her snow-white limbs hang helpless from the bed;
> While with quick sighs, and suffocative breath,
> Her interrupted heart-pulse swims in death.

—Then shrieks of captured towns, and widows' tears,
Pale lovers stretch'd upon their bloodstain'd biers,
The headlong precipice that thwarts her flight,
The trackless desert, the cold starless night,
And stern-ey'd Murderer with his knife behind,
In dread succession agonize her mind.
O'er her fair limbs convulsive tremors fleet,
Start in her hands, and struggle in her feet;
In vain to scream with quivering lips she tries,
And strains in palsy'd lids her tremulous eyes;
In vain she *wills* to run, fly, swim, walk, creep;
The will presides not in the bower of SLEEP.
—On her fair bosom sits the Demon-Ape
Erect, and balances his bloated shape;
Rolls in their marble orbs his Gorgon-eyes,
And drinks with leathern ears her tender cries.
                                        (III.59–79)

This long passage on the victim's involuntary corporeal motions suggests the ambiguous response to such motions that Darwin implicitly prescribes to his readers. To the extent that readers experience the hallucinatory suspension of the poem as described in the "First Interlude," they find themselves in the position of the demon's helpless and eroticized feminine victim. At the same time, her passivity testifies to her innocence and distinguishes her from scandalous figures of monstrous female sexuality in the poem, reinforcing the readers' identification with the poem's gendered ideologies. The poem thus offers a gendered poetics: the proper reading of poetry is defined as an experience of effeminization. The aesthetic discourses of the "Interludes" thus reinforce the subtextual disciplinary program of the poem: to hallucinate, to be powerless, to manifest involuntary motions—in short, to read *The Loves of the Plants*—is to be ideally feminine.

Other victims are emblems of a specifically maternal bathos. Darwin explains that in the case of some bulbs and tubers, a "parent-root" dies annually, giving life to the next year's growth. Thus the orchid is personified in an account of maternal victimization focusing on the breast: a soldier's wife Eliza, and her two children are watching a battle in which her husband is fighting. At the moment of victory, she is killed by a stray bullet. When the soldier rejoins his family, his little son runs to meet him, lisping,

> "Eliza sleeps upon the dew-cold sand;
> Poor weeping Babe with bloody fingers press'd
> And tried with pouting lips her milkless breast.

Alas! we both with cold and hunger quake—
Why do you weep?—Mama will soon awake."
(III.312–16)

The cyclamen, a plant that roots from its flower or, to use Darwin's terms, "inhumes" its seed "Nursling" (III.382, 383), is represented by another mother in extremis: burying her seventh and last child during the Great Plague, she throws herself after the little corpse into the communal burial pit: "'I follow next,' the Frantic mourner said / And living plunged amid the festering dead" (III.409–10). For Darwin's victims, the exercise of autonomy is limited to self-destruction.

In contrast with these properly feminine figures, Darwin's representations of active and powerful women dwell on and rebuke their monstrous sexual desires. Given what seems to be his marked preoccupation with the maternal, the description of the gloriosa may be taken as Darwin's idea of a female moral nadir. The gloriosa represents the class Hexandria, with one female, six males, and its stamens are arranged in two sets of three that mature one after the other:

> Proud Gloriosa led three chosen swains,
> The blushing captives of her virgin chains.
> —When Time's rude hand a bark of wrinkles spread
> Round her weak limbs, and silver'd o'er her head,
> Three other youths her riper years engage,
> The flattr'd victims of her wily age.
>
> (I.119–24)

This suggests to Darwin the story of Ninon de l'Enclos, whose sexual desire outlives what conventional gender decorum permits: she is still sexually active when her son has reached adulthood, and the result, Darwin implies, is just what one might imagine. Ninon announces that she is her lover's mother: "First on that bed your infant form was press'd, / Born by my throes, and nurtured at my breast" (I.129–30). In horror, the young man commits suicide, affirming the strength of masculine moral self-discipline in the face of monstrous female sexual appetite.[35]

Canto III, as we learn in the "Second Interlude," is particularly devoted to examples of the tragic and horrid intended to test the boundaries of Darwin's aesthetics of readerly suspension (96); here Darwin reshapes classical accounts of Circe and Medea to emphasize the monstrousness of their sexuality. To personify nightshade (two males, one female), he offers a lurid Gothic scenario in which Circe, desecrating a church at midnight, conjures

up "two imps obscene" in clerical drag for an orgy in which they "plite alternate their Satanic love" (III.38). Medea, used in Canto I to represent the
madder plant, is invoked a second time in Canto III to personify the impa-
tiens, which broadcasts its seeds phytodynamically by a kind of spring or
coil. Darwin pulls out all the stops in describing Medea's murder of her children by Jason after he abandons her for Creusa:

> Thrice with parch'd lips her guiltless babes she press'd
> And thrice she clasp'd them to her tortur'd breast;
> Awhile with white uplifted eyes she stood,
> Then plung'd her trembling poniards in their blood.
> "Go, kiss your sire! go, share the bridal mirth!"
> She cry'd, and hurl'd their quivering limbs on earth.
> (III.167–71)

In both cantos, Medea's criminal destruction of familial order is implicitly
linked to her monstrous sexuality.

Canto IV explores vegetable phenomena that are most remote from the
paradigm of human heterosexuality: "vegetable mules"; the possibility of
plant volition; and pollination by insect. It also offers examples of Linnaeus's
twentieth class, Gynandria, or "masculine Ladies," as Darwin translates Linnaeus's term; the twenty-third class, Polygamia; and numerous examples of
the twenty-fourth class, Cryptogamia. To close this chain of monstrous floral
personifications, I will cite Darwin's illustration of the twentieth class. The
exemplifying flower, the arum or cuckoo-pint, is represented by a vignette of
double gender reversal: Dejanira appropriates Hercules' lion-skin and hands
him her distaff. Darwin's note insists on the monstrosity of the arrangement
of the arum's sexual organs: "The pistil, or female part of the flower, rises
like a club, and is covered above or clothed, as it were, by the anthers or
males. . . . The singular and wonderful structure of this flower has occasioned
many disputes among botanists. . . . The stamens are affixed to the recepta-
cle amidst the germs (a natural prodigy), and thus do not need the assistance
of elevating filaments; hence the flower may be said to be inverted" (note to
IV.281). Ovid's account emphasizes Dejanira as Hercules' inadvertent murderer (she is tricked by Nessus into giving Hercules a poisoned robe), but in
Darwin's version it is not her crime but her transvestism, her appropriation
or impersonation of male power, that is shown as terrifying to animals and
satyrs alike:

> O'er her white neck the bristly mane she throws,
> And binds the gaping whiskers on her brows;

Plaits round her slender waist the shaggy vest,
And clasps the velvet paws across her breast.
Next with soft hands the knotted club she rears,
Heaves up from earth, and on her shoulder bears.
Onward with loftier step the Beauty treads,
And trails the brinded ermine o'er the meads;
Wolves, bears, and pards, forsake the affrighted groves,
and grinning Satyrs tremble as she moves.
(IV.285–78)

As Nessus's pawn, Dejanira fits the category of victim-surrogates, but it is as a gender- and even species-transgressing monster that she serves as a disempowering emblem of sexualized female agency.

Ultimately, none of the poem's formally distinct elements remains exempt from the hallucinatory vision of monstrous female sexuality that seems to migrate out of the original cordon sanitaire of the footnotes. Even the appendix, which reprints a Dutch colonist's protoethnographic account of the Javanese upas tree, participates in the poem's struggle to recontain the female in the feminine. The upas tree was said to be a botanical anomaly, a "unique" organism, meaning one that reproduces itself nonsexually (like the phoenix). Travelers' accounts claimed that the exhalations of the tree destroyed life for miles around, and noted that its sap was used for ritual executions. Not by chance, I think, the account at the end of *The Loves of the Plants* describes the execution of, specifically, sexually transgressive women. The Dutch writer attests to the efficacy of the poison after having observed the punishment of "thirteen of the Emperor's concubines . . . who were convicted of infidelity to the Emperor's bed" at Soura-Charta in February 1776 (156). The women were stripped to the waist and lanced "in the middle of their breasts"; his description of their agonized death-contortions is detailed and clinical, down to the Latin medical phrase that provides a final example of Darwin's fascination with involuntary motions: "in about five minutes after they were lanced, they were taken with a tremor, attended with a *subsultus tendium,* after which they died in the greatest agonies, crying out to God and Mahomet for mercy. In sixteen minutes by the watch, which I held in my hand, all the criminals were no more." Examined some hours later, the corpses' deterioration seems to manifest the hidden criminal characters of the dead women, realigning surfaces and depths in support of the gendered conventions that assign sexuality to monsters: "I observed their bodies full of livid spots, much like those of the Petechiae, their faces swelled, their colour changed to a kind of blue, their eyes looked yellow, etc. etc." (193).

The story of the concubines' execution emblematizes what I am claiming to be Darwin's purpose in *The Loves of the Plants:* the recuperation of Nature, or female sexuality, by the male natural historian's successful discursive ordering of the "involuntary motions" of female bodies, according to a feminine ideal that is intended to function as a "second nature," replacing the dangerous original. *The Loves of the Plants,* like *The Plan for the Conduct of Female Education in Boarding Schools,* is an example of the disciplinary print technologies devised by later-eighteenth-century writers and theorists who sought to convert the female into the feminine, or, put more tendentiously, to sublimate female sexual agency into passive feminine "character."[36] But if Darwin intended these monitory images of monstrous women to discipline and recontain the threatening autonomy of a sexually aggressive female nature that seeps out of the scientific footnotes into what was originally the romance register of the couplets, his effort must be ruled a spectacular failure. Not only is the bifurcated formal structure of the poem compromised by the migration of the sexualized female into the spaces of femininity, but more subversively the fundamental epistemological model that separates femininity from femaleness, grounding Darwin's society and his science in a gendered hierarchy, is undermined.

What I have described here as internal incoherence, as an ideological failure in *The Loves of the Plants,* has been read differently by others. Darwin's contemporaries took the poem to be a revolutionary invitation to radical free love, even to female emancipation, monstrously successful on its own terms; this was precisely what provoked both Polwhele's frothing denunciation of Linnaeo-Darwinian botany and the intermittently amusing parody "The Loves of the Triangles" in the *Anti-Jacobin* (1798). But such an emancipatory reading requires, among other things, the suppression of that lurid parade of female monsters and victims and the erasure of their variously sexualized and desexualized bodies. This tendency, which might be called the "pastoralization" of Linnaean botany, has continued in some recent criticism: one essay claims that *The Loves of the Plants* contains "no sexual victims, no rape or violence of the kind found in Ovid or, for that matter, in some of Linnaeus's work. . . . All is clean, healthy, and pastoral."[37] Bewell's more nuanced assertion, already cited, that "plant sexuality seemed to provide botanists with a means of entering visually into the innocent sexuality of an Edenic world, of recovering the unfallen Eve in an unfallen pastoral world," nonetheless leads him to read *The Loves of the Plants* as "a revolutionary kind of pastoral writing aimed at subverting conventional wisdom about gender and sexuality."[38] Such readings suppress the anomalies and monstrosities, the generic and ideological inconsistencies of this poem, flattening out its ambivalent and complex commentary on the relations between feminine character and female sexuality. To the extent that Darwin's attempt at constructing the female as a sexualized negative of femininity is part of the larger cultural work of natural history, and beyond that of our contemporary ways of understanding how the scientific, aesthetic, and moral discourses of nature shape our own perceptions of the world, it is critical to see how its representations of women's sexualized bodies ground modern notions of gendered subjectivity.

NOTES

1. The feminine/masculine pair does not exhaust the gender identities available to eighteenth-century Anglo-Europeans, as Randolph Trumbach, among others, has argued. See particularly his "London's Sapphists: From Three Sexes to Four Genders in the Making of Modern Culture," in *Body Guards: The Cultural Politics of Gender Ambiguity,* ed. Julia Epstein and Kristina Straub (New York: Routledge, 1991).

2. Thomas Laqueur, *Making Sex: Body and Gender from the Greeks to Freud* (Cambridge: Harvard University Press, 1990), 150.

3. The *OED* notes that the name of the pistil, now invariably described in botany handbooks as the female reproductive organ of a plant, came from its resemblance to a pestle, while the stamen or male organ took its name from the Latin word for a fabric's warp thread. See François Delaporte, *Nature's Second Kingdom: Explorations of Vegetality in the Eighteenth Century,* trans. Arthur Goldhammer (1979; Cambridge: MIT Press, 1982), 116.

4. Our historical incapacity to deal with what current biomedical discourse calls human "intersexuality," the sexual/gender identities of individuals with ambiguous or mixed physical structures and/or chromosomal and hormonal conditions, including hermaphroditism, is discussed in Julia Epstein's *Altered Conditions: Disease, Medicine, and Storytelling* (New York: Routledge, 1995), 79–122. The translation of plant hermaphroditism into human heterosexuality in popular accounts of plant reproduction supports Epstein's point that "a historical examination of the understanding and treatment of these conditions discloses the ideological power of ideas of normativity in relation to sex" (80).

5. Cited in Wilfrid Blunt, *The Compleat Naturalist: A Life of Linnaeus* (New York: Viking, 1971), 34.

6. Blunt, *The Compleat Naturalist,* 56.

7. Alan Bewell, "'On the Banks of the South Sea': Botany and Sexual Controversy in the Late Eighteenth Century," in *Visions of Empire: Voyages, Botany, and Representations of Nature,* ed. David Philip Miller and Peter Hanns Reill (Cambridge: Cambridge University Press, 1996), 177.

8. Ruth Bernard Yeazell, *Fictions of Modesty: Women and Courtship in the English Novel* (Chicago: University of Chicago Press, 1991), 65–80.

9. This is a point Foucault does not adequately consider in his analysis of "clas-

sical" taxonomy in *The Order of Things: An Archaeology of the Human Sciences* (1970; reprint, New York: Vintage, 1973, chap. 5, "Classifying") which emphasizes the tabular, static aspect of Linnaean botanical systematizing.

10. Londa Schiebinger has suggested that Linnaean taxonomy should be related on the one hand to contemporary Anglo-European models of marriage, exemplified by Linnaeus's own courtship of a well-dowried wife to whom he referred as his "monandrian lily," and on the other to innovations in contemporary pornography emphasizing relatively detailed descriptions of genitalia. See *Nature's Body: Gender in the Making of Modern Science* (Boston: Beacon, 1993), 25–26. Consider, for example, a text entitled "The Natural History of the Frutex Vulvaria," by one Philogynes Clitorides, or a poem blandly called "The Sensitive Plant," a pseudobotanical description of the penis dedicated to none other than Joseph Banks (Bewell, "On the Banks," 182).

11. A very few traveled to the New World colonies, including Maria Sibylla Merian, born into a German family of illustrators, whose studies of insect metamorphoses combine still-life naturalism and detail with a protoecological awareness of the plants with which the insects interacted. See Natalie Zemon Davis, *Women on the Margins: Three Seventeenth-Century Lives* (Cambridge: Harvard University Press, 1995), 140–202; see also Schiebinger, *Nature's Body*, 203–4.

12. Ann Shteir cites a poem celebrating Charlotte as ideal wife, parent, and female scientist that was included in the first issue of the *Lady's Poetical Magazine* of 1781: "Happy for England, were each female mind, / To science more, and less to pomp inclin'd; / If parents, by example, prudence taught, / And from their QUEEN the flame of virtue caught! / Skill'd in each art that serves to polish life, / Behold in HER a scientifick wife!" (*Cultivating Women, Cultivating Science: Flora's Daughters and Botany in England, 1760–1860* [Baltimore: Johns Hopkins University Press, 1996], 36).

13. On the history of phytodynamism in the second half of the eighteenth century, see Delaporte, *Nature's Second Kingdom*, 149–86.

14. Cited in Schiebinger, *Nature's Body*, 30.

15. Cited in Shteir, *Cultivating Women, Cultivating Science*, 17.

16. Cited in Schiebinger, *Nature's Body*, 29, 30.

17. Cited in Blunt, *The Compleat Naturalist*, 245.

18. Polwhele sets up botany as a recursive trap: even to be interested in it is to be already corrupted (one is reminded of Rousseau's claim that, for a young girl, simply opening his novel *Julie* accomplished her ruin). Unwilling to waste a good pair of couplets, Polwhele records in a footnote to the lines quoted here an even more lurid original version, in which coeducational botanizing is the prelude to orgy: girls "Eager for illicit knowledge pant, / With lustful boys anatomize a plant; / The virtues of its dust prolific speak, / Or point its pistill with unblushing cheek." Polwhele comments pointedly, "I have, several times, seen boys and girls botanizing together" (*"The Unsex'd Females" and "The Female Advocate,"* ed. Gina Luria [New York: Garland, 1974], 8). For a further discussion of representations of Wollstonecraft's relation to botany see Bewell's "'Jacobin Plants': Botany as Social Theory in the 1790's," *Wordsworth Circle* 20 (1989): 132–39.

19. A less dramatic antisexualist strategy involved trying to suppress the sex while keeping the system. In his *Botanical Arrangement of All the Vegetables Naturally Growing in Great Britain* (1776), which became a standard text, William Withering, a member, like Darwin, of the Lunar Society of Birmingham, acknowledged the practical advantages of Linnaean nomenclature but rejected its explicit sexuality as unsuitable for female readers: "From an apprehension that botany in an English dress would become a favorite amusement with the ladies, . . . it was thought proper to drop the sexual distinctions in the titles to the Classes and Orders." So Withering substituted English words intended to be without sexual connotation for Linnaeus's Latin: for example, "stamen" became "chive" and "pistil" became "pointal." Seven years later, the Botanical Society of Lichfield, one of whose three members was Erasmus Darwin, published English translations of Linnaeus's *Systema Vegetabilium* and *Genera Plantarum*. Throughout the *System of Vegetables*, the translators criticize Withering's *Botanical Arrangement* for confusing both Latin- and English-speaking botanists. Ducking the question of sexuality, they argue that it is more straightforward to anglicize the Latin terms than to translate them. Withering finally gave in, reluctantly adapting Linnaean terms in his third edition of 1796. Shteir gives a full account of this exchange (*Cultivating Women, Cultivating Science*, 21–24).

20. Cited in Shteir, *Cultivating Women, Cultivating Science*, 29.

21. Prefiguring the "infomercial" videotapes that colleges send out today to prospective applicants, the frontispiece of the *Plan* is an engraving of a garden scene labeled "From the Garden of Miss Parker's Boarding School." The blending of ostensibly disinterested information and specific product promotion is typical of Darwin, who immodestly puffed his own poetry in the *Plan* and asked his friends Matthew Boulton and Josiah Wedgwood how they wanted their factories commemorated in his industrial poetry.

22. Darwin was himself a lifelong stammerer, as was his oldest son, whom he sent abroad to speak French only for two years as a cure (Anna Seward, *Memoirs of the Life of Dr. Darwin* [London, 1804], 63–64). He was therefore surely particularly attuned to questions of bodily self-control and self-discipline.

23. Marcia Pointon, *Hanging the Head: Portraiture and Social Formation in Eighteenth-Century England* (New Haven: Yale University Press, 1993), 194–98.

24. Deidre Lynch, "Overloaded Portraits," in *Body and Text in the Eighteenth Century* (Stanford: Stanford University Press, 1994), 119, 142. Lynch details the pervasiveness and intensity of debates over Garrick's acting. An actor's face was ideally the "screen on which the operations of a natural semantic system might be viewed with special distinctness," as Lynch puts it, and it was for the "ductility" of his facial muscles that Garrick became so famous. Diderot and others extolled his representations of the whole taxonomy of the human passions: for example, in one famous scene his face displayed within five seconds the signs of delight, pleasure, tranquility surprise, astonishment, sorrow, fright, horror, despair, returning to delight. His detractors found this facial play "too much": it was overloaded, excessive, caricatural, kitschy (136–41).

25. Peter de Bolla, *The Discourse of the Sublime* (New York: Blackwell, 1989), 131, 161.

26. Lynch, "Overloaded Portraits," 142.

27. Pointon, *Hanging the Head,* 194–203.

28. The same point could be made about images of flowers, which for all their intensity of detail inevitably become allegories of the transience and ephemerality of the material. This reading of the feminine individualized as monstrous suggests a somewhat less egregiously misogynist, if still distinctly antifeminist, reading of the opening couplet of "Epistle to a Lady": "Nothing so true as what you once let fall, / Most women have no characters at all." I thank Helen Deutsch for suggesting this connection; see her chapter on Pope's anxieties about male and female character in *Resemblance and Disgrace: Alexander Pope and the Deformation of Culture* (Cambridge: Harvard University Press, 1996), 83–135.

29. *A Plan for the Conduct of Female Education in Boarding Schools* (1797; New York: Johnson Reprint Corp., 1968), 12. Further citations to this edition are given in the text.

30. *The Botanic Garden,* vol. 2 (New York: Garland, 1978), I.51–56. Further references to this edition are given in the text.

31. To some extent Darwin would have encouraged such a slippage: in his *Phytologia* (1800), Darwin argues for plant sensitivity and indeed for some form of vegetal consciousness. See Delaporte, *Nature's Second Kingdom,* 157–58.

32. This, I think, would be consistent with the claim of Janet Browne that "in writing of the passions as if the human beings who experienced them were mere plants" ("Botany in the Boudoir and Garden: The Banksian Context," in *Visions of Empire,* 164), Darwin sought to bring human behaviors into line with "natural" plant behaviors in an age in which "fear of the wilderness was gone" and "natural processes" were seen as "free of imposed moral value" (169). Browne claims that Darwin's "descriptions of the sex life of plants glorified the unsophisticated virtues, the uncomplicated naturalness of plant reproduction, and pointed up the shortcomings of human conventions" (169). I read Darwin as far more ambivalent about "natural" female sexuality in both plants and humans than does Browne or Bewell, a point I return to in my conclusion.

33. See Felicity Nussbaum's *The Brink of All We Hate: English Satires on Women, 1660–1750* (Lexington: University Press of Kentucky, 1984) for a comprehensive cataloging and analysis of such tropes in Augustan satire.

34. In nodding to Marvell's "To His Coy Mistress," "vegetable loves" invokes another highly ironic body of poetry on nature, sexuality, and gender conventions. On Pope, see Ellen Pollak's discussion of how the supernatural machinery supports the "metaphysics of femininity" of *The Rape of the Lock* (*The Poetics of Sexual Myth: Gender and Ideology in the Verse of Swift and Pope* [Chicago: University of Chicago Press, 1985], 86–88).

35. In her *Memoirs of Dr. Darwin,* Anna Seward has six pages on her attempt to moderate Darwin's representation of this "celebrated female voluptuary" (286), which turns into a disquisition on chastity as the key to all virtues in women.

36. In this sense, the *Loves of the Plants* is among a range of print material, including conduct books, housewifery manuals, educational treatises, advice columns, ladies' magazines, and marriage manuals, as well as what Nancy Armstrong calls

"domestic fiction," that seek to construct a new "domestic woman." See *Desire and Domestic Fiction: A Political History of the Novel* (Oxford: Oxford University Press, 1987), 59–95. Armstrong specifically cites Darwin's *Plan* as an example.

37. Janet Browne, "Botany for Gentlemen," *Isis* 80 (1989): 615.

38. Bewell, "'On the Banks,'" 179, 184. Armstrong's reading of the *Plan*, if extended to *The Loves of the Plants*, would also tend to refute Bewell's suggestion that Darwin seeks unequivocally to subvert. She notes that Darwin acknowledged the viciousness of many mythological figures, but insisted that explication would prevent their being taken as bad examples: "Darwin could allow his reader to consume almost any kind of information provided that reader knew how to interpret it"—that is, in accordance with the ideal of the domesticated subject (105).

Obedient Faces: The Virtue of Deformity in Sarah Scott's Fiction

Robert W. Jones

It has long been recognized that the literature of the Hanoverian period—perhaps particularly the fictions of the midcentury—exhibits a profound fascination with the faces and bodies of its leading characters.[1] What is striking in all the varied manifestations of this interest is that the face is generally imagined to have a moral significance or at least to give a key to the moral standing of the man or woman who possesses it. Works by Fielding, Richardson, Mackenzie, and Sterne all feature prominent descriptions of the faces of major players that the reader was expected to understand in terms that are ultimately more ethical than physical. This semiotics of character is more often applied to women: witness Sophia Weston and Amelia Booth among Fielding's heroines and the scrupulous attention to appearance that determines the presentation of Clarissa and Pamela. To the eighteenth-century novel reader skilled in the nuances of such pictorialism, if a woman's face was formed in one way it might denote her sly and grasping nature; if shaped in another, presumably more pleasing way, it would reveal her to be chaste and modest; perhaps an eligible match or a worthy mother.[2] The practice of reading the face was not confined to the adventures of *Tom Jones* or the comedy of men of feeling. There is now ample evidence that similar assumptions had a bearing on the conduct and judgment of men and women in eighteenth-century society. As Roy Porter has argued, in a society in which encounters between young men and women remained highly regulated, physical appearance was one of the few indicators available to intending marriage partners. The ability to distinguish between the face of the scheming coquette and the visage of a virtuous woman was therefore a skill thought advantageous to a young man's education. Women were not expected to be merely the passive objects of this scrutiny; via the media of advice literature, they were urged to compose their faces so as to allow their better natures to shine through. In such a climate physiognomists flourished, and texts giving counsel to intending partners and to other interested parties were published in profusion.[3]

Midcentury periodicals rarely felt inhibited when it came to giving advice on this grave matter, and the eighty-second issue of the essay-periodical *The Adventurer*, first published in August 1753, is no exception. The writer, beginning what is unquestionably an address to a middle-class readership assumed to contain a high proportion of women, soon warms to his task and announces his intention of teaching all the ladies "the art of being PRETTY." In so doing the essay attempts to account for the presence of a virtuous woman in terms that both accepted, and yet sought to distance themselves from the age-old notion that a beautiful countenance discovered a beautiful mind. The elegantly fashioned and gently admonishing argument strolls through a familiar terrain of condemnation and praise. The writer by turns decries folly, delights in the dimples of a smiling girl, and questions the ineffable nature of love, before settling on the premise that beauty resides more in the passions than in a "smear of paint."[4] Beauty, because it "depends principally on the mind," that is to say, not on looks but on "SENTIMENTS and MANNERS," may be considered a moral good. The *Adventurer*'s intention is to counter the idea that the sight of beauty leads always to vice:

> NEITHER does beauty which depends upon temper equally endanger the possessor; "it is," to use an eastern metaphor "like the towers of a city, not only an ornament but a defence": if it excites desire, it at once controuls and refines it; it represses with awe, it softens with delicacy, and it wins to imitation. The love of reason and virtue is mingled with the love of beauty; because this beauty is little more than the emanation of intellectual excellence, which is not an object of corporeal appetite. As it excites a purer passion, it also more forcibly engages to fidelity: every man finds himself more powerfully restrained from giving pain to goodness, than to beauty; and every look of a countenance in which they are blended, in which beauty is the expression of goodness, is a silent reproach of the irregular wish.[5]

A charming physical appearance is presented here as a figure of constancy and virtue. True beauty speaks the virtuous form of woman; a vision that "excites the purer passion." It is a presence that charms without dissembling, and provides a compelling spectacle while remaining chaste and modest.

With this image in place, the essayist finds it comparatively easy to assert that, "those who wish to be LOVELY, must learn early to be GOOD."[6] Despite earlier assurances that beauty could and would be defended, what is occurring in this passage is a subtle changing of the terms of the argument. The beauty of women is kept as an essentially questionable property unless it is

allied with proper moral sentiments, with a propriety that chastens the desires beauty might otherwise be thought to evoke. Certainly the "Beauties"
to which the article later refers are taken to be less than virtuous, and represent merely the vain appearance of good looks combined with tasteless co-
quetry. Their appearance is described as a "wretched . . . substitute for the
expression of sentiment."[7] That beauty and prettiness appear to be distinguished by this rhetoric represents a telling alteration in the way in which
the notion of the beautiful is articulated. Texts written in this period repeatedly effect the transposition of an aesthetic category into the polite or familiar discourse that marks the *Adventurer*'s advice. Once moved, the term
becomes a prescriptive, as well as a descriptive appraisal of women. It is here
that the *Adventurer* hopes both to frustrate the power play of the "factitious
beauty" and to teach its audience "an art by which their predominant passion may be gratified, and their conquests not only extended, but secured."[8]
Underlying such an assertion is a consideration of how women might be represented both in the private sphere of the drawing room, and in the public
world of ballrooms and society assemblies.[9]

My reading of the *Adventurer* essay suggests that by the mid-eighteenth
century, accounts of a woman's physical appearance, her beauty or otherwise, had been transformed into a vocabulary that marked out the proper or
the obscene nature of feminine display. Shaping this discourse is the assumption that beauty is the term that best represents the moment of a
woman's public visibility; functioning as an image that declared her moral
and sexual role. However, despite the complacency of the *Adventurer*'s pre-
cepts, many midcentury discourses are more readily characterized by a contradictory investment in and yet disavowal of femininity and the female
body. For many commentators, to suggest a connection between virtue and
beauty was to place morality on a very questionable footing. The equation
not only granted a tremendous authority to the viewed object, but relied on
an inherent legibility in the beautiful body that was often hard to find. Too
frequently the beautiful woman was discovered to be unreadable; the signs
making up her face and body found to be too singularly wonderful to permit a detailed examination of her character. Men, such as those who wrote
rather bitter articles for periodicals like *The Connoisseur,* confessed that they
could no longer distinguish fine ladies from prostitutes and appealed for legislation to clarify the situation.[10] Most problematically, the physical presence of beautiful women was thought of as acting upon the mind of the male
viewers with a sudden and overwhelming effect. As such the experience was
conceived of as the sensation of an instantaneous excitement, a thrill to the

senses that prevented male spectators from acting responsibly and that further suggested a loss of potency equally damaging to their masculinity.[11]

Given these anxieties, novels of the period place particular yet uncertain stress on the appearance of their heroines. Tassie Gwilliam's reading of Samuel Richardson's *Pamela* has shown the complexities and ambiguities raised by bodily illegibility to be many and various. Gwilliam's close analysis of the text exposes the degree to which Richardson's writing and subsequent editing sought to stabilize what was an unhelpfully vague visual language.[12] Other novelists, of which Fielding is perhaps the best example, sought to resolve this problem by contrasting the looks and behavior of the dissipated beauty with her more ugly sisters, adding to this narrative a corresponding investment in the plain or ugly face as the sign of true worth and virtue. For the face of an ugly woman represented a physiognomy that, while it could not seize the attention of the male gaze or awaken a woman's sexuality, could be read by the more discerning eye of the moralist. Fielding's last novel, *Amelia*, is one among many texts that gave moral weight to the ugly or deformed face. Although suspicious of physiognomy as a guide to moral character (it is satirized in both *Tom Jones* and *Amelia*), Fielding was keen to draw attention to the damaged nose of his heroine as an indicator of her social and moral transparency. To underline this association, Fielding's wayward hero, Booth, describes his beloved Amelia in enthusiastic tones, claiming that her damaged nose gives him an indication of her greater worth.[13] In her fine analysis of Fielding's novel, Jill Campbell has explored how Amelia's awkward face is positioned in relation to what she describes as the "proleptic cultural dream" of the mother as "domestic heroine." As Campbell makes clear, Amelia's damaged nose is central to Fielding's representation of her as thoroughly domesticated and yet morally self-sufficient.[14] While Campbell succeeds in exploring the disjunction between Amelia's homely virtues and the sexual license of society ladies such as the disreputable Lady Bellaston of *Tom Jones,* a focus on the unbeautiful face and its relation to the meaning of virtue and to the nature of feminine sexuality may also yield worthwhile insights. For it is in the presentation and discussion of the ugly woman that a distinctly middle-class account of virtue is made most emphatically.[15]

An Ugly Resemblance of My Father

These connections are most vividly realized in the work of Sarah Scott, a writer from the midcentury whose fiction is now receiving much critical interest.[16] In many of Scott's works faces that are scarred or plain, and bodies that are twisted or deformed feature prominently. Certainly, physical deformity plays an important part in Scott's most famous novel, *Millenium Hall* (published in 1762) in which a number of the women have bodies that are variously damaged or deformed. Key moments in other novels, such as *The History of Sir George Ellison* and *The History of Cornelia*, also place an emphasis on the imagined distinction between the ugly and the beautiful woman. It is, however, in *Agreeable Ugliness*, first published in 1754, and to which Scott added the telling subtitle, *or the Triumph of the Graces*, that Scott makes her commitment to ugliness most apparent.[17] It is on this now unfamiliar work that this essay focuses. A reading of *Agreeable Ugliness* will reveal that for Scott ugliness had an almost moral quality as the sign of virtuous femininity. Throughout the novel, which is a loose translation of Pierre Antoine de la Place's *La Laideur Amiable et les Dangers de la Beauté*, Scott focused precisely on the issue of a woman's physical appearance in relation to her social as well as sexual identity.[18] The narrative, told in the first person, details the life of a gentlewoman living in France at the end of the seventeenth century. In many respects the life of the narrator (who is never named) fulfills the reader's expectations of a sentimental novel of this period. She has her lovers whom her father's prohibitions deny her; she has escapades (unwillingly) at masquerade balls; and finally, belatedly, is offered a reward in the form of a loving and virtuous marriage to her first admirer, a local aristocrat. What is distinctive about *Agreeable Ugliness*, however, is that the narrator defines herself, quite clearly and deliberately, as "ugly." Furthermore, she makes her lack of visual significance the foundation of her relationship with her father. Building on the formidable filial identification, Scott makes physical ugliness the principal object in an examination of the nature of female propriety; an inquiry that manipulates ugliness as the exemplary sign of gender difference.

In a perceptive essay on Scott's novel, Caroline Gonda has begun to explore the connections between virtue and ugliness that I have described here.[19] However, Gonda's focus is on the father-daughter relations represented by Scott, and not upon ugliness itself. What her essay lacks therefore is a sense of how the perception of the narrator's ugliness coincides with an increasingly forceful middle-class account of feminine subjectivity and individual integrity. Neither does Gonda attribute any particular meaning to ugliness beyond its opposition to the sexuality condemned by conduct books. This is a mistake: ugliness and deformity are at the center of Scott's moral program, functioning as both the sign and the guarantee of moral worth. By contrast, beauty is fickle and duplicitous; worse still, beautiful women are ambitious and adventurous:

> A Handsome Woman is, by her Beauty, placed in a more distinguished, and more conspicuous Light in the World, than a Dutchess is at Court. The Seat of Honour is due to a Woman's Birth, to the services of her Husband, or to the Favour of the Prince, the sovereign Dispenser of Ranks and Titles; but for our Charms we are indebted to Nature alone, and yet we are apt to think we owe them to ourselves. . . . At the play, the Opera, or at any public Assembly, observe on one Side a Lady of the first Fashion, whose only Recommendations are her Title, the Richness of her Cloaths, and the Sparkling of her Jewels. On the other, A Woman much her inferior in Birth, Title, and Dress, but who is distinguished by the Elegance of her Shape and the Resplendency of her Beauty. You will find Nature's fair Workmanship shall engross the Eyes and Attention of all the Spectators. . . . a fine Woman is watched, sought and followed. (*Agreeable Ugliness*, 1, 2–3)

The issue here is the relationship between personal magnificence and individual worth, a distinction that would have been familiar to most readers in the 1750s.[20] The rise of the fine or beautiful woman is seen as outrageous to an emerging sensibility that on the one hand endorses a woman's visibility as exciting and enlivening, yet also damns that presence as a source of enervating femininity and social corruption. By omitting a discussion of this aspect of the text, Gonda underestimates the class or social significance of Scott's separation of private ugliness from public beauty.

The Physiognomy of Obedience

The strength and ambiguity of this moral investment in physiognomy is emphasized when the narrator describes the physical differences between herself and her sister. Throughout the passage the narrator's physical appearance is considerably more elusive than her account of her "native Ugliness" has suggested:

> My Sister was fair, I was very brown. She was a Picture of my Mother with every Beauty heightened, I an ugly Resemblance of my Father. She had the Superiority in Beauty, I had the Advantage over her in Shape. Her Eyes were of a dark blue, large, and finely formed, but without Fire or Expression, in short they were fine Eyes without Meaning; mine were black, a little too much sunk, tolerably large of very uncommon Vivacity, and seemed to indicate more Sense than perhaps I really had.

The narrator continues in much the same vein throughout the passage noting that, while "my Sister's Nose was well-shaped, but rather long; mine was the best feature in my Face." The overall effect of the passage is to suggest a curious balance; implying that for every one of her sister's charms the narrator has a corresponding advantage: for example, "my Sister's skin was as white as possible, it was neither so smooth or as soft as mine" (*Agreeable Ugliness*, 19–20). What is striking in this passage, however, is the way Scott's narrator has appropriated the conventions through which a beautiful face is generally described and has inverted its procedures, so that it is the distinction and difference associated with an ugly woman that comes to the fore. Instead of endorsing the beautiful woman's preeminence (the dubiousness of which Scott had already underlined), the passage champions the unattractive face; a physiognomy that indicates its "Vivacity" and "Sense," not despite its deformities, but because of them. The reason for this is that, unlike her sister's superficial charms, the narrator's face requires a more discerning examination if its very real charms are to be discovered.[21]

As the *Adventurer* essay indicated, the face of a virtuous woman required careful decoding. More forcefully, the face had to be of a kind that permitted a prolonged and discriminating gaze without unmanning the spectator. The artist William Hogarth's attention to, and enjoyment of, the detailed lines that compose the face and dress of virtuous but sensuous women, confirms the importance of this ideal in midcentury culture.[22] Indeed, Hogarth's description of a beautiful face is uncannily like the one offered by Scott. Hogarth writes:

> The face indeed will bear a constant view, yet always entertain and keep our curiosity awake, without the assistance either of a mask or veil; because the vast variety of changing circumstances keeps the eye and the mind in constant play, in following the numberless turns of expression it is capable of. How soon does a face that wants expression, grow insipid, though it be ever so Pretty?[23]

Hogarth's depiction of the sensuous woman, like his depiction of a country dance, evidences a pleasure that, while undoubtedly alluring, offers no threat to the viewer's masculinity. Furthermore, a woman's face offered Hogarth a pattern of features and expressions from which he could read the "index of the mind."[24] Like the narrator of *Agreeable Ugliness* or Fielding's *Amelia*, Hogarth's readable face offers both pleasure and definition, chastity and a more ambiguous pleasingness to the right-thinking spectator, who is able to understand the nuances of the face and is able to see the real virtues represented by such an appearance.[25]

Apparently aware of this debate, Scott's narrator endeavors, when de-

scribing herself and her sister, to emphasize her own distinction and sepa-
rateness without appearing to endorse the showy distinction that characterizes her sister. Most importantly, the association with her father ensures that
the narrator's face is, in a distinctive fashion, doubly inscribed; signed, as it
were, in two ways: first by her own presence, her unique and "native Ugliness," and secondly because that ugliness is in the form of a "Resemblance"
to her father. The place of the narrator is as such both verifiably her own yet
continues to be determined by her relationship with her father. Indeed the
moral disjunction between the sisters is underlined by the resemblance to
their parents: the Fair Villiers is "the Picture of my Mother"; while she is "an
ugly Resemblance of my Father." In terms of the difference from her sister,
the narrator has a countenance and a character distinctly her own; yet the
narrative seeks to keep that distinction in abeyance, suggesting that it exists
as an obedient mimic of Monsieur de Villiers.

The reader is only given the narrator's word for this state of affairs. Literary critics are wont to pause over such a problem (and certainly it cannot
easily be dismissed); however, it is important to note the enormous stress that
is laid throughout the novel on the *ideal* of ugliness. Even if this commitment
were offered only as the narrator's self-persuasion, it would remain instructive in that it seeks to connect virtue, not with beauty, but with plainness and
humble simplicity. However, the narrator's self-appraisal is supported by her
recollection that her mother "never gave me any other Name than the *Shocking Monster*" (*Agreeable Ugliness*, 13). Her father, by contrast, offers a more
subtle confirmation of her predicament. Wishing to ensure her obedience, he
insists upon the facts of her plainness:

> He could not indeed conceal from me the Misfortune of having been so ill-
> treated by Nature, but far from chusing to make it the Subject of Vexation,
> he talked to me of the Charms I wanted, only to excite in me a desire of ac-
> quiring such, as were more valuable and lasting: These were Advantages he
> was well qualified to give me; and while Madame *de Villiers* had no other Em-
> ployment than the pursuit of Pleasure, he made it both his Pleasure, and his
> Duty, to instruct me in all the useful knowledge which he possessed. (14)

By returning to the fact of her absent beauty, her father hopes to instill in her
the impossibility of transgression and to suggest that even if she sought to
act improperly, she lacks the wherewithal to do so. De Villiers's advice is intended as a remonstration of his daughter; by keeping her ugly he hopes to
keep her loyal. Secured by habit and a shared nomenclature, the notion of
her ugliness is crucial to the way in which the narrator forms her self-image,
as an obedient, retiring daughter. Curiously, it is an identity that is only partially individuated, becoming almost a nonidentity, a mere resemblance.

However, her father's teaching, the virtues and charms he wishes her to adopt, encourages her to conceive of herself as a uniquely moral individual (62–63, 91–92). The strategy works because Scott's narrator is not keen to make a "Noise" in the great world, which on the evidence of her mother's conduct she knows to be ruinously dissipated. As a result, the social world—the realm of beauty and the visual—is rejected in favor of companionable obscurity, the native place of the ugly.

This emphatic faith in the virtue of not being beautiful is made consistently throughout the novel, and key scenes are used to give its dramatic realization. Initially the narrator uses her ugliness to support her claims of honesty, stating that "when a woman confesses her own ugliness, we may believe her sincere." The conjunction of being truthful with being ugly is striking, particularly when the duplicity of the mother and sister is considered. Yet the narrator concedes that it is beauty, not honesty, that is most likely to arouse "public curiosity." "Handsome Woman is," she writes "by her Beauty, placed in a position more distinguished, and in a more conspicuous Light in the world than a Dutchess." In comparison, to be ugly is to be "reduced to a kind of Non-existence" (*Agreeable Ugliness*, 5, 1, 3, 6). It is statements such as the last that have prompted some critics, such as Elizabeth Bergen Brophy, to conclude that *Agreeable Ugliness* is best read as an attack on the judgment of women's physical form.[26] However, such a lack of visual significance is endorsed by Scott's novel as a means to virtue. Ugliness, because it has no pretence to public visibility, produces a temper at once mild and amiable; and these are virtues "wherein Beauty is often deficient." The misfortune of ugliness—that it fails to signify—is then balanced by the fact that it appears well suited to the heterosocial world of her public and private life: for this reason the narrator appears to find her own deformity consoling.

The connections these passages establish between seclusion, paternal authority, and ugliness are not uncommon within Scott's work. In the *History of Sir George Ellison,* the sequel to *Millenium Hall,* the youngest Miss Tunstall is congratulated, albeit cruelly, on the loss of her beauty to the ravages of smallpox. The disease, by obliterating the pliancy and vivacity of her character, has, according to Sir George, kept her virtue by excluding her from the public diversions into which pretty women are naturally drawn.[27] Like the narrator of *Agreeable Ugliness,* Miss Tunstall acquires virtue and understanding as a result of her loss; finally, however, she finds a suitor who is not only rich, but sensible enough to find her ugliness "agreeable" (*Ellison,* 2:287–88). In these terms the striking aspect of Scott's work is the degree to which she disrupts the conventional correspondence—advanced by the *Adventurer*—between femininity, beauty, and virtue. In both *Agreeable Ugli-*

ness and *Sir George Ellison* beauty is made into the disruptive term encouraging young women to become coquettish and daring schemers. In terms of an emerging discourse on female sexuality what seems to be at issue is the degree to which women, and particularly unmarried daughters, should have identities constructed beyond the confines of the paternal home.[28] Any movement beyond the domestic sphere of the de Villiers's paternal and private authority can therefore only be undertaken with a great deal of anxiety.

Indeed, despite the clear separation between beauty and ugliness envisioned by Scott at the outset of the novel, the two terms become increasingly interdependent as the plot unfolds. Although the narrator initially describes herself as ugly, or "not formed" for marriage, *Agreeable Ugliness* chronicles a life in which that identity is under constant threat of renegotiation. Her entrance into fashionable society, and most tellingly her depiction by a portrait painter, disturbs her sense of herself by making her the object (and the subject) of a sexualizing as well as socializing gaze. As the plot evolves, therefore, the narrator becomes engaged in a series of rearguard actions designed to preserve and restate her seclusion and ugliness. She reiterates the fact of her ugliness because it defines her self-image as both chaste and unattractive. It is an identity that is placed under threat by the men in the novel who, because they interact with her socially and visually, reconstitute her position in society. They look at her, either from attraction or admiration, and in so doing begin to give the impression that she is less than entirely ugly, propelling her toward the identity she seeks to resist: that of a beautiful woman. Crucially, this drama is played out through a moral discourse that locates its terms of reference in the opposition between obedience and desire, deformity and beauty.

A Picture Which Could Not Be Drawn for a Monster

The moment when the slippage between public and private identity is most apparent is the scene in which a portrait painter is commissioned to paint the narrator. Occurring halfway through the novel, it is an event constructed around the competing claims of feminine modesty and the need for self-display. The narrator's appraisal of events is indicative of this competition:

> I do not know whether the relating of these trifling Circumstances about my Picture, will not lead my Readers to accuse me of some Self-conceit; but they will hereafter be sensible that it was necessary they should be acquainted with Part of them. I therefore enter a Caveat against every Jest that People may be inclined to make upon me, and I continue to tell the Truth, in frankly

confessing, that I was very pleased to find that a Picture, which could not be drawn for a *Monster* was acknowledged by my Friends to resemble me. (*Agreeable Ugliness,* 120)

There is in this short passage a complex working of what it is to be both private and feminine. The stakes are raised because of the way these ideas seem to pose, quite explicitly, a question of truthfulness. The problem arises because the narrator tries to maintain a clear distinction between public and private codes when, in the context presented by the novel, no such separation can be achieved. The "trifling Circumstances" of the painting's production are, as the phrase suggests, a relatively intimate affair, comprising a private contract and an arrangement to sit at a friend's house. However, the demands of the novel require their publication. In a sense the narrator is caught in a trap of her own making: the publicizing of events is "necessary," otherwise the reader will lose the sense of what is being related, yet it requires a "caveat" and a further declaration of truth in order to make it properly acceptable. And here lies the rub: for by opening the events to a wider audience the narrator is exposed to the charges of imprudence and vanity, and accordingly only a confession will resolve the problem. By declaring her pleasure, the narrator hopes to turn the unrealized distinction of public and private to her advantage. Because she acknowledges her private pleasure at the portrait—making it the subject of a public declaration—she dismisses the suggestion that she harbors such gratification and the desires from which they spring in secret. She is therefore open and honest, and hence virtuous. Furthermore, the narrator has been careful to place the sensation of her pleasure, and the reader's awareness of it, at one remove from any immediate gratification arising from her own physical appearance. It is only because the resemblance between portrait and sitter is "acknowledged by my Friends" that the narrator is satisfied. The rhetorical function of these friends is to mediate between that which is overtly public and the narrator's more immediate sphere. By making the recognition of the semblance, and the pleasure it gives, the act of a third party, the process of making it public has been reduced in danger, if not in significance.

The problems of portrayal remain, however, especially as the degree to which the security of a "Resemblance" is undermined by the intrusion of individuality and desire. As Marcia Pointon has argued, for a woman to have her portrait painted was a serious business. The exercise necessarily involved a dramatic reformation of her identity upon the painted space of the canvas. Pointon further suggests that it is through the constructed image of the portrait that women enter the world. She situates portraits of women in a further context, that of marital property and exchange between fathers and husbands.[29] The circumstances depicted by Scott operate within a comparable social and discursive environment, and they raise similar kinds of problems for the woman portrayed. In this context, it might be profitable to keep in mind William Hazlitt's enthusiastic appraisal of the pleasures of portrayal: "The fact is, that having one's picture painted is like the *creation of another self;* and that is an idea, of the repetition or reduplication of which no man has ever tired, to the thousandth reflection."[30] Hazlitt genders his account throughout; the subject of this passage neither aspires to, nor deserves, universality. He makes it clear that while men can experience representation as pleasure, women must endure the uncertainty of exposure. The production of "another self" for women is a more anxious moment, marking an entrance into a complex play of glances that constructs the sitter as a sexual subject. Throughout Scott's novel it is possible to see these problems as those that the narrator is attempting to avoid with her caveats and confessions.

In the present context it is worth noting that William Hay, the hunch-backed author of *Deformity: An Essay* (published the same year as *Agreeable Ugliness*), found the problems of portrayal similarly acute. The following passage forms part of Hay's account of the misfortunes visited upon those afflicted by deformity:

> When I was a Child, I was drawn like a Cupid, with a Bow and Arrow in my Hands, and a Quiver on my Shoulder: I afterwards thought this an Abuse, which ought to be corrected: and when I sate for my Picture some Years ago, I insisted on being drawn as I am, and that the strong Marks of the Small Pox might appear in my Face, for I did not choose to cover over a Lye. The Painter said, he was never allowed such liberty before; and I advised him, if he hoped to be in Vogue, never to assume it again: for Flatterers succeed best in the World; and of all Flatterers, Painters are the least liable to be detected by those they flatter. Nor are the Ladies the only Persons concerned for their Looks.[31]

Hay's complaint concerns the imprisoning effect of painterly convention, the fact that, in Hazlitt's phrase, a portrait creates another self; one that is neither expected or welcome.[32] It is therefore crucial that in *Agreeable Ugliness*, the painter is only commissioned after he, like the narrator's first husband Dorigny, has been captivated by the sweetness of the narrator's disposition. Within the terms of the novel's ideological parameters he is set a difficult task, as he must blend the claims of modest ugliness with those of painterly portrayal. It is striking therefore that his promise to the narrator is to make her, or at least to represent her, as the "handsomest woman in *Paris.*" He does not stop there, however, as he asserts that "this Lady, has one of those countenances—of which I would be happy to draw an exact Likeness." The perhaps unlikely combination of verisimilitude and pleasingness is seized upon with some enthusiasm by Dorigny, who declares a wish to know whether the painter's "Eyes are as good as mine" (*Agreeable Ugliness*, 116, 118).

The painting once begun is rapidly completed, and Dorigny "charmed" with the result. His pleasure, and those of other close friends, is such that they order a number of copies. It is during this private act of purchase and praise that the Count de St Furcy, the narrator's former lover, enters the room. It is a telling moment:

> We had just settled this Point when the young Count *de St Furcy* came to visit the Countess; in vain I endeavoured not to see him, [but] the Viscountess and my Husband obliged me to stay. The Count turned pale at the Sight of me, I red at the Sight of him, but after the first Compliments were over, Mr. *Dorigny* would have Monsieur *de St Furcy* consulted about my Picture, which put me quite out of countenance. The Count thought it exactly like. (*Agreeable Ugliness*, 120–21)

It is by no means clear what de St Furcy's comment is meant to indicate. There are, I think, three interpretations available. Most obviously he could mean merely to congratulate the painter on the veracity of his art; to say, in effect, "yes, this is indeed how she looks, exactly like." He could, however, like Dorigny and the painter, mean something more ambitious. He could be saying, without discounting the possibility of applause for mimesis, "well done, this picture has captured what I know to be her true character and nature." Third, and most dangerously, he could mean, although he may not know it, "truly this is a wonderful picture, it conforms to my desire of, and for this woman. This is what she is like, this is what I desire."

But what really seems to be at issue is that the portrait, which is "acknowledged by my friends to resemble me" and yet "cannot be taken for a *Monster*," represents the narrator not as an obedient daughter but as an attractive young woman. Everybody is pleased with it, and though they do not comment on whether or not it makes her appear as "the handsomest woman in *Paris*," as the painter had claimed, we know this to have been his intention. This is new territory for the narrator, for it takes her away from her "native Ugliness." She has been displayed before, when earlier she sang in a privately performed opera; significantly, her performance made her desirable to both Dorigny and de St Furcy (54, 57). But now she is both desired and displayed, and not through her own devices, or desires, but through a painting. Indeed, in attempting to avoid having the painting done at all she had exclaimed, "I should be very sorry to have a Picture so much handsomer than myself" (117). And it is for this reason that she is "quite out of countenance."

The effect of the painting's exhibition on the narrator is equally ambiguous. She is, by her own testimony, "out of countenance," alienated from her own face, separated from herself. What she appears to mean is that the occasion of de St Furcy's reappearance has taken her beyond the normal range of her emotions and morality, leaving her disconcerted, distracted. However, the sight of de St Furcy, of his face turning pale—hers turning red, hence not being of itself—has not been the sole cause of this division. She is discomposed morally by the conjuncture of a former lover and a new portrait, and the result will later be "a Breach between my Inclination and my Reason" (*Agreeable Ugliness,* 207). It is not only the return of the Count, unexpected though it is, that has been the cause of this; rather it is the precise moment at which he has walked in that is vital. It is a moment of her utmost vulnerability and exposure. Hung up as a portrait, she exists for another, for de St Furcy: for a man who is not her father, and who has no interest in her resembling him. So displayed she solicits, even if unwillingly, the gaze that will represent her as a sexual subject. It is a radical displacement (she is out of herself, between the portrait and her own body), and she is no longer an "ugly Resemblance" of her father—but looking like herself, or rather looking "like" she does to de St Furcy.

In these terms the new portrait's status is unclear, as it pleases both husband and lover. The issue is one of propriety, as it is throughout the novel. This concern is already evident in what the narrator has recorded about the event: the obligation to "see" de St Furcy and the scrupulous attention to the protocols of polite and wifely behavior—an observance of forms as fully hers as her husband's. What could conceivably be proper and improper in these terms is a complex question; one that seems allied to the question of who owns the face and its painted resemblance. In this context, the propriety or otherwise of the portrait could conceivably entail nothing further than an assessment of its success as a "likeness." In this sense the portrait would have to include the distinctive presence or mark that is characteristic of, or special to, a particular person; apparent "ugliness" in this case. In this context however, the notion of that which is proper appears more capacious in its meaning. That which is proper also entails that which is in conformity to the rules of polite society. The importance of propriety is ever present in *Agreeable Ugliness,* and the reason for this insistence appears to lie in the crucial intersection of class consciousness (represented by the obsequious concerns of Monsieur de Villiers) and the transgressive potential of women, who can break this stratification. In the realm of previously arranged aristocratic marriages that the characters inhabit, the management of desire is particularly necessitous, and women who are seen to provoke unwanted sexual longings are scrupulously policed by both the narrator's own moralizing and by other characters in the novel (40, 62, 73, 239–42).

This is the problem that this portrait represents, because it is improper on both these counts as the image is neither wholly chaste nor securely owned. The narrator has been at pains to reiterate her ugliness, her status as a "Shocking Monster." This is her "native" quality, that which makes her different from her mother and sister physically and morally, and which marks the location of her sincerity: in her person, and at home. The painting would seem to threaten that intimate connection. Commenting on the image in more detail, she reflects:

> Tho' one is not the best Judge of one's own Picture, I could not mistake mine. I saw in it some Beauties which I did not suspect in myself, and whose momentary Appearance in my Countenance there must have been great Art in seizing when I was gay and happy; and in short, when without knowing why or how, it endeavoured to render itself agreeable. This was what the Painter had so well expressed, that agreeing to the Resemblance the picture bore to me, I thought myself obliged to accuse him of having greatly flattered me. (*Agreeable Ugliness*, 119)

It resembles her—it is in agreement with her face—but she cannot, or will not fully recognize it. This description of the painting is inlaid with what is either an attempt to evade the implications of the portrait or an inability to comprehend how such a production might represent herself. What the canvas depicts is therefore said to be something unsuspected, whose fleeting appearance is testimony to "great Art"—in the sense of artifice—rather than to any great perspicuity on the painter's part.[33]

To agree that the portrait represents, or, worse still, resembles, her would be to concede that she is pleasing; and therefore more like her mother than her father. This is the dilemma that she faces. It is an ambiguity that is underscored by the syntax of the passage, as the second *it* is uncertain in its reference and could refer either to her face or to the portrait. Such an ambiguity, while suggestive, is more likely to be the product of a questionable prose style than any intention on Scott's part. What remains striking, however, is the deep sense of alienation the passage instills; the narrator appears wholly divorced from herself, referring to her face, painted or physical, merely as an "it." It is that "it" which, in the narrator's testimony, is assumed to have endeavored to become agreeable and not herself. The narrator cannot deny, however, the force of the resemblance, and this leaves her to charge the portraitist with flattery. What the narrator seems most fully distanced from is the desire to be desired, the wish to be sought after. Or rather she wants to love, or to be loved, but cannot, or will not, find a place in which that wish can be fulfilled. She is denied it on several points, and on numerous occasions. There have always been her father's instructions, which are combined with her own deep sense that his teachings are correct. In his terms, to be desired is not to be esteemed. Significantly, the new portrait embodies a form of display that entails becoming available, not only to a desiring male gaze, but to gaze at oneself; it is to consider oneself as sexual. The portrait scene indicates that display acts as a moment of sexual awakening, one that is experienced as a process of being split or divided. Indeed throughout *Agreeable Ugliness* passion is represented as a painful disembodiment or multiplication (163–65, 207–10).

No Oil Painting: The Charms of Agreeable Ugliness

What the portrait scene demonstrates is the ways in which female sexuality and feminine self-display were regarded by Scott as monstrous when not held within their due bounds. This is a position that is shared by both the narrator and by the discourses that shape the overall narrative structure of *Agreeable Ugliness*. Viewed from this perspective, de St Furcy's return during the portrait's exhibition serves as a warning about the dangers of self-display: women who seek the male gaze, it is suggested, will disorder themselves, confusing and confounding the men around them in the process.[34] In accordance with these strictures, the narrator spends much of the novel striving to maintain her ugliness, insisting on her plainness as the sign of her goodness. Given the extent of Scott's commitment to this ideal, it is surely revealing that Fanny Burney used Scott's title-phrase when describing the appearance of fellow novelist Frances Brooke whom she met in 1774:

> Mrs Brooke is very short & fat, & squints, but has the art of shewing Agreeable Ugliness. She is very well bred, & expresses herself with much modesty, upon all subjects—which in an *Authoress*, a woman of *known* understanding, is extremely pleasing.[35]

Burney seems to be saying three related things about her fellow novelist. First, that she is an ugly and afflicted woman; poor eyesight is combined unattractively with an unappealing physical form. Second, that despite this handicap she has a manner—an art—of yet being pleasing. Finally, that even as a woman of known and admired talents, Brooke remains modest and gracious. The effect of this combination is to suggest that Brooke's "Agreeable Ugliness," her plainness, responds to her conspicuous talent. Most forcefully, her lack of physical attraction appears to provide the foundation upon which a properly feminine modesty can be established. This makes her, despite or rather because of her ugliness, a more attractive woman: indeed it makes her "extremely pleasing." In some respects, Burney's use of the image was in keeping with her rather tart attitude toward other women, yet it is also illustrative of what can be thought as the morality of ugliness, a sentiment that is found throughout Scott's work. For both women ugliness and decency seem irrecoverably connected.[36]

However, while Burney's representation of Brooke indicates that she shared Scott's assumptions about the connection between apparent ugliness and moral worth, her anecdote can also reveal the greater ambiguity of Scott's position. Burney's recollection turns upon a clear distinction between notorious publicity (that which she fears Brooke may exhibit) and the more placid charms of feminine modesty. On one level, Burney seems to be rehearsing a commonplace notion that women should be discrete and retiring, while also acknowledging that Brooke succeeds in maintaining an acceptable public role. Crucially, Brooke's virtue relies upon her ability to retain her private virtues even when she has become a public figure: "a woman of *known* understanding." Private virtue and public respectability are not therefore hypostatized options: the line between them is more often blurred. Scott's fiction—even a text as apparently programmatic as *Agreeable Ugliness*—contains a similar blurring of public and private positions. Crucially, *Agreeable Ugliness* revolves around the disjunction between the "native ugliness" that the narrator believes (and wishes us to believe) she possesses, and the strangely attractive "agreeable ugliness" that determines the conduct of the novel. Significantly, "agreeable ugliness" is, as Burney's use of the phrase suggested, a description best suited to an individual who, while publicly visible, retains the attitude and demeanor of feminine retirement. In the case of Brooke, it was her good breeding and modest expression that transformed her unfortunate body into something more agreeable.

What Burney's remarks indicate is that the significance of ugliness as a marker of moral well-being was generally understood and perhaps widely employed in mid- to late-eighteenth-century Britain. Clearly ugliness had a relation to female virtue and to social place; however, this seems insufficient to account for the tortuous syntax or the sense of Scott's depiction of ugliness in the novel generally and in the portrait scene in particular. The representation of ugliness and monstrosity elsewhere in Scott's work suggests something more complex still. Indeed the display of the individual who retains virtue, declines exhibition, and yet remains visible is something of a trope in Scott's writing. In many respects Sir George Ellison's first visit to the society of ladies in *Millenium Hall* typifies this recurring dual movement. Millenium Hall is remarkable not merely for its idyllic setting, but also for the spectacular wealth and the peculiar ugliness of its domestic staff. In the novel it also images a scene where women's worth (and wealth) can operate, even conspicuously so, without address to the necessity of display.[37] Early in Ellison's stay both he and the foppish Lamont are taken round the park and gardens of the house. In the course of their tour they pass an enclosure that "bore some resemblance to one of Lord Lamore's, where he kept lions, tigers, leopards and such foreign animals" (18). The two men are intrigued; the ladies, however, protest that the kinds of cruel exhibition Lamont wishes to enjoy are not practiced on their land, rather the reverse. The "inclosure" is indeed for "monsters," but for dwarfs and giants of the human variety. The purpose though is to shield them from display, to remove them from the cruel gazes to which they had hitherto been exposed. However, Sir George's narration serves to make the lack of exhibition exemplary. His zeal to portray the ladies' virtue ensures that he must expand on the appropriateness of their conduct; in effect he displays what is hidden. Moreover, the shrouded "inclosure" first attracted Lamont's gaze because it appeared to be constructed for display, and the people it contains also retain the name *monsters*, designating them as those individuals destined for display.

Sir George's narrative of the monster's enclosure is not the only instance of this doublethink in *Millenium Hall*. The histories of the women who make up the society evidence similar rhetorical habits. Miss Trentham's story suggests that a woman's beauty disrupts her domestic arrangements, in this case by making it impossible to live with her childhood friend Mr. Alworth. Her charms made him desire her, and confused her own sense of her place and her virtue. Her sociable intentions are consequently destroyed by the fact of her own appearance (194–95). Confused Miss Trentham catches smallpox:

> When she came to her senses, she at first seemed mortified to think Mr Alworth had seen her in that disfigured condition; but on reflection told me she rejoiced in it, as she thought it must totally extinguish his passion; and her greatest solicitude was for his happiness. . . . When she recovered, she perceived that the small pox had entirely destroyed her beauty. She acknowledged she was not insensible to this mortification; and to avoid the observation of the envious or even of the idly curious she retired, as soon as she was able to travel. (199)

Like the narrator of *Agreeable Ugliness*, Miss Trentham finds ugliness consoling: "she became perfectly contented with the alteration this cruel distemper had made in her . . . and she regained the quiet happiness of which flutter and dissipation had deprived her." The purpose here is twofold: to display to Sir George, and by extension to the reader, the femininity of Miss Trentham; and to call attention to the fact that Miss Trentham does not display herself. Furthermore, as an ugly woman Miss Trentham may retire into Millenium Hall, a community of similarly persecuted and virtuous women.

Despite their seclusion, the zeal of the women, and the vision of virtue they embody, form an alluring spectacle precisely because they appear to resist the desire to the seen.

A consequence of this investment is that the public sphere—the world of vision and beauty—is rarely virtuous for women; typically, as in the case of Millenium Hall's inhabitants, what is proposed is a modest retreat, albeit one framed by the published discourse provided by Sir George (175–76, 202–7).[38] In this sense, virtue predominates in *Millenium Hall* not because the women abolish display; rather, they invert it, and virtuous seclusion exists only to the extent that it can be meaningfully displayed: a total disguise would have no rhetorical impact. This is important because Scott did have a reformist agenda when writing this novel, as many critics have begun to point out. Through her work she hoped to improve both sexes; men, like Lamont, were to becomes less foppish, and women were encouraged to adopt chaste maternal and sentimental roles.[39] As such Scott's fiction defines a description of a woman that, while according her a place in a refined society, does not attribute to her physical appearance excessive importance nor place her in a position of undue prominence. The concept of agreeable ugliness is the means of holding that precarious balance. In a culture in which an increasing stress was placed upon the conduct of polite sociability, "native ugliness" with its associations of isolation and seclusion could have little value. By contrast a woman's agreeable ugliness could connote a modest yet pleasing disposition that offered refinement without luxuriance. Considered in this context, the twists and turns of *Agreeable Ugliness* illustrate not the folly and self-deceit of the narrator but an anxious attempt to define the social position of a virtuous woman, a definition that at once accepts the need for her retirement and yet must display that very retreat. Scott's fiction responds to this paradox by implying that the best way to signal a woman's moral integrity was to consider her as ugly, plain, or at the very least unbeautiful. In fact ugliness is recommended by Scott as a more attractive quality than beauty—more attractive because, curiously, it is more regular and more obedient. As such Scott's representation of ugliness cannot be read as a redemptive or liberating ideal; it is no counterdiscourse, for it is too thoroughly implicated in the morality that causes feminine beauty to be repudiated. Indeed the notion of "agreeable ugliness" is part of an eighteenth-century discourse about society that, although it celebrates the inclusion of women as the guarantee of society's gentility, fears the authority of women over men in what Lady Wortley Montagu disparagingly called "the imaginary Empire of Beauty."[40] In contrast to her beautiful sister, the ugly woman can have no territorial ambitions, preferring instead a sophisticated retreat and a more delicate assertion of influence.

NOTES

1. A version of this paper was first presented to the Eighteenth-Century Research Group at the University of York in June 1995 and was later published as chapter 4 in Robert W. Jones, *Gender and the Formation of Taste in Eighteenth-Century Britain* (Cambridge: Cambridge University Press, 1998). That chapter, with some revisions, is reprinted here by kind permission of the Press. I am grateful to Harriet Guest, Angharad Penrhyn Jones, Mary Peace, and Shaun Regan whose criticism of this essay has improved it immeasurably. I would also like to thank Helen Deutsch and Felicity Nussbaum for providing the perceptive and tactful editing that the essay needed.

2. For an overview of the significance of the face in eighteenth-century literature, see Graeme Tytler, *Physiognomy in the European Novel: Faces and Fortunes* (Princeton: Princeton University Press, 1982). See also Barbara M. Benedict, "Reading Faces: Physiognomy and Epistemology in Late Eighteenth-Century Sentimental Novels," *Studies in Philology* 92 (1995): 311–28; and Michael G. Ketchum, "The Arts of Gesture, *The Spectator* and its Relationship to Physiognomy, Painting, and Theater," *Modern Language Quarterly* 42, no. 2 (June 1981): 141.

3. Roy Porter, "Making Faces: Physiognomy and Fashion in Eighteenth-Century England," *Etudes Anglaises* 38, no. 4 (1985): 385, 392–93. See also Benedict, "Reading Faces," 312, 316–19; and Tassie Gwilliam, "Cosmetic Poetics: Coloring Faces in the Eighteenth Century," in *Body and Text in the Eighteenth Century,* ed. Veronica Kelly and Dorothea von Mücke (Stanford, Calif.: Stanford University Press, 1994), 144–59.

4. *The Adventurer* no. 82, August 18, 1753, 3d ed., 4 vols. (London: C. Hitch and L. Hawes, J. Payne, 1756), 3:105, 109.

5. *The Adventurer,* 3:110.

6. *The Adventurer,* 3:111.

7. *The Adventurer,* 3:109.

8. *The Adventurer,* 3:110, 105.

9. For a discussion of the connection between aesthetic discourse and the morality of the conduct book, see Robert W. Jones, "The Empire of Beauty: The Competition for Judgement in Mid-Eighteenth-Century England," D.Phil. thesis, University of York, 1995, 123–73.

10. George Coleman et al., *The Connoisseur. By Mr. Town, Critic and Censor General,* no. 21, June 27, 1754, and no. 52, June 26, 1755, 4th ed., 4 vols. (London: R. Baldwin, 1761), 1:172–78 and 3:21–28.

11. Edmund Burke's notorious treatise on taste and the aesthetic is perhaps the most blatant formulation of this problematic. See *A Philosophical Enquiry into the Origin of Our Ideas of the Sublime and the Beautiful,* ed. J. T. Boulton (Oxford: Basil

Blackwell, 1987), 114–15; see also Frances Ferguson, *Solitude and the Sublime: Romanticism and the Aesthetics of Individuation* (London: Routledge, 1992), 51–53.

12. Tassie Gwilliam, *Samuel Richardson's Fictions of Gender* (Stanford, Calif.: Stanford University Press, 1993), 15–49.

13. Henry Fielding, *Amelia*, ed. David Blewett (Harmondsworth: Penguin, 1987), 57–58. The initial reception of Fielding's novel was mixed, however. Not every reader was convinced that the heroine's deformed nose was the sign of virtue Fielding had intended. For an indicative selection of responses to Fielding's work see Ronald Paulson and Thomas Lockwood, eds., *Henry Fielding: The Critical Heritage* (London: Routledge and Kegan Paul, 1969).

14. Jill Campbell, *Natural Masques: Gender and Identity in Fielding's Plays and Novels* (Stanford, Calif.: Stanford University Press, 1995), 204, 211–12; see also George E. Haggerty, "Amelia's Nose; or, Sensibility and Its Symptoms," *Eighteenth Century: Theory and Interpretation* 36 (1995): 139–56.

15. In *The Origins of the English Novel, 1660–1740* (Baltimore: John Hopkins University Press, 1987), Michael McKeon discusses the role of progressive ideas of moral character in relation to the opposition between "aristocratic" and "bourgeois" ideas and literary forms found in early novels. For a specific discussion of Fielding's novels in relation to middle-class ideology see John P. Zomchick, *Family and Law in Eighteenth-Century Fiction: The Public Conscience in the Private Sphere* (Cambridge: Cambridge University Press, 1993), 130–53.

16. For a discussion of Scott's work see Vincent Carretta, "Utopia Limited: Sarah Scott's *Millenium Hall* and *The History of Sir George Ellison*," *Age of Johnson: A Scholarly Annual* 5 (1992): 303–26; George E. Haggerty, "'Romantic Friendship' and Patriarchal Narrative in Sarah Scott's *Millenium Hall*," *Genders* (spring 1992): 108–22; Melinda Alliker Rabb, "Making and Rethinking the Canon: General Introduction and the Case of *Millenium Hall*," *Modern Language Studies* 18, no. 1 (1988): 3–16; Johanna M. Smith, "Philanthropic Community in *Millenium Hall* and the York Ladies Committee," *Eighteenth Century: Theory and Interpretation* 36 (1995): 266–82.

17. Sarah Scott, *Agreeable Ugliness: or, the Triumph of the Graces. Exemplified in the Real Life and Fortunes of a Young Lady of Some Distinction* (London: R. and J. Dodsley, 1754). All subsequent references to this work are given in the text.

18. Pierre Antoine de la Place, *La Laideur Amiable et les Dangers de la Beauté: histoire veritable* (Londres [i.e., Paris]: Rollin, 1752).

19. Caroline Gonda, "Sarah Scott and the 'Sweet Excess of Paternal Love,'" *Studies in English, 1550–1800* 32, no. 3 (1992): 511–35.

20. Very similar sentiments to those advanced by Scott can be found in Charlotte Lennox's novel *The Female Quixote; or, the Adventures of Arabella*, ed. Margaret Dalziel (Oxford: Oxford University Press, 1989), 144–53. For both Scott and Lennox the recent celebrity of the Gunning sisters, whose beauty did secure them great prestige, may well have been an implicit reference.

21. Felicity Nussbaum has argued that Scott's attention to the details of her heroine's deformed or disfigured faces represents a demand that male spectators reform themselves, becoming in the process more refined and more sympathetic. See *Torrid*

Zones: Maternity, Sexuality, and Empire in Eighteenth-Century English Narratives (Baltimore: John Hopkins University Press, 1996), 150, 155, 157–58.

22. William Hogarth, *The Analysis of Beauty. Written with a View of Fixing the Fluctuating as Ideas of Taste* (London: J. Reeve, 1753), 123–31. For a discussion of the relationship between Hogarth's account of beauty and the sexual politics of the 1750s (especially the Marriage Act of 1753), see Ronald Paulson, *Hogarth*, vol. 3, *Art and Politics, 1750–1764* (Cambridge: Lutterworth Press, 1993), 85–92.

23. Hogarth, *The Analysis of Beauty*, 36. See 80, 126, 130.

24. Hogarth, *The Analysis of Beauty*, 125–26. The precise and discriminatory descriptions found in the work of Scott can also be discovered in other eighteenth-century texts; see, for example, Oliver Goldsmith, *The Vicar of Wakefield*, ed. Arthur Friedman (Oxford: Oxford University Press, 1992), 11–12; Charlotte Lennox, *Sophia*, 2 vols. (London: James Fletcher, 1762), 1:2–4, 25–26; 2:236–37.

25. For a discussion of this aspect of eighteenth-century culture see Deidre Lynch, "Overloaded Portraits: The Excesses of Character and Countenance," in Kelly and von Mücke, *Body and Text*, 112–43.

26. Elizabeth Bergen Brophy, *Women's Lives and the Eighteenth-Century Novel* (Tampa: South Florida University Press, 1991), 16–17.

27. Sarah Scott, *The History of Sir George Ellison*, 2 vols. (London: A. Millar, 1766), 2:223–30.

28. This issue has in recent years received extensive critical work. See, for example, Susan Staves, "British Seduced Maidens," *Eighteenth Century Studies* 14, no. 2 (1980–81): 109–34; Erica Harth, "The Virtue of Love: Lord Hardwicke's Marriage Act," *Cultural Critique* 9 (spring 1988): 123–54.

29. Marcia Pointon, *Hanging the Head: Portraiture and Social Formation in Eighteenth-Century England* (New Haven: Yale University Press, 1993), 141–58.

30. William Hazlitt, "On Sitting for One's Portrait," in *The Plain Speaker* (London: J. M. Dent and Sons, Everyman's Library, n.d.), 108 (emphasis added).

31. William Hay, *Deformity: An Essay* (London: R. and J. Dodsley, 1754), 37.

32. Sadly, I have not been able to able to gain sight of either of the portraits mentioned by Hay. Certainly neither corresponds to the rather conventional portrait that served as a frontispiece to Hay's *Complete Works*, published under his daughter's auspices in 1794.

33. See Lynch, "Overloaded Portraits," 126–28, 140–41.

34. Gonda, "Sweet Excess," 514–15.

35. Fanny Burney, diary entry for February 20, 1774, *The Early Journals and Letters of Fanny Burney*, vol. 2, *1774–1777*, ed. Lars E. Triode, 3 vols. (Montreal: McGill-Queen's University Press, 1988), 2:4–5. As Margaret Anne Doody has shown, this caustic attitude was perhaps particularly true of her relationship with other women; her early acquaintance with Mrs. Thrale bears this out admirably. For an account of Burney's relationship with the Thrales, see Doody, *Frances Burney: The Life in the Works* (New Brunswick, N.J.: Rutgers University Press, 1988), 9–35.

36. It should be noted that Burney did not always connect ugliness and virtue in quite the same way in her published fiction. In *Camilla*, for example, descriptions of Eugenia's scarred and twisted body represent her as a woman painfully excluded from

normal social intercourse and yet able to gain integrity and a degree of emancipation precisely because of this exclusion. Equally, in *Evelina* Mrs. Selwyn is emancipated, clever, and not conventionally attractive; a conjunction that is far from accidental.

37. Sarah Scott, *A Description of Millenium Hall*, ed. Jane Spencer (London: Virago, 1986), 4–8, 12–13, 68–69, 205–7. All subsequent references are given in the text.

38. For a discussion of the "improving" agenda of Scott's novel, see Dorice Williams Elliott, "Sarah Scott's *Millenium Hall* and Female Philanthropy," *Studies in English Literature* 35 (1995): 535–53; see also James Cruse, "A House Divided: Sarah Scott's *Millenium Hall*," *Studies in English Literature* 35 (1995): 555–73.

39. Nussbaum, *Torrid Zones*, 149–62. See also Irene Q. Brown, "Domesticity, Feminism, and Friendship: Female Aristocratic Culture and Marriage," *Journal of Family History* 7, no. 4 (1982): 406–27.

40. Lady Mary Wortley Montagu, *The Nonsense of Common Sense*, no. 2, December 27, 1737, in *Essays and Poems and "Simplicity," a Comedy*, ed. Robert Halsband and Isobel Grundy (Oxford: Clarendon Press, 1977), 109.

Afterword: Liberalism, Feminism, and Defect

Cora Kaplan

Rooted in the developing narratives of liberal humanism and the natural and human sciences, nourished both by their overt arguments and their less visible contradictions, the discourse of defect has adapted, flourished, and proliferated in the last two hundred years. In this brief afterword I want to focus not on the murderous twentieth-century history of defect as a pretext for genocide but on the everyday presence of deformity and disability in public narrative as an unremarked but insistent motif in the liberal, humanist—and feminist—imagination. For human anomaly, especially the wide range of visible differences that have historically elicited a reflexive repulsion, continues to trouble the rhetoric of liberal individualism, testing both its ethics of tolerance and its fetishization of autonomy and agency as a condition of human status and civic participation.

The complementary fantasies of unrestricted agency and group purity that fed the rise of eugenicist models of a healthy nation or superior race were, for example, less an "antihumanist" ideology than the reactionary end of a spectrum of humanisms.[1] More generally, the pursuit of human perfectibility as a normative physical or psychological standard, involved a curious disavowal of variation and mortality. Such a denial of difference and death pathologizes not only ethnic others, but the inevitable anomalous differences *within* relatively homogenous social groups or national populations, highlighting those fears about hereditary defect that are always positioned at the uncanny moment when the familial becomes strange.

From the nineteenth to the mid-twentieth centuries these anxieties were characteristically fostered and focused through the conflicting imperatives of laws of kinship that forbade inbreeding on the one hand and phobic responses to certain kinds of exogamy on the other. The fear—and the shame—of defect was meant to deflect unions too close to home or too "hybrid."[2]

Today, in the affluent countries of the West, wider environmental and health issues and the threat and promise of genetic engineering supplant exogamy and endogeny as reproductive anxieties. Reproductive fears are, in any case, only one strand of this century's negative discourse of defect. These discourses may have a global impact, but their imagining is always local, deeply tied to the wealth and social policies of different nation states. Although medical skill dramatically improves the survival rate of children in some countries, disease and famine continue to decimate them elsewhere, so that the image of the emaciated child, ever before Western eyes on the "cold" screen of the television, makes dying children a spectacle of racialized deformity. As populations continue to age, or, conversely as diseases like AIDS demand treatment available only in prosperous regions and continue to outrun prevention and cure, defect and dependency become an abiding pragmatic issue for fin-de-siècle societies. The United States and Great Britain have resorted to a discourse of fiscal responsibility in which dependent disability is expressed as an intolerable economic burden on governments and therefore on "normal" citizenry. Residual fears and superstitions about defect give silent support to policies that flow from such seemingly rational economic analyses. Viewed from a long term perspective, the continuing debate about the rights of citizens, and the price of increased agency for them, is itself a legacy of liberalism's historically mixed messages about autonomy and social justice, an ongoing paradox that remains as radically unresolved in the liberalisms that characterize late-twentieth-century social democracies as it did in the "classic" liberalism of the nineteenth century.

Nowhere is that paradox more fully visible or more freighted with affect than in those debates about gender and sexual difference initiated by feminism. If we look at discrete moments in the development of feminism, we can see that those tensions within feminism were articulated with the long-standing association of "woman" with human abnormality and anomaly, a figurative linking strengthened and expanded in the nineteenth and twentieth centuries, as well as reimagined in terms of the ethics and aesthetics of both modern political theory and scientific discourse.[3]

Marked by its volatile relationship with the emerging liberal discourses of the self and its possibilities, the feminism of the last two centuries confronted this damaging association head-on by preemptively introducing the question of disability as the mark of femininity into its arguments. Contesting the current belief that women's "degraded" character is not open to amelioration, that she is a "*fair defect* in creation," Mary Wollstonecraft, for example, boldly turned the figure against itself.[4] In her classic analysis of bourgeois femininity as an elaborate culture of "dependency" she associated the dominant customs that degraded women's moral sense with the gendered aesthetic that restricted their physical activity, and therefore rendered their physical growth stunted and their "organs" affected with a "sickly soreness" (117). Women's "weakness" and "dependence" are the signs of their corruption by contemporary mores. Yet this brazen transference of gendered defect from woman as a category to the society that makes them was mobilized, in Wollstonecraft's argument, exclusively on behalf of middle-class female autonomy, a limitation that undermined its radical thrust. Hovering at the borders of *A Vindication* and of her posthumous novel *The Wrongs of Woman* are prostitutes, servants, anonymous members of Eastern seraglios, even working-class women whose ignorant, abject, or corrupt condition of being was not the immediate object of Wollstonecraft's reforming project, and whose "defect" could not be theorized in terms of a disabling socialization into leisured femininity and the "weakness," physical and moral, that were its inevitable effects. These other women could, indeed they were forced to, "act a little for themselves" (117) within the limits of their economic situation, but, lacking the forms of moral agency and informed rationality that Wollstonecraft is championing, their activity is as problematic as that of the unreconstructed middle class. Wedded, therefore, to an idea of moralized female independence that was as rule-governed as the debased subjectivity it wished to supplant, shadowed by the innate "defect" of sexual difference that it argues so powerfully against, but cannot quite dispel, *A Vindication* succeeded textually in making dominant bourgeois femininity ethically and aesthetically monstrous. Yet this inversion of gender's deformity, even if now situated firmly in culture rather than nature, left in place the association of defective femininity with the failure or deformation of female agency, a symbolic coupling that would be used across the nineteenth century to attack both Wollstonecraft and feminism.

In the succeeding century, dependency and autonomy, defined ever more in the terms of maturing liberal thought, increasingly troubled protofeminist argument. Wollstonecraft's creative attempt to make the normal socialization of women a process of cultural disabling and deformation becomes recast in a more conservative mould in new stories in which tropes of deformity, disability and monstrosity are used as characteristic devices for the splitting of femininity into "good" and "bad" subjectivity. In line with Wollstonecraft's aggressive introduction of defect into such discussions, defect would appear on either, or sometimes both, sides of this binary—on the one hand as a kind of counterdiscourse distinguishing the protofeminist subject at odds with, but superior to, contemporary social and moral values, and on the other as a theatrical personification of the amoral and irrational femininities that threaten both emergent feminist agendas and the social body. Nature, too, characteristically serves both denominations of female subjectivity: the superior protofeminist figure's innate qualities, improved by moral education, are seen to triumph over a debased social and cultural environment, while monstrous feminine nature in its most frightening guises often overcomes, with fatal effects, a surface socialization. Even in these midcentury decades, before Darwinism became the leading evolutionary paradigm, certain popularizing theorists of human origin and difference had broad ambitions to compete with economic and social arguments about the causes of class and national conflict. The ubiquitous racialization of physical and psychological difference between women was part of a wider set of arguments in which "race" became a signifier of unalterable differences within the category of the human.[5] "Race" as the irreducible mark of human hierarchy and of social cohesion becomes of paramount concern in the 1840s, the decade after the abolition of colonial slavery in Britain, when the status and future of newly freed persons of African descent was an abiding concern of English government and society, testing the limits of Christian emancipatory doctrine.[6] The issue of how far such persons were qualified to become liberal subjects with full economic and civil rights frequently became posed as a relative question, one that placed the free men and women of the African diaspora in direct competition with the working poor in the British Isles and, more obliquely, with the aspirant women of the English middle classes. It is at the juncture where these claims were seen to conflict that deformity and race in combination and competition erupt as highly favored figurative devices in protofeminist narrative in which female agency, virtue, and sometimes equality are being argued.

Disability and deformity are recurring themes in the nonfictional writing of England's most important liberal and feminist writer of the mid-nineteenth century, Harriet Martineau, who was also, from the mid-1830s through the 1840s, a committed, crusading abolitionist. Deaf from early adolescence, and by her own account missing a sense of smell and taste as well, Martineau wrote occasionally about deafness, and more generally about defect and illness.[7] In her childhood she had a friend, a lame little neighbor with a "wasted" limb, who underwent its amputation with such "great courage" and "composure" that she was "the talk of the whole city."[8] Envy of and identification with "little E." led Martineau to "exciting and vainglorious dreams" of physical "martyrdom." These fantasies of martyrdom Martineau believed damaged her "nervous system" and helped to bring on her deafness, whose gradual advent, alas, brought none of the public sympathy and local celebrity that greeted "little E.," but rather cruel criticism from her family for her supposed deficiency in attention.[9] A source of transgressive quasi-erotic identification as well as painful humiliation, a site where both omnipotent and abject fantasies of the self were engendered, defect finally works as a fortuitous moral testing ground for the development of ethical and autonomous selfhood. The identification and abjection associated with defect find another, related, set of narratives in Martineau's encounters with slavery and with other races. Her most fascinating and disturbing use of defect occurs passim in her extensive antislavery writings in the 1830s and 1840s, and in her narrative of her trip to Egypt, *Eastern Life Present and Past* (1850). In her abolitionist polemic, anxiety over the status of the racialized subject becomes textualized in terms of their bodily integrity—she dreads her first sight of slavery, and surprised when she discovers that the "tall, handsome mulatto" who had served her the night before was indeed a slave.[10] Martineau's abolitionism rested on a didactic insistence on the irreconcilable difference between slavery, a status that rendered subjects not only legally bound but barely human, and freedom, in which they were, in every sense, autonomous liberal individuals. The "miserable restlessness" she felt in the presence of slaves seems similar to the "weakness and uneasiness" aroused by disability that she ascribes to the parents of defective children.[11] In her travels in the American South, she depicts the "negro quarter" as something between "a haunt of monkeys and the dwelling-place of humans";[12] she notices the "walloping gait and vacant countenances" of the slave women in the field, and wishes "to see breathe his last" (unlike little E.) a young slave whose attempt to escape had ended in the amputation of his frostbitten legs.[13] A combination of anxiety, disgust, and a kind of unconscious violence accompanies Martineau's encounter with slaves. In Martineau's later travel writing too, those populations or legal categories of persons—the modern Egyptians of both sexes and Egyptian women in the harem—who cannot aspire to the status of free rational subjects, are seen as both less than human, and better off dead.[14] Although Martineau moves through several different religious and philosophical positions in her lifetime, beginning as a Unitarian and ending as a freethinking positivist, her strong belief in the ameliorative social effects of free-market economies and in individual liberty and progress are a leitmotif in her work from her influential popular series of the 1830s, *Illustrations of Political Economy,* onwards. Martineau's committed and eloquently argued liberalism together with her biographical implication in the history of disability makes her uneven negotiation of the discourse of defect particularly poignant, but, in its most negative expression, politically disturbing as well.

Two related protofeminist fictions written in the late 1840s further suggest the political complexity of narratives in which tropes of race and deformity were intertwined. Charlotte Brontë's *Jane Eyre* (1847) and Dinah

Mulock Craik's *Olive* (1850), a novel that revisits and revises *Jane Eyre*'s story and argument, produce, as their leading figure, a dream of defect, of monstrous, deformed, and disabled humanity as a corollary to their demand for female agency or gender equity. But each novel produces this relationship differently.

Defect is a hard-worked trope in *Jane Eyre*.[15] Children, women, and men, from little Jane to her icy cousin and sometime suitor St. John Rivers, are identified by both themselves and others as anomalous, deformed, or defective in spirit and body. Jane calls her child self "a heterogeneous thing" (12); the servants spell it out in her hearing—"if she were a nice, pretty child, one might compassionate her forlornness; but one really cannot care for such a little toad as that" (21). Rivers refers to his "cold, hard ambition" as a "human deformity" covered by Christianity's "blood-bleached robe" (330).

Most familiar to its readers are the novel's cruder, gothic representations. Bertha Mason's degeneration into madness and bestiality includes her loss of a fixed gender identity and her implied transmutation from apparent whiteness to blackness. Her insanity is visually marked by her "discoloured face," "a savage face" with a "fearful blackened inflation of the lineaments" (249). But just as racialization degrades Bertha, so disability saves her husband, the erring Edward Fairfax Rochester, who rediscovers his moral agency through being maimed and blinded. Minor characters, especially those who turn against Jane with an atavistically negative or aggressive response, require no such traumatic mutilation; they arrive on the page already disfigured into caricature—Jane's aunt Reed and her son John with their "thick lips" and "muddy complexions" (12) are racialized grotesques; a telling passage from *Gulliver's Travels* precedes by only a few pages the entry of the sinister governor of Lowood school, the Brobdingnagian Reverend Brocklehurst with his "great nose" and "large prominent teeth" (27). Both Englishness and foreignness are part of the spectrum of female defect—mental, moral, and physical. Rochester's European mistresses, Celine, Giacinta, and Clara, and the "coarsely clad" peasant girls in St. John Rivers's parish are, at least in Jane's eyes, part of Brontë's gallery of repulsive femininities, the first exciting Rochester's lust, followed soon enough by repugnance, the latter provoking involuntary and somewhat shamefaced degradation and disgust in Jane, their teacher (316). An "innate" response of repulsion or disgust to perceived human defect is the novel's most ambivalent signifier. At some points it marks Brontë's own assent to conventional prejudices, at others it indicates that her characters are insensitive and vulgar. At yet others, as in Jane's reaction to her peasant pupils joined with her immediate resolve to struggle against her feelings, both instinctive revulsion and principled resistance to it indicate the responder's innate and learned superiority to inferior or flawed humanity. While both Jane and other characters in the novel identify her with bad and defective femininity, she is extricated from these associations by virtue of her own "instinctive" aversions. In *Jane Eyre* both defect itself, and the response to it, are developed as a complex grammar, expressed as a universal language of selfhood and relationship, that becomes the novel's difficult, sometimes impossible, task to parse into an ethically recognizable system.

Brontë's insistent and contradictory response to difference and defect in *Jane Eyre* was indicative of a more general tendency in cultural representation. In the ethnological theories of polygyny advanced by the anatomist Robert Knox and others, part of staple middle-class reading in the forties and fifties, an "aversion" to difference was an essential element of the argument that "races" were, in fact, as distinct and immutable as "species." While "aversion" played a key role in the theory of multiple origins of the human, by the forties *both* monogynist and polygynist theorists assumed that aggressive and aversive responses to collective and idiosyncratic difference were instinctive human behaviors; where they differed was as to the meaning of that response. It is within this ideological field that Jane's constellation of defects, her difference from bourgeois Victorian gender ideals—diminutive size, unfashionable coloring, "irregular" physiognomy, intelligence, aspiration, and anger—works as a defensive counterdiscourse against a supposed norm in which virtue and beauty are seen to be coincident. Passive female beauty, usually blonde and blue-eyed, was represented as Saxon or Scandinavian, and female ugliness equated with deformity.[16]

In *Jane Eyre* however, even more than in Wollstonecraft, such an inverted use of defect in which the protofeminist heroine is ultimately the sign and agent of a regenerated middle class, and the savior or conscience of its men (who are themselves prone to various deformities of morals and feeling), depends on the evocation of a surprisingly normative and racially inflected view of human deformity and monstrosity. The fullest expression of the monstrous is Bertha, the "goblin" with a "gaunt head," whose "giant propensities" and "pigmy intellect" (269), are the dual effects of hereditary taint both through her mad mother and the degenerative influence of tropical, colonial environment. The discourse of "dependence" and "independence" in *Jane Eyre* is blurred by the novel's conservative adherence to class, if not gendered deference, and its relationship to individual autonomy and liberty is consistently mediated by the novel's national/racial imperatives, which determine which female subjects can aspire to civil freedoms. Within the grotesque spectrum of femininities in *Jane Eyre,* to which Jane is constantly exposed and explicitly compared, *her* physical and psychological differences emerge as minor faults at one register, at another as necessary to her survival, and, in the final pages, as the triumphant sign of racial, national, and ethical superiority.[17] Both Jane's and Rochester's "irregular features" (a code, perhaps, for Brontë's Irishness in a period when the comparison of Celts to monkeys is not uncommon) figured a form of "English" heterogeneity and hybridity—vigorous, virtuous, and productive—sent to supplant a superficial norm of racial purity. At the same time, through the blunt instrument of narrative homicide and intranational containment, the novel's discourse of defect polices its own boundaries against the collective deformity of inferior European and African races, and the threat in particular of exogamy with degraded femininities.

Jane Eyre's orchestration of liberalism includes a stinging critique and gendered revaluation of some of its terms, especially as it pertains to the market in women and the ideological and economic forms of imperialism; issues that this essay cannot address.[18] Yet Brontë's questioning of what we might think of as masculinist market thinking does not necessarily contradict the way in which the novel does severely restrict the social field in which toleration and sympathy for the deformities and defects of gender are to be extended, and narrow the class, race, and national base in which Jane's cry from the rooftops of Thornfield for gender equality—"woman feel just as men feel" (96)—may be implemented. Against the grain of the text, which offers Bertha Mason no sympathy at all, indeed lends its sympathies to the rakish Rochester at the expense of her horrifying transformation from stately white woman to "clothed hyena" (258), modern readers might read a feminist, anti-imperialist allegory in which forced marriage, transportation in a simulacrum of a slave ship, and incarceration in the attic of an English country house are the causes, not the consequences, of her degeneration. But if that is indeed the novel's unconscious, its overt narrative offers few opportunities for it to surface.

Yet within a couple of years the eclectic mix of conservatism and radicalism in Brontë's textualization of deformity found an admiring yet critical response in fictional form. Craik's reworking of Brontë's plot and figures in *Olive* (1850), a novel in which the heroine's birth defect, her "curse of hopeless deformity," is highlighted as specifically physical, a curvature of the spine that leaves one shoulder higher than the other, implies an awareness and a critique of *Jane Eyre*'s strategies.[19] In *Olive,* the "innate" response of repulsion to deformity is immediately challenged as ethically and emotionally flawed. Toleration and sympathy toward disability and toward cultural difference are supreme virtues in *Olive,* and its eponymous heroine

becomes their guardian. Nor are physical and psychic defect as closely allied as they are in Brontë's text, a distinction made simpler by Craik's own
more conservative ideas about femininity, which emphatically disassociate
agency and anger. The crippled Olive is a suitably patient, passive Victorian
heroine, but not a willing victim. Her reforming agency is a matter of example, gentle persuasion and nurturance practiced on her mismatched parents and her husband to-be Harold Gwynne, a minister who has lost his
faith. For a good half of its length, *Olive* almost accepts its heroine's deformity as the unambiguous, positive sign of her virtuous femininity. Indeed
deformity itself, in the opening page of the novel, is adumbrated as infancy
itself, in the "purple, pinched-up withered face" of the "nameless concre-
tion," the "helpless lump" of the newborn child, and this semigrotesque,
half-formed physical state, Craik ask us to remember, is the one in which
all humans come into the world, and should be the basis of our tolerance
to those who are "poor, mean and degraded" (3). But as Craik develops her
trope and pursues her critical rewrite of *Jane Eyre*, the radical thrust of her
argument becomes distinctly more confused. In place of Bertha Mason,
Craik introduces a woman of African descent, Christal Manners, the illegitimate and mixed-race child of Olive's father and his Caribbean quadroon
mistress. Beautiful, and apparently "white," her defect emerges as purely
temperamental. Like Bertha she has inherited a "violent and unreasonable
temper" (*Jane Eyre*, 269)—discovering her doubly degraded origin, she attacks her innocent and loving half-sister in a "demoniacal," sorocidal rage.
And while Christal is allowed to survive, albeit in the convent that she herself chooses as self-imposed exile, the denouement of the story reasserts, as
does *Jane Eyre*, a more normative discourse of defect than its opening suggests. This shift is signaled not only by the displacement of Olive's physical
deformity onto the mental debility of the unfortunate Christal, but by the
gradual blindness that, belatedly, punishes Olive's mother for her early rejection of her imperfect child. As the novel moves toward a happy matri-
monial conclusion, the dynamic of comparative defect provides a narrative
resolution. Olive's physical "curse" becomes less and less noticeable.[20] Nevertheless, the novel strikes an early eugenicist note, for neither Olive nor
Christal are allowed to bear children, that is, to reproduce their particular
familial taint. In *Olive*, Craik poses defect at once as the universal human
condition, and as the effect of specific forms of exogamy—the mésalliance
of Scots and English, British and African. Arguing against the kind of feminist individualism that suffuses *Jane Eyre*, but against, too, Brontë's illib-
eral contraction of tolerance and sympathy for difference, *Olive* nevethe-
less ends, as does *Jane Eyre*, by using the discourse of defect comparatively

and conservatively to regenerate and safeguard British, if not English, bourgeois culture.[21]

In Martineau's retrospective account of attitudes toward "personal infirmity," especially deafness—her own and others—in the early decades of the nineteenth century, the "dread and dislike" that met the deaf is described as an unthinkingly unsympathetic social response composed largely of annoyance and irritation at the effort involved in relating to deaf relatives or acquaintances, rather than the instinctive revulsion to racialized defect, inferiority, and legal disability that surfaces elsewhere in her writing. Deafness, she argued, may make the sufferer from childhood who cannot be properly trained "sly and tricky, selfish and egotistical,"[22] but these character faults Martineau regarded as effects of parental failures of knowledge and management—not as psychological flaws that inevitably accompany disability. In her account of her own development Martineau turned that absence of wise parenting that accompanied her growing disability into a fortunate accident that allowed her a triumphal experience of character building, one whose outcome shored up both her liberal self-fashioning and her strong social conscience. At fifty-five, when she mistakenly thought herself "on the borders of the grave, at the end of a busy life," she was "confident that this same deafness" had been

> the best thing that every happened to me;—the best in a selfish view, as the grandest impulse to self-mastery; and the best in a higher view, as my most peculiar opportunity of helping others, who suffer the same misfortune without equal stimulus to surmount the false shame, and other unspeakable miseries which attend it.[23]

The theme of self-mastery, of an exultant if moralized transcendence of both physical and psychological defect, rendered as a narrative of liberal and humanist self-fashioning, is common to all three of the midcentury women writers and thinkers discussed here and is deeply connected to their aspirations for their sex as well as themselves. Yet this trajectory is bounded, culturally and psychologically. Martineau and Brontë are intermittently aware that the counterdiscourse of defect has its dangers; too enthusiastic an identification with the individually or collectively disabled or victimized (as others or selves)—whether these are martyrs, saints, or rebels—threatened mental and moral stability as well as the danger of a permanent stigmatizing association with defect. These identifications with defect—Martineau's fantasmatic investment in the saintly, crippled "little E." or Jane's imagined child persona as "any other rebel slave" (9)—are seen as supporting children's amoral, if not always innocent, dreams of power or revenge, to be replaced, at least superficially, by the hard graft of a more socialized and ethical becoming.

When we move forward to a later moment in which liberalism and feminism are articulated, and turn to the first decades of the twentieth century, the configuration of these issues changes again, now combined with women's collective demand for the franchise and economic and professional equity, but situated also in the context of debates on eugenics and immigration. Virginia Woolf's diary entry of January 9, 1915, "On the tow path we met & had to pass a long line of imbeciles. . . . everyone in that long line was a miserable shuffling idiotic creature, with no forehead, or no chin & and imbecile grin, or a wild suspicious stare. It was perfectly horrible. They should certainly be killed,"[24] may, as her biographer Hermione Lee argues, have been related both to her impending breakdown a month later and the need to distinguish herself "violently, fearfully" from her disturbed and backward half-sister Laura, who was placed in an asylum in her early twenties and died there many years later.[25] But the insertion of the word "certainly" in Woolf's lethal judgment relates the passage suggestively to the contemporary public debates on negative and positive eugenics. In the spectrum of eugenicist views, it should be remembered, the legal extermination of the mentally and physically defective was, in Britain, considered the view of an extremist outer fringe.[26] Although Woolf, like Martineau, suffered in body and spirit from her own "curse" of defect, and shared Martineau's feminism, if not the full range of her social concerns, what is noticeably absent—and we might say much less available to her historically and culturally, as well as psychologically in an age of secular modernity—is the compelling trajectory of self-improving Protestant-inspired struggle against adversity, which transforms impediment and humiliation into a bracing moral challenge. At the same time Woolf lived through those positive changes in women's lives that the mid-Victorians only dreamed of. In Woolf's euphoric view in 1929, a kind of gender utopia was just round the corner, one in which, because "the woman writer would be no longer angry," her books, unlike those of Charlotte Brontë, would not emerge "deformed and twisted." Her subject would now be social and global, her potential unlimited, as long as she did not write from the site of "personal discontent," that is from the position of collective "disability" that included women, working-class men, and Negroes.[27]

Woolf deployed the language of defect more vividly, and less self-reflectively perhaps, than other feminists of her generation, but her writing is suggestive of a more general critical tension between a new spacious view of female human possibility and a tolerance for the whole spectrum of human ability. We can indeed see a trace of that tension hovering over Lee's own astute discussion of Laura's illness, Virginia's consistently hostile view of her "vacant-eyed," "idiot" sibling, and the critical and biographical linking of the illness and fate of the two girls.[28] For although Lee points out that Virginia Woolf frequently describes herself in "fearful opposition, not identification" with Laura, Lee herself repeats and reproduces that opposition, arguing with those critics and biographers who want to see the two sisters "as parallel victims of patriarchal cruelty" not now on the grounds she gave earlier, that this analysis is too crude, but because it is "demeaning to the half-sister who repeatedly overcame her condition (which was quite different from Laura's) in order to do her life's work."[29]

"Life's work" seems an innocent enough synecdoche for the writer's vocation and genius that Lee values, but the transcendent value placed on working lives has meant that work and defect have become ideologically yoked, as I suggested at the beginning of this essay, in ways that have to do with the downsizing of the welfare state and the setting in place of various forms of social triage. Western feminism's own divided stake in, on the one hand, women's independence, sometimes too narrowly defined in terms of traditional working lives and forms of upward mobility, and, on the other, support for a more fully communal response to social needs in which dependency of all kinds can be recognized and respected, becomes particularly painful when it comes to consider the targeting of poor single mothers as defective citizens. This assault has gathered legislative steam not under the overt neoliberals of the Reagan-Bush or Thatcher-Major governments, but in the Clinton/Blair "third way" regimes that have followed them. Unregulated maternity coupled with poverty has become a kind of social crime, whose punishment extends to children as well as mothers.[30]

One of the first acts of Tony Blair's New Labour Party after its triumphant electoral victory and accession to government in the spring of 1997 was to announce, as expected, a program of modernization of Britain's welfare provision. While there was widespread agreement that welfare was due for systematic reform, there was some alarm that the first two categories of recipients whose rights to benefits were to come under review with an eye to possible cuts and curtailment were single mothers—and the disabled. An audible outcry from many quarters followed the announcement of the targeting of these particular groups of citizens for new and draconian forms of surveillance and regulation. However outmoded the postwar philosophies of social distribution had become in the eyes of almost all political parties, surely the nation had not rejected nearly two decades of Conservative hegemony with its bleakly punitive legacy of doctrinaire hostility to the welfare state in order that Britain's most obviously vulnerable subjects would be set up as the trial populations for instant economic reform? Attacked by a principled if politically suicidal few of its own backbenchers as well as by Liberal Democrats and gleeful Conservatives and faced with well-organized and well-publicized demonstrations by disabled action groups, Blair's government quickly began to soft pedal its initial aggressive stance, spin-doctoring its retreat as a sensitive response to public opinion.[31] Yet once the wave of publicity had receded, it was hard not to see in the scum of bad faith left behind on the political shoreline a cynical wish to test the hard edge of New Labour policy on what the modernizers perceived as not only the least powerful but least entitled groups within society—women, children, and the physically and mentally impaired. The initiative itself came, after all, from a government whose humanitarian rhetoric still drew, however reluctantly, on its mixed inheritance of socialist, social democratic, and liberal thought. The vigorous debate that followed it suggests how alive and well the contested discourse of defect remains at the end of the 1990s, its gendered associations still present within it, and its antidemocratic impulse fed as much perhaps by the prescriptively modern assumptions about universal agency and autonomy as by a more pragmatic or elitist stance.

NOTES

1. See Etienne Balibar, "Racism and Nationalism," in Etienne Balibar and Immanuel Wallerstein, *Race, Nation, Class: Ambiguous Identities* (New York: Verso, 1991), 54–56.

2. For the nineteenth-century history of hybridity, see Robert J. C. Young, *Colonial Desire: Hybridity in Theory, Culture, and Race* (London: Routledge, 1995), esp. chap. 1. Young, however, argues that the reactionary history of the term in racial science precludes its positive late-twentieth-century use, a view that has, in turn, been heavily critiqued by other theorists and historians.

3. For a full discussion of the relationship between emergent feminism and racial science in Britain in the mid-nineteenth century see my essay, "'A Heterogeneous Thing': Female Childhood and the Rise of Racial Thinking in Victorian Britain," in *Human, All too Human*, ed. Diana Fuss (New York: Routledge, 1996), 169–202.

4. Mary Wollstonecraft, *A Vindication of the Rights of Woman*, ed. Carol H. Poston, 2d ed. (New York: W. W. Norton, 1988), 45 (page numbers for further quotations are given in the text). The phrase "this fair defect / Of nature" is from *Paradise Lost*, book 10, and is referred to again on page 55. Neither appropriation directly cites Milton. On page 62, in a related argument, she misquotes from Pope's *Moral Essays* II, 44, on women as "Fine by defect, and amiably weak" (Pope says "delicately weak").

5. For these developments on race and science see George W. Stocking Jr.,

Victorian Anthropology (New York: Free Press, 1987), esp. chaps. 2–7; Michael Banton, *The Idea of Race* (London: Tavistock Publications, 1977); and Nancy Stepan, *The Idea of Race in Science: Great Britain, 1800–1960* (London: Macmillan, 1982).

6. For the background to the problems of the 1840s see Robin Blackburn, *The Overthrow of Colonial Slavery* (London: Verso, 1988); for the increasing racial conservatism of British governments see Philip Curtin, *The Image of Africa: British Ideas and Action, 1780–1850* (London: Macmillan, 1965).

7. Harriet Martineau, *Autobiography* (London: Virago, 1983), 1:72–78 and *Life in the Sick-Room* (London: E. Moxon, 1844).

8. Martineau, *Autobiography*, 1:45.

9. Martineau, *Autobiography*, 1:76.

10. Harriet Martineau, *Retrospect of Western Travel* (London: Saunders and Ottley, 1838), 1:232.

11. Martineau, *Retrospect of Western Travel*, 232; *Autobiography*, 1:76.

12. See Martineau's similar figure of disgust represented as an elision of the human and the animal in *Eastern Life Present and Past* (London: Edward Moxon, 1850), when she describes the governor of Thebes, "crouching on his haunches on the filthy shore among the dung heaps, feeding himself with his fingers among a circle of apish creatures like himself" (217).

13. Harriet Martineau, *Society in America* (London: Saunders and Ottley, 1839), 302, 305, 309–11. The overt topic of this passage is antislavery, as an occasion for liberal homily. Martineau severely criticizes a Southern proslavery woman who wishes the same slave dead not on Martineau's supposed compassionate grounds but because he had wished to "be free," defied the system and his masters, and run away.

14. Martineau, *Eastern Life*. For a brilliant analysis of the genocidal impulse in travel writing about Egypt in the nineteenth century, including Martineau's *Eastern Life*, see John Barrell, "Death on the Nile: Fantasy and the Literature of Tourism, 1840–1860," *Essays in Criticism* 41, no. 2 (1991): 97–127. Barrell's illuminating discussion of the psychic and political anxieties suggested by Martineau's account of her bizarre encounter with the "monstrous," "ugly," noseless Sphinx is particularly germane to my argument about the way in which contradictions within liberalism and feminism produce forms of textual violence directed at racial subjects and rationalized through the discourse of defect.

15. Charlotte Brontë, *Jane Eyre*, ed. Richard J. Dunn, Norton Critical Edition, 2d ed. (New York: W. W. Norton, 1987). All further citations appear in the text.

16. See Robert Knox, *The Races of Men: A Fragment* (Philadelphia: Lea and Blanchard, 1850; reprint, Miami: Mnemosyne, 1969). This American edition came out in the same year as the London edition, published by Henry Renshaw. For the best account of the monogynist argument as put by Britain's most influential ethnologist of the first half of the century, James Cowles Prichard, see George W. Stocking, "From Chronology to Ethnology: James Cowles Prichard and British Anthropology," the introduction to Stocking's edition of Prichard's *Researches into the Physical History of Man* (Chicago: University of Chicago Press, 1973), ix–cx. For an analysis of articulation of ethnology and women's fiction, see my essay "A Heterogeneous Thing."

17. See, for the novel's most extreme example, Rochester's staged comparison of Bertha to Jane in chapter 26: "Compare these clear eyes with the red balls yonder—this face with that mask—this form with that bulk" (258).

18. Implicit in the novel's treatment of its leading male figures is a critique of a colonial expansion, which degrades or kills the English metropolitan subjects who go abroad for economic or altruistic reasons. Rochester is contaminated by his contact with the "hell" of the West Indian tropical environment and its degenerate Creole populations, and Jane fears, with good reason, the sure death that St. John Rivers meets in India.

19. Dinah Mulock Craik, *Olive,* ed. Cora Kaplan (Oxford: Oxford University Press, 1996), 14. All further references are in the text.

20. For similar narrative strategies that diminish physical defect, see the partial recovery of Rochester's sight in *Jane Eyre,* and the lessened prominence of Esther's smallpox scars in Charles Dickens's *Bleak House* (1853).

21. However, Craik published a more daring, radical tale about racialized defect, written about the same time as *Olive,* and included in the Oxford University Press edition. "The Half-Caste" has as its heroine a mixed-race Indian child abused by her white English relations. Nurtured by her governess, she develops from a child with a "dull, heavy face," the sign of the "ultra-stupid" (337), whom her uncle calls an "ugly little devil" and the narrator, at first, "demoniac" (341), into a beautiful, talented young woman who marries her English guardian.

22. Martineau, *Autobiography,* 1:73.

23. Martineau, *Autobiography,* 1:78.

24. *The Diary of Virginia Woolf,* ed. Anne Olivier Bell and Andrew McMeillie (New York: Harcourt, 1982), 1:13.

25. Hermione Lee, *Virginia Woolf* (London: Chatto and Windus, 1996), 104.

26. See Richard A. Soloway, *Demography and Degeneration: Eugenics and the Declining Birthrate in Twentieth Century Britain* (Chapel Hill: University of North Carolina Press, 1990). Soloway writes,

A variety of schemes to segregate, institutionalize, incarcerate, punish, deny the right to marry, and even to sterilize degenerates, as some American states were starting to do, were proposed throughout the Edwardian period. If all else failed, some people were prepared to entertain a "gentle, painless" policy of extermination. . . . With the exception of the "lethal chamber," which only appealed to the rabid fringe, most eugenicists, including Galton, had little difficulty with the majority of these proposals. But other than the institutionalizing of the feebleminded, whose affliction was generally acknowledged to be hereditary and whose segregation was assured by eugenically inspired legislation in 1913, they recognized that the implementation of such restrictive measures was politically and logically impossible for the foreseeable future. (64)

27. Virginia Woolf, *A Room of One's Own* (Harmondsworth: Penguin, 1973), 70; "Women and Fiction," in *Women and Writing,* ed. Michèle Barrett (London, 1970), 47. See my discussion of these passages in "Pandora's Box: Subjectivity, Class

and Sexuality in Socialist Feminist Criticism," in *Sea Changes: Essays on Culture and Feminism* (London: Verso, 1986), 170–75.

28. Lee, *Virginia Woolf,* 104.

29. Lee, *Virginia Woolf,* 103–4.

30. The policy of withdrawing welfare support from single mothers who gave birth to subsequent children out of wedlock was an explicit part of Clinton's reforming agenda in his 1992 presidential campaign, and advanced by Hillary Clinton as early as the spring of 1992.

31. Neasa Macerlean of the *Observer* reported disability cuts in store as early as June 15, 1997, only six weeks after the election of New Labour ("Money Matters: Disabled People Face Crackdown on State Benefits," 17). The row over single parents blew up in early November 1997. See Patrick Wintour, "Women MP's Drafted in by Labour to Cut Single Parent's Benefits," *Observer,* November 9, 1997, 8. The debate on disability cuts raged from late November 1997 through mid-December. See also articles in the *Guardian* on November 21, December 12, 15, and 16 of 1997.

Contributors

Barbara M. Benedict, Professor of English at Trinity College, Connecticut, has published *Framing Feeling: Sentiment and Style in English Prose Fiction, 1745–1800* (AMS Press, 1994) and *Making the Modern Reader: Cultural Mediation in Early Modern Literary Anthologies* (Princeton University Press, 1996), as well as articles on eighteenth-century physiognomy, popular culture, literature, and book history. Her current project explores curiosity and curiosities in English literature and culture.

Jill Campbell, author of *Natural Masques: Gender and Identity in Fielding's Plays and Novels* (Stanford University Press, 1995), is an Associate Professor of English at Yale University. She is now at work on a book about satire and self-representations of Lady Mary Wortley Montagu, Lord Hervey, and Alexander Pope, which explores the construction and expression of individual "character" in historical persons as well as within literary works.

Elizabeth Heckendorn Cook, Associate Professor of English at the University of California, Santa Barbara, is the author of *Epistolary Bodies: Gender and Genre in the Eighteenth-Century Republic of Letters* (Stanford University Press, 1996). She is embarked on a project about discourses of nature in the long eighteenth century.

Lennard J. Davis is Professor and Graduate Director in the English Department at Binghamton University (State University of New York). In addition to several books on the origins and theory of the novel, he is the author of *Enforcing Normalcy: Disability, Deafness, and the Body* (Verso, 1995), *The Sense of Silence: Memoir of a Childhood with Deafness* (University of Illinois Press, 1999), and the editor of *The Disability Studies Reader* (Routledge, 1997). A founding member of the Modern Language Association's Committee on Disability, he has written essays on disability issues for the *Nation, Chronicle of Higher Education,* and other publications.

Helen Deutsch, Associate Professor of English at UCLA, is the author of *Resemblance and Disgrace: Alexander Pope and the Deformation of Culture* (Harvard University Press, 1996). Her work continues to explore the connection between literary authorship and physical difference in eighteenth-century British culture. Her present book project, *The Case of Doctor Johnson,* investigates the relationship of Johnson's material body to his monumental literary corpus and authorial canonization.

Robert W. Jones lectures in the department of English at the University of Wales, Aberystwyth, and is the author of *Gender and the Formation of Taste in Eighteenth-Century Britain: the Analysis of Beauty* (Cambridge University Press, 1998). The review editor for the *British Journal of Eighteenth-Century Studies,* he has published articles and reviews in journals including *Textual Practice, Oxford Art Journal* and *English.*

Cora Kaplan is Professor of English at Southampton University in the United Kingdom. A feminist cultural critic, her books include *Sea Changes: Essays on Culture and Feminism* (1986). She has recently coedited, with Joan W. Scott and Debra Keates, *Transitions, Environments, Translations: Feminisms in International Politics* (Routledge, 1997). She is currently finishing a book on gender and racial thinking in Victorian Britain.

Nicholas Mirzoeff is an Associate Professor of Art and Comparative Literature at SUNY Stony Brook. Among his publications on issues relating to the body and disability are *Silent Poetry: Deafness, Sign, and Visual Culture in Modern France* (Princeton University Press, 1995), *Bodyscape: Art, Modernity and the Ideal Figure* (1995), and "Intersections" for the catalog to Joseph Grigely's exhibition *Body Signs* (1993).

Felicity Nussbaum, Professor of English at UCLA, is the author of *Torrid Zones: Sexuality and Empire in Eighteenth-Century English Narratives* (Johns Hopkins University Press, 1995), *The Autobiographical Subject: Gender and Ideology in Eighteenth-Century England* (Johns Hopkins University Press, 1989), and co-editor of *The New Eighteenth Century: Theory/Politics/English Literature* (Methuen, 1987). She is presently finishing a book on race, gender, and monstrosity.

Stephen Pender is writing a dissertation on rhetoric and medicine in the early seventeenth century, particularly in the work of John Donne, at the University of Toronto. He has published an essay on early modern conjoined twins in *Monster Theory: Reading Culture,* ed. Jeffrey Jerome Cohen (University of Minnesota Press, 1996).

Joel Reed teaches at Syracuse University and is coeditor of *The Eighteenth-Century: Theory and Interpretation.* His previous work includes essays on eighteenth-century scientific culture, eighteenth-century English nationalism, and postmodern theories of nationalism. He is completing a book, *Academic Discourse: Instituting Nationalism in Seventeenth- and Eighteenth-Century England.*

Index

288; about monstrosity, 14–19, 96, 100–113, 141–42; sexual, 131–32. *See also* spectacle; wonders
curiosity cabinets, 17, 102–3, 110–11, 125n. 93, 173. *See also* collection; medical museums
Curran, Andrew, 13–14

Darwin, Erasmus, 20, 253–54, 260–62, 264–75, 277–79
Daston, Lorraine, 3, 13, 18, 118–19n. 15
da Vinci, Leonardo, 88
Davis, Lennard J., 3, 16–17, 21, 54–74, 177, 319
deafness, 3, 34–35, 72n. 30, 75–92, 206n. 50, 306, 312; education and, 8, 60, 76, 77–80, 84, 86, 87; sign language and, 22, 57, 75–87, 91
de Beauvoir, Simone, 214, 244n. 6, 248n. 41
de Bolla, Peter, 263
de Certeau, Michel, 87
defect, 10–11, 18–19, 303–18; anomalies grouped together as, 3, 127, 229–30; as comic spectacle, 2–3, 18, 116, 194; cultural context of, 3–4, 11–12; definitions of, 1–2, 6, 19, 21, 154–55; double, 34–43, 45, 50, 213–51; gender and, 1, 10, 12, 31–53, 127, 195, 304–9; geography of, 7–8, 9; natural versus man-made, 45. *See also* disability; imperfection; literature of defect; monstrosity
Defoe, Daniel, 54
de Fontenay, M., 57
deformity, 57–59, 303; acquired, 20–21, 45, 59, 213, 235; anomalies grouped together as, 3, 127, 229–30; cause or sign, 21, 115–16; definitions of, 2, 6, 35–36; as divine intention, 59–60, 95, 127; feminization of, 12, 32, 195; and form, 179–89; of old age, 20–21, 213–51; racialized, 8–10, 42, 304, 306–11, 316n. 14; and virtue, 11, 20, 21, 69, 280–302, 311. *See also* defect; monstrosity
Deformity: An Essay (Hay), 2–3, 21, 35, 60, 97, 115–16, 291

degeneracy theories, 9–10, 145–46
de Guyon, Abbé, 42
dependency, 304–5, 309, 314
depression, 54, 55, 61, 64–65
Derrida, Jacques, 75, 76
Description of a New World, called the Blazing World (Cavendish), 111
desire: deafness and, 87; and eunuchs, 46, 52n. 21; female, 21, 36–41, 235, 239–44, 262, 271; in fictions of defect, 36–41, 46–48; monstrous, 129, 137–38, 140–41; sentimentalized, 132–33, 146, 148n. 3, 150nn. 21, 22. *See also* sexuality
Desloges, Pierre, 72n. 30
Deutsch, Helen, 19, 21–22, 177–209, 249n. 58, 320
difference, 18–19, 76, 303. *See also* aging; anomaly; class; gender; race
disability, 19, 29–92, 54–74; deafness as, 78–79; definitions of, 3–4, 56, 57–58, 71n. 8; versus deformity, 57–59, 60; as identity, 2–3, 287–95, 312; madness versus, 72n. 34; politically activist, 3, 4, 314–15
dissection of monsters, 14–15, 99–100, 102, 111, 166–67
divine intention, deformity as, 59–60, 95, 127
dress, old women's, 229, 230, 231–32, 236
Dublin Physico-Historical Society, 155–75
The Dumb Virgin: or, The Force of Imagination (Behn), 36–41, 46, 47–48
Du Plessis, James Paris, 3, 103, 113
du Puy, Claudius, 103
dwarfism, 58, 59, 60, 103

Eamon, William, 101
Earle, John, 99, 110
education, 4; for deaf, 8, 60, 76, 77–80, 84, 86, 87; for girls, 20, 253, 262–66
Elias, Norbert, 23
empire building, 10, 12, 50, 52n. 19, 82, 310
Enforcing Normalcy (Davis), 16–17
epigenicists, 11

literature of defect *(continued)*
31–53, 280–318; Lady Mary, 21,
213, 214–15, 236–43; Shakespeare,
55, 58, 133. *See also* authorship,
monstrous; Boswell, James; Fielding,
Henry; Johnson, Samuel; Pope,
Alexander; Scott, Sarah
Locke, John, 115, 223–24, 225–26
Loves of the Plants (Darwin), 20, 254,
260–61, 266–75, 278–79nn. 36, 38
Lynch, Deidre Shauna, 246n. 26, 247n.
35, 263, 277n. 24

Macaulay, Thomas Babington, 64,
190–91
Mahoney, Cnogher O., 161
Making Sex (Laqueur), 19
marginalization of socially aberrant, 23
Martin, Felix, 80
Martineau, Harriet, 306–7, 312, 313,
316nn. 12, 13, 14
masculinity: anxieties, 12, 16–17; cultural authority, 22; enfeebled, 43;
and female beauty, 282–83; as monstrosity, 22, 129–30, 147; as moral
and aesthetic criteria, 1, 32–33; plant
sexuality and, 254–55. *See also* men
Massieu, Jean, 84
Maty, Matthew, 66–67
Maupertuis, Pierre Louis Moreau de,
8–9
Mayne, Judith, 87
McKeon, Michael, 46, 300n. 15
Meades, Anna, 42
medical community, 10, 13, 304;
anatomists, 10, 33, 164–65; and
monstrosity as pathology, 7–8,
13–18, 119n. 15, 155–75
medical museums, 15, 17, 18, 19,
102–3
Medicinal Dictionary (James), 193–95,
198–99
Meige, Henry, 192–93, 197
Memoirs of Martinus Scriblerus, 4,
110–11, 112–13, 125n. 81
men, 10–11; aging, 244, 247n. 29; deformed by women, 43; effeminate,
43–44, 45; eunuchs, 11, 32, 42–49,
53n. 24; monsters born to, 10–11;

and old women, 213; and sexual
monstrosity, 127, 130–31, 135–36;
women as deformed, 10, 13, 31–32,
49, 71n. 9. *See also* gender;
masculinity
menstruation, 34, 165, 235
mental illness, 23, 43, 54, 55, 61–62,
64, 72n. 34
mental retardation, 34
Michelet, Jules, 159
middle class: degeneracy theories, 9–10,
145–46; dependent femininity,
304–5; female virtue, 20, 283,
284–85, 311; feminist agency and autonomy, 23, 303–14; Monster of
1790 and, 128, 132–35, 140,
143–44, 146; and "moral monstrosity," 12–13, 132–35
Millenium Hall (Scott), 5, 20, 69, 284,
288, 296–99
Milton, John, 55, 183, 184
miracles, 6–7, 113
mirrors, aging and, 213–50
Mirzoeff, Nicholas, 8, 21, 22, 75–92,
320
misogyny, 11, 243; and femininity as
defect, 32, 33–34, 39, 43, 44; and
monstrous sexuality, 129, 269–70,
278n. 28
Molyneux, William, 157–58, 168–69,
170
monogynists, 309, 316n. 16
Monster of 1790, The. *See* Williams,
Renwick
Monster Theory (Cohen), 19, 172
monstrosity, 3, 10, 12, 19, 60, 93–209;
and acquired deformities, 20–21, 45,
59, 213, 235; botanical, 260; curiosity about, 14–19, 96, 100–113,
141–42; deafness as, 75, 86; definitions, 21, 129; differentiated categories of, 127; dissected, 14–15,
99–100, 102, 111, 166–67; exhibitions of, 18, 19, 59, 70, 95–126; imposters of, 21, 105–10; masculinity
as, 22, 129–30, 147; as medical
pathology, 7–8, 13–18, 119n. 15,
155–75; "moral," 12–13, 33–36,
132–35; national, 22–23, 117n. 7,

sign language, 22, 38, 57, 75–87, 91
slavery, 8, 306, 307, 316n. 13
Sloane, Sir Hans, 103, 111–12, 113, 122n. 45, 157
smallpox, 2, 3, 5–6, 8, 69, 224–26, 247n. 31; Johnson, 54; Lady Mary, 21, 214, 236; in Scott novels, 69, 288, 297
Smart, Christopher, 61
Smellie, William, 260
Smith, Charles, 155–75
Snell, Hannah, 42
socioeconomics, 40, 46–50, 62. *See also* class; race
Soemmerring, Samuel Thomas von, 33
Soloway, Richard A., 317n. 26
spectacle, monstrosity as, 2–3, 6, 18, 21, 22, 194, 196. *See also* comic spectacle; curiosity; human exhibition; wonders
Spectator, 2, 111, 149n. 13, 188, 215, 224–26, 240
Spencer, John, 100–101, 109, 118n. 10
Sprat, Thomas, 98, 101, 104, 122n. 50
Stafford, Barbara Maria, 15, 18, 125n. 93
Staring Back (Fries), 3
Steele, Richard, 2, 149n. 13
Stoler, Ann Russell, 9–10
subjectivity, 18, 19; in body, 19, 20, 38–39, 252, 263–64; gendered, 20, 32, 46–50, 252, 263–64, 275, 305–6
suicidal impulses, 54, 260
Sutton, Daniel, 5
Swift, Jonathan, 4, 59, 104, 132, 158, 182

temporality: and appearance, 20–21, 214, 222–35, 239–43, 247n. 31. *See also* aging
teratology, 13, 14, 16, 60, 105–6, 144; Monster of 1790 and, 128, 131, 138, 144
Theophrastus, 110
Thomson, Rosemarie Garland, 4, 7
Thoresby, Ralph, 102
Thornton, Bonnel, 67
Thrale, Hester, 61, 62, 70n. 1, 190, 221–22, 301n. 35

tics, Johnson's, 54, 55, 178, 186, 191–202, 204n. 16
Tics and Their Treatment (Meige and Feindel), 193, 197
Todd, Dennis, 16–17, 27n. 60, 59, 82, 125n. 81
Toft, Mary, 4, 16, 59, 104, 113, 141, 189
Torrid Zones (Nussbaum), 19
Tourette's syndrome, 55, 178, 197, 199–200, 207n. 73
Truth, Sojourner, 50
tuberculosis, 54, 70n. 1

ugliness, 2, 6, 20, 35–36, 309; as identity, 287–95; virtue linked to, 5, 11, 20, 35, 227, 283–302; women's double defect of, 34–35, 45. *See also* beauty
Unfortunate Bride: Or, The Blind Lady a Beauty, The (Behn), 36, 39–41, 46
United Nations, 4
universalism, 1, 23, 157, 159, 303–15, 311

Valerius, John, 102, 121n. 38
Vanity of Human Wishes (Johnson), 178, 181–89, 200
violence, 42, 52n. 19, 128
virtue: beauty as, 11, 281–82, 288, 309; deformity linked to, 11, 20, 21, 69, 280–302, 311; "involuntary motions," 20, 254, 261–62, 264–66, 270, 273–74; ugliness linked to, 5, 11, 20, 35, 227, 283–302. *See also* character
visibility, 3–4, 21, 23, 137, 187, 303; aging and, 21, 216, 217–18; virtue and, 20, 282, 285, 288, 296–98. *See also* beauty; human exhibition; spectacle

Walpole, Horace, 132, 213, 234–36, 249n. 54
Ward, Ned, 100, 103
Waterman, John, 99–100
Weldon, Anthony, 57
Wendorf, Richard, 221
Whytt, Robert, 199, 208n. 81